MELTDOWN

HOW THE 'MASTERS OF THE UNIVERSE' DESTROYED THE WEST'S POWER AND PROSPERITY

STEPHEN HASELER

Also by Stephen Haseler

The Gaitskellites
The Death of British Democracy
Euro-Communism (Joint Author)
The Tragedy of Labour
Anti-Americanism
The Politics of Giving
The Battle for Britain: Thatcher and the New Liberals
The End of the House of Windsor
The English Tribe
The Super-Rich: The Unjust World of Global Capitalism
Super-State: The New Europe and its Challenge to America
Sidekick

First published in 2008 by Forumpress

Forumpress
c/o The Global Policy Institute
London Metropolitan University
31 Jewry Street
London EC3N 2EY, UK

ISBN: 978-0-9554975-6-8

A catalogue record for this book is available from the British Library.

The publisher has used its best endeavours to ensure that the URLs for websites referred to in the book are correct and active at the time of going to press.

For further information on Forumpress, visit our website: www.forumpress.co.uk

Cover Design and Layout: Ben Eldridge ben@somethingdesign.co.uk

Printed by Lightning Source www.lightningsource.com

MELTDOWN

HOW THE 'MASTERS OF THE UNIVERSE' DESTROYED THE WEST'S POWER AND PROSPERITY

STEPHEN HASELER

Contents

Preface

This is a story of an era – an era spanning two decades – that is now ending. It started with the leadership of the western world – on Wall Street and in Washington (and in London) believing they could rule the world. And – as can be seen at the time of writing (in September 2008 with the collapse of Wall Street) – it ended with their failure, a failure with catastrophic consequences – not just for West's financial system and its world role, but also for the living standards of everyone in the western world.

It is a classic tale of hubris – of how, following the cracking open of the Berlin Wall, and the West's victory over communism in the Cold War in the late 1980s, America's leaders allowed it all to go to their heads. Unable to handle success, and with the world at their feet, they went for broke – with no sense of limits and no sense of perspective or history (indeed, in 1990, the former State Department policy planner Francis Fukuyama 'abolished history' to much acclaim).' And for the next twenty years all the talk out of Wall Street and Washington was of 'new world orders' – run by a hegemonic America – and a 'new economy' that would secure continuous growth fuelled first, in the late 1990s by a 'hi-tech' revolution, and then by an endless credit revolution. And all with new rules, rules of course that would be written by Wall Street and Washington. It was to be called, misleadingly, the 'neo-liberal' or 'free market' revolution.

This book has its origins in my earlier, 2001, book *The Super-Rich: The Unjust New World of Global Capitalism* when I first outlined how in the post-cold war era the emergence of 'globalisation' had changed our capitalist system out of all recognition, slowly sowing the seeds of its own destruction (which, as I finish this book, looks to be underway). In the earlier book I also argued that this 'neo-liberal' capitalist revolution had unleashed a global super-rich class which, working through the great institutions of Wall Street (and the City of London), had become the driving force in refashioning the Anglo-American and global economy to suit its own needs.

Between 2000, when I wrote *The Super-Rich*, and 2008, as I write *Meltdown*, the trends I originally described have continued uninterrupted. I have updated the data – and refined some of my arguments.

This is not just a book about economics. It is an attempt to place the rise and fall of the new global capitalist revolution in a broader – essentially political, or geopolitical – context. An intriguing aspect of the last two decades is that both Wall Street and Washington have developed what amounted to a shared vision of the future. This vision was much broader than a dry economic philosophy. Rather, it was a worldview encompassing a moral, political and social as well as an economic perspective. In essence it saw the future – the future of the world no less – as an American future. The belief was fervent and simple: that with the Soviet Union having imploded, it was 'the American way' – the 1990s American world of 'markets' and 'democracy' – that would ultimately triumph everywhere.

So, it is a thesis of this book that, although Wall Street may have led this new globalist vision, both the financial elites in Wall Street (and The City of London) and the political elites in Washington were in it together. An economist, Federal Reserve Board Chairman Alan Greenspan, may well have been the revolutionary era's guide and guru, but both President Bill Clinton and President George W. Bush signed on as well, as did some European political leaders – most notably Tony Blair in Britain and Jose Maria Aznar in Spain.

Americanising the world was, in essence, what the famous, or infamous, 'neo-conservative' era was all about. The 'neocons' were originally a smallish group, mainly New Yorkers, who painted the left, whence many of them came, as soft on communism and essentially 'anti-American'. They sought a reassertion of American power in the world – a sentiment that was to grow into mainstream thinking during the 1990s, and, after 9/11, was to dominate. During the presidency of Bill Clinton it took the form of 'globalisation' as markets and money would Americanise an increasingly integrated globe; and then, after 9/11, George W. Bush added a military component as 'democracy' in Iraq was to be imposed at the barrel of a gun.

There was a messianic quality about Wall Street and Washington during these times. Like other messianic groups – the French revolutionaries after 1789 or the communist generation in the 1920s and 30s – the American financial and political elites were gripped by a universalist ideology that sought to change, to remake, the world. I lived and worked in Washington (in think tanks and universities) over the years from 1982-97, and looking back, I am now able to see what amounted to a slowly gathering messianic quality in the outlook and thinking of elites. It had started way back during the Reagan/Thatcher 'free-market' revolution in the 1980s, but it was only after the fall of communism at the end of the 1980s that the Washington think tanks and institutes began to develop ideas about how their 'American revolution' could spread further and ultimately remake the world.

It was, of course, bound to fail. And it did so, spectacularly. One turning-point came some time in 2004 in Iraq when it finally became obvious that, in the Middle East at least, imposing the American version of 'democracy' through the barrel of a gun would simply not work. And then, in August 2007, the 'new economy' came to grief as the volcano at the heart of the great American debt mountain began to erupt in the form of the housing and banking crisis. This crisis was so dire that by the late summer of 2008 we had witnessed the collapse of several of the Wall Street investment banks and the effective nationalisation of large tracts of the banking, mortgage and insurance industry. And then, in late September 2008 came the startling proposal from the Bush administration that the whole banking system was to be semi-socialised.

This revolution was always built on illusions – principally illusions about American power in the world. For the West, particularly the US, was simply not as strong as its leaders thought it was. The GDP and population of the USA was simply not such as to warrant its 'lone superpower' status. And Americans were, in fact, living beyond their means, funded by loans from abroad. With wage and income levels stagnant the only way that the US could keep up its growth rates and its standard of living was by debt – huge amounts of it, both public and private – coming from Asia. This whole construct has now come apart at the seams.

Following the implosion of the Soviet empire, although all the talk was of a 'uni-polar world' and of American 'hegemony', the US was in truth only one amongst several equals. And this multipolar character was to be further enhanced when the West's leaders, under pressure from its corporations, brought China into the western-led global economic system. It was a fateful decision; and the West now needs to accommodate to a world in which an ascendant new superpower does not share our democratic values.

It also needs to accommodate to the fact that 'globalisation', or the era of global capital, is now coming to a close. The downturn we are facing will inevitably take its toll on trade flows and will increasingly produce domestic political pressures in favour of some form of trade protection – making trading blocs virtually inevitable.

And the main question remains. Can we adjust? And, can the West reorganise itself to meet these great challenges? Much will depend on the Americans. And Americans – unlike Europeans – are not used to decline. Indeed, the words 'America' and 'decline' sit badly together. Yet, as the banking crisis in 2007 raged into the slump of 2008 the idea of American economic decline – comparative if not absolute – was beginning to resonate, as was the realisation that this particular downturn was not just another dip in American economic fortunes, a recession that Americans would bounce back from. Nor was it like the great depression of the 1930s – a serious and ugly downturn, but one which saw America recover and then lead the world. This time it appeared to be quite different. This time it appeared highly unlikely that the America economy would lead the world out of the slump.

So I raise in this book a question about how Europe will respond to this meltdown of American leadership. It would seem that we in Europe can do very little without unity, at least the unity of Europe's core members, France and Germany. The fact that the Franco-German alliance has stuck together over the seminal Russo-Georgian crisis in 2008, and have begun to charter a separate policy from that of the US is, potentially at any rate, the beginning of a more independent and unified European geopolitical position.

But the question remains: whether, in the current downsizing of the West in the world, America and Europe need, instead of separate paths, to come together. Do we need one West or two?

And, just as important, as the new global capital revolution now winds down, is there an 'alternative capitalism' available? Of course, there already exists an alternative to the Anglo-American 'free market fundamentalist' model. The 'European social model' of capitalism – with its greater emphasis upon stability, its greater acceptance of social welfare, its more relaxed view of the state, and its scepticism about 'financiali-sation' – has always been a viable alternative, and is now look-ing more attractive. And the fact that it has been so derided over the years by supporters of Wall Street and the City of London should not stop us from adopting it.

In the turmoil to come the policymakers who will pick up the pieces from the Wall Street catastrophe will need to set aside the values of the system now in meltdown – short-ter-mism, quick money and 'innovation'. It will be important to remember what and who got us into this quagmire. And we will need to remember too what went before – when capitalism was more stable, balanced and better regulated. This alternative capitalism – social democratic or 'social market' capitalism – has built postwar Western Europe. It was less dynamic than Wall Street capitalism and may also be facing dislocations, but it is surely more stable and sustainable.

And we should remember too the America of the postwar years. The past cannot be recreated, at least not exactly, but, as the three decades since 1945 now testify to, the leaders of the USA – even amidst all the aspirational and bombastic rhetoric and cold war fear and anxiety – knew that their power had limits.

I would like to thank my colleagues at the Global Policy Institute, particularly Professors Chris Dixon and Sam Whimster, for their support both intellectual and organisational, and Professors Peter Gowan and David Carlton for their highly informed insights on financial and banking issues. I would also like to thank Dr. Henning Meyer, Chris Luenen and Jon Temple for their invaluable research assistance.

Stephen Haseler
London, September 2008

Some Notes on Terms Used

The era now coming to a close has been a time of excessive 'spin' and manipulation in which words and political terms have often either changed accepted meaning or been misused. Therefore throughout the text some of the well-worn political and economic terms like 'free market', 'globalisation', 'neo-liberal' and 'neo-conservative' have been placed in quotation marks.

'NEO-LIBERAL'

The term 'neo-liberal' derives from the older nineteenth century English usage 'classical liberal' which was opposed to state and trade union influence in the economy and took a fundamentalist 'free-market' view of the world. Today, though, the word 'liberal' means the opposite – at least in the American context. For 'liberal' implies a social democratic approach to economics. It involves a tax policy conducive to funding a welfare state, a relaxed attitude to the character of ownership, be it private or public, as long as in the economy as a whole there is a balance, the need for regulation of business in a modern capitalist system, a strategic, as opposed to an ideological, view of trade policy, and a balance between freedom and social justice.

Supporters of 'free-market' fundamentalism are not therefore 'liberal' in the contemporary sense. Instead it is better to describe them as 'conservative'. And it is also more accurate to call them 'neo-conservative' – because they are truly 'new conservatives'. This will distinguish them from the older, traditional conservatism, which, rather like modern social democrats, was content with a mixed economy and a 'social capitalist' system that embraced the idea of social justice.

'NEO-CONSERVATIVE'

'Neo-Conservative' is normally used to describe a geopolitical, not an economic, persuasion. Neo-conservatives, who in the 1970s were on the left of American politics but broke with 'liberal' orthodoxy on détente with the Soviet Union, later broadened out their critique of the American 'liberal' worldview and advocated American leadership of the world and the use of American power – both economic and military – to advance the US position in the world.

As the 1990s progressed there was a coming together of these 'neo-conservatives' with the economic 'free-market thinkers'. There were exceptions (like the Cato institute in Washington D.C.) but those who professed support for 'markets' also tended to support an aggressive and forward US foreign policy, whether based on soft power 'globalisation' or hard power military means (the invasion of Iraq and the continued occupation of Afghanistan).

Hence 'neo-conservatism' is a better term than 'neo-liberal' to describe the Clinton and Bush administrations, their economic and foreign and defence policies.

'GLOBALISATION'

'Globalisation' is a term that is normally used to describe the global integration of economies (and also of communications and, to some extent, culture). I place the term in quotation marks throughout the book because 'global' economic integration is incomplete (where it exists it is primarily a USA-Europe-Asia phenomenon) and politically it is virtually non-existent (with nation-states and regional blocs showing no tendencies to form a global government).

Yet it is real in the sense that between the West and Asia the extent of economic transactions are now huge, with lower Asian costs having fuelled huge Asian surpluses, some of which are transferred back to the western financial system. This is the limited sense in which I use the term 'globalisation' in this book.

'FREE MARKET'

I usually place this term in quotes because so-called 'free markets' are often neither 'free' nor 'markets' in any serious or pure sense. In the real world markets are distorted either by governments or by big market players or by inheritance. They remain an aspiration only. But the term 'free market' is often used to describe the economic philosophy that resists a serious role for the state in the economy.

RULING THE WORLD

In December 1996 Alan Greenspan, the Chairman of the Federal Reserve Board, addressed the luminaries of the neo-conservative thinktank the American Enterprise Institute (AEI) at their annual dinner in Washington D.C. Wall Street was meeting the Pentagon; looking back on the evening, the gathering was more than just a meeting of minds. It would turn out to be a joining of destinies. For whether Greenspan or the neo-conservative politicos in the AEI knew it or not, their two worlds, Wall Street and the Pentagon, were about to be joined together in a great new cause – a bold, revolutionary attempt to remake the world in their own American image.

Greenspan, well into his stride by the mid-1990s, was giving leadership to the global market revolution that, through what was being called 'globalisation', would open up the world to American capital as never before. And behind the scenes at the AEI the neo-cons, though still in opposition, were nonetheless sharpening their swords, developing the arguments for the day when Pentagon hard power would drive US foreign policy.

TRIUMPH IN THE COLD WAR

Greenspan and the AEI neo-conservatives represented the two strands of emerging American triumphalism. The neo-cons' sense of triumph was the most upfront. Their trumpets made a clean, certain, sound. America, they argued, had won an unambiguous victory in the 40-year world contest with Soviet Russia. Michael Gorbachev once faulted US leaders for suffering from the 'disorder' of 'a winner complex', but following the dramatic events of 1989-90, with the USSR and the Warsaw Pact dissolved and the US and NATO still standing – it would have been difficult to come to any other assessment.[1] But the neo-cons also believed that America's victory had been American made, and had little to do with democratic change in Russia. It was, they argued, the result of hard power geopolitics – of Ronald Reagan's arms buildup which the Soviet Union's 'basket case economy' could simply not match.

And, in the early 1990s as the dust settled following the collapse of the Berlin Wall and US emergence as the pre-eminent and unchallenged military power, the AEI scholar warriors began articulating and polishing the case for what had now become possible – a new assertive American foreign policy based around unilateral action and pre-emption.

For the neo-cons the battle of ideas had always been an important component of the geopolitical contest. And for them, the victory in the Cold War had been a great ideological victory – of 'democracy and freedom' over 'communism'. Francis Fukuyama's book title *The End of History* captured this sense of ideological triumph as he argued that the way was now open for 'democratising' the world.[2] This neo-con mix of the need to use hard power in the service of great, universal, ideas – 'democracy at the barrel of a gun' – was classic Napoleonic revolutionary stuff and was to become the rationale for the invasion of Iraq and the attempted reordering of the Middle East.

Broader American public opinion was not so triumphant, nor that interested in remaking or ruling the world. There was certainly a general idea around Main Street that America had 'won' the Cold War; and this melded nicely into an underlying perception of America as a highly successful, even exceptional, country. It also fitted in with the strong strain in American thinking that American history is one long march of progress – from the founders through to the victory of Lincoln in the Civil War, the taming of the frontier and the making of a continent, two victorious world wars, the successful civil rights campaigns, and other postwar achievements such as putting 'a man on the moon' and, in the Cold War, the unrivalled merits of American capitalism and democracy.

This American 'Whig' version of history, as 'onward and upward' progress, and of America as, in Thomas Jefferson's famous words, 'the last, best, hope for mankind' still ran deep in early 1990s America. But, crucially, such beliefs in an 'exceptional' America did not normally translate into an impulse to rule the world – certainly not by imposing values by the use of force, Americans, like other publics, could usually be sold on the use of force only in order to defend the country – not change the world. The Pentagon was the 'Defense Department'. Americans certainly liked to think of themselves as 'leading' but by example only.

In any event, in the mid-1990s the American public and mainstream elite opinion were not yet ready for neo-con new hard-power thinking – no matter how cloaked in great universal values. Also, any sense of triumph in the Cold War was seriously tempered by the economic downturn of the early 1990s which had put an ostensible left-of-centre president into the White House with an agenda wholly dominated by domestic problems. In his early years in the White House Bill Clinton (still sensitive over his opponents attacks on him for draft dodging during Vietnam) was loathe to put American soldiers in harm's way. He was initially extremely hesitant over any American involvement in the Balkans and, later, determined to limit American casualties.

The Clinton formula is simply put: that American world power influence, of which he was in favour, would best be secured through American global economic power. And, as 'globalisation' spread and became embedded, so too would American interests – and all without one shot being fired. In sum, the 'Masters of the Universe' on Wall Street, rather than the generals in the Pentagon, would do the job.

MASTERS OF THE UNIVERSE

On Wall Street a triumphal mood had been building ever since the late 1980s and the successes of the Reagan/Thatcher deregulatory revolution. And, in the 1990s, following Bill Clinton's failure to reform healthcare, it was becoming clear that the new Democratic president's 'Third Way' policies were destined to deepen, rather than undermine, the revolution. And it was a revolution that was making finance king of capitalism.

Furthermore, this new finance capitalism was going global. With communism defeated and Euro-style social capitalism deemed 'sluggish' or 'sclerotic', the 'dynamic' Wall Street model was carrying all before it. And triumph built upon triumph when this new Wall Street capitalism managed to survive the serial shocks of the dot.com crash, the Asian crisis and the Russian default.

It was an atmosphere in which Wall Street knew few constraints, possessed no sense of the limits and limitations which had previously, from Roosevelt to Reagan, governed western capitalism. It was heady stuff, and it unleashed an arrogance, selfishness and irresponsibility that fuelled a 'boom' – but also would, later, cause a great 'bust'.

In 2007 the economist Paul Krugman argued that 'around 25 years ago, American business – and the American political system – bought into the idea that greed is good.'[3] 'Greed is good' was the famous line of Gordon Gekko, the fictional character in the 1987 film *Wall Street*. Gekko was a new type of capitalist, a 'master of the universe' – a financial speculator and manipulator with huge financial assets at his disposal. He was ruthless, asocial (unanchored in any society), cynical and highly opinionated.

In the film, Gekko tells it like it is, with no frills. He tells his young sidekick Buddy about the money that can be made: 'I'm not talking about some four-hundred thousand dollar a year working Wall Street stiff, flying first class, being comfortable, I'm talking about liquid. Rich enough to have your own jet, rich enough not to waste time. Fifty, a hundred-million dollars, Buddy. A player...or nothing'.

Gekko sets out, more pithily than any commentator or economist, the harsh new reality – that 'the richest one percent of this country owns half our country's wealth, five trillion dollars. One third of that comes from hard work, two thirds comes from inheritance, interest on interest accumulating to widows and idiot sons'. 'And what I do' he says is 'stock and real estate speculation. It's bullshit.' As early as the late 1980s he could assert a horrible truth: 'You got ninety percent of the American public out there with little or no net worth. I create nothing. I own.'

And with greed and money goes power. 'We make the rules pal,' says Gekko. 'The news, war, peace, famine, upheaval, the price of a paper clip...now you're not naïve enough to think we are living in a democracy, are you Buddy?'

Yet Gekko was no extreme caricature. For in real Wall Street life there were plenty of Gekkos, flesh and blood examples of the genre. One such was Michael Milken the 'junk bond king' whose company Drexel Burnham Lambert arguably started the Wall Street spree. The financial lawyer Martin Lipton has argued that 'the financial crisis we're in today stems from the invention by Drexel Burnham Lambert of the junk bond. You can draw a straight line from Drexel Burnham to the financial world today'[4] Milken, who exemplified the greed and excess of the 1980s, helped discover 'securitisation' and today's fancy financial instruments. He was convicted of racketeering and securities fraud in 1989.

Another example of Wall Street's limitless vaunting ambition was Victor Neiderhoffer. More cerebral than most, Neiderhoffer was a hedge fund manager, statistician and economist. Like Alan Greenspan he was an extreme Randian individualist. His key characteristic was to push life to its limits. Like many on 1980s and 90s Wall Street his watchword was 'freedom' – a 'freedom' unconstrained by any sense of social obligation. Even basic manners were constricting: Neiderhoffer would eat meals in restaurants with his hands (including, on one occasion in a London restaurant, mashed potatoes).

But, intriguingly, Gekko, Milken and Niederhoffer were inspirational. They were men to emulate – at least on Wall

Street. And their 'philosophies', style and appetites became part of the acceptable culture of the new capitalism as it was emerging around the globe – from Wall Street to the City of London and the Far East.

GRAND MASTERS OF THE UNIVERSE

Wall Street was this new capitalism's engine room. But the course was set on the bridge by America's political and financial leadership. And at these controls was the Chairman of the US Federal Reserve Board, Alan Greenspan. Greenspan, a Reagan appointee, had become Chairman in August 1987 just as communism was imploding. He survived the 1987 stock market crash and was to assume the status of financial statesman as he guided the US – and the global economy – during four Presidencies, those of Ronald Reagan, George Bush Snr, Bill Clinton and George W. Bush.

During the 1990s, as the US economy powered ahead in the new world now free of communism, Greenspan's growing stature served to legitimise the new Wall Street. Greenspan was soft-spoken, sophisticated and possessed of an academic air, which together with his power and status, gave him an aura of gravitas. (He was to be bestowed with honours – awarded the Presidential Medal of Freedom by George W. Bush and, from Tony Blair's New Labour government in 2002, the Knight Commander of the British Empire). Yet, at bottom, he was an ideologue – a quiet ideologue. A student of the market fundamentalist Ayn Rand, Greenspan was seriously committed to the world of 'free markets' and to the 'neo-liberal' world order. He once described himself as a 'libertarian Republican'.

'Free markets' – with light touch regulation – was an ideology, and a bias, that sustained Greenspan throughout his tenure. It was his foundational structure and compass that would give him the confidence both to guide the American economy for over two decades and to lecture his competitors – primarily the social capitalists of Europe – on their system's shortcomings. But it was also a bias that blinkered him in his dealing with his beloved markets.

This limited vision was most clearly on display when, at a critical juncture in American economic history, he turned his back on the need to regulate the mounting housing debt crisis that, after he left office, was to lead to the banking crash of 2007.

In 2002 he lowered the interest rate (Fed Funds Rate) to 1 per cent and set out to give a boost to the housing market. In late 2002, as the housing bubble was beginning to get underway, Greenspan praised the mortgage industry – arguing that 'besides sustaining the demand for new construction, mortgage markets have also been a powerful stabilising force over the past two years of economic distress by facilitating the extraction of some of the equity that homeowners have built up over the years'.[5] In 2004, with the housing bubble building up pressure, he actually recommended Adjustable Rate Mortgages to the public.[6] And, as late as 2005, he was praising 'the multitude of new products such as sub-prime loans' and justifying lending on the grounds of spreading equity more widely. He suggested that 'where once more marginal applicants would simply have been denied credit, lenders are now able to quite effectively judge the risk posed by individual applicants and to price that risk appropriately.'[7]

Critics were later to suggest that the welcome rise in 'marginal applicants' for mortgages was only exceeded by the number of dispossessions.[8] One commentator suggested that 'in Greenspan's world, predatory lending – like…poison toys and tainted seafood – just doesn't happen'.[9]

GRAND MASTER BILL CLINTON

In all the adulation, and searing criticism, of Alan Greenspan, it is often forgotten that American presidents appoint the Fed chief, and Greenspan holds a record – of being appointed by four successive presidents. And not surprisingly so, as Greenspan's approach to economics was their approach – one dominated by the market revolution. In this sense Greenspan's long tenure was simply the reflection of the dominant political mood of the time.

Of the four presidents, only Clinton presented Greenspan with a possible problem. Clinton was a 'poor boy' and had developed a left-of-centre agenda for America in which 'big government' and 'high taxes' (for better public services) were not public enemies. He came into office in 1992 committed to real reform of the American health system. But by the time Greenspan came up for renewal, Clinton's Presidency was in its third year – and the white hope of the American liberals had abandoned healthcare, come under the sway of corporations and become a devotee of 'the new economy' – and the ambitious idea that America was entering a new economic age with new rules – or no rules.

The 'new economy' was all the rage during the 1990s and Greenspan was 'very open to the possibility that we have entered a new economic age' reported Judy Shelton (a scholar who regularly met Greenspan) and 'he really believes in the organic nature of the market economy'.[10] Clinton was reported to 'share Greenspan's view on the New Economy'. Early in his second term the president said that 'I believe it's possible to have more sustained and higher growth without inflation than we previously thought.' Mundane words, but a revolutionary thought. Clinton and Greenspan had discovered a 'new economy' – a whole new economic paradigm that was going to change the rules and change the world. In fact the rest of Clinton's presidency and Greenspan's tenure was built on this intoxicating idea of a new economic age with new rules of economics. Clinton secured his 'sustained higher growth' but it was to be fuelled by debt-led housing boom consumption which in turn would be fuelled by low inflation and low interest rates out of the growing China project. Thus the 'new economy' was both a global economy and a market economy – indeed a more extreme version of the market economy that had been ushered in under Ronald Reagan.

The Clinton administration's main contribution to the construction of this 'new economy' is best described by its keenness to deregulate – particularly in the banking and financial services sector. The Nobel prize winning economist Joseph Stiglitz, himself a former Chairman of Clinton's Council of Economic Advisors, has pointed out how the Clinton administration opened the way for the emergence of the huge 'shadow banking' sector with its loose regulatory framework, a move that undoubtedly contributed to the boom of the roaring nineties and the bust of 2007.[11]

Clinton deregulated the banking sector by repealing the Glass-Steagall Act – a Roosevelt New Deal measure introduced in the aftermath of the bank failures following the 1929 Great Crash. By separating the functions of commercial and investment banks it barred all banks from both lending money and selling securities. Clinton's Treasury Secretary Robert Rubin took the lead in the repeal even though he was an investment banker himself (a former co-Chairman of Goldman Sachs). Following the repeal the way was clear for conflicts of interest to emerge, not least the ability of the same (big) institution to both push stocks in a company and at the same time drive up the price of the shares being promoted by lending money to the same company. As well as banking, the telecommunications industry saw yet another major act of deregulation introduced by the Clinton administration. This deregulation 'unleashed a gold-rush', and the parallel deregulation of the banks allowed the rush to get out of control'.[12] Clinton's successor George W. Bush also became a champion of the new economy and the new capitalism – the growth rates of this great new economy would help him launch a war, and pay for it.

GRAND MASTER TONY BLAIR

The Greenspan/Clinton 'new economy' was not short on fervent supporters overseas – leaders like Britain's Tony Blair, Spain's Jose Maria Aznar, and Italy's Silvio Berlusconi. Chief amongst them, though, was the British New Labour administration of Tony Blair. His own version of the 'new economy' was built around the City of London's financial services industry which, deregulated in the 1980s under Margaret Thatcher in order to compete in the global economy, became, in the late 1990s, a major success story. But, as with Wall Street, it unleashed the new culture of unrestrained money, untold riches and greed – what Susan Strange called 'casino capitalism'. The Blair government was 'intensely relaxed about people getting filthy rich' and Britain saw the 'rise of celebrity mansions, private aircraft and Highland sporting estates.' In Blair's Britain 'any sense of decent restraint has become meaningless in a country invaded by overseas billionaires, and homemade ones who would never deign to pay income tax and so keep a flat in some tax haven overseas.'[13]

Blair continued and deepened the privatisation programme; he developed a relatively low tax regime but his tax take, and therefore public expenditure, was rising – whilst, that is, the boom (the housing boom) lasted. And the housing boom saw, as it was meant to, a gargantuan growth in British private debt levels, debt which in turn fuelled consumer-led growth – and so on. But it, too, was to burst in 2007.

'CLEVER MASTERS': DEBT AND CHINA

The 'masters of the universe' in Washington, Wall Street and the City of London during the two decades of boom succeeded in one major respect. They managed, against many predictions, to sustain impressive economic growth levels. During the late 1990s and into the twenty-first century the Anglo-American 'neo-liberal' economies were growing well – on paper at least. And it was this growth that persuaded the American leadership, post 9/11, that a new, limitless economy could drive new limitless western global power.

But the truth was that America was living beyond its means. As we see in Chapter One the super-rich were doing very well and were driving the economy and setting its rules. But American wages were stagnant (or falling), and imports from China and Asia were displacing jobs (and keeping wages low).

So only the miracle of debt – both mortgage and credit card – could keep consumption up and sustain growth. Future generations would later pay the price as millions of ordinary consumers – their hugely inflated house prices inducing a 'wealth effect' – kept the economy growing by debt-financed shopping and holidays. And the debt mountain was of Himalayan proportions. The US Bureau of Economic Analysis tells the incredible story. The ratio of debt to GDP stayed at a steady 1.2 during the 1950s, 60s and 70s; in the early 1980s it started to rise significantly and did not stop rising, until at its height it reached well over 3.1; that is, 200 per cent higher than in 1979.

The late Professor Susan Strange has argued that this bubble was the product of what she termed 'casino capitalism' run by 'mad money'.[14] It had two main features. The first was the extreme 'financialisation' of the system – a term meaning more credit, more banks, more lending to new types of institutions like hedge funds, private equity funds and the like, and lending through an array of new and exotic types of financial instruments. Secondly, the thing that made 'financialisation' possible was deregulation, and particularly, deregulation of financial markets (including global markets).

But this great Wall Street debt mountain could not possibly have been built without the US-sponsored entry of China into the global labour and capital market. The 'fall of communism', and the emergence of a billion Chinese into the world economy, was an historic opportunity for the 'neo-liberals' on both Wall Street and in Washington – for it would produce a secure low inflationary global environment. Old rules and norms could be torn up as Americans (and their 'neo-liberal' allied economies) could begin to live way beyond their means. The cheap Chinese would keep prices low; and this endless low-inflationary environment would allow an endless low interest consumer boom (with endless profits), based on endless debt. As long, that is, as house prices, kept rising,

GRAND MASTER BUSH: RULING THE WORLD

In Europe the 'neo-liberal' trio of Tony Blair, Jose Maria Aznar and Silvio Berlusconi, saw not just a new economy but a new world coming. The new system had ended old rules of economics; and, following 9/11 and George Bush's response, the old geopolitical rules were changing too – ushering in a new global order. Blair spanned the presidencies of both Bill Clinton (when he signed up to the 'new economy') and George W. Bush (when he signed up to the new American-led global political order). Where Clinton (and Blair) had seen a vision of a new world order based upon 'soft' American-led western economic power, Bush (and Blair), particularly after 9/11, saw Pentagon power, to be displayed to the world by the invasion of Iraq and the removal of Saddam, as a necessary reinforcement in establishing this new order. The full doctrinal framework of the new order was outlined in the 2002 National Security Strategy of the USA issued by the White House.

The 2003 invasion and occupation of Iraq was supported by an array of American leaders and opinion-formers – conservatives, neo-conservatives, moderates, liberals. Indeed, the extent of 'liberal' support for the invasion and occupation is often underestimated. The invasion was supported by almost all serious Democratic presidential candidates in the two elections of 2004 and 2008. Bill and Hillary Clinton, John Kerry, John Edwards (with only Howard Dean and Barack Obama, then an Illinois legislator, opposing). It was also supported by a wide array of liberal journalists and by much of the mainstream American media owned by the large media corporations. And in Britain the Labour cabinet (there was only one cabinet resignation) and the majority of Labour MPs joined the Conservatives in supporting Britain's invasion of Iraq.

The invasion of Iraq has since been portrayed as the work of a small unrepresentative group – primarily of neo-conservatives and their Christian fundamentalist allies. And the failure to meet the objectives of the invasion has been blamed on post-invasion policies. 'Blaming Bremer' – Jerry Bremer the ruler of Iraq before the formation of the Iraqi government – was the standard response of many of those who sought to distance themselves from their support for the original invasion. Others, like Senator John Edwards, announced that he had taken the wrong decision.

The invasion of Iraq and the 'global war on terror' may have been a strategy made in Washington but it was eagerly signed on to by some of Washington's European supporters, principally Tony Blair. Other supporters included Jose Maria Aznar of Spain and Silvio Berlusconi of Italy and a host of pro-American East European leaders An intriguing aspect was that Europe's supporters of the invasion tended also to be those who supported the American Wall Street 'neo-liberal' economic model and were critical of 'Social Europe'.

By early 2003, with US opinion and key Europeans supportive, the scene was set for the event which would show that the US meant what it was saying. And on 21st March 2003 – as 40 cruise missiles were fired from the Abraham Lincoln battle group in the gulf into southern Baghdad – the gloves finally came off with the 'shock and awe' of the American-led invasion of the heart of Arabia and the subsequent removal from office, and execution, of Iraqi President Saddam Hussein. By the late spring of 2003 – in the immediate aftermath of this spectacular assertion of US military power in Iraq – it seemed to many that the US had indeed now become the 'full spectrum' global 'hegemon' – militarily, economically, politically. Finally, Wall Street and Washington were as one: Wall Street's economic globalisation and Washington's global military reach would allow 'the lone super-power' to guide, if not rule, the world.

THE CRASH

But it was not long before it all fell apart. By the turn of the New Year of 2004 it was becoming clear that American troops were never going to be welcomed with flowers (as some neocons had predicted) and that Iraq was not going to become a beacon of democracy that would spread democracy and stability throughout the Middle East (as many in Washington had foreseen).

And then, on 7th October 2004, Charles Duelfer, the head of Washington's Iraq Survey Group, formally made the stunning announcement that Iraq had no stockpiles of biological, chemical or nuclear weapons before the 2003 invasion. And from then on American public support for the invasion and for the continuing occupation began to slide away.

Yet, even after the Iraq imbroglio, whilst the American economy was seemingly powering ahead, the idea of America as the 'lone superpower' could still resonate. Critics were pointing to the growing housing bubble, the debt mountain and the huge imbalances between Asia and the USA; but these were still marginal voices.

But then, suddenly, on 9th August 2007 interbank lending throughout the western banking system essentially dried up – and the great 2007 credit crunch began. The trigger point was the sub-prime mortgage bust; but it soon became clear that the crisis was much wider, and deeper – involving the busting, or 'de-leveraging', of the whole credit system of the USA (and US linked enterprises abroad). Wall Street had crashed. And would not be repaired, or recover, any time soon.

As the dimensions of the credit crisis emerged it soon became apparent that the credit and debt bubble had been the result of a deregulatory binge that had allowed all kinds of predatory lending based on weird and wonderful lending vehicles. 'Deregulation' had been a key aspect of the market revolution – and the fundamentalist market ideology – that had so dominated Washington and Wall Street during the Greenspan/Clinton/Bush era. Consider the press conference held four years before the bust on 3rd June 2003 – just about the time sub-prime lending was starting to go wild – to announce a new US government initiative aimed at reducing the regulatory burden on banks. Representatives of four of the

US government agencies responsible for financial supervision used tree shears to attack a stack of paper representing bank regulations. The fifth representative, James Gilleran, of the Office of Thrift Supervision, wielded a chainsaw.'[15]

WHAT THE TRIUMPHALISTS HAVE WROUGHT

The triumphalist years since the fall of communism – years which were marked by a combination of hubris, greed and unlimited ambition amongst the West's elites – have ended badly. The 'masters of the universe' in Washington and Wall Street sought to remake, if not rule, the world; but in so doing, and in so failing, they left America and the West much weaker. For all the bombast, the net result has seen a reduction in the power and reputation of the United States and, to an extent too, that of the broader western world.

At the heart of the new weakness of the West is the growing dependence on foreign money to fund living beyond its means. America's Treasury has been kept afloat by China's purchase of T-bills. But the fact that China is also tied into this dangerous and unhealthy co-dependency relationship does not diminish America's loss of freedom of action.

This growing dependence has been fed again during the credit crisis when the West's troubled banks were bailed out by politically-controlled Asian and Middle Eastern funds, many of them purchasing an ownership role. There were few questions asked about this foreign 'sovereign wealth'. In a sign of how 'low in the water' the western financial system had sunk American and British leaders – who fiercely rejected public ownership at home – fell over themselves to encourage the buying of western banks by money controlled by dictators, sheiks and communists. The UK was unworried – or was so exposed that it could not afford to worry – and in January 2007 it revealed that Goldman Sachs, the investment bank which had been selected by the British government to find financing for the stricken Northern Rock Bank, was seeking money to bail-out British banks from cash-rich governments in the Middle East. The Abu Dhabi Investment Authority and the Qatari Investment Authority were being approached to 'invest' – the same Abu Dhabi Investment Authority that had already poured millions into Citibank.[16]

This growing economic dependence was a natural part of the Wall Street 'neo-liberal' globalisation project. Globalisation leads to integration, and integration leads to co-dependencies. But when such integration is forged quickly – in historical terms in 'the blinking of an eye' – and between such utterly diverse economies as the USA and China, then integration comes at a huge price. And the price was to be paid by the growing numbers of western citizens – no longer just the unskilled – who were 'uncompetitive', and either lost their jobs or saw their wages and conditions worsen. The upshot of the great 'neo-liberal globalisation' of the 1990s onwards was that the West's societies became more and more divided between the 'winners' – the new mobile global super-rich class – and the much larger number of 'losers' – drawn increasingly from the fracturing middle classes. And, following the bank crisis of 2007, with the debt unravelling, the West was standing on the brink of even worse social divisions as, should some forecasts be believed, millions more were slated to lose their homes and jobs.

But financial collapse and economic weakness at home was only half of the story – for the triumphalist years also saw a major western geopolitical failure in the Middle East. The 2003 invasion and occupation of Iraq was still, in 2008, provoking a debate in Washington about how the US should leave; but there was a general recognition that the war had been a failure

– with sizeable majorities of Americans believing that the US had 'made a mistake' in sending troops or 'should have stayed out of the war'.

It was obvious too that the broad objective of 'democratising' and 'remaking' the Middle East' through force had failed. It was also becoming clear that the Middle East region was no more 'democratic', and much less stable, than before the invasion, and that the only real winner was Iran, who, with Iraq seriously weakened, was well on the way to becoming the regional superpower. Yet, pulling western armed forces out of Iraq will be difficult, not least because of issues of credibility. But the longer the US stays in Iraq the greater the long-term toll on domestic support for armed interventions abroad – perhaps even for America's global role. And, importantly, the loss of American honour and reputation caused by the false premises for invasion had hurt the standing of America (and her allies in the adventure) – a reputation that will not be recoverable any time soon.

DELUSIONS

Such a record of failure, however, needs an attempted explanation. And it is one of the theses of this book that the American elites' so-called victory over world communism in 1989 simply went to their heads – producing a consequent deluded view of the world and their position in it. The key delusion lay in the assessment of America's (and the West's) power. In the 1990s all the talk in Washington and Wall Street was of the 'unipolar moment', 'American hegemony', 'America as the lone superpower' and of the superiority of the American economic model and the 'new economy' which was rewriting the rules.

Yet, the reality was of an America in long-term comparative decline. This decline was real. America's share of global GDP halved between 1945 and 2000. But this fall was masked by America's leadership of the West during the Cold War, by the collapse of communism, and, then, by a series of military successes in the first Gulf War and in the air war over Serbia. The idea of American economic ascendancy was then given further life by the spin surrounding the dot.com bubble and the 'new economy'. By the turn of the century economic commentators were regularly describing the early twenty-first century 'new economy' – the US economy – and the US economic model, as uniquely dynamic and flexible, certainly when compared with the 'sclerotic' European economies which needed 'a reform agenda'.

These plaudits, though, hid another reality – one only fully revealed when the credit crisis rocked Wall Street. For the fact was that, contrary to the mood of triumphalism, American capitalism itself was in trouble. The American 'free enterprise system', historically so dynamic, inventive and productive, was simply no longer its old self – it had slowly degenerated. The greatest achievement of the American economic system in the twentieth century, compared that is to all the other systems, was that it had spread wealth quite widely – enough to create and sustain a large, stable and vibrant middle class – the backbone, and life-blood of America. But Chapter 8 points out that the middle class is now fracturing, and as we see in Chapter 9, the values which underpinned it – individual merit and enterprise, driven by the Protestant ethic – are giving way to an unproductive inheritance culture which is producing, of all things in republican America, a super-rich aristocracy shorn of any social concern or responsibility. A business class living off the state and, because the state is so important to it, increasingly trying, through politics, to buy it.

Yet, with the US in comparative decline (and social divisions growing at home), the two decades since 1989 saw the triumphalist generation in Wall Street and Washington power ahead as though nothing was happening. America was the 'lone superpower', the 'hyper-power', the 'hegemon'. In the view of Condoleeza Rice this was the 'unipolar moment'. A Democratic predecessor, Madeleine Albright, said as well that 'America was the indispensable nation'. Yet the reality was very different. Rather than a 'unipolar' world order, the US and the West were facing the clear emergence of a multipolar world in which, as we see in Chapter 11, the rise of China presented real challenges. As did CHINUSA, the term I coin to describe the co-dependency relationship developing between China and the USA.

And with power diffusing throughout the world – rather than the other way round – the other reality, which the Bush administration was to come up hard against in Iraq, was the growth of resistance around the world to US global power projection. The American triumphalists were for real: so they truly believed their own rhetoric – including the neo-con prediction that American troops would be greeted with flowers like 'liberators'. Yet the Washington neo-conservatives were to learn that bringing democracy, even through the barrel of a gun, was not always popular, and that people abroad did not like being invaded and occupied even if a dictator was removed in the process. And it was also to learn that domestic opposition to foreign invasions and occupations – if they were protracted – could grow quickly, with domestic political consequences.

RESCUING THE WEST

The question now is no longer about how Washington can 'manage' the changing world – whether it be rising Asia or enlarging Europe or unstable Islam. This approach – that America needed to 'manage' global change – was always both unrealistic and patronising on Washington's part. The question now is somewhat different: it is whether the US can easily adjust to her weaker global role? And whether she can become more realistic in her ambitions? And, as far as the broader West is concerned, the urgent question is whether there can be, or should be, and will be, two Wests rather than one? And, also: what role for a Europe that has been sitting on the sidelines for far too long.

With the western elites' post-cold war fling now subsiding, a damaged West has the opportunity to develop a more realistic grand strategy. But I argue here that we also need an ideological change in direction. The project of remaking the world was always flawed, but remaking it in the image of a dysfunctional and degenerate Wall Street capitalism was the height of arrogance.

Thankfully, though, during these triumphalist years, there was always 'an alternative West' out there. Today's Wall Street greed, excess and deregulatory paradise is historically not the only American way. And, though it galls many an advocate of 'Anglo-American' neo-liberal economics, it now seems fair to argue that Europe's social democratic variety of capitalism has proved more sustainable than its Wall Street 'mad money' capitalist cousin. It has certainly not allowed its societies to run up the dangerous debt levels now unravelling. It has allowed a better more balanced relationship between state and market and also created a more sustainable – because less divided – society. And because the European business class, though powerful, is not rampant, there is less 'special interest' opposition to universal healthcare and welfare – and less constant pressure to cut costs and switch jobs overseas.

And geopolitically, although the neo-conservative ideologues may have carried the day during the last twenty years, the American and European leaders who are now taking over from the disastrous triumphalist generation still have the West's more realistic traditions to draw upon.

The last time Americans found themselves on the winning side of a world war – with the world at their feet – was in 1945. Then the American leadership was quite able to win without triumphalism and braggadocio and deluded visions of ruling the world. When Marshall, Truman and Acheson – the 'masters of the universe' of their day – found themselves 'in at the creation' of a new world they acted with strength certainly, but also judiciously and with a sense of limits. During the Cold War they constructed a defensive alliance, they recognised Soviet communism's sphere of influence, and they firmly resisted the 'roll-back' (of communism) and the delusions of 'remaking the world'. In today's world, with so much about to change, such realism is sorely needed.

CHAPTER ONE

WALL STREET UNBOUND

THE SUPER-RICH

When in 1989 the Berlin Wall cracked open, and the iron curtain parted, the end of the forty-years-long Cold War was a political triumph for the West and for America. It was a great victory for freedom and pluralism over command communism, but it also heralded a more dubious outcome. For with communism defeated and great new markets (principally China and Eastern Europe) opening up, the way was clear for a new unfettered form of western capitalism – global capitalism – to emerge. And with it a new global elite, indeed a new global class.

In the early years of the new century this new class was commanding wealth beyond imagining. It is potentially wealthier than any super-rich class in history (including the famed 'robber barons', those 'malefactors of great wealth' criticised by Teddy Roosevelt, and the nineteenth century capitalists who inspired the opposition of a century of Marxists). And it is also assuming the proportions of over-lordship, that is of an over-class – as powerful, majestic and antidemocratic as the imperial governing classes at the height of the European empires.

A troublesome aspect of today's super-rich – one which separates them sharply from earlier super-rich – is that they owe little or no loyalty to community or nation. In previous eras the wealthy used to be grounded and bound within their nations and societies – a constraint that kept aggregations of wealth within reason and the rich relatively socially responsible. Now, though, the rich are free: free to move their money and their assets around the world. In the new global economy super-rich wealth (capital) is now freer than ever before to seek out the most productive – that is, high profit, low cost – haven; and with the entry into the global economy of China, India and Eastern Europe – these opportunities have multiplied. The super-rich are also free to move themselves. Although still less mobile than their money, they too are becoming less rooted, moving easily between many different locations. And all this freedom means one thing: an increase in the power of wealth over that of democratic politics – to the point now where wealth can buy, and is owning, politics.

ORDINARY MILLIONAIRES

This essential mobility of the rich separates them from the rest of us – who remain rooted to the locale where we work. Indeed, it is the ability to escape from the world of work (and its rootedness) which effectively defines the modern super-rich. Ordinary dollar millionaires are by no means lavishly well-off, particularly if they are in three- or four-people families or households. However they are able to be financially independent – as one commentary put it, they can 'maintain their lifestyle for years and years without earning even one month's pay'.[1]

It has been estimated that in 1996 there were as many as 6 million dollar millionaires in the world, up from 2 million at the end of the Cold War. By 2006 the number had risen to 9.5 million. Intriguingly they were spread relatively evenly across continents – with 3.2 million in North America, 2.9 million in Europe and 2.6 million in Asia-Pacific.[2] The European breakdown includes: Germany with 798,000 and the UK with 485,000. This World Wealth Report uses the term 'High Net Worth Individual' instead of super-rich, and it defines net worth as including the values of private equity holdings, publicly quoted equities, bonds, funds and cash. It excludes primary residences and collectibles.

MULTIMILLIONAIRES

These ordinary dollar millionaires, however, find themselves at the *very* lower reaches of the world of the super-rich. They often work – if not for a living, then for extras – and their lifestyles are often not particularly extravagant or sumptuous. They are, in fact, poor cousins in comparison with the more seriously rich families and individuals who are now emerging in the global economy.

In 2004 the top 1 per cent of the American population possessed a mean net worth of around $15 million each – a wealth holding that could produce an *unearned* annual income of say $750,000.[3] And in 2007 The World Wealth Report issued annually by Capgemini/Merrill Lynch reported that the number of 'Ultra-High Net Worth Individuals', that is people with $30 million or more, amounted to 94,970 worldwide (roughly 39,000 in the USA, 21,000 in Europe and 19,000 in Asia-Pacific).[4]

These households are the truly super-rich, whose net worth, much of it inherited, is the source of considerable economic power and produces an income (mainly unlinked to work) that allows, even by affluent western standards, extraordinarily sumptuous lifestyles. Although huge amounts of the money of these multimillionaires are held outside the United States, in Europe, Asia and Latin America, this tells us nothing about the nationality of the holders. In a sense these super-rich multimillionaires are the world's true global citizens – owing loyalty to themselves, their families and their money, rather than to communities and territorial boundaries. Their money is highly mobile, and so are they themselves as they move between their various homes around the world – in London, Paris and New York; in large houses in the Hamptons in the United States, in the English and French countryside, and in gated communities in sun-belt America, particularly Florida, southern California and Arizona – as well as on yachts traveling between tropical paradises not scarred by local poverty.

'THE 950 BILLIONAIRES'
Amongst these multimillionaires there is a distinction to be made between those at the lower end – say the $30 million net worth households – and those at the higher end – say the $500 million plus households. The distinction is one of power, not lifestyle. From most perspectives the income from $30 million can, at least on the face of it, produce the same kind of lifestyle as income from the net worth of the more serious multimillionaires (for there is arguably a limit to the number of homes, yachts and cars that can be enjoyed and consumed in a lifetime).[5] $30 million in net worth, however, simply cannot command as much economic power – over employment, over small businesses – as do the resources of the really big time multi-

millionaires, much of whose money is tied up in big transnational corporations.

At the very top of this mega-rich world are the dollar billionaires, those who command over $1,000 million in net worth, a fortune that can secure an *unearned* annual income, depending on inflation and interest rates, of $50 million a year before tax – staggeringly well over 1,000 times more than the average *earned* US income. In 1997 estimates of the number of these mega-rich individuals varied from 358 to 447 worldwide.[6] By 2007 the Forbes 'Wealth List' estimated the number of billionaires to be 946, with 178 'newcomers' (from the previous year). 415 of these billionaires were from the USA and, intriguingly, 20 were from China (a number that had grown dramatically during the year to reach 66, with some estimates suggesting 106!)[7] In 2007 *The Sunday Times* estimated that Britain had about 65 billionaires, up from 54 the previous year – although many of these were foreigners living in the UK.[8]

WHO ARE THESE BILLIONAIRES?

These 950 or so billionaires in the world are a varied lot. In one sense they are like the rest of us (and like those who will read this book). They are overwhelmingly western, primarily American or European, and male, but they represent no single ethnic group, no single social background, and certainly possess no single business acumen or financial secret which can explain the acquiring of these awesome fortunes.

Many, indeed most, of these billionaires, though, would not be in the mega-rich category without the aid of a substantial inheritance – for 'inheriting' remains the well-trodden route to great multimillion dollar wealth. The crucially central role of inheritance in wealth building is often underplayed by the super-wealthy and their supporters. It is also downplayed by supporters of the 'entrepreneurial society' and the 'free-market' who need to argue that money and success comes through hard work, creativity and intelligence rather than unearned privilege. In Britain in 2007 it was claimed that as many as 78 per cent of those on *The Sunday Times'* 'Rich List' had 'made their money themselves through business'.[9] Yet the true origin of the wealth of today's super and mega-rich families normally always involves some start being given to the super-wealthy through inheritance. For instance, in the late 1990s a survey claimed that of the top 400 wealthiest people in the United States, 39 made the list through inheritance *alone* – and many of the others had some inheritance to help get them started.[10]

The British Queen, Elizabeth Windsor, is perhaps the most famous example of such massive unearned wealth. In 1997 Phillip Beresford (in *The Sunday Times'* 'Rich List', (*Sunday Times*, 6th April 1997) put her net worth at a staggering $10.4 thousand million in 1992 (double the 1997 figure for top-listed Joseph Lewis). However, after she took a rival 'rich list' to the Press Complaints Commission over its valuation of her assets, *The Sunday Times'* Wealth Register excluded from its calculations the royal art collection, which, had it been included, would have given her a $16 billion figure, making her the world's wealthiest woman and the second wealthiest person in the world, with half the net worth of the Sultan of Brunei but more than the Walton family.'[11]

In contrast to the inheritors, there are some 'self-made' men (very few women) in the billionaire class. Yet even these men of merit have not necessarily made their inordinate fortunes through extraordinary amounts of work and talent – certainly not its continuous application. Many of the self-made mega-rich are certainly talented and creative (and often ruthless), but many of them have become mega-rich through one-off bursts of insight or risk or luck.

William (Bill) Gates is seen as 'self-made', very much the American entrepreneurial hero. His vast resources – *Newsweek* calls him 'the Croesus of our age' – have been built upon the meritorious image of having run a successful company which provides a real service, a real addition to human understanding and communication. In 2007 his huge net worth was listed as $56 billion by *Forbes* magazine (up from $36.4 billion in the 1997 listing) – and is based upon the value of his shares in his company Microsoft. It was Gates' original burst of imagination that created his fortune – the initial stock offering in 1986 of 100 Microsoft shares cost $2100 but by the first trading day in August 1997 this had risen to 3600 shares at $138.50 each! Gates' personal share of the company rose from $234 million to $37.8 billion in the same period.'[12] Certainly Gates has managed the company and taken many crucial decisions. Yet as Microsoft grew he needed the more 'routine' skills exhibited by thousands of major company directors – such as managerial aptitude and the ability to stave off competition. As with all established businesses, less and less risk and less and less creativity was needed (and a junior hospital doctor probably put in more hours).

Paul Raymond is a different type of self-made billionaire. Described by academic John Hills as Britain's richest man – in 1995 he placed him ahead of Joseph Lewis – Raymond's fortune in the mid-1990s was thought to be well over £1.65 billion. Having founded Raymond's Revue Bar in the Soho district of London, with topless dancers, he made his money by investing in soft pornography and property.[13] Like Gates he had the talent to spot a coming market – albeit one that was less elevating and educational. And also like Gates, and the other mega-rich, once the original burst of inventiveness (perhaps amounting to his one great insight) was over, the rest of his working life has consisted of simply managing his empire and watching his money grow – as long that is as the great boom worked its will.

Intriguingly, no person whose talent has been put to continuous use throughout his or her career or vocation – such people as writers, sportsmen and women, professionals such as accountants, architects, professors, teachers, engineers, even distinguished physicians and pop stars – makes it to the higher reaches of the mega-rich. Even the pop star Paul McCartney of the Beatles, with a mere £400 million, is only the thirty-seventh richest Briton.

The truth remains that the key to entering today's world of the mega-rich, and certainly the billionaire class, is not work or talent or risk-taking (millions have those attributes in abundance). Rather it is access to capital. For capital, once attained, can both grow and be lost very quickly – neither outcomes needing much work, flair or intelligence. For the mega-rich it was the getting of the capital start that was all-important; for in the last three decades – of seemingly endless finance-led growth – *keeping* capital, and *growing* capital, is nothing special. It needs none of the skills, character and hard work associated with running and growing an old-style business.

Perhaps the most perfect exemplar of modern capitalism – finance capitalism – is Joseph Lewis. By 1997 he had arguably become Britain's richest person, overtaking both the Queen and David Sainsbury and family, and he was approaching the foothills of America's 'top twenty' mega-rich. His lifestyle conforms to the popular image of the global capitalist, virtually a parody of the genre. He lives in a Bahamas villa and owns a 62 metre yacht that is four storeys high. He plays the exchange markets in front of a bank of computer screens. Whereas fellow finance capitalist Jimmy Goldsmith built an estate in South America, Lewis has bought a whole village. He has invested in British football and in the auctioneers Christies (which, along with fellow auctioneers Sotheby's probably own the most impressive intelligence records on the world's high-net-worth individuals).

Born in the East End of London, Joseph Lewis made his fortune in foreign exchange dealings. Starting out as a London caterer laying on medieval banquets for rich tourists (with a sideline in cashmere shops) Lewis only made real money when he went into foreign exchange dealing. He, as well as other mega-rich dealers such as George Soros and the Barclay brothers, use relatively small amounts of money to move markets, and profit from the changes. This is often condemned as 'speculation' or worse (the prime minister of Malaysia once called Soros 'a devil').

Yet 'speculation' conjures up the idea of considerable risk. The reality, however, is very different. It normally takes rather small amounts of money – particularly if the big players cooperate – to start the ball rolling (that is, create a selling spree in a marginal market) in an overvalued currency. In this 'Canute Play' the super-rich currency players find a central bank that is 'playing Canute' – trying against all the odds to bolster an ailing currency – and then target its home economy. When the process gets going, devaluation becomes inevitable; and in such an environment it takes very little intelligence (or risk), though considerable capital, to make huge profits. And in these 'Canute Plays' the capital often comes not from the individual himself but from huge lines of credit made available by foreign currency trading banks. (One estimate has it that credit lines of up to £6 billion are available for Joseph Lewis's currency operations.) Britain fell to a 'Canute Play' in 1992 when the British government handed £5 billion to 'the market' in an attempt to shore up the unshoreable.

Lewis's fortune is certainly the result of talent. For all self-made, mega-rich people, capital needs to be earned, and often their own work and talent (together with considerable luck) help to create the precious capital in the first place. However, once an initial amount of capital has been acquired, life suddenly becomes much easier. Moving further up the line from super-rich to mega-rich to billionaire – hardly requires extraordinary talent, hard work or even risk (certainly no more talent, hard work or risk than that offered and encountered by millions of the non-wealthy). As a fortune builds it can often assume a dynamic all of its own, with the owner of the original wealth simply being carried along as the fortune grows and grows. In a relatively stable economy it is very difficult to lose a fortune. In a bust, though, the super-rich can lose big money (Lewis himself lost a portion of his fortune in the Bear Stearns collapse in 2008); but what is left at the bottom of the cycle is often more than enough to 'make' another fortune in the up-swing.

THE SHEER MAGNITUDE OF SUPER-RICH WEALTH

This group of early twenty-first century billionaires are, by any standards, outlandishly rich. They not only dwarf their 'ordinary' super-rich contemporaries but also the earlier race of mega-rich 'robber barons' who were so identified with the burgeoning capitalism of the early twentieth century. In terms of resources at their personal command, in 1997 William Gates was three times richer than John D. Rockefeller (Standard Oil) was in 1918, Warren Buffet was over ten times richer than Andrew Carnegie (Steel) was in 1918, and it was estimated that in 1992 the British Queen was ten times richer than Henry Ford (automobiles) was in 1918, although some of these early-twentieth century super-rich probably commanded a greater percentage of their nations' resources.[14]

The resources at the disposal of these billionaires, and the broader swathe of super-rich families, represents a huge pool of the globe's wealth and is beyond the wildest imaginings of most people. In 1996 the high net worth individuals (HNWIs, as they are depicted by the financial services sector that serves them) accounted for almost $17 trillion in assets in 1996. By 2007 they accounted for a staggering $37.2 trillion.[15]

These mammoth sums are not just a measure of wealth, they are also a measure of power. And this power derives from the command over resources that wealth brings. Measuring this egregious concentration of power now enjoyed by the world's super-rich is difficult, but it can be given some meaning by making comparisons. For instance, even though it is not exactly comparing like with like, there exists an astounding statistic: it shows that in 2006 the combined wealth of the world's dollar millionaires ($37.2 trillion) is almost three times the entire gross national product of the United States ($13.2 trillion) and also much higher than the combined GNP of the 'Group of Seven' countries – the US, Japan, Germany, France, Britain, Italy and Canada. What's more, figures show that this gap – between the super-rich and the USA is growing – for in 1996 the super-rich had only twice the gross domestic product of the USA.[16]

By comparison with the broad super-rich, the mountain of wealth owned by the 950 billionaires assumes Himalayan proportions when comparisons are made. For instance, the world's richest 500 billionaires together have an income greater than the world's poorest 420 million people. Also, the 950 billionaires have combined wealth a third bigger than the gross domestic product of the whole continent of Africa and three times the size of South America's MERCOSUR (whose members include Argentina, Brazil, Paraguay, Uruguay and Venezuala). Nearer to home, the combined wealth of the 950 billionaires amounts to a third more than the total US federal budget and two thirds more than the US government's combined Social Security, Medicare and Education budget.

Individual wealth comparisons are even more invidious. In 1998, a good decade into the 'globalisation' process, it was calculated that 84 of the world's richest people had a combined worth greater than that of China, so that the wealth of *just one of these super-rich individuals is equal to that of about 12.5 million of his fellow humans.*[17] And since then the figures have become even starker. For instance, in 2007 it was claimed that Lakshmi Mittal – the Indian-born steel magnate and the 'the world's fifth richest person' – has a personal net worth larger than 30 countries listed in the World Bank's GDP table, and that Bill Gates's $56 billion of personal wealth gives him greater resources than 50 countries.[18]

On some counts the world's richest individual (at the turn of the century) was not Gates, but rather the Sultan of Brunei who it has been estimated commands more resources than the combined GNP of 40 nation-states. To give his wealth some form of reality, it was also estimated to be larger than the GNP of the Czech Republic (population 10.3 million); and William Gates was estimated to command more resources than the GNP of Africa's oil-rich giant, Nigeria (with a population of 111.3 million), the Walton family more than the GNP of Vietnam (peopled by 73.5 million), Paul Sacher and the Hoffmann family more than the GNP of Bulgaria (population 8.4 million), Karl and Theo Albrecht more than the GNP of

Panama (with its 2.6 million inhabitants); and Joseph Lewis more control over resources than his country of residence, the Bahamas.[19]

Get the world's top 3 mega-rich (dollar billionaire) people into one room at the turn of the century and you would have assembled command over more resources than the GNP of Israel; the top 4 and you would tie with Poland, the top 10 and you would beat Norway and South Africa. Europe's 20 richest families command around $113 billion, a little more than the whole Polish economy; America's richest 10 and Britain's richest 1000 families together command more resources than the GNP of the entire Russian Federation.[20] And if the top 200 or so billionaires could ever be assembled together, then the command over assets, in that one room, would outrank the GNP of each of Australia, the Netherlands, Belgium, possibly even Brazil; and with 400 or so billionaires the one gathering would outrank Britain and almost overtake France!

Another way of looking at concentrations of wealth is through the proportions of national wealth of the western nations held by their own passport-holding super-rich. In 2004 the top 1 per cent of American households owned 34.4 per cent of the US. More striking still, the top ½ per cent of households (500,000 households) owned well over a quarter of the US. Super-rich concentration in Britain – the world's most globally-oriented large economy – is also striking, as is its growth. In Britain in 1998 its 'top 50' owned $69 billion – but by 2007 the same amount was owned by the 'top 10'.[21]

A particular feature of the British super-rich scene is the concentration in very few hands of land ownership. Britain – or rather the land area known as the United Kingdom – is, quite literally, owned by a very small caste; as is the capital city, London. It remains a poignant commentary on wealth concentration that large tracts of London are owned by just a few individuals. The Duke of Westminster, through the Grosvenor Estate, owns around 200 acres of Belgravia and 100 acres of Mayfair – a dynastic inheritance created by the seventeenth century marriage of Cheshire baronet Thomas Grosvenor to Mary Davies, the '12 year old heiress to a London manor that at the time included 200 acres of Pimlico'. Viscount Portman owns 110 acres north of Oxford Street. Lord Howard de Walden's four daughters, through a holding company, own 90 acres of Marylebone. Elizabeth Windsor, the Queen, remains the 'official' owner of 150 acres of 'crown estates' in central London, as the eight crown estates commissioners address their annual report to her. Andrew Lycett has argued that although 'millions of pounds are exchanged every week in leasehold property deals...London still has no sizeable new landowners' with the exception of the Sultan of Brunei and Paul Raymond.[22]

It is these kinds of statistics that bring into sharp focus the economic power of the global super-wealthy compared even to that of politicians, presidents and prime ministers – who have to share their economic power with cabinets and parliaments. Later in this Chapter I look at how the super-rich can, in essence, buy political power in a democracy. But there is a whole array of ways of influencing policy – both indirectly and directly. One such was on display when the American media billionaire Ted Turner decided to donate at the stroke of a pen $1 billion to the United Nations and 'to put on notice...every rich person in the world...that they're going to be hearing from me about giving money'.[23] For a western politician to similarly move a billion dollars in the direction of the UN would have involved months and months of negotiating and a bruising campaign.

RICHER STILL, YET RICHER

And the super-rich continue to get richer. Alan Blinder, a former vice chairman of the US Federal Reserve Board, said in 1997 – only a few years into the Wall Street globalisation era – that 'I think when historians look back at the last quarter of the twentieth century the shift from labour to capital, the almost unprecedented shift of money and power up the income pyramid, is going to be their number one focus.'[24] It was a prophetic analysis. The figures are indeed dramatic – showing not just the success of the rich, but also the squeezing of the middle classes. Using a very modest definition of 'rich', then in the US in 1979 – at the beginning of the Thatcher-Reagan age – the incomes of the richest 10 per cent (90th percentile) were 110 per cent greater than the middle 10 per cent (50th percentile); but by 2004 they had become 147 per cent greater. A more accurate definition of rich – say the top 1 per cent or the top ½ percent – would have shown much greater rises by the rich over those of the middle class.[25]

Another way of looking at the 'richer and richer' story is to note the continuous growth in the sheer number of the world's super-rich – that is, the so-called High Net Worth Individuals (HNWIs) together with the growth in their combined wealth. In 1996 – when the era of the super-rich was just getting underway – HNWIs numbered 4.5 million and their wealth amounted to $16.6 trillion. By 2001 the rich had grown to 7.1 million and their wealth to 26.2 trillion. By 2006 they had risen to 9.5 million persons and their wealth to $37.2 trillion.[26]

And the global distribution of these rich folk is changing – away from America and Europe and towards Asia. Intriguingly the 1996 super-rich 'market' grew more rapidly in Latin America than anywhere else – perhaps a function of the ease with which millionaires can be created where a traditionally stratified social structure is melded with global capitalism. Yet it is in Asia where the most consistent growth in the new millionaire super-rich has taken place – an incredible 15 per cent annual growth rate in the HNWI market over a decade up to the Asian market collapse in early 1998. In the 2007 World Wealth Report 'Singapore, India, Indonesia and Russia witnessed the highest growth in HNWI populations' and China recorded a huge growth of billionaires (from 20 to 66 during the one year of 2006-7).[27]

AND GREEDIER?

As well as larger and richer, the new super-rich class are getting greedier. Whereas 'old capital', bounded and constrained by nation and social responsibility, tended to seek preservation of capital and a long-term goals, 'new wealth' – particularly that generated in the post-cold war era – seems concerned with immediate investment performance. In an era of low inflation (where there are small returns from deposit markets) the performance-driven super-rich seek out securities, futures and options. In the Chinese-led low inflationary environment they are more able to take risks than their forebears, they diversify more easily, and buy and sell more readily.

Above all – in the post-communist environment – they are driven by profit, and it is this insistent search for return and profit that makes them global – and 'offshore' – in their reach and interests. And this new need for performance (mainly of profits) was a major cause of the growing private banking market – Goldman Sachs, Credit Suisse, UBS, JP Morgan, Merrill Lynch – as it catered to the new millionaire class by diversifying their investments across both asset classes and the globe.

GOOD AS WELL AS RICH? ANYONE FOR NOBLESSE OBLIGE?

Yet when the investment has been a success, and the profits are made, can we expect our new global wealthy to develop the social obligation that infused the more traditional upper classes and helped to create the social cohesion and welfare states of modern continental Europe?

It is unlikely. Traditional western capitalism's essential individualism and cultural egalitarianism always placed great limits on the feudal instinct of *noblesse oblige*, but the new global capitalism can be expected to expunge it altogether. Not only is modern global capital less rooted in a social or moral sensibility, in the 'greed is good' culture, but increasingly it also has fewer and fewer roots in the community or the nation – or indeed, the civilization. Robber barons with a social conscience giving back to their nation has become something of a curiosity. And as capital moves easily from nation to nation and from west to east in search of profits, local identities and obligations fade away.

No doubt generous and compassionate feelings exist within many a super-rich breast. But the growth of so-called 'giving' has become less a true sign of moral sense or old-fashioned compassion and more a strategic business operation – primarily a good way to improve one's public relations. The Prince of Wales – as a part of his campaign to become King – has mastered this art of 'giving' as a form of public relations.[28] As has Bill Gates. Indeed, 'giving', particularly 'mega-giving' (none of which actually hurts or even limits the lifestyle of the 'giver') serves the continuing human need to be 'good', or seen to be 'good', as well as rich and powerful. It certainly used to be more difficult for 'the rich man to get into heaven than for a camel to enter the eye of a needle', but 'giving' can perhaps make it a little easier.

Yet, at root, this kind of high profile 'mega-giving' remains yet another instrument of power. In a sense the super-rich have it both ways-not only the power of the possessor of egregious accumulations of wealth but also the power derived from 'giving it away' to charities of their choice, thus further imposing their tastes and values on the wider public; and, in the case of political 'giving' and influence, helping to determine the politics of nations.

WHERE IS THE MONEY?

What the new global super-rich actually do with their money is no idle speculation. For in the new global economy decisions about how to deploy these gargantuan portfolios can move economic mountains, change governments, even regimes. By a stroke of a pen, as mighty as that wielded by any politician, the super-rich can touch and change real lives of real people the world over – whether it be creating or destroying jobs, building or guiding charities, supporting culture or investing or disinvesting in sport.

Intriguingly, the super-rich hold their wealth in very different ways from average middle-income households. The mass of middle class Americans hold a large proportion of their net worth in their principal residences and in cars – and of course their debt liabilities, through mortgages and non-mortgage consumer debt, is alarmingly high and unsustainable. By comparison, only a small per cent of the net worth of the global super-rich is in principal residences, and a miniscule amount in cars themselves. As for debt – the bane of the middle classes in America and Britain – the global super-rich do not like it and do not need to have it.

The super-rich are conspicuous for their love of the stock market – and during the great post-communist Wall Street bonanza many fortunes have been made in equities. In 2006 the global super-rich invested 31 per cent of their financial assets in equities, 24 per cent in real estate (including commercial real estate – a market that collapsed on them in late

2007, 21 per cent in fixed income investments, 14 per cent in cash, and, intriguingly, only 10 per cent in the 'alternative investment world' of hedge funds, private equity and derivatives (down by 100 per cent over 2005).[29]

There is also a growing amount of super-rich money going into luxuries and collectibles (and the annual Forbes's Wealth Report has produced a tasteless 'Cost of Living Extremely Well Index' – the CLEWI – to monitor the rising cost of super-rich living. These luxury investments – dubbed 'investments of passion' by analysts – include 'cars, boats and planes' (accounting for 26 per cent of super-rich 'passion' spending), art (20 per cent), jewelry (18 per cent), and a new entrant – investments in sports, including football teams (6 per cent). A recent development in Britain has been the investment by foreign billionaires – such as Roman Abramovich (in Chelsea, in London) and the Mittall family (in QPR, also in London) – in football teams.[30]

RICH FAMILIES AND THE CORPORATIONS

It is not surprising that super-rich individuals and families hold a considerable part of their wealth in and through corporations. Some sociologists, though, point to a subtle though crucial difference in shareholding between the mega-rich and the super-rich. At the very top of the globe's social pyramid the mega-rich – probably amounting to no more than a few hundred families – own sizeable, mainly minority, interests in large enterprises, and effectively control them.

However, because of the growth and dispersal of shareholdings – held by pension funds, banks, even universities – even the mega-rich do not tend to have outright control of large corporations. One expert has suggested that 'it is doubtful whether family holdings of less than five per cent can signify "control", and there are few examples of such concentration.'[31]

Alongside these large enterprise stockholders there are a group of investors – many of them just as mega-rich – who come nowhere near to controlling companies because they diversify their portfolios into a variety of enterprises. The number of these 'rentier shareholders' (essentially big time coupon clippers) has grown dramatically with the rise of stock exchanges and the ability to spread financial risk around the world. These 'rentiers' were described by Edward Luttwak as those who:

> live off dividends, bond interest…and real-estate rentals, rather than the active conduct of a business or profession. When seen on the golf courses and boat docks of the fenced in and carefully guarded residential enclaves they so greatly favor, from Palm Springs, California to Hilton Head, South Carolina…rentiers kitted out in their Ralph Lauren clothes superficially resemble businesspeople or professionals on vacation. But their vacation never ends.[32]

A further strand of the globe's mega-rich – some of them bordering on being only super-rich, some of them even believing themselves to be 'middle class' – are the salaried executives or directors of some of the large corporations. To these super executives need to be added the new race of those who hold multiple part-time directorships and executive positions in a variety of enterprises (what the Marxists call 'finance capitalists').' The salaries of these executives are so huge that they themselves can build up considerable shareholdings or pension funds, receiving almost the kind of income available to the big time owners of capital.

And, of course, some of these mega-rich people can have multiple identities. 'A rentier capitalist may also be a finance capitalist…the daughter of a rentier capitalist may marry an entrepreneurial capitalist, and an executive capitalist may regularly play golf with a finance capitalist.'[33] And what have been called 'kinecon groups' build up over the generations. These are sets of 'interrelated kin who control the corporation through their combined ownership interests and strategic representation in management'.[34]

Below these mega-rich individuals and families the majority of the ordinary super-rich – the top 1 per cent of wealthy Americans – also hold a large proportion of their wealth in businesses, but normally in small and medium-sized businesses, often their own (many of which, though, are dependent for their future upon the large corporations and the mega-rich).

THE RICH PRIVATISE THE CORPORATIONS

During the global financial bonanza of the 1990s the corporations began to lose out in the affections of the super-rich to a new kind of capitalism – private equity. New folks began to appear on super-rich lists (whilst, of course, many of the old super-rich got even richer) – and what in 2004 *The Economist* described as 'the new kings of capitalism' began to be crowned.[35] Private equity served two purposes for the super-rich: first it purchased major corporations from shareholders, thus releasing the new owners from legal obligations such as disclosure and, secondly, it 'leveraged' the acquired companies. Stewart Lansley in his extremely well-researched 2006 book on the super-rich revolution in Britain described Philip Green as a 'classic example' of one of these new 'kings of capitalism'. He reported that 'Green has built his fortune by buying up underperforming companies, often on the cheap, pumping them full of debt, stripping them down, refinancing them and making a pretty tidy profit in the process.'[36] By 2005 private equity had become so controversial in Europe that when the Chairman of Germany's SPD described private equity as 'locusts' his remarks were greeted with general applause. He said 'they remain anonymous, they have no face and descend like a swarm of locusts on a company, devour it and then fly on'. And even the British held a parliamentary investigation in which some of the major figures in the City of London's private equity world – such as Damon Buffini of Permira and Mike Smith of CVC – answered their critics in public.

The Carlyle Group has perfected the art of global private equity investment for the super-rich. With offices around the world from New York to Tokyo and Barcelona this US-based firm describes themselves unabashedly as having a 'mission to be the premier global private equity firm leveraging the insight of Carlyle's team of investment professionals to generate extraordinary returns.' It reports that it has $75 billion of equity capital under management – more, that is, than the fortune of Bill Gates. With investment money coming from the super-rich of the US (65 per cent) and Europe (25 per cent) Carlyle invests across the world in a range of industries, including aero-space and defense, energy and power, and telecommunications and transportation.

Carlyle specialise in political influence – indeed it remains a text book example of how the mega-rich can influence the world of politics which in turn can influence business and profits. Present and one-time members of the board include a glittering array of the globally powerful – including two US presidents (George H.W. Bush and George W. Bush), a former British Prime Minister (John Major), a former US Secretary of State (James Baker III), a former US Secretary of Defense (Frank Carlucci), a former Premier of Alberta and a former president of the Philippines. Carlyle's political acumen was on display when it engineered a remarkable – indeed, on its own terms, admirable – raid by its super-rich investors on the public assets of the British government. In 2002 an agency of Her Majesty's Government had been split up and turned into a company called Qinetiq and the Carlyle Group moved swiftly to invest £42 million at auction in the new company. By February 2006 its share value was worth £351 million and Carlyle sold half its shares at a profit of over 800 per cent. As it had bought its shares through a series of 'special purpose vehicles' based in the off-shore tax-haven Guernsey these profits were tax-exempt. A former Defense Procurement Minister, John Gilbert, described Carlyle as having taken 'The Ministry of Defense…like a lamb to the slaughter'. He considered that 'all the value [in Qinetiq] was built up by public servants using public money' and that the whole operation was 'a complete outrage, a scandal'.[37] In the Qinetiq affair Carlyle had certainly lived up to one of its objectives in its mission statement: that of 'generating extraordinary returns' for its investors. Yet, maybe it had fallen short in another: that of maintaining 'our good name and the good name of our investors'.

INHERITANCE AND THE RICH

This perfectly legal financial play by the Carlyle Group in the Qinetiq affair is simply one amongst a myriad of techniques used to make the super-rich even richer. The post-cold war world of finance (together with governments that provide light-touch regulation) have allowed big money to make bigger money – quite easily as it happens. Yet, an even more fundamental question needs asking. Where do those who have the money 'to play' – and therefore to grow – get it from in the first place?

The myth has it that today's super-rich fortunes are largely the product of the merit and enterprise of the 'self-made' as they work in the market. Thus periodically when inequality becomes an issue, the western media tend not to highlight the size of private capital but rather 'excessive' top salaries and remuneration. Corporate pay is easy to grasp, and outlandish corporate remuneration is a real feature of modern capitalism. The heads of America's 500 biggest companies took home an aggregate pay raise in 2004 of 54 per cent, and Forbes reported that the compensation of these 500 amounted to $5.1 billion (up from $3.3 billion in 2003). Intriguingly, the bulk of the compensation of CEO's now takes the form of stock gains — thus allowing the CEO's to build up a large capital sum which transports them from well-paid salaried officers into the realm of capitalist 'movers and shakers'. Two examples of the huge amounts involved in 2004 were Terry S. Semel, CEO of Yahoo, who received total 5-year compensation of $230 million made up of salary, bonus and stock (which amounted to $229); and Edwin M. Crawford, CEO of Caremark Rx, who received 5-year compensation of over $77 million (of which over $69 million was in stock gains).[38] Other examples include: Stephen Hubert's $39.6 million from Conseco Inc., Lawrence Coss's $28.9 million from the Green Tree Financial Corporation and James Donald's $25.2 million from the DSC Corporation. Some spectacular examples of those also feeling no pain were Andrew Grove of Intel, paid a salary of $3,003 000 and $94,587 000 in long-term compensation in 1996, Edward Pfeiffer of Compaq Computers, paid a salary of $4,250,000 and $23,546,000 in long-term compensation in the same year, and, a mere twentieth in one rich-list in 1996, Drew Lewis of Union Pacific, paid a salary of $3,131,000 and $18,320,000 in long-term compensation.[39]

So 'excessive' were corporate compensations becoming during the 1990s that even the market-oriented British Labour Party campaigned against 'exorbitant' top corporate salaries in the run-up to the British general election of 1997. Gas chief Cedric Brown's salary — then at £475,000 — and perks sparked off a national controversy, and the CBI set up a Commission to look into 'top people's pay'. Since then, and during the time of the corporate-friendly Blair government there has been no noticeable lowering of top company remuneration.

The often outlandish remuneration of corporate executives clearly creates pockets of wealth that can often lead to significant capital accumulation. Yet, this route to riches is at least linked to some form of effort, skill and intelligence – and the sums involved are miniscule compared to those that are inherited or essentially derived from inheritance. The fact is that the new global rich are a mixture of 'new' and 'old' money, of 'earned income' and inheritance – but with inheritance playing by far the larger part. The old adage that 'it takes money to make money' holds true – more so now than ever – as does the other rueful popular belief that 'To Him That Hath...'

'Old money' is still very prominent in New Labour, free-market Britain; and the traditional aristocracy remain a highly privileged group. Tom Nicholas has suggested that 'becoming a business leader in Britain is still largely determined by the interconnected characteristics of a wealthy family and a privileged education...there has been no democratisation of British business over the last century and a half.'[40] For all the rhetoric of 'the need to reward enterprise and skill', 'old money' has done extremely well out of the Thatcher-Reagan revolution and the global market economics that it spawned. Like all capital, 'old capital' was bound to survive and prosper in a low-tax, deregulated economy. And 'new inheritance' – that is the wealth of the sons and daughters of the self-made of the post-war years – has now joined 'old inheritance' in an economy (and culture) dominated by inherited wealth.

The amounts are staggering. The economist Robert Avery of Cornell University argued at the beginning of the 1990s that 'we [in the US] will soon be seeing the largest transfer of income in the history of the world' as the older generation leave wealth to the baby boomers.[41] Some guesstimates place inheritance at 6 per cent of US GDP each year![42] Apart from straight gifts during the lifetime of the giver, there is also the mammoth transfer of unearned wealth – including whole businesses – upon the death (or retirement) of the super-rich giver.

And this inheritance culture will continue to grow. Two dynamics will see to that. First, the global economy has made the present generation of super-rich wealthier than any before. Second, this burst of super-wealth coincides (or, is the cause of) the increasing financial pressures on the young. Hence, leading political scientist Kevin Phillips has argued,

> for young Americans, those under thirty or thirty-five, two decades of polarization had brought a special, though widely unappreciated, irony: not only were they (and those younger) in danger of being the first generation of Americans to suffer a lower standard of living than their parents, but they would be the first generation to receive – or not receive – much of their economic opportunity from family inheritance, not personal achievement.[43]

A troublesome feature of this new economy and culture of inheritance is the growth in the number of recipients of unearned cash income – the use of inherited money to consume and live on. There are a considerable number of people within super-rich families whose unearned annual income is not derived from their own net worth, but rather from their parents' or grandparents' net worth. One estimate suggested that 46 per cent of the US 'affluent' give at least $15 000 a year to their adult children or grandchildren.[44] But partly because it is often shrouded in mystery some of the egregious sums involved are, unlike huge salaries, rarely exposed to public view.

Also, the sting is often taken out of attacks on super-rich inheritance because in the modern economy many middle class families and individuals now inherit money themselves (albeit fairly small amounts). And this inheritance – normally the family house – is a very welcome addition to the stretched household economies of millions. The great housing and debt boom of the early twenty-first century priced many younger middle class people out of housing altogether, and, as a result, passing housing down the generations was the least the older generation could do for their off-spring. The middle class housing crisis creates a considerable constituency for inheritance, from which the super-rich inheriting classes benefit. So, politicians in the West (particularly in the housing boom and bust lands of America and Britain) either accept inheritance as untouchable – except at the margins – or even support it ideologically as creating 'islands of independence' from the state.

Neo-liberals and 'free-marketeers' – who philosophically may remain meritocrats – nevertheless often support the idea of wealth as 'cascading down the generations' as a bulwark against socialism. Yet, ironically, what has now begun to emerge is a capitalist version of the much derided state welfare 'dependency culture'. For too many dependency upon the family inheritance has been substituted for dependency on the state.

A GLOBAL RULING CLASS?

These super-rich families and individuals possess huge personal wealth and command considerable influence over resources. They have control of, or influence over, the great corporations, and they hand their extraordinary wealth down through the generations. But, do they amount to a new ruling class?

Certainly the new class regime of global capitalism is very different from the old class model. Today's mega-rich are not like the 'old style capitalists' who owned great businesses out-right and could – and did – personally direct huge resources and thousands of workers. These traditional 'mogul' capitalists (the popular image derived from nineteenth century capital-ism) still exist, but are now called 'entrepreneurial capitalists' and run their own shows (in Britain people such as the late James Goldsmith, Alan Sugar, the founder of Amstrad, and the late Anita Roddick of Bodyshop are good examples). Yet the wealth of the world's richest people is no longer held in this way – rather it is held 'impersonally', primarily in the form of stocks and bonds.

The nineteenth century Marxian notion of 'a class' of capi-talists – based upon highly concentrated capitalism – is also now redundant. A modern socialist analysis has appeared that argues that the control of corporations is still highly concen-trated in 'knots of financial power' by small numbers of finan-cial capitalists operating interlocking directorships and cross-shareholding – in other words, concentrated shareholder power. However in today's huge and diverse global economy, such traditional concentration simply does not exist. The emer-gence of the modern globalised corporate economy has dis-persed shareholdings and separated ownership from control.[45]

So, given the size and variety of today's global super-rich, is it fair to describe them as a class at all, let alone a ruling class? Historically, capitalist societies, such as the first one – imperial Britain – have produced what amounts to a class: a cohesive, self-conscious, self-confident, socially exclusive, super-rich upper class possessed of a community of feeling. Yet, today's global super-rich are too numerous, too fragment-ed nationally, ethnically and geographically, and too divided into different types to be an old-fashioned class in the Victorian sense. And as for a 'ruling' class, modern global capitalism – too individualistic, too lacking in team spirit – is rather bad at rulership. However, there is some evidence to suggest that a US 'business establishment' did exist in the early decades of post-World War Two America. Then many amongst the American super-rich held multiple directorships and many 'key positions in the intercorporate network' tended to be drawn from a more integrated social background – exclusive boarding schools, a listing in the Social Register ('the crucial indicator of social exclusivity') and membership of exclusive big city clubs.[46] And of course in Britain (with cohesion amongst the super-rich secured by public schooling and the shared experience of land ownership), in France, and amongst the Japanese zaibatsu, the sense of class or caste was always pronounced, and this was reflected in their postwar business culture as well.

However in the US in the 1970s and onwards, with the rise of Dallas, Chicago, San Francisco and Los Angeles, the American business establishment, historically grouped along the eastern seaboard, became even less cohesive – certainly in geographical terms. And with new generations coming on stream, capital inheritance can often mean dispersal. As well as disputes over money – which may sour fellow 'class feeling' – the average size of individual holdings within the inheriting family group falls, and dynasties dissipate into a number of rentier families.

In one of the most systematic and sophisticated analyses of postwar capitalism, John Scott argues that this more dispersed shareholding has led to 'a consequent reduction in, though not a disappearance of, family control and influence'. He suggests that those with less than 5 per cent of the shares of a company have little purchase on decision-making, and those with 5-10 per cent have only a 'potential for control'. Very few super-rich have such a concentration of shares – in fact they usually disperse their shareholdings among a variety of enterprises – thus lowering risk but diluting the sense of ownership.

Of course the dispersal of the character of share ownership developed apace with the huge growth of pension funds during the 1970s, 1980s and 1990s. In reality, modern global corporations are now controlled by 'constellations of interests' – families, banks, pension funds.'[47]

So the big question remains: who drives these great corporations? For if corporations run the world and shape our lives – certainly more than other institutions – then those who run the corporations are truly a new ruling class. For a time a new 'managerialist' theory emerged which argued that shareholders no longer controlled corporations; rather there was a separation of ownership and control, and the decisions of these great corporate behemoths were now taken by a new managerial class – 'captains of industry' such as Britain's Sir Peter Waiters or John Browne of BP, and Ian Valiance of BT. Such managers or 'executive capitalists' can virtually write their own huge incomes, but can only enter the ranks of the super-rich by accruing, through their remuneration packages, large amounts of shares and bonds. These executives are in capitalist locations that give them power as well as high personal reward.

In 1941 James Burnham, in his famous book *The Managerial Revolution*, argued that this growth of managerialism was bringing family capitalism to an end. And in 1963 A. A. Berle argued that 'the transformation of property from an active role to passive wealth has so operated that the wealthy stratum no longer has power'.[48] However, the new global capitalist order has rendered this debate somewhat redundant. Whether the power to direct the affairs of the corporation resides amongst the 'capitalists' or the 'managers' hardly matters anymore. For it is the logic of the market – and increasingly the global market – which dictates. And both capitalists and managers have to dance to this new tune. The great decisions of the corporations are informed and determined by short-term market profitability – 'performance' in the lingo – and not by the particular preferences, tastes or style of individuals or families or managers! There used to be room for these preferences – many of them of them reflecting a social or moral concern. In the modern Wall Street regime those days are now over.

A GLOBAL OVERCLASS (WITHOUT A COUNTRY)

If the new global super-rich do not amount to an old-style ruling class, they are certainly becoming an overclass: the mirror image of the more discussed urban underclass. In a very real sense the new super-rich are becoming transcendent – removed from their societies, separated from the rest of us. This is happening physically. The higher levels of the super-rich have always lived apart: within their walled estates or in wealthy ghettos in the centre of Manhattan, London and other cities. They have always owned possessions that have singled them out. Today, of course, mere diamonds, helicopters and expensive cars no longer signify the apex of great wealth. Now it is the luxury yacht (normally personally designed by John Banneman), the personal aeroplane – the Sultan of Brunei has a Boeing 747 – (normally supplied by Grumanns), and one or two of the highest valued paintings that signify someone has reached the top.

Although the ordinary super-rich – including simple dollar millionaires – cannot afford this mega-rich lifestyle, they too are increasingly becoming separated, removing into wealth enclaves. Some estimates suggest that by 1997 there were 30,000 gated communities and that in parts of the US a third of all new homes were being built behind walls. These gated communities are home to over eight million Americans, and thus have become a normal aspect of the lifestyle of the vast majority of the top 10 per cent of US wealth holders and their families.[49] Their gated communities have their own security forces and amenity centres and their own codes of what is acceptable – ranging from the colour of doors and the planting of shrubs to rules against political posters – which residents accept as part of the local social contract. It amounts to an embryonic privatised local government, an epochal development that will inevitably lead those inside the gated communities to demand deep cuts in local taxes and services. Schooling still exists outside the gated communities, although the demand for private schooling within the walls can be expected to grow. Such a separated existence found its extreme form in Yeltsin's capitalist Russia, where the new super-rich mafia were not only separated by money but were also essentially above the law.

The American journalist and writer Thomas Friedman has written that we should 'never trust a country where the rich live behind high walls and tinted windows. That is a place that is not prospering as one country', and that such 'fragmentation undermines the very concept of civitas – of organised community life...which is the notion behind the US.'[50] Yet such separatism is increasingly the reality. And if the perceptible growth of inequality within western societies continues much longer, then for the super-rich the world outside the ghettos of the wealthy will become even more unattractive – and hostile.

'ONLY THE LITTLE PEOPLE PAY TAXES'

Of course one test of loyalty to a society is a willingness to pay its taxes, particularly if they are not onerous. Yet increasingly the super-rich are dodging the taxes of their countries of origin. The late Leona Helmsley, the billionaire New Yorker, famously made her name by putting this well known fact into the public prints when she bragged that 'we [the super-rich] don't pay taxes. Only the little people pay taxes'.

In 1997 the *New York Times* reported that:

nearly 2,400 of the Americans with the highest incomes paid no federal taxes in 1993, up from just 85 individuals and couples in 1977. While the number of Americans who make $200,000 or more grew more than 15 fold from 1977 to 1993, the number of people in that category who paid no income taxes grew 28 fold or nearly twice as fast, according to a quarterly statistical bulletin issued by the IRS.[51]

So difficult was it for the US authorities to collect taxes from the super-rich that Congress introduced a new tax altogether – the Alternative Minimum Tax – to catch them. With the American 'middle classes' – the middle income groups – paying a larger percentage of their earnings in taxes (including sales taxes, property taxes and social security payroll taxes), super-rich tax evasion and avoidance is becoming a growing cause of economic inequality and social fracture. And during the George W. Bush administration tax cuts made the super-rich even richer. And some Republicans wish to further benefit the wealthy. The Republican politician John McCain, by no means a low-tax extremist, argued during the 2008 presidential campaign that 'entrepreneurs should not be taxed into submission...John McCain will make the Bush income and business tax cuts permanent' and 'will fight the Democratic plan for a crippling tax increase in 2011'. As the economist Paul Krugmam commented this 'crippling' plan was the proposal to let the Bush tax cuts for people making over $250,000 a year expire.[52] Also, the push for the abolition of the income tax – proposed by the Republican politician, libertarian and champion of the super-rich, Steve Forbes – may help a range of people but, should it ever be enacted, is also a clear win for the wealthy.

In Britain the super-rich also escape paying their fair tax share. The British Queen – who until 1994 was allowed by her government to pay no taxes at all, and since then has only had to pay some of them – is literally above the law as far as tax is concerned and remains a role model for tax dodging. As does her son, the heir to the British throne, Charles Windsor, who has also been placed above the law by British governments as he is specifically exempt from paying corporation tax, capital gains tax and death duties. The Duchy of Cornwall, the territory owned by Charles and run as a company, has not been liable for tax since 1921.

Other British super-rich, who unlike the royals are not 'above the laws' of taxation, nonetheless manage to avoid their share of taxes. Lloyd's 'names' are a striking example. 'According to Robson Rhodes, the accountants, the most striking advantage is that Names are treated like businesses...so losses incurred in the market can be offset against other earnings...they enjoy business property relief for inheritance tax purposes on their deposits and funds which support their underwriting.'[53] Dodging taxes – even in global capital's highly friendly tax environment – is final proof, should it be needed, of the lack of even a residual loyalty to nation and home society on the part of many super-rich families.

During the Blair government in the late 1990s London became a haven for a species of super and mega-rich called 'non-doms' – a term used as shorthand to describe non-domiciled rich people. These 'non-doms' paid no tax at all to the British government – who refused to tax them, unlike other countries including the US, on their worldwide income. And whilst the 'little people' were compelled to pay their taxes, in Britain, under the Labour government elected in 1997, private equity partners paid tax on income at 10 per cent and 'entrepreneurs', who turn their income into capital gains, also got taxed at 10 per cent of their income. As the economist and commentator Martin Wolf argued this super-rich tax haven had become so egregious that it was 'subversive of any enduring political compact amongst citizens' leading to a situation in which the 'political community will collapse'.[54]

Companies – huge, large and medium-sized – are also well into the tax dodging game. One scam, made possible by global economics, is 'transfer pricing', which allows companies to pay tax where they want to, which naturally is the country or haven with the lowest tax regime. They can engineer this by doing much of their spending in the high-tax countries, thus cutting their tax obligations, and making most of their profits – using subsidiaries with little more than a front office with a few staff – in low-tax countries.

For super-rich tax dodgers a helpful dynamic often sets in. Home governments, in order to keep what money they can within their borders, make even more strenuous attempts to keep money at home by lowering even further the tax burden on rich people. The idea, not always fanciful, grew that more tax money could be attracted by taxing less. In Britain the top rate of tax was reduced from 98 per cent to 40 per cent during the country's move to market capitalism, and in the US, even after a decade and a half of falling taxes for the upper income groups, by the late 1990s the authorities were still struggling manfully to lower the burden even further by even lower capital gains taxes.

This timidity of national governments in their relations with the super-rich takes many forms. For instance capital flight is conducted primarily via computers – cash in suitcases smuggled on board aircraft bound for exotic places are now fantasies from the past – and national governments can therefore, if they really want to, get at records stored on hard-disks in headquarters in New York, London, Paris and Frankfurt. But the threat by banks and financial institutions to relocate in the event of such an oppressive intrusion into their 'secrecy' keeps local governments from doing anything more than administering the occasional slap on the wrist.

In this environment it is hardly surprising that the amount of 'offshore' money is growing rapidly. The IMF reported that a staggering $2000 billion is located beyond the reach of the countries in which the money was made – in the growing number of safe-haven tax shelters, ranging from the Cayman Islands, through the Channel Islands and Lichtenstein to Singapore. In the late 1990s German commentators estimated that 100,000 tax-evading rich people have transferred many of their assets to a new favourite safe haven: the rock of Gibraltar.[55] 'Trickle down' – the 1980s public relations term for the idea that wealth trickles down to the masses from those who make and own large chunks of it – has now been replaced by 'gush up and out'.

Another sign of the detachment of the super-rich from their domestic societies is their decreasing involvement in those societies. Potential economic and social changes in their countries of origin and residence used to be of great concern to the wealthy. They saw their destinies as linked to their countries of birth, and they spent considerable amounts of money (and willingly acquiesced to relatively high tax regimes) in order to stabilise and ameliorate social changes that might otherwise threaten their interests. This strategy was at the root of much of the progressive, centrist politics of the western world in the twentieth century.

Now, though, domestic – that is, national – social and economic changes are no longer of such urgent concern. Should a
local environment turn hostile to them – not just because of a
government's economic policy, but also, say, because of its law
and order or policing strategy – then they can simply up sticks
and leave, both financially and in person. And often the mere
threat, or assumption of a threat, to withdraw their assets and
patronage is enough to persuade the domestic politicians to
secure a friendly environment. Such threats are now regularly
made, either implicitly by corporations (who take jobs with
them) or explicitly by high-profile, super-rich individuals, as
was the case before the 1997 British general election with the
musical entrepreneur Andrew Lloyd Webber, the actor Michael
Caine and the boxer Frank Bruno.

Of course emotional ties to the land of their birth are bound
to remain; and there will doubtless be a certain discomfort in
being forever on the lookout or potentially always on the run –
not, like the Jews, because of persecution, but because of the
possibility of advantage and gain. However the arrival of global communications – particularly satellite television for entertainment and the internet for financial transactions – and the
increasing number of locations that are overclass friendly, has
made mobility, even expatriation, much easier to handle.

This twenty-first century overclass is being built upon a fundamental divergence of interest between the global super-rich –
both members and aspirants – and the rest of us. Simply, there
will be those whose interests are tied to the performance of the
global economy and those, the majority of people in the West,
rooted in their own communities and dependent upon local
jobs and welfare, who will continue to depend upon the success or failure of their own countries, regions or cities. George
Orwell's aphorism that 'the poor are the only true patriots' may

take on real meaning, but will need to be amended to include, as well as the poor, large sections of the western middle class.

Whereas 'the locals' will need skills in order to be employed and avoid the minimal (or worse) welfare systems, the new global overclass, many of them not needing to work, will need financial advice, and will be catered to by professionals, some of whom themselves will get rich and make it into the overclass.

And there is a further frightening twist. The dread prospect exists that for those who need jobs – those who have only their labour to fall back on – even this haven will be removed. Old-style capitalism, as Eric Hobsbawm and others from a Marxist perspective have argued, may have exploited the masses, but it also, crucially, included them. Now, though, new global capitalism in its search for 'performance' places cost-cutting and outsourcing above jobs. Thus, as China and India produce more and more, the demand – the need – for American workers may well be over. And in the market system, little or no demand for labour means low or no wages – and a pauperisation of whole sections of the middle class in an era when the pressure on the welfare systems of the West are already becoming acute.

CHAPTER TWO

THE GLOBALISATION GAME: 'HOLLOWING OUT THE WEST'

UP, UP AND AWAY: CAPITAL GOES GLOBAL

The new super-rich business class that now dominates the American empire is, of course, the product of the early 1990s worldwide triumph of capitalism in the Cold War. It was this victory that allowed capital to go global. And going global was a godsend for Wall Street. The financiers – and their political supporters – called it 'globalisation', which sounded more high-minded. But what this 'globalisation' gave western capital was unheard of profits – profits based upon mobility.

Whilst capital became mobile, those forces that had previously constrained it – the state (governments) and the trade unions – remained local. Thus global capital won the battle with the state by allowing capital and the corporations to play one western government off against another; and it weakened the trade unions by undercutting western wages (through the new pool of labour now available in Asia and Eastern Europe).

The upshot was a new world – one in which western capital could lower its costs and raise its profits almost at will. This was the great trick that during the Clinton/Greenspan era built up unprecedented profitability for the western money men – as it ushered in a world of minimal regulation, massive capital flows and, with the addition to the global market of China, low inflation and gigantic debt, and the consequent unprecedented scope for leveraging. It was a world where profits would fall from the tree like over-ripe fruit.

That the new 'globalisation' was good for profits became clearer by the year. A good measure of profitability was the remorseless rise of the New York Stock Exchange's Dow Jones Industrial Average in the globalising years. On 19th October 1987, after its largest one day fall, the average was 1,738. A decade later, by 19th October 1997, it had risen to 7,161. And a decade later still, by 9th October 2007, it had risen to 14,164. The era of high globalisation had seen it rise by a gigantic factor of 14 – little wonder that Forbes's High Net Worth individuals in their search for profitability, have been very keen on stocks.[1]

Access to global capital movement – and to profits – is typically and primarily bought through shares and bonds which since the end of the Cold War have become the main conduit for capital mobility. By investing in shares – particularly those of multinational companies – western capital (including the money of the super-rich) stepped off the local platform onto the up escalator which lifted it to an altogether new level – the promised land of global profits and higher and higher returns.

The spectacular growth in the operations of the great stock markets of New York, London, Frankfurt, Paris and the leading markets in Asia show how millions upon millions were taking this shareholding route onto the up escalator. The percentage of net worth of both Americans and Britons held in stocks and bonds has risen considerably in the post-cold war years.[2] And millions of non-super-rich western individuals and families have placed, or have had placed for them by managers, at least a portion of their assets on the up escalator to this higher, global, level of economic return. Many 'ordinary' families, too, have had their pension money moved from the domestic economies to the global arena.

'Performance' or 'high-return on profit' for these millions of shareholders was (and is) increasingly likely to be found in low-cost areas in Asia where the wage levels are much lower than in the western societies from which the money originally came. Exact figures on Asia's lower wage levels and costs are difficult to discern, but World Bank figures for 2006 show that, even after almost twenty years of 'globalisation' Chinese per capita income is a staggering twenty times lower than that of the US and eighteen times lower than Germany and France. A decade earlier China had been over fifty times lower – a dramatic catch-up but still leaving lots of room for big cost savings by western capital.[3]

It was always obvious that producing goods with any sizeable labour content in low-cost areas will provide much greater profits for the shareholders of the companies involved. James Goldsmith, a major global financial capitalist himself, put it this way in the early years of the 'global rush' – as early as 1994:

In most developed nations, the cost to an average manufacturing company of paying its workforce is an amount equal to between 25% and 30% of sales. If such a company decides to maintain in its home country only its head office and sales force, while transferring its production to a low cost area, it will save about 20% of sales volume. Thus a company with sales of $500 million will increase its pre-tax profits by up to $100 million every year.[4]

Lower social costs – the taxes on business and capital that governments force corporations to pay in order to finance various aspects of the welfare state – are a key gateway to profitability, and thus share performance. As long as countries can provide a secure political framework (democratic or undemocratic it hardly matters) and a pool of relatively skilled workers, then shareholders will increasingly demand investment in low-social-cost areas – Asia, Russia and Eastern Europe and those western locations where costs and taxes are still competitive by western standards. And within the West there have also been 'low-cost' countries seeking to undercut. The Thatcher/Blair plan for Britain since the end of the Cold War has included a strategy of keeping social costs (primarily taxes) low as a way of competing with Britain's European neighbors without increasing real productivity. British social security costs as part of indirect labour costs are significantly lower than those of France, Sweden, Germany, the Netherlands and Portugal.[5]

'GLOBALISATION' IS FINANCE AND CAPITAL-LED

The frantic search during the 'global rush' years for lower and lower costs, and for lower and lower taxes, by the western super-rich is the engine which has driven the increasingly integrated global market for capital. The really big money is made by speculative capital – often borrowed or 'leveraged' – that dips in and out of countries making money either by exchange rate changes or by the 'carry trade' – borrowing on lower interest in one place, loaning on higher interest in another. This speculative finance is huge, and makes people very,

very rich. And, like George Soros, famous too. The amounts involved, though, are difficult to measure. Much easier to measure is the less glamorous, though just as deadly, end of the capital market where jobs are immediately made and lost – and, from the western perspective, are shipped overseas. The figures for foreign direct investment (FDI) – that is, investment which takes a longish term, if not exactly lasting, interest in foreign enterprises – are impressive. FDI, that is the inflow and outflow capital from locations in one country to locations in another, continues to grow. UNCTAD reported that foreign direct investment reached $1,306 billion in 2006, the third successive year in which it rose, almost equalling its record high in 2000.

During the 1990s the proportion of FDI going to low-cost areas in non-western countries had risen to 27 per cent in 1991 and 40 per cent in 1993, and remained at or around this record level for some time (it was 35 per cent in 1995) And FDI inflows into all developing countries rose from $31.9 billion in 1995 to $38.5 billion in 1996, falling back marginally to $37.2 billion in 1997. But by 2005 South, East and South East Asia *alone* was receiving $165 billion in 2005 with East Asia accounting for three-quarters of the total Asian figure. South, East and South-East Asia are still the main magnet for these inflows into 'developing countries' with most of this increase going to a handful of countries – the bulk of total 'Third World' FDI investment ended up in China, Singapore, Malaysia, Thailand, India, Hong Kong, Taiwan, Mexico, Brazil, Argentina and Egypt. China – with $108 billion – was the single biggest player in this league.[6]

During the boom years of the 'global rush' the West also received significant inflows (with the UK at the top of the western list). And it may well be that – initially at least – these inflows to the West will reach much greater heights following the banking and credit crash as western banks – with the connivance of western governments – both seek and accept 'sovereign wealth funds' from Asia and the Middle East. As of writing Citigroup was putting the finishing touches to a big capital raising exercise as it sought up to $14 billion from both China and Kuwait. As the news commentary in *The Financial Times* put it in what was the understatement of the year: 'The deal underscores the depth of the problems faced by banks that suffered heavy losses in the US sub-prime mortgage crisis.'[7] (One of the investors in this case, was called the China Development Bank, in reality the Chinese Communist Party, which as well as financing infrastructure products at home also funds Chinese companies as they develop abroad. This 'bank' has also taken a stake in the British-based bank, Barclays).

However, much of the capital inflow into the West still comes from other western countries, much of it based on intra-western mergers and acquisitions (M&As). In 2005 UNCTAD reported that cross-border M&As rose to $716 billion close to that of the merger boom year of 2000. Of course many of these mergers and acquisitions, and often privatisations too, may be intra-western, but they also serve to reduce costs (involving the laying off of domestic labour or the employment of new labour at lower rates).

FEAR AND BLACKMAIL. 'THE FAUSTIAN PACT'

Although the new globalised world is being built upon mobile capital, debates about its size are not the whole story. For the future of jobs and living standards are influenced not just by the amount of capital flight, but also by its *possibility* – indeed its increasing probability. For the tough fact is that in the 'global rush' mobile capital (and the corporations that wield it) can blackmail whole nations. The threat to any government is clear: if a corporation does not get its way – that is, if wages or the social costs to business (taxes) are too high, or if the tax-breaks or local skills are not appropriate – then capital can (and does) simply up sticks and move to more accommodating areas. This kind of blackmail – by corporations, by mega-rich individuals threatening to go into tax exile – is now routine, and is mostly conducted in secret. Sometimes it is public. And sometimes it is used to attempt to change general public policy. The Swedish government is a case in point. In the 1990s it was successfully and blatantly publicly intimidated by both Peter Wallenberg of Scania trucks, who threatened to move his headquarters unless the government brought down the budget deficit, and Bjorn Wollrath, of the insurance company Scandia, who threatened to boycott Swedish government bonds.[8]

More often, though, such threats are not articulated. They do not need to be as the effect is the same. As *Newsweek* magazine has argued, governments are induced into what it calls 'a Faustian pact': they can have access to global capital as long as they obey the imperatives of corporations, and the super-rich behind them, about the need to constantly provide capital with a low cost environment.[9] The shareholders are believed to demand it.

CORPORATIONS AND COMPANIES:
'ALIEN' STATIONS CIRCLING THE EARTH

This free movement of capital – out of the domestic economies and into the global system – is largely made possible by the great arteries of the system carrying the life-blood of big mobile money. These arteries are the corporations – what used to be called multinationals but are now more accurately termed transnationals.

These modern corporations are great political power centres in their own right. Even in the early 1950s the chairman of the editorial board of *Fortune* magazine was arguing that corporations had become so powerful that the president of the United States had a dependence on them that was, 'not unlike that of King John on the landed barons at Runnymede, where [the] Magna Carta was born'.[10] And by the 1990s *Financial Times* columnist Joe Rogaly could tell us to 'forget governments – companies rule, OK', and spoke for a growing number of opinion formers when he argued that the corporations now 'matter more than ever' and 'are heading for dominance over the lives of most advanced countries'.[11] For a time the role of the corporations became so controversial that even mild liberal opinion in the West flirted with ideas of restructuring corporate governance – with more say by an array of 'stakeholders' and less by managers and shareholders. The English journalist Will Hutton pioneered this idea in his book *The State We're In* and his idea was apparently taken seriously by new Prime Minister Tony Blair whilst he was in opposition (but soon dropped when he entered Downing Street).

The size of these transnationals is awesome. And it was unsurprising that they were powerful enough to punch their way into a global future – powerful enough to override political resistance and forge the new world of global capital. According to UNCTAD, in the 1990s, as the 'global rush' was getting well underway, about one third of all private productive assets in the world were under the 'common governance' of transnational corporations, and many, many more were linked to and reliant upon them. It has also been calculated that the sales of each of the top ten transnational corporations amounted to more than the GDP of 87 countries. General Motors, Ford and IBM almost outranked Britain in terms of

GDP (and, of course, when calculating the GDP of Britain the productivity of British-based transnationals is counted in!).[12] Staggeringly, of the 100 largest economies in the world at the time, more than half were corporations, not countries. General Motors' sales figures were higher than the GNP of Denmark. Ford's were higher than the GNP of South Africa. Toyota's were higher than the GNP of Norway; and the top 200 firms' sales added up to more than a quarter of the world's economic activity – and have been growing ever since.[13]

These transnationals are no longer simply domestic commercial operations that increasingly operate abroad, as did many British corporations during the empire or the great American corporations during the period of the Cold War. In truth the modern transnationals should no longer be viewed-as they have been since the inception of capitalism-as commercial entities owing a loyalty to, and even deriving an identity from, their nations.

Robert Reich, as early as 1991 in his path-breaking book, *The Work of Nations*, saw clearly how in the new corporate-run global order corporations were unconstrained by national loyalties. To believe that the big transnationals are loyal to their countries of origin, he argued, is 'charming vestigial thinking'. He suggested that what he called 'the new organisational webs of high-value enterprise' were replacing the old core pyramids of 'high-volume enterprise' and they are reaching across the globe in such a manner that there will soon be no such organisation as an '"American" (or British or French or Japanese or West German) corporation, nor any finished good called an "American" product'.[14]

Some fifteen years later such 'charming vestigial thinking' is still prevalent. Much popular journalism still treats the big corporations as though they were national businesses. Even when it is clear that great icons of Britishness are owned by foreigners (as of writing Rolls Royce is owned by BMW, HP Sauce and Lee and Perrins Worcestershire Sauce are owned by Heinz, Jaguar is owned by Tata Motors of India and Rowntree Chocolate is owned by Nestlé) it takes time for the public to see the corporations in a new light. Can you get more 'American' than General Electric, Proctor and Gamble or IBM, all of which are now essentially stateless, with highly decentralised 'corporate webs' spreading around the globe with foreign profit centres and employees? As are the foreign-owned Doubleday, RCA, Giant Foods, Pillsbury or Goodyear? Can you get more 'British' than the ocean liner *Queen Elizabeth II* (in the 1990s owned by Norwegians) or *The Times* of London (owned by Rupert Murdoch, formerly an Australian but now a US citizen)?

Robert Reich has given life to all this by drawing a vivid picture of what – and from where – consumers are actually buying when they deal with one of the big cosmopolitan corporations:

When an American buys a Pontiac Le Mans from General Motors...he or she engages unwittingly in an international transaction. Of the $10,000 paid to GM, about $3,000 goes to South Korea for routine labour and assembly operations, $1,750 to Japan for advanced components (engines, electronics), $750 to West Germany for styling and design engineering, $400 to Taiwan, Singapore and Japan for small components, $250 to Britain for advertising and marketing services and about $50 to Ireland and Barbados for data processing. The rest – less than $4,000 – goes to strategists in Detroit, lawyers and bankers in New York, lobbyists in Washington...and General Motors shareholders – most of whom live in the United States, but an increasing number of whom are foreign nationals.[15]

This depiction, written at the beginning of the 1990s, is now, in the first decade of the new century, underdrawn. So diverse (and, in terms of nationality, often unknown) is their ownership that almost the only certain link between a transnational corporation and its supposed nationality is the city of its headquarters. Both in their ownership and their activities transnational corporations are now wholly independent world actors. Instead of being a part of a nation they are increasingly nations themselves – in competition with nations for resources. In their tactical operations they may live within the laws of nations, but strategically they operate on a global basis. They float above the domestic economies as majestically as alien spacecrafts circling the Earth.

They may need 'the people' below in the domestic economies – for skills, and as consumers of their services and products. But they are now autonomous beings, able to rise above their national base, bargain with their current 'host' nation as well as other nations, and shift resources from one to another.

THE WALL STREET BANKERS' REGIME

These transnationals produce goods, and are not, technically, financial institutions. Yet, in the 1970s and 1980s as they forged new global markets and created global networks – in what came to be called 'globalisation' – they were but a part of a deeper global conquest being established by the great American banks and finance institutions on Wall Street and their satellites in the City of London.

The great investment banks – Merrill Lynch, Morgan Stanley, Goldman Sachs, Lehman Bros., Bear Stearns, Credit Suisse – were the dynamo of the emerging global financial system, but the traditional banks – Citigroup, Bank of America, UBS,

Deutsche Bank, Barclays – although depository institutions, were also adopting some of the features, the flexibility and 'innovation' of the investment houses. As these banks went global, they only did so on the strength of the American hinterland base. About half their revenues still came from their operations in the American economy and about a third from Europe.

Wall Street got its first big break during the Nixon presidency when in 1971 the link with gold was broken and the dollar was allowed to float against other currencies. This early example of US unilateralism ended the role of nation-states managing currency exchanges, and meant that, as the US government controlled the one reserve currency, the dollar, US dominance over the dollar area was embedded. With the petro-dollar recycling of the mid-1970s as a kind of dry run, the 1980s, with Reagan in the White House and Paul Volker at the Fed, saw the end of capital controls and the beginning of the era of huge flows of private finance around the non-communist world. And with the collapse of communism these flows spread wider and wider.

At the same time Wall Street was getting large new amounts of money to play with. The American political leadership in Washington opened the door for Wall Street by opening up the wallets and savings of Main Street to the banks. They called it the 'liberalisation' of the US economy. Through a major change in tax law US private pension funds ballooned and created a huge new pool of money for Wall Street to use. By the turn of the century it amounted to around $2 trillion.[16]

It is the pension funds that give Wall Street capital its democratic face, for pension funds represent the savings of millions of ordinary people, who indirectly (and unknowingly) take part in the stock markets. 'When the Cold War ended in 1989 there were less than one hundred million people in the world economy who owned shares through pensions. If present trends continue, then in twenty-five years time this number could expand to 2 billion'.[17] In Britain in 1957, pension funds owned 3.9 per cent of beneficial shares in British enterprises; by 1993 this had risen to 34.2 per cent.[18]

Pension funds were becoming truly enormous. In Switzerland, Denmark, Holland, the United States, Britain and other Anglophone countries private pension programmes have assets that equal 50-100 per cent of GDP. And pension funds are set to grow. Demographic changes already mean that two thirds of all people who have lived to the age of 65 are still alive today.

Pension funds were also in the vanguard of the internationalisation – and globalisation – of money. They are as mobile and footloose as other capital. And they – or rather pension fund managers – encourage corporations to promote a higher return on capital for their shareholders, a process that reinforces the search by corporations for low-cost production centres. Pension money has considerable power in the stock markets of the world. Take the US mutual fund industry. One reason why it has grown from $1.1 trillion in 1990 to $14 trillion today is the growth of defined-contribution retirement savings programmes which now account for about one third of all mutual fund assets (for the giant Fidelity group, 65 per cent of its assets in 1997). As David Hale argues, 'Instead of the Japanese and Anglo-Saxon forms of capitalism encouraging different investment agendas, pension fund trustees will require managements everywhere to focus on maximising the return to corporate shareholders, not stakeholders such as corporate suppliers, main banks or employees.'[19]

Thus the desire for performance, for profits as the key economic need, can no longer simply be dismissed as the product of the greed of the super-rich; it is now emanating from those who act for the ordinary man and woman – the pensioner and future pensioner. Should pensioners ever be asked, they would obviously want – maybe even demand – that their fund manager invest their pennies in the most profitable manner, and therefore globally.

Yet in a very real sense this pension money was (is) a hostage. Although the Wall Street 'globalisation' regime – as this book argues – increases divisions in the West and, potentially at any rate, threatens the living standards of vast swathes of the West's population, responsible politicians (those who agree with this analysis) can do little to limit its effects. The living standards of pensioners and future pensioners – the very living standards that the political critics of Wall Street 'globalisation' tend to worry about most – would, paradoxically, be put at risk if the pension industry could no longer invest globally to secure the biggest immediate return. It creates a very hard choice.

Along with the pension money of America, Wall Street's resources were also hugely boosted by the 1980s growth in the global bond market, which by 1997 was estimated to be $23 trillion, the majority of which was US government bonds. Thus, the way things worked in the weird and wonderful world of Wall Street, as the US deficits grew, so too did the market for bonds, and every loan by the banks improved the assets of the Wall Street banks.

The banks now had big resources to make profits from. And the golden key to making money on Wall Street was 'arbitrage'. Just as the transnationals made money by exploiting differences in national conditions, so too, and on a huge scale, did (do) the financial capitalists of Wall Street. Professor Peter Gowan of the Global Policy Institute in London outlined how arbitrage works. The key was that the there may have been a global order, but the world was not 'flat' – that is, not the same:

> The world remained broken up into radically different financial markets in radically different economic, regulatory and institutional configurations, as before; but now the big Wall Street institutions could enter and exit these markets at will and exploit differences between the conditions in each. In short, the new architecture provided enormous scope for arbitrage, exploiting the differences between these still segmented markets...Arbitrage of all kinds has thus become an enormous new field for profitable activity...'[20]

Arbitrage needs a world canvas – for it needs to be able to dip in and out of the nations of the world, making profits at each entry and exit. Above all it needs open borders and 'free trade'.

ONE 'FREE TRADE' WORLD

Preventing government – any government, national or global – from interfering with the world of trade is a major aim of the new Wall Street order. Ever since the Bretton Woods agreement 'free trade' – including, crucially, the free movement of capital – has been a sacred cow, And any attempt to replace this 'free trade' market by thinking and acting strategically and politically about trade (usually dubbed 'protectionism') has been considered by supporters of the Wall Street global order as economically injurious, indeed one step away from war.

The formidable coalition supporting 'free trade' in the West was headed up by the great US-based corporations and their supporters in both parties on Capitol Hill. Every single president since 1945 has supported the policy of free trade. As have all US trade representatives. The George W. Bush administration's trade philosophy was standard fare – said its trade representative's office: 'free trade is good for American workers, because when American workers compete on the world stage, American workers win.'[21]

Opposition to 'free trade' was not absent in the US, but was very much a minority sport – coming from the weakened labour movement and from marginalised political figures such as 1992 independent presidential candidate Ross Perot and conservative columnist and two-time presidential candidate Pat Buchanan. In postwar Europe 'free trade' has also been the orthodoxy – led by the powerful German export industry, and supported by the global financial interests in the City of London. Although some European political leaders–particularly in France – often flirted with a measured protectionism (latterly called 'economic nationalism') none would ever seriously and frontally challenge the idea of 'free trade'.

As 'free trade' critic Ravi Batra commented in the early 1990s 'the idea [of free trade] is now embraced as economic theology around the world'.[22] Its powerful grip on the minds of western intellectuals is reinforced by a particular view of history – principally the belief that interwar 'protectionism' was a cause of the 1929 financial crash, the interwar depression and then the war itself. The fact that the Smoot-Hawley Tariff Act – demonised in the West during the 1990s – followed, not preceded, the great Wall Street crash, and the fact that US unemployment rose from 3.2 per cent to 8.7 per cent long before the effects of the tariffs were felt, has little effect upon this powerfully embedded received opinion.

Another part of the governing mental construct about trade was that protected markets hinder economic growth. Much of this comes from the British experience in the nineteenth century when the flourishing protected imperial market system was mistaken for 'free trade'. So well propagated was the benign character of 'free trade' and the malign nature of 'protectionism', that the fact that the United States protected its home market for most of the period of its spectacular economic growth during the nineteenth century is often overlooked – as is the role of 'protectionism' in the postwar Japanese economic miracle, and the rise in the 1980s and 1990s of the newly industrialised 'tiger' economies of Asia, particularly Taiwan and South Korea.

During the global boom 'free traders' relied on the powerful theory of comparative advantage which dictated that two countries forming a trading partnership (that is a single market without trade restrictions) should specialise in the production of goods and services in which they have an absolute or comparative advantage, and that together they are more productive than they are separately. Yet this theory has always rested on the proposition that companies are part of a country's economy – that is, capital is essentially national, rooted in place. As John Gray noted 'in the classical theory of free trade capital is immobile', and he quoted David Ricardo as arguing that 'every man...has a disinclination to quit the country of his birth...[and this] checks the emigration of capital'.[23] But in the age of footloose, mobile capital, the world is very different. Gray himself is one of a number of theoreticians who believe that 'both in theory and practice the effect of global capital mobility is to nullify the Ricardian doctrine of comparative advantage', and according to Martin and Schuman, 'Ricardo's basic postulate [comparative cost advantage]...is now completely out of date.'[24]

THE HOLLOWING OUT OF THE WEST: THE LOSER POPULATIONS

Yet, theoretical disputes about 'free trade' aside, the overwhelming new characteristic of the Wall Street-driven global trading order was the sheer scale of change – and its sudden-ness. Its size and speed had no historical precedent; and in comparison the previous bursts of globalism, of capital moving beyond the confines of its home in North-West Europe (through western colonialism and the paced migration into North America), looked paltry. This time there was the 'China factor' and the 'India factor' – the 'six billion factor'. The emerging Wall Street world order, as seen from the early 1990s through the turn of the millennium, was of a world economy that virtually overnight embraced an additional 4-6.5 billion people, a quantum leap not seen before in economic history.

In the early 1990s the late magnate and activist James Goldsmith became a prescient and eloquent critic of this new world – and like other magnates he was often more incisive than the academics in the field. In a series of slim volumes he drew the attention of anyone who would listen to the fact that with the end of the Cold War four billion people had suddenly entered the world economy, and that these newcomers would 'offer their labour for a tiny fraction of the pay earned by work-ers in the developed world'. And in a none-too-veiled shaft at his fellow global super-rich he argued that 'it must surely be a mistake to adopt an economic policy which makes you rich if you eliminate your national workforce and transfer production abroad, and which bankrupts you if you continue to employ your own people.'[25] Goldsmith had sounded an early warning about how what was later to become known as the 'hollowing out' of the West.

The writer, Edward Luttwak, was another early critic of the new global order and its 'free trade' fundamentalist assump-tions. In his 1998 book *Turbo Capitalism*, Luttwak conceded that 'free trade' theory may be more efficient globally – pro-ducing the same goods by replacing expensive workers with cheap workers – but adds that 'in affluent countries...now increasingly afflicted with the return to poverty in the most vulnerable fraction of their population, it is not necessarily a good idea to enrich the kingdom by turning some of its subjects into paupers'. And he criticised the 'free trade' economists for 'leaving the scene' whenever compensation schemes for the unemployed and low-waged – which are 'never implemented' – are mentioned.[26]

These early critics of this 'hollowing out' process were reacting to the loss of manufacturing jobs. But the western political establishment could see off these critics because it was only the lower skilled sections of the populations of the West that were being affected – either by being replaced or by facing stagnant wages and fewer benefits.

It was also an article of faith that the West's losers would never outnumber the West's winners. And this hopeful prognosis was stuck to stubbornly as each passing year the real job situation worsened throughout the West. In Europe the losses showed up in higher unemployment numbers throughout the larger continental economies; in the United States the losses were hidden by the creation of less well-paying jobs without benefits, and by very odd survey methods of employment; and in Britain hidden by a low wage economy embedded by the invasion of massive numbers of cheap foreign labour.[27]

And the Wall Street 'free traders' continued to serve up large doses of fatalism. They argued that western nation-states could do very little about the loss of jobs, and that the jobs, when lost, would not be returning. (In 2008, John McCain, then Republican presidential candidate, made this clear as part of his 'straight speaking' campaign.) Some put the loss of jobs and growing inequality in the West down to technology, and not to global capital and trade. Robert Lawrence of

Harvard University, in a scholarly defence of free trade, made the argument that 'technological changes and changes in management practices, rather than trade, are the source of growing inequality'.[28]

All that the politicians could do, they argued, was to try and relocate the loser populations in new jobs – in 'services', although where these jobs were coming from, and what kind of jobs they would be, was not normally spelt out in any detail.

The general policy of the 'free-market' governments was to prepare their populations for the tough new world of the global economy by encouraging new 'skills' – 'training and skills' – so that both the loser populations and the new generations could compete with the Asian competition. (Although the rhetoric remained, long gone were the old-fashioned, Victorian-utopian ideas of creating an 'educated population'.) This task of maintaining and enhancing the skills of local populations was conveniently not assigned to global capital itself, but rather to the western public sector. British Prime Minister Tony Blair once went so far as to argue that such 'skilling' and 'reskilling' was nothing less than the 'greatest single priority' of government in the global economy. (Global capital would of course play its part in this process – as a kind of umpire, picking and choosing between nation-states as to which ones have performed best, and rewarding the winners by investing, for a short period, in their local populations.)

Some market enthusiasts though disagreed with 'reskilling' being a proper function of the state. Pressures on public expenditure – and the need to maintain a low tax regime – would limit the amount of resources that could be afforded. And in a sign of the tenor of the 'free market' times, the following suggestion was seriously made: 'market forces will do this automatically...for instance, if workers with low levels of education in OECD countries saw their wages fall to levels equal to those of workers in developing countries, they would have a tremendous incentive to invest [personally] in education'.[29]

BUT, WHAT ABOUT SERVICES?

But low-skilled manufacturing loss was to be only half of the story. As the new century got underway it was becoming clear that rising Asia was offering more than sectoral competition – it was making a general and strategic challenge to the West.

The complacent view that China and India could never be able to compete with the West in the service sector, particularly financial services, and in hi-tech, died hard. Consider this, from a study commissioned by the OECD: 'some processes and technologies can be moved internationally...the most significant sources of higher productivity in the developed countries – the superior levels of skills and the tacit knowledge of the workforce – cannot move abroad.'[30]

But this complacency slowly began to lose its hold as it became clear that Asians were quite capable of competing across the board. As Australian writer-diplomat Gregory Clark could argue that 'for East Asia the western myth of free trade is a good joke', and that 'today, in Asia at least, some [countries] are equal or superior to the West in work ethic and ability to absorb technological skills'.[31] And it was also becoming apparent that Chinamen, and Chinese women, might well also be able to do banking! And that, over time, they could also do virtually anything else that westerners could do – and at a lower cost.

Yet, the pioneering American political thinker Michael Lind was something of a lone voice when he argued, in 1995, in a passage which deserves quotation at length, that:

Within a generation, the burgeoning third world population will contain not only billions of unskilled workers, but hundreds of millions of scientists, engineers, architects, and other professionals willing and able to do world class work for a fraction of the payment their American counterparts expect. The free trade liberals hope that a high wage, high skilled America need fear nothing from a low wage, low skill Third World. They have no answer, however, to the prospect – indeed, the probability – of ever increasing low wage, high skill competition from abroad. In these circumstances, neither better worker training nor investment in US infrastructure will suffice...It is difficult to resist the conclusion that civilised social market capitalism and unrestricted global free trade are inherently incompatible.[32]

By the turn of the century it also becoming apparent that China in particular was not necessarily going to play the free-trade game – and fully open up its own market to the West's service sector; and that ultimately it would be able to serve its own growing market – and serve other markets – through its own financial service sector. The were lessons here for the financial services sectors of Wall Street and the City of London, but also for the hi-tech engineering industry of Germany and the computer industry of California.

THE WEST IN DANGER

By the late 1990s the writing was more than etched upon the wall. It was carved into it. The world, in Gabor Steingart's words had 'seen the integration of millions of Asians but the disintegration of millions more westerners'.[33] And 'globalisation' was not going away; indeed was only in its early stages. And it was not a difficult call to predict that China was likely to retain a huge competitive advantage over the West as

China's billions – its large pool of reserve labour – were still massing on the edges of the coastal areas waiting to enter the labour market. Nor was it difficult to see a real danger for the West in the fact that China's increasingly skilled urban population could easily begin to move into the service sectors.

Yet, western financial capital still had (still has) the prospect ahead of it of a deep, rich seam of cheap labour and cheap costs to mine. In sum, there were many more western jobs to lose and much more western wealth to be transferred. And as for the politics of it all, China remained an enigma. The predominant western view was that integration in the global economy meant integration into the West, including into its political and cultural system. It would take time, but China would be westernised. So, confronting the Chinese political, and geopolitical, question could best be left until later. And, anyway, after 2001, radical Islam was the greater problem.

By century's turn it was clear that Wall Street's new economic order would continue on into the new century. As William Greider, after writing his long critique of the global system could argue: 'the [western] elites of media, business, academia and politics have already made up their mind on...the global economic system – and [about] defending it from occasional attacks from angry, injured citizens'.[34]

LOW INFLATION AND DEBT SAVES THE DAY

There was to be no popular rebellion in the West against 'globalisation' and global capital – and the slow but remorseless hollowing out of the West. There were numerous violent protests on the streets outside some big global governance meetings, and these were played up by the media. But during the 1990s not one serious western political party ran on an anti-free trade platform. And there was to be no equivalent of the early twentieth century British Conservatives who adopted 'protectionism' as their platform and campaigned on the issue. Today's equivalent – a political party in a major country advocating economic protectionism as a way of maintaining living standards – has simply not appeared.

The fact was that during this early phase of the new global order the bulk of the American and European populations suffered no loss of living standards. By the late 1990s the West was in the middle of boom times. The boom was interrupted by a sharpish recession at the turn of the century, but the boom was to return with even greater intensity until it burst in 2007.

It was a party fuelled by cheap prices from Asia. These Asian-driven low costs were a godsend. For cheap Chinamen and cheap Chinese women – working away in low-standard sweatshops in greater Shanghai – provided a low inflationary global environment in which westerners could live well beyond their means. It was this Chinese-led global low inflationary environment that allowed the West's leaders to temporarily keep their peoples' living standards up by creating massive private – and public – debt. Western workers – middle class and blue collar – may have found their pay packets shrinking, but their credit cards came to the rescue. Low inflation meant low interest rates, and low interest rates meant low sub-prime mortgage rates and easy money to buy houses; and as the house prices rocketed in value 'globalisation's losers', now feeling the 'wealth effect', could run up their low interest credit cards and car loans.

For 'globalisation's losers' – those out of work, or those in work with few benefits, or those in work with two or three low-paying jobs – low inflation did them another favour. It provided the growing legions of the working poor with the wonderful world of Wal-Mart: low prices for most everything for the house. Low prices to suit low wage packets.

For the West's smaller number of winners this Chinese-induced low inflationary world was also a real boon. Inflation has always been a deadly enemy of the super-rich – the global rentier class of wealth holders. As the columnist Bob Herbert saw it 'Alan Greenspan's purpose is to protect the assets of the very wealthy. The value of those assets erodes with every up-tick in the rate of inflation.'[35] The assets of the less wealthy are also devalued by inflation, and for the middle classes, and those on fixed incomes, inflation can also be deadly. Roger Bootle in *The Death of Inflation*, a pioneering book on the consequences of what he believes may be the coming age of zero inflation (or even disinflation), has argued that a zero inflation economy – as long as it doesn't tip over into serious disinflation – can be generally beneficial, but is specifically good news for shares, the engine room propelling the growing wealth of the rentier super-rich. He argues that zero inflation 'would imply a higher level of real equity prices at each stage even if the level of bond yields and the rating of equity risk were the same'[36]

In any event the free market revolution of the 1980s and the Wall Street world order that followed it were built upon the foundations of low inflation – indeed upon an anti-inflationary zeal. During the decades of the social democratic (post-Second World War) era the West lived with inflation. Anyone born after the 1920s has known a world in which prices rise every year. Yet suddenly counter-inflation became a political if not a populist issue, gathering a degree of public support. Post-Second World War German opinion was always hostile to inflation, indeed obsessed by it, because of the Nazi experience in the 1930s. But a broader anti-inflation constituency throughout the West emerged following the oil price crisis of the 1970s when unusually high price rises led to serious social unrest and political instability (this was particularly marked in Europe, where radical political change, including the possibility of 'Euro-communist' governments, was only just averted).

As a reaction to this inflationary dislocation the anti-inflation campaign – led in the early 1980s by Federal Reserve chairman Paul Volker and politicians Reagan and Thatcher – took hold. And since then the goal of low or zero inflation has become orthodoxy, and any policy that can be attacked as 'inflationary' hardly stands a chance of a serious hearing. The arguments against an inflationary society remain strong, even for social democrats, but so too do the arguments against deflation.

Yet the Wall Street global capitalist orthodoxy still appears prepared to take risks for one course, but not the other. And so fixated on low or zero inflation have the western economies become that those who question the orthodoxy of low inflation are few and they tend to argue their corner rather tentatively. Yet they are beginning to emerge. The late 1990s centre-left political regimes in Germany and France tolerated somewhat higher levels of inflation than their predecessors. Even amongst economists some heads are beginning to appear above the parapet. James Tobin of Yale University has argued that a small amount of inflation helps 'grease the wheels' of the economy.[37] Also, the highly experienced former British Treasury minister Joel Barnett recently suggested that 'it seems untenable to put inflation on a unique pedestal', and that it should be considered alongside other objectives such as 'growth and exchange-rate management'.[38]

Yet the western consensus was (is) still a long way from replacing anti-inflation as dogma with inflation as technique – as merely a mechanism to help secure economic prosperity and social and political goals. And we are still a very long way indeed from understanding that the large internal western markets (in the US and the European Union) can, partly because of their still relatively low exposure to trade, easily tolerate rather higher inflation levels than those which prevailed in the 1990s.

HOLLOWING OUT: 'SELLING THE ROPE'

So, by century's turn, all was seemingly well in the western garden. The new global system appeared to be working well for almost everyone. The winners were making money; and the losers were saved by low prices and the credit boom.

In the West, capital was boss, and the world its playground. And Asia remained the new frontier. Big western capital had gone global and was beginning to make prodigious profits and the prospect was of much more to come from where that came. The constraints on Wall Street doing exactly what it wanted had been removed. Governments were weakened by 'globalisation'; the trade unions were dead men walking; rampant individualism reigned, and 'greed was good'.

What's more, although serious trade imbalances with China were beginning to show up, China was helping the West by recycling its huge surplus into US government securities – thus allowing the Americans and their British and other economic satellites in the West to party some more, and continue to live beyond their means.

Perhaps though the biggest, and darkest, cloud on the horizon was the growing pauperisation of the loser populations in the West. But the good news for western capital was that the high costs of doing business – and the expensive western jobs and high taxes that caused these high costs – could now be jettisoned without any comeback from the impotent western governments and peoples. So began the historic hollowing out of the West.

In a previous era Vladimir Lenin could catch a sort of truth when he asserted that 'the capitalists will sell us the rope with which we will hang them'. Today's communists, the much more peaceable leaders of rising China, are, almost a century later, still being sold the rope.

CHAPTER THREE

THE 1990S: RENEWING THE GLOBAL REVOLUTION

CLINTON AND BLAIR JOIN WALL STREET

1997 was an important year for the 'masters of the universe' in Wall Street and Washington. In January Bill Clinton took the oath of office for a second term, and a few months later Tony Blair became British Prime Minister. These two new world leaders – both of them left-of centre politicians – had sought to draw a line under the Reagan/Thatcher revolution and had set out on a new course – which they called the 'third way'. And they had the wind at their backs. In 'Anglo-America' the 'free market' years were becoming controversial, increasingly seen as the 'decade of greed'; and pollsters were finding that publics were more willing to contemplate paying higher taxes for better services.

Yet, both Clinton and Blair were to turn out to be very good news for the big players on Wall Street and the City of London

– and for the 'globalisation game' that was their ticket to unheard-of riches. The poor boy from Arkansas and the youthful radical from Islington had come to power at a time when some of the structural economic changes – that would open the way to the full flow of 'global capital' – had already been secured. Yet they both had a clear opportunity to limit, and even reverse, the process. Yet, neither Clinton nor Blair showed even the remotest inclination to do so. Instead, with the super-rich riding off into the 'globalisation' gold rush, Clinton and Blair, and the western political class to which they gave leadership, decided to ride shotgun.

Clinton's opportunity came first. He was elected in 1992 during a sharp recession when a major milestone in globalisation, the North Atlantic Free Trade Association (NAFTA), was top of the American agenda. It was an election in which Ross Perot had achieved a record-breaking 20 per cent of the presidential vote as a third party candidate dedicated to ending the free-trade agreement. Perot built his whole campaign around the 'hollowing out' argument, famously, and presciently, declaring that once NAFTA was in being 'you will hear a giant sucking sound' as jobs are 'sucked out' of the US.

The anti-NAFTA campaign had many supporters in the Democratic party, and with presidential leadership, NAFTA could easily have been emasculated, if not completely abandoned.

But Clinton had made his bargain with corporate America and, as president, both introduced, and became a stalwart defender, of NAFTA and the next great burst of 'globalisation'. Also, Clinton's abandonment of any serious attempt to bring in a comprehensive health service to America – which would inevitably have created an incentive for corporations to pay taxes at home instead of investing abroad – meant that Clinton was even abandoning the attempt to 'shape globalisation' to American needs. Rather, Americans would, in effect, be told to 'accept it', shape up and compete in the world.

The truth was that Clinton had, long before becoming president, embraced US big business and their linked agendas of market reform (deregulated markets and low taxes) and economic globalisation. His first term assured corporate America that their revolution was safe in his hands. And he made clear there would be no going back when in 1995, as president, he reappointed the intellectual godfather of the revolution, the Randian economist Alan Greenspan, to yet another term at the Federal Reserve.

Tony Blair, who came into office some five years after Clinton, also had a window of opportunity through which to bring a halt to the rampant globalisation then already underway. Blair's route, should he have decided to take it, would have been through Europe – and Europeanisation. When Blair took over in Downing Street the City of London was already the major player in British politics and was seeing its future as inexorably global. Yet, at the same time, a majority of City opinion was in favour of the country joining the euro-zone. It saw the City as being able to combine global influence with a future as the financial centre of the European hinterland (like Wall Street to the USA). And Blair's New Labour, ever sensitive to City opinion, had fought the election on a pro-euro platform. He had pledged a referendum, and would have won one – particularly if it had been held fairly soon into the new New Labour regime.

Yet he lost his nerve. Had he gone for it, and won the referendum, then Britain, melded into the European economic scene, would, inevitably, been set on a course in which British economic policy would become Europeanised. It would have involved some serious adjustments, but it would also have ended up with a country less dependent upon the global economy, less leveraged, less imbalanced than the Wall Street model which it was later destined to follow.

From his earliest days as Leader of the Labour party Blair had, like Clinton, made his pact with Britain's corporate business community. Blair had proved his market credentials when, before becoming Prime Minister, he formally dumped socialism (and social democracy) in rewriting the Labour party constitution. He later went on to become a true disciple of 'free market' themes and big corporate business, and his attraction to the American economic model, the Wall Street model, weakened his desire to commit Britain to a European future. As British prime minister he would regularly lecture the 'sclerotic' social capitalists in Europe about the virtues of the American model.

Both Clinton and Blair gave their considerable rhetorical gifts and public relations expertise to the cause of 'globalisation'. They both argued that economic globalisation was 'inevitable', and could not, Canute-like, be turned back; rather, it needed to be 'accepted', and adapted to. But they tended to avoid making the case solely by reference to economics, profits and cheap consumer goods. They sought instead to create domestic support for globalisation by stressing its positive moral content. Clinton saw it as a great progressive force unleashed to save humanity. For him it was 'world without walls' – 'the only sustainable world; and globalisation was 'an explosion of democracy and diversity within democracy'.[1] Tony Blair regularly made the same kind of case – and even some months after leaving office he was setting globalisation in a slightly mystical, moralistic and religious, context during a speech entitled 'Faith and Globalisation'.[2]

By the mid-1990s 'globalisation' was all the rage amongst western opinion-formers – as an army of academics, economists, journalists and pundits also saw 'globalisation' as a positive force in the world. A strong moral case was consistently proffered with many analysts believing that 'one world', fuelled by the communications revolution, mass tourism, and growing trade, was finally in the making. The leading academic of globalisation, the sociologist Anthony Giddens (who influenced much of Blair's thinking) saw globalisation in these terms – as a truly transformative agency. 'We have a chance' he said in 2001, 'to take over where the twentieth century failed, and a key project for us is to drag the history of the 21st century away from that of the 20th.'[3] Amongst western journalists *New York Times* columnist Thomas Friedman, also led the way in seeing globalisation as progress – with its 'inexorable integration of markets and nation-states'.[4]

Economists and economic commentators tended, as is their wont, to take a narrower, more precise, perspective – seeing globalisation through economic, rather than political and moral, eyes. Indeed, as Ralston Saul argued, they saw 'civilisation as a whole through an economic prism'.[5] And, for a time, there was a near unanimity of opinion amongst economists on the subject – in globalisation's favour.

There was also a very strong correlation between 'free market' supporters and advocates of 'the global market' and globalisation. Leading 'free-market' economists Martin Wolf and Jagdish Bhagwati saw globalisation as both inevitable and good for aggregate global living standards and good, too, for western prosperity (after suitable 'reforms' and adjustments, particularly in Europe). The overwhelming consensus was that the West needed to adjust to the new global reality and that the forces that opposed such adjustment, protectionists and pro-welfare politicians, would, by interfering in the workings of the global market, end up causing even lower living standards. Even Joseph Stiglitz, a trenchant and bitter critic of prevailing ortho-doxies, only went as far as criticising how globalisation was managed – in part under his tenure as Chairman of President Clinton's Council of Economic Advisors. His primary criticism appeared to be that the US used globalisation to advance her own interests. Looking back in 2003 he suggested that 'we had no vision of the kind of globalised world we wanted, and we weren't sensitive enough about how what we wanted would be viewed by the rest of the world'.[6] Stiglitz developed a powerful critique of a world of economic globalisation without global economic governance – but with global governance still an impossible dream, his readers were left not quite knowing whether he believed that the whole post-cold war project of economic globalisation, and its free trade component, had been wrong in principle.

THE WASHINGTON CONSENSUS

In the real world of money-making, globalisation was much more than a nice theory – for it was the practical method of opening markets, deregulating commerce and finance, and raising profits worldwide. For Wall Street and Washington it was heady stuff. The West's capitalists were setting rules and norms for the whole world – their own rules and norms.

These rules were to be set out in what became known, appro-priately enough, as 'the Washington Consensus'. This 'consen-sus', unveiled in 1989, was a ten-point programme setting out what western bankers wanted from indebted Latin American countries. It amounted to a regime that would be imposed on countries which fell into debt, a regime that took advantage of distress in order to impose ideological market solutions.

A precursor to this 'Washington Consensus' was the Structural Adjustment Programs (SAPs) of the World Bank instituted following the oil crisis of 1973. These programmes ended the passive (and short-term) loan role of the international financial authorities, substituting a more direct and controlling approach, restructured the market of debtor countries to open them to foreign investment and to promote exports in order to repay the debt. Looking back, in 2006, W. Easterly, a World Bank official and supporter of these SAPs, has argued that 'the over-ambitious reforms of shock therapy and structural adjustment were the flight of Icarus for the World Bank and the IMF. Aiming for the sun, they instead descended into a sea of failure.'[7]

Icarus regularly fell to earth in Africa where there is considerable evidence that these SAPs were big-time failures, for the fact was that those countries that implemented the most SAPs either had neutral or negative growth. The same was true for the countries of the former Soviet Union who agreed to SAPs. Also, The World Bank funded a number of SAP projects that caused considerable environmental damage as in Brazil and Indonesia.[8]

The bottom line was clear: the West, through the big international organisations, sought to draw the less-developed countries into an integrated market-based global economic system which the West led and controlled and were run according to the West's economic precepts. These 'emerging' economies were forced to rise and fall with the West; and were not allowed to develop indigenous markets, the key to long-term economic growth and success. The idea was 'one world, one market' – but 'one world, one market' run from Wall Street.

The man who drew up the blue-print for the 'Washington Consensus', economist John Williamson, later argued that although he never intended his plans to work out the way they did, they implied and then led to 'policies like capital account liberalization, monetarism, supply-side economics, or a minimal state...getting the state out of welfare provision and income distribution.' (And he added that, for his part, he now hoped, in 2002, that 'we can all enjoy its wake'.)[9]

The 'Washington Consensus' regime was to be tried out in a big way in the Asian crisis in the late 1990s. Malaysians, Thais and Indonesians were all to get the treatment– what one critic called 'redemption' through 'economic and social self-flagellation'. In other words, in return for being bailed out countries would need to introduce a full 'neo-liberal' 'reform programme' based upon 'opening' markets and 'liberalising' economies. And in the process the way would be cleared for western economic and financial elites to do business and to make money. And to continue to make money – as through this global 'reform programme' the whole world would turn into one giant Main Street serviced by Wall Street.

As the Asian countries dutifully 'reformed', then western hedge-fund money swept in, and western hedge-fund money swept out; and left in its wake a devastated and debilitated terrain.

However, not all was plain sailing for western mobile capital. Malaysia rebelled. Its maverick and articulate leader Mahathir bin Mohamad broke ranks and reestablished capital controls and trade protection. It was a rare act of defiance; and was treated in the West as an act bordering on sacrilege. His heresy unleashed 'a tidal wave of contemptuous condemnations' from around the world 'writing off Malaysia as a basket case and [Prime Minister] Mahathir as mentally unstable'.[10] Mahathir returned fire with sarcasm. He declared the Malaysians to be 'stupid' but asked the market liberals to 'leave us to do the wrong things we want to do'.[11] Of course, the

Malaysian leader did not believe that the rebel course he had set was wrong, and soon Malaysia was doing well even by the economic indicators used by the western-dominated international organisations. George Soros could predict that 'if Malaysia looks good in comparison to its neighbours, the policy may easily find imitators.'[12]

Intriguingly, during the Asia crisis, China was not one of the countries that western market 'neo-liberals' were able to dictate to – in part because the Asian giant's currency remained pegged. In the world of 'free trade' China was the proverbial 'elephant in the room'. For the Asian giant has been growing by doing all the things 'free traders' were telling them not to. It had a pegged currency, it has capital controls, and it has refused to 'liberalise' many key sectors of its economy. China, as it emerged, was going to work to its own, not the West's, rules and agenda.

SURVIVING THE CHALLENGES

Yet, the Wall Street-led globalised order was to display considerable resilience. It ultimately survived the Asian crisis. And it also survived three other serious challenges – the 1998 bail-out of the mammoth hedge-fund LTCM, the Russian default crisis of 1998 and, most importantly, the 2000-1 bursting of the dot.com bubble.

On 10th March 2000 the dot.com's main index NASDAQ peaked at 5132, more than double its value of a year before. Its rise had been accompanied by extravagant claims about how the Californian-based technology 'new economy' was a wholly new economic phenomenon – a 'new paradigm' – that was going to rewrite the rules of economics and change the world. Yet, on 10th March the prick was administered and for the rest of the year and into 2001 the dot.com bubble burst. The IT revolution had run its course – an important new technology but not one that was going to sustain the global economy.

Yet Wall Street did recover. The Dow Jones bottomed out at 7,286.27 on 9th October 2002 and it was then onwards and upwards again. By the end of 2003 it had reached 10,000 (and by January 2006 it broke through the 11,000 barrier).

THE VISION OF GLOBAL AMERICANA

In this climate the 'masters of the universe' in Wall Street and the new imperial leaders at court in Washington could be forgiven for believing that America financial genius when married to its military power was an unstoppable combination. And they could be forgiven too for believing that the global economic order that had been fashioned in their image, had been tested and had survived, was now unstoppable. The world had indeed become Main Street.

Thus economic globalisation and Americanisation (of the Wall Street business variety) became one. And supporters of this Global-Americana were not bashful. For America was good for the world as America stood for capitalism and democracy. It was a compelling vision. Robert Samuelson has described its outlines when he argued that 'after the Cold War, global capitalism offered a powerful vision of world – prosperity and, ultimately, democracy. Multinational companies and investors would pour technology and capital into poorer regions, creating a transnational mass market of middle class consumers who would drive Toyotas, watch CNN, eat Big Macs – and, incidentally, demand more freedom.'[13] This was Wall Street's economic counterpart to Francis Fukuyama's famous political and cultural vision of one world in which 'western liberal-democracy' reigned as 'the end-state of the historical process'. For both Fukuyama and the Wall Street visionaries, although they would not say so openly, something like America (or more like America than anywhere else) was what the 'end of history' would look like. (Although Fukuyama was, much later, to say that he had in mind the EU rather than the USA).

No wonder that in that spring of 2003 the conservative historian Niall Ferguson could be moved to declare that the United States had the world at its feet, and that the republic was not only an imperial power but was *good* as well. 'The reality,' he argued, 'is that the United States has – whether it admits it or not – taken up some kind of global burden...And just like the British empire before it, the American empire unfailingly acts in the name of liberty, even when its own self-interest is manifestly uppermost.'[14]

AMERICAN CAPITALISM AND THE MINIMAL STATE

And 'liberty' was to be advanced by the market. Indeed the market was American global capitalism's great universalist idea. And this belief in the market developed a visceral quality, a militant conviction that a brave new world was being born. It amounted to a certainty of religious dimensions. Indeed, it became a secular religion. William Greider argued that 'the utopian vision of the marketplace offers...an enthralling religion. Many intelligent people have come to worship these market principles, like a spiritual code that will resolve all the larger questions for us, social and moral and otherwise'. And Edward Luttwak described the orthodox monetarism at the heart of the new capitalism as having 'like all religions a supreme god-hard money – and a devil, inflation'.[15]

This new religion was 'Gekko's world' view. It was the vision too of Ayn Rand and her student Alan Greenspan, of Keith Joseph and his student Margaret Thatcher, and of a host of aca-

101

demic economists who followed in their footsteps and were beginning to populate the think tanks. They called themselves 'neo-liberals'. And it was this 'neo-liberal' world which in the mid-1990s Bill Clinton and Tony Blair had signed on to renew.

This religion of the market made few conversions amongst the West's masses, but it did enthral and entrance many of the West's elites – and not just the opinion-formers in the big corporate media outlets and at the annual World Economic Forum in Davos. For it even lit fires in the minds of the men in the staid world of officialdom and policymaking. True believers could be found not just in the White House and Downing Street, but in the great international institutions like the IMF, the World Bank, the WTO, and even in key parts of the European Commission.

These true believers saw the market – the global market – as being nothing less than an expression of American freedom itself. 'Freedom' was what America stood for, and this 'freedom' could only be guaranteed by the 'free market' because, so the argument ran, entry to the market – unlike to the state – was essentially voluntary, and this ensured the liberty of the individual. Thus in the mind of the believer the ethical idea of the sovereign individual fighting a great battle for liberty translates easily into a more prosaic and materialistic economic individualism.

In this way 'free markets' became one of the security and foreign policy goals of the West. For instance, NATO was no longer to continue as a defence pact but would instead become a military alliance dedicated to changing, to remaking, the world on western lines. It would, according to Colin Powell, testifying before the Senate Foreign Relations Committee in 2002, 'promote democracy, the rule of law, and promote free markets and peace throughout Eurasia.' For the first time NATO possessed a specifically economic agenda. In a big win for the market revolutionaries, 'free markets' were to be backed up by bayonets, another example of Wall Street's objectives signed on to by the Pentagon.

Thus the market developed a moral and political content, for it was not only by far the best way of allocating resources, it was also virtuous – both efficient and good. And the roots of its goodness lay in its protection of the individual – the sovereign individual. Thus, the market and individualism became one. The market was as American as apple pie.

And, for the true believers, if the market was an essential engine for individual freedom then, by contrast, 'the state' – in all its guises, federal, state and local – was a serious threat. Thus was 'the state' demonised as 'un-American'.

A flavour of the near-religious fervour – indeed vehemence – behind much of this contemporary anti-state impulse is provided by this intriguing passage from a 1980s new right propagandist:

> The New Right must propagandise mercilessly against the state. It must stress unremittingly the enduring moral bankruptcy of government. It must constantly compare the burden borne by the taxpayer, to fill the government trough from which the interest groups are feeding with the benefits received by the swine at the trough...we must underscore relentlessly to our un-organised fellow taxpayers their direct interest in the unremitting attenuation of the state.[16]

REWRITING THE HISTORY OF THE STATE

A religion – even a secular one – needs a favourable history. And the winners, of course, write the history books. So global capitalism's victory over socialism – and the market's victory over the state – became the occasion for such a new history. In this new history the state took a veritable drubbing. The state came to be associated with limiting freedom, with oppression, even with persecution. Socially it induced sclerosis and politically it automatically centralised and bureaucratised. And most cutting of all, the state was an expropriator – of property and, worse still, of taxes. In such an environment the contrary idea of the state as helping to forward pleasing images such as enabling, helping, opening, democracy and rights could not get house room in government of western opinion.

The gravamen of the new globalist history was the view that raw capitalism – the Anglo-American model of free market, minimal government capitalism – is the world's great success story. This well-entrenched thesis was built around the extraordinary economic success of the western world, and in particular, in the twentieth century, of the United States. The received wisdom had it that the US (and to a lesser extent Britain), the two great examples of high, free-market Victorian capitalism, uniquely ushered in the industrialism (and later the commercialism) that made the West the predominant civilisation of the world; and that through the good graces of global capitalism this huge success story will be repeated worldwide.

This history of private and market triumph completely undervalues the role of the state – the public sector – in the success story. Britain in Victorian times was by no means the raw capitalist society of myth. Its great free-trade, free-enterprise, free-market system, it should never be forgotten, was built upon the back of a worldwide empire – an empire sustained by government and its agencies in the military and civil services.

Likewise, the history of the economic development of the US is hardly a story of undiluted capitalism. That great engine of American capitalism, the continent-wide internal market, was the result of government – the geopolitical expansion of the US 'feds' through military conquest. The British Royal

Navy the military arm of a foreign state – but a state nonetheless – ensured the protection of the US capitalist economy during the formative decades of the nineteenth century. And American *state* craft helped defeat US capitalism's great enemy – the imperial protectionist system of the old European colonialists. And of course it was the state – the US state (with its *public sector* military, diplomatic and political arms) – that, by prevailing over the Soviet Union and its command economy, preserved western capitalism and gave global capitalism its lift-off. In the face of such overwhelming evidence it is impossible not to see the history of the US as the history of capital and state working together.

Of course, one of the primary reasons for US capitalism's great leap forward in the twentieth century had nothing at all to do with its economic system, and everything to do with politics and the international game of states. Unlike its competitors in Europe, the US was relatively unscathed by the two world wars – the great conflicts that destroyed the European empires and set back the European nations for over half a century. It was the wisdom of politicians, the leaders of the US state – primarily General George C. Marshall and President Harry Truman – who, by pouring public sector money into the regeneration of the European economies, provided an expanded market and represented the single greatest boon to US corporations in their history, and made them the global players they are today.

The clash of political ideologies and state interests that was the Cold War also helped US capital and capitalism to make their mark. The post-1945 bipolar global political framework, with the US as the leader of the West, helped US capital to penetrate global markets; and the military confrontation with Russia helped create a huge market for American business –

the big business of defence procurement and the small businesses it generated.

State and capital worked together in another way too. The American success story in the twentieth century – 'the American century' – is too often attributed to the economic dynamism unleashed by bustling entrepreneurs, tough-minded robber barons and, later, the efficient management of global American corporations. Yet this is only half the story. For there was a political dimension too – a governmental genius was at work as well. To create, and then to bind together this geographically and socially diverse, continent-wide federation was no small achievement. It was a political document, the US constitution (liberal, flexible, adaptable) that helped keep a fractured nation – and thus a single economy – together. It was the political genius, too, of President Abe Lincoln and his supporters, who, by keeping the union together after the defeat of slavery and the south, preserved a single internal market – perhaps the most important of all the reasons for the later blooming of the US free-market system.

Rewriting – that is, talking down – the history of the state, and of government itself, often involved depicting the state as simply a phase of history. In an echo of historical Marxist determinism, supporters of the market see 'stateless' global capitalism as the end-point of history. 'Prehistory' was the history of nation-states; these nation-states may have been progressive in their way (they did, after all, serve to organise democracy and introduce concepts such as rights and accountability), but they were riddled with contradictions, and were unstable. This instability has given way to a new, stable system of globalisation. Globalisation is historically inevitable and represents 'the end of history'.

THE MINIMAL STATE

Global capitalism is a godsend to such anti-statists. By weakening the hold of the 'interfering' and 'expropriating' nation-states, state power is automatically marginalised. In the great clash between market and state, power thus swings decisively towards the market.

In an unusual alliance with libertarians, big corporate capital saw all too clearly the advantages of a weakened state: the unhindered mobility of capital (so those who invest can punish those states and societies that do not encourage sufficiently acceptable returns), low or zero inflation (in order to ensure low interest rates and thus boost the prices of shares and bonds), low taxation (so that the returns from capital remain high), and 'flexible labour markets' (in order to keep costs, particularly social costs, low and therefore raise profits and the return on shares).

Most serious proponents of the 'free market', however, did not waste their time arguing for the abolition of the state – the campaign objective was more limited: it was to shrink the state, to reduce it further and further until it became a 'minimum state'. Adam Smith's aphorism that governments should do only what cannot be done in the market – or what cannot be done by individuals – became the central idea; and that injunction is now interpreted as limiting government to a small number of 'absolutely necessary' functions, leaving the rest to the market. And in our own time the libertarian philosopher Robert Nozick in his famous 1974 work *Anarchy, State and Utopia* has argued that these 'necessary functions' are very few, including defending the country and enforcing contracts.[17]

In practical terms, minimalists want the state to withdraw not only from economic life through lower and lower levels of taxation, through privatisation and deregulation, but also from the four main welfare services: education, housing, medical care and insurance for income in retirement. As Arthur Seldon declared, 'the vision of capitalism is the prospect of minimal government. It excludes the state, or its agencies, from the production of goods and services...The vision thus requires the eventual withdrawal by government from most of its accumulated activities.'[18]

In Britain during the late 1960s and 1970s advocates of such a minimal state began to put policy flesh on these bones – with some very practical proposals. Clustered around the Institute for Economic Affairs in London, and led by Arthur Seldon, they pioneered many of the ideas that, in the 1980s, conservative politicians began to introduce to a wider public. B. G. West wrote *Education: A Framework for Choice* in 1967, F G. Pennance wrote *Choice in Housing* in 1968 and Charles Hanson wrote *Welfare before the Welfare State* in 1972. Later, in 1981 Arthur Seldon wrote *Wither the Welfare State*, and in 1985 David Green wrote *Working Class Patients and the Medical Establishment.*[19]

Some extremist minimalisers even wanted the government to withdraw from law and order functions, even from controlling the currency. Another school of thought amongst the minimalisers argued that although government should be largely withdrawn from economic life, it should nonetheless be used to liberate 'the poor' by a gift of money to enable them to acquire the means – money – to exercise choice and to take responsibility for their health, education and old age provision. This was the plan behind Seldon's provocative 1977 pamphlet 'Charge' in which he advocated charging everybody for all kinds of erstwhile services. It amounted to using the state in a sort of enabling function – and it assumed that the 'poor' would remain a relatively small section of society.[20]

THE MINIMAL STATE PROJECT

This vision of minimal government – that governments should do only what cannot be done in the market – was, until the 1990s, just that: a vision, a distant goal. Certainly the late 1970s and the 1980s saw a major tilt in the US political world (and consequently in Britain) away from social democracy and towards the market. Ronald Reagan and Margaret Thatcher gave political leadership to a conservative movement that used simple and populist terminology to get its anti-state case across. Politically powerful sound-bites – such as 'get government off the backs of the people' and 'government is the problem, not the solution' – skillfully associated the state with bureaucracy, officialdom, 'red tape', inflexibility and, most witheringly of all (as I have argued earlier), compulsion.

Reagan and Thatcher also led an *intellectual* revival. Unlike many of the more centrist presidents and prime ministers who preceded them – most of whom who took a managerialist view of leadership – they saw the long-term value of ideas. They used their offices to introduce to a wider public a host of classical liberal theorists who, marginalised during the postwar social democratic consensus, finally came into their own. Ludwig von Mises, Frederick von Hayek, Milton Friedman and Karl Popper, if not exactly becoming household names, did become the new gurus of the age (taking over from John Maynard Keynes and John Kenneth Galbraith).

In the US a new generation of free-market 'conservative' intellectual leaders emerged in the think tanks and universities – economists such as George Stigler and George Gilder, sociologists such as Charles Murray, public choice theorists such as Mancur Olsen and J. M. Buchanan, and philosophers such as the former socialist Robert Nozick. In Britain, in an intriguing parallel eruption, theorists such as Arthur Seldon, Madsen

109

Pirie, Anthony Flew and William Letwin, economists such as Samuel Brittan, Peter Bauer, W. H. Hutt, Patrick Munford, Gordon Tullock and Alan Walters gave Thatcherism a vibrant intellectual underpinning. These Reaganite and Thatcherite intellectuals wrote with verve and confidence, and with a sense that they were part of a new tide of ideas. And indeed they were. It was a period in which the governing social democratic consensus was seemingly breaking down, and the left's response to these insurgent thinkers seemed tired and bereft of fresh thinking.

One intriguing aspect of this renaissance of the 'free-market' was the number of former socialists and social democrats who began to break cover and support market solutions and a reduced role for the state. The initial issue for many of them was non-economic – they supported the defence build-up during the Cold War and rejected what they considered to be their fellow socialists' growing anti-western attitudes. But this was a time when the social democratic consensus – built by Roosevelt in the USA and the Attlee government in Britain – was seemingly failing on the economic front. Big government welfare had not solved the American inner-city problems which were literally going up in flames; and in Britain many of the country's economic problems were put down to the 'over-mighty' public sector – with its powerful 'over-mighty' public sector unions. It was an environment tailor-made for a systematic critique of the mainstream left's assumptions, not just about defence and NATO, but also about the role of the state and the market. And the list of 'left' public intellectuals who moved across to associate themselves with many aspects of the broad Reaganite and Thatcherite 'revolution' was considerable. It included Robert Nozick, Peter Berger, Norman Podhoretz, Robert Skidelsky, Evan Luard, Irving Kristol and – less so –

Sidney Hook, Daniel Bell, New York Senator Daniel Patrick Moynihan and European Commission President Roy Jenkins.

In the US a new political term took hold to describe these former Roosevelt and LBJ social democrats. They were called 'neo-conservatives'. And, although they were later to divide – between those who went on to throw their lot in with Republicans and Conservatives, and those who stayed Democrat or Labour – they played a major role in the 1980s in moving the centre of political gravity towards a more market-based world.

Two magazines became the home for this transatlantic generation of 'neo-cons' – as they came to be dubbed by the American media. In the US the American Jewish Committee's *Commentary* magazine – edited by the redoubtable Norman Podhoretz – not only focused on winning the Cold War but also, month after month, systematically attacked the social and economic agenda of the American 'liberals', including what they considered to be the overblown US welfare state. In Britain, *Encounter* magazine, led by the equally redoubtable Melvyn Lasky, did not set itself against social democracy quite so strongly (in the early 1980s it supported the social democrats' political exit from the increasingly leftist Labour Party), but it did provide a platform for serious arguments from Thatcherite economists and social scientists.

As well as these social democratic allies, the anti-statist market revolution secured support from another, somewhat surprising quarter. Traditionalist conservatives – numerous in Europe, less numerous in the US – were always suspicious of individualism and consumerism, tended to be neutral about the power and reach of the state, and saw the market as destructive of traditional values and ways of life. Yet a number of these 'paleo-conservative' thinkers – such people as Michael

Novak, Roger Scruton and John Casey – got swept up in the market revolution and rode shotgun with the free-market conservatives who saw few contradictions between capitalism – even the rawer kind – and tradition.

LOWER AND LOWER TAXES

The intellectual case that sustained the market revolution was both systematic and, in an era witnessing the collapse of the authority of socialism, appealing. But the war for the market was really won on the more practical, and populist, terrain of taxes. Market politicians noticed something that the socialists and social democrats of the 1970s and 80s had ignored. One of the most pronounced social changes since the 1950s was the hugely increased number of people paying taxes. Low, and even average, wage earners were not really in the income tax brackets in any numbers until well into the 1960s. But as they, and the growing army of women in the workforce, flooded onto the labour market in the 1970s the anti-tax appeal of conservative politicians achieved a previously unknown resonance.

But it was the world of business that harbored the real resentments against the high-tax regimes of governments. And as globalisation got underway tax competition by governments, anxious to keep and attract global capital, assumed serious proportions. The name of the game was to keep companies sweet. So, from the late 1980s onwards the tax rates for companies fell throughout the world. It has been estimated that between 1991 and 1995 Europe's largest engineering conglomerate, Siemens (including its subsidiaries), was able to reduce its worldwide taxes from 50 per cent of its profits to 20 per cent. This new power relationship between corporation and nation-state was summed up neatly in 1996 by the reported comments of Daimler Benz chief Jurgen Schremp, who announced that he did not expect his company to pay any more taxes on profits in Germany, and told parliamentarians bluntly that 'you won't be getting any more from us'. Schremp summed up the clear, new, market capitalist idea that companies, not the state or society, have the ultimate right to ownership of money and resources – it is 'our' money, not 'yours'.[21]

So successful, so total, was this victory of business over government on the issue of taxes that by the turn of the century not a single politician in the West was even trying to associate him or her self with a regime of higher taxes. Gone too was the mid-1990s rhetoric – tried out for a bit by 'left-of-centre' politicians like Bill Clinton, Tony Blair and Gordon Brown – about how public services should come first even if it meant slightly higher tax rates. New Labour's public sector spending did involve tax increases – the so called 'stealth' taxes – but business pressure for lower taxes continued into the new century, and was only contained so long as growing amounts of tax money was being spent on the private sector through the growth of outsourcing.

In 2006, towards the end of his premiership, at the CBI conference in London, prime minister Tony Blair was still acting as a cheerleader for the low tax regime desired by business; and he was selling it by appealing to the well-worn formulae: We must, he argued, 'keep our tax system here competitive...with the new economies as well as the more traditional economies against which we compete.'[22] In other words, 'globalisation', which we must 'accept', demanded it. It was still difficult for any aspiring politician to say otherwise.

MINIMUM WELFARE

Of all the projects of the minimum state, reducing welfare was the most difficult to sell. Most of the leading continental European nations had serious welfare states that, though reformable at the margins, were (are) so entrenched that any dismantling – particularly in health provision – would lead to political revolt. And in the US the welfare system was so bound up with inner-city, underclass politics that any major surgery would, even though unintended, produce real racial divisions.

In the push for a minimum welfare state market fundamentalists argued on two levels. On the moral and ideological level they continued to assert that there was simply more dignity in providing for yourself than relying on 'handouts' from the state. Those relying on welfare become supplicants. This argument was spelt out clearly by a leading free-market theorist, who argued that the welfare state turned 'paying customers in the market' into 'importunate supplicants in the political process'. It represented a clear contrast with the traditional social democratic view, set out by Will Hutton, that 'the vitality of the welfare state is a badge of the healthy society; it is a symbol of our capacity to act together morally, to share and to recognise the mutuality of rights and obligations that underpins all human association'.[23]

Yet at the heart of the minimalist view of welfare was the question of efficiency and cost. Minimalists fervently believed that the four main services of the welfare state – education, medical care, housing and pension income in retirement – could be provided much better by the private sector – through insurance and charging – than by the state through taxation. Indeed taxes are the real point here. Capitalism used to be able to sustain a welfare state through taxes on businesses – the so called 'social costs'. Yet with the growth of demand in some welfare areas – such as health and pensions – the same level of service can only be provided by increasing taxes, and in the absence of punitive taxes on consumers, that means raising these 'social costs' on businesses. And the minimalist reformers of the welfare state argued (argue) that such social costs are no longer sustainable – certainly not at the level operating in continental Europe in the so-called 'European social model'. Unless prices or employment take the strain, then by eating into profits they threaten share performance.

In the 1990s, with the Wall Street minimalists' campaign against Europe's welfare capitalist system in full swing, British and American supporters of the new capitalism regularly focused on late-twentieth century France as the prime example of the unsustainability of this 'high social cost' model. In 1997, under a headline 'Will Europe Face Up to Coming Reality', the American-owned *International Herald Tribune* investigated a French decorating company, BDM, in the Normandy town of Bray-et-Lu and found that 'employing a worker at a gross monthly salary of 10,111 francs ($1,702) ends up costing a total of 15,306 francs, or an additional 51%'. The paper revealed that these 'social costs' go towards family allowances, low-cost housing loans, unemployment insurance, work accident compensation, pensions and professional training, and even towards reducing the social security budget; and the clear implication emerged that in the Anglo-American market model much of this kind of provision cannot be expected to be funded by businesses.[24]

In a future minimalist state there would be a trade-off between welfare and unemployment. If social costs remained high then companies would simply lay off workers in order to keep profit margins high. A leading French banker argued in 1997 that 'if costs in America were the same as in France...perhaps 25% of Americans would be unemployed.'[25] Of course, in such a regime the minimal state would not be able to afford much in the way of unemployment benefits. So low-remunerated – very low-remunerated – part-time work for millions of people might be the answer. And in the late 1990s, at least in Anglo-America, it was indeed becoming the answer, and the grim reality.

MINIMAL REGULATION (OF THE BANKS TOO!)

This minimal state would also be a minimal regulator. The minimalist revolutionaries based their deregulation agenda on the need to 'free up' business from the 'dead hand' of state regulation – a freedom that would lead, in financial services as much as elsewhere, to higher levels of innovation and productivity – and profits. One of the leading voices behind the campaign for deregulation was the American Nobel laureate and minimal-statist George Stigler who argued that regulation too often ended up favouring the regulated through cosy deals between the private and public sectors and led business into the inadequacies and corruptions of the political process.[26]

In the Anglo-American world in the 1990s the deregulators won the battle. In both the US and Britain the so-called 'light regulatory touch' ruled the day particularly in the banking and financial sector. And it was this 'light touch' that, in essence, opened the door to the massive over-leveraging that, over a decade later, was to lead to financial catastrophe. So powerful was this push for deregulation that, even after 2007 – even after the banking failures, and even after the fall-out from Enron and WorldCom – the voices of the minimalists could still be heard from Wall Street to the European Commission urging a new round of deregulation – this time in the labour market.

A key demand of the minimalists had been a deregulation of the labour market – in order to create a 'flexible' workforce. And the key point of the 'flexibility' advocates was the need to establish a legal ability of corporations to hire and fire at will so they could respond quickly to changing profit margins caused by changes in demand. Some extreme supporters of these 'reforms' saw an end-game in which corporations not governments would determine the labour market, and would be free not just to hire and fire but to employ a whole range of labour – full-time, part-time, hourly, full benefits, no benefits, and so on. 'Reforming' the labour market – making it more 'flexible' – was a policy propounded far beyond Wall Street, most prominently by the European Commission.

If the power of a religion can be measured in adversity, then the religion of the market – and its central doctrine of deregulation – was strong indeed. For, even by 2008, when it was clear that deregulation had been a major contributor to bringing low the western financial system, and with it the living standards of the West, the true believers were still believing. The God of the market was still very much in his heaven – and was receiving souls. In the US, Democratic presidential candidate Barack Obama may have edged towards blasphemy when he argued, in a speech in March 2008 to the Cooper Union in New York, that 'a free market was never meant to be a free license to take whatever you can get, however you can get it'. But, at the very same time, and in the midst of the 2008 banking crisis, the then Treasury Secretary Hank Paulson was still in a deregulating mood. He brought forward proposals to further deregulate some SEC functions, and still refused to force hedge-funds and banks to hold capital proportionate to the risks they were taking.[27]

Even the new Labour administration in Australia was, some months into the banking crisis, still buying into the necessity to deregulate. On 26th February 2008 Lindsay Tanner, the incoming 'Minister of Finance and *Deregulation*', no less, accused Australia's Conservatives of 'letting the deregulation agenda in this country lie dormant for most of their eleven

117

years in office' and believed that 'relieving businesses and con-sumers of the burden of inappropriate, ineffective or unneces-sary regulation will build Australia's productive capacity...'[28]

GLOBALISM AND THE MINIMALIST BREAKTHROUGH

Market extremists and 'minimalists' did not, though, get it all their own way. Although possessed of a considerable *esprit de corps*, and a sense of being on the winning side, for most of the 1990s they were ascending rather than ascendant. They were never fully able to dislodge the mechanisms of social democ-racy – the state, the welfare society, or the mixed economy. President Ronald Reagan presided over a huge budget deficit, and, no matter the rhetoric, did not succeed in lowering the public sector in the US economy; and the same was true for Prime Minister Thatcher, who, for electoral reasons, was at one point reduced to proclaiming that 'the National Health Service is safe in my hands'. Public spending remained high but was increasingly spent by the private sector.

What is more, as the 1980s progressed it became clear that the European social model was still intact – as was the Japanese model – both representing something of a beacon for those who wanted a more cooperative public-private (and manager-labour) system, and an active, involved, and enabling, welfare state.

Even the marked growth of privatisation, which was partic-ularly dramatic in late 1980s and early 1990s Britain, did not fully marginalise the state. It weakened the public sector by depriving it of the assets of ownership. Yet at the same time the newly-privatised companies paid taxes to the state, and when they reduced their workforces the state was still there to pick up the social security bill. By the end of the free-market 1980s most western states were, intriguingly, taking as much in taxes as they had at the beginning of the decade; and of course the state was still a power in the land by virtue of the huge military budgets – and the payrolls it still deployed.

It was not privatisation, but rather 'globalisation', that made possible the real breakthrough for the minimalists. Although privatisation deprived the state of assets, the state could still tax them. 'Globalisation', or the mobility of capital, meant that assets could move. During the 1990s – almost overnight, as it were – capital, freed from nation, began to establish a marked ascendancy over the state. Capital mobility, or the threat of mobility, allowed the market, for the first time, to punish and reward nation-states according to its requirements. It weakened the state *vis-à-vis* the market more effectively than any proselytising or privatising by Reagan or Thatcher and their army of market intellectuals.

AND A MINIMAL INTERNATIONAL POLITICAL ORDER

The key prize for minimalists always lay beyond the water's edge. For in order to succeed they needed to weaken government. Their very best possible world was one single global order comprising no government at all. But they would settle for a world in which a host of states were all competing with each other for capital's favour.

A type of global governance existed during the post World War Two Bretton Woods regime, when the world financial system – with its fixed exchange rates, regulated financial markets and currency risks borne by the public sector – provided some form of political, and thus democratic, authority as a balance against markets. This era ended when, in response to the pressures of the early 1970s, the US government decided to dump Bretton Woods; during the following two decades exchange controls were abolished, domestic limitations on cross-market access to finance were removed and controls on credit were scrapped. During the 1980s, amidst a quantum leap in speculative financial flows, financial risk was privatised and a global market in monetary instruments emerged. And in the 1990s this flow became a tide.

Today's capital globalisers, though, seek a world order that is far more minimalist than Bretton Woods – and one that is also far slimmer than the *ad hoc* internationalism of the earlier era. And they are getting it. With the state weakened at the national level, their aim is to ensure that the state does not regroup at the global or regional level – that the world order remains fragmented into a host of states, none of them too big to establish political authority over global finance, and all of them competing with each other for capital's favour.

It remained at once both an ennobling and dangerous vision. It sought a world in which international relations – the essential characteristic being relations between nation-states – will, in all but a rudimentary, residual sense, cease to exist. In its place we will inhabit what John Burton, way back in 1972, described as a 'world society'. And 'the units of the system [of this 'World Society'] will not be billiard ball states but can be corporations, overlapping ethnic groups, classes or even individuals'.[29] The danger lies in there being no off-setting global government. And thus no global democracy. In fact, no democracy at all.

The American business economist Joel Kotkin also caught the flavour of this modern global vision when he introduced the idea of global tribes – he talked of the British, the Japanese, the Jews, the Chinese and the Indians – establishing global networks 'beyond the confines of national or regional borders'. And, as for global tribes, so too for global corporate units and global individuals – our super-rich. In this idealised global society there is no government. The state is not minimal, it is non-existent. In short, no one is willing to regulate the casino.

As things stood at the turn of the century, to believe in a future for this 'global society' – a society without effective global government and therefore effective regulation – was not utterly fanciful. Nor was it over the top to see the reality behind the vision: that the only serious form of government in this 'global society' would be that of the one superpower, the government of the United States of America. And with the US government as the only state with any power in the world, business and the dollar would rule. And so too would 'democracy'.

CHAPTER FOUR

RULING THE WORLD: THE PENTAGON UNLEASHED

'AMERICA CAN REMAKE THE WORLD'

In the 1990s the Clinton-led vision was of a global exercise of soft power – of America remaking the world through the power and allure of its Wall Street-driven capitalist economy. But, at the same time, and largely behind the scenes, American conservatives were also beginning to have ideas of remaking the world. But, this time, not by soft power alone.

The central figure of 1990s American conservatism was new Republican Speaker of the House of Representatives, Newton Leroy Gingrich. In the summer of 1995 Newt Gingrich made a foreign policy speech. He went boldly to the big question. 'We have to lead the world' he declared, and 'if we don't lead the world I think we have a continuing decay into anarchy.'[1]

Gingrich was effectively 'co-president' (with President Bill Clinton) and spoke for the newly invigorated conservatives who were dominating Washington following the Republican victory in the Congressional elections of 1994. Gingrich was an historian who, although a standard free trader, also saw the world through a broader geopolitical focus. He was also highly Pentagon-friendly – a supporter of big defence spending, he was a personal friend of Donald Rumsfeld, President Ford's Defence Secretary from 1975-77, who was later to appoint him to the Pentagon's Defence Policy Board.

Gingrich's speech was a sign that the American right had finally shaken off the ideas of the conservative 'anti-globalists'. The Republican party had always had its share of those who were sceptical about US interventionism around the world. And sceptical too about the exercise of global hard power. From the inception of the republic the dominant American view was set against 'entangling alliances'; and even after America became the world's leading economy, powerful voices, primarily Republican, continued to argue for an essentially 'isolationist' foreign policy. They had been particularly insistent in the run-up to American involvement in the Second World War, and had been grouped around the 'America First' movement.

However, World War Two and its aftermath reduced these voices to a whisper – as a near-total US consensus gathered behind an internationalist and interventionist strategy. Corporate America sought global markets; and most everybody supported the US as the new global super-power in its contest with the Soviet Union – and also its worldwide bases structure tied to a worldwide series of interlocking global alliances (from NATO through CENTO to SEATO). It was an era in which anti-communism and the 'red threat' became political culture; and non-interventionism, and certainly 'isolationism', were considered eccentric, or sometimes worse.

But with the end of the forty year Cold War, and the end of the Soviet threat, American non-interventionism could resurface. And those who sought a more modest role for the US were provided with a real opportunity. Prominent amongst them was the social conservative commentator Pat Buchanan. Buchanan, a former Nixon speech-writer, had run for president in 1996 and again in 2000 on an overtly non-interventionist and anti-'free-trade' platform. He had opposed American involvement in the Gulf War in 1991, and later in the 1990s would go on to oppose American intervention in the Balkans and in Kosovo, and he opposed the American air strikes in Serbia. He was also to oppose the US invasion of Iraq in 2003, arguing that the US had embarked on 'a neo-imperial policy that must involve us in virtually every great war of the coming century – and wars are the death of republics.'[2]

Buchanan had also opposed the North American Free Trade Agreement (NAFTA) which he argued would cause American job losses. As well as a serious writer he could become a populist controversialist, and he drew on the image of a peasant's revolt against big corporate 'free trade' and became known as 'pitchfork Pat'. He once argued that 'we love the old republic and when we hear phrases like "the new world order" we release the safety catches on our revolvers'. The Los Angeles Times described him in very un-American terms, as a 'class warrior'.[3]

As well as Buchanan, supporters of the American libertarian right, best exemplified by the Cato Institute in Washington D.C., were also articulating a non-interventionist foreign policy. But, unlike Buchanan, they based their approach on libertarian principles, rather than geopolitics. Opposed to big government in principle they attacked lavish Pentagon spending – an approach which the Republican primary candidate Ron

Paul would articulate in the 2008 presidential primary campaign. Paul argued for a policy of 'non-intervention' and opposed the 2003 invasion of Iraq.

Yet this conservative scepticism about America's world role was not to carry the day in the post-cold war Republican party. For by the mid-1990s Speaker Gingrich and the new Republican mainstream had made up their minds about America's future role in the world: their 'free-market' reservations about big government (and big Pentagon spending) were to be put aside in favour of supporting American power in the world and the Pentagon-driven politics of empire that, after 9/11 under George W. Bush, would be given free reign.

Gingrich's call for American 'global leadership' had, though, tapped into a broad strand of cross-party American thinking that had been building ever since the collapse of the Soviet Union. This new thinking reached across all political opinions and walks of life – it was held by Democrats as well as Republicans, business leaders as well as labour union officials, and Main Street as well as Wall Street. It amounted to a straightforward belief that in the post-cold war environment America needed to continue to be engaged in the world (and could not afford to retrench). It was a renewal of the internationalist instinct – at its most modest it saw America having a global leadership role; at its most extravagant it believed in America's global mission.

For a time this emerging consensus for global leadership found few echoes in the new Clinton administration which came into power in January 1992. President Clinton had made an unsure start in foreign policy. Tensions in Bosnia, Somalia and Haiti had dominated the agenda distracting the new administration from developing a serious grand strategy. What was clear was that the newly-elected president was

worried about US intervention abroad. He had been pum-
melled by the Republicans in the election for his 'draft dodging' in Oxford during the Vietnam war and was anxious not
to put US troops in harm's way if he could avoid it. The mood
in Clinton's Washington was cautious. There was no talk of
retreat from global responsibilities, but much talk about a
new 'multilateralism', and also marked concern about how
many casualties US public opinion would tolerate in any unilateral US intervention.

In the early months of the Clinton Presidency NATO
enlargement was being pushed forward as a big test for the
new administration – and for whether it truly sought a global
leadership role in the post-communist era. And Washington
was initially rather reticent. Clinton's predecessor, George
Bush Snr., with his realist outlook, had rebuffed the Reagan era
neo-cons and refused to take them into his administration; and
his government took the view that 'an enlargement of NATO to
include eastern Central European states, would be a provoca-
tion for Moscow and was thus out of the question.'⁴ And new
President Bill Clinton initially agreed. And for a a time in early
1993, political Washington seemed that it was not taking the
'world leadership' idea too seriously.

However, whilst Washington dithered the world of economics and profit – both Wall Street and leading American economists – were taking a very different tack. Wall Street was in the
grip of a 'we won the war' mentality, and with a sense that the
world was at their feet their attitude to the 'defeated' Soviet
Union was brutal. The influential American economist Jeffrey
Sachs was talking about 'shock therapy' in Russia being necessary – meaning the quick and ruthless introduction into reel-
ing post-communist Russia of the globalist free market mantra
of trade liberalisation, large-scale privatisation, and the ending

of state subsidies. And as the full extent of the Russian and East European 'basket case' economies became public knowledge, this only reinforced the Wall Street view of American capitalist superiority. And as the Russians under Yeltsin actually began implementing the capitalist 'shock therapy' – with massive privatisations, Wall Street's sense of new found power took hold. The talk was all about American capitalism, and American capitalists, leading and changing the world, and knowing best.

And then in the early spring of 1995, just a few weeks *before* Gingrich's speech, Warren Christopher, the doyen of the Democratic party's foreign policy establishment, and Clinton's Secretary of State, joined the rising chorus. 'America must lead' he proclaimed, and then went even further: 'American leadership is our first principle and a central lesson of this century.'[5] And with both the Democratic administration and the Republicans in the Congress ringing the bell for American leadership – 'America must lead' – Washington had finally decided to follow Wall Street.

This mid-1990s Gingrich/Christopher, Republican/ Democrat consensus amounted to a radical new view of America's role in the world. It represented a clear break with the post-1945 global settlement. In this settlement the United States, through its alliances and its corporate interests, became the dominant power in the western, and allied, system. But, at the same time, this settlement denied the US any influence over most of Eurasia. Both the Soviet Union and its satellites, and China and its sphere, were off-limits to US influence, as were the many third-world nations that aligned themselves with them. US strategic policy accepted this division of the world; and Washington strategic approach was 'containment' not global expansionism.

So, what both Gingrich and Christopher were now advocating was wholly new in the history of the American republic. They, and the new consensus they represented, saw the United States as graduating from its 1945-89 role as leader of the West, or leader of 'the free world', to an altogether higher calling – nothing less than the leadership of the whole globe. It was, in fact, a breathtaking quantum leap, but, interestingly, such were the times, that it was not seen as such.

This new American strategic vision was born out of the view that the post 1989 era had placed the US in a wholly new position. No longer bounded by the bipolar world, now, in the new world, the US had a genuine strategic choice. It could review its worldwide involvements, and take a decision to limit them to new clearly defined, though narrower, interests. One area for redefinition could have been Europe and western Eurasia. The US, as in the White House days of George Bush Snr., could have opted for encouraging, indeed forging, EU unity and its emergence as a fully-functioning western superpower which could take up some aspects of the American global role.

Yet, instead, the Clinton administration finally opted for a resolute policy of NATO expansion. It pushed the boundaries of the western alliance deep into the old Soviet empire, as NATO incorporated all the states of Eastern Europe, including Poland, an expansion which took NATO (and the American sphere of influence) right up to the Russian border. It was a bold geostrategic move – but not nearly as bold as what was to follow when at the Prague NATO summit in 2002 the US insisted upon starting negotiations for Latvia, Lithuania and Estonia (as well as Romania and Bulgaria) to join. When, two years later, the Baltic nations formally joined the alliance NATO's borders had extended into three former states of the

Soviet Union itself, states with very large Russian minorities. It was a bitter pill for the Russians to swallow; and left a searing resentment that was to fully surface, once the former super-power was flowing with oil, a decade or so later.

In reality, though, the 'retrenchment alternative' for the USA, though theoretically plausible, was far too exotic. George Bush Snr. – as the victor of the Gulf War – had some tri-umphalist capital in the bank and could probably have used it, as he would have wanted to do, should he have won a second term. But Clinton had a real need to prove himself. And to refuse to expand the 'victorious' NATO alliance would have seemed weak. It would also have been seen as a step back-wards. Also, and crucially, too many domestic US interests – not least the big American corporations – continued to be engaged around the world making profits, and the great new markets of the old communist world were beckoning. The interests grouped around the Pentagon, both commercial and electoral, were also rooting for an American forward strategy. What's more, the intellectual zeitgeist, the governing idea of the American foreign policy establishments of both left and right, was all for global involvement; anyway, as many American told themselves, Europe was simply not ready to 'step up to the plate' of global leadership – a powerful theme that would be developed later during the Kosovo crisis in the late 1990s and Iraq in 2003.

By the mid-1990s, with this cross-party agreement now established, the debate was no longer about global involve-ment or retrenchment. Rather, it was about the best way to secure America's global role. Democrats and liberals, and some moderate Republicans, tended to favour what they called 'the multilateral' route. 'Multilateralism', though, had differing meanings. For some it meant a wide multilateralism – that

America should work through the great international institutions – the United Nations, the GATT, the IMF and the World Bank, that the US had set up after the war. For others multilateral meant a narrower grouping, mainly of western nations in western organisations like NATO or in American-led 'coalitions of the willing' cobbled together for specific objectives. Republican Bob Dole best set out this kind of 'multilateral' case in 1995. He argued that 'the choices facing America are not...doing something multilaterally, doing it alone, or doing nothing. These are false choices. The real choice is whether to allow international organisations to call the shots – as in Bosnia or Somalia – or to make multilateral groupings work for American interests – as in Operation Desert Storm.'[6] (Intriguingly, not one leading American politician ever actually proclaimed that the US should accept a foreign country's veto power over US foreign policy.)

Yet during the late 1990s frustration with 'multilateralism' of all kinds was growing. The UN was becoming a subject of criticism and ridicule. Republicans had always seen the UN as either irrelevant or inimical to US interests, and many Democrats still took their lead from Senator Daniel Patrick Moynihan's 1970s blistering attacks on the UN for its growing opposition to Israel.

There was frustration with NATO too – particularly with the Germans and French and others who dragged their feet over NATO enlargement. Whilst the foreign policy professionals in the State Department and some in the Pentagon saw NATO as the linchpin of American security, an increasing number in the Washington political world saw the alliance as limiting America's freedom of manoeuvre both diplomatically and militarily. And operationally too – for during the air war over Serbia in 1999 American commanders were to complain about how every small European NATO country could effectively veto targeting.

In consequence, American conservatives began thinking unilaterally. The idea began to grow that rather than seek multilateral alliances and solutions, the US should decide on a course of action, then call for support, then form a 'coalition of the willing' – no matter how small. It was to become the formulae later used by the Bush administration during the invasion of Iraq.

'REMAKING THE WORLD': PART ONE

As opinion in Washington was shifting during the mid-1990s President Bill Clinton himself remained sceptical about the rising chorus for global leadership and intervention. His presidency, born in a recession, had concentrated on domestic policy, and his first inaugural was all about 'renewing America' rather than global leadership. He would often remind those, often foreigners, who wanted America to intervene more around the world, that there were serious limits to America's influence. The idea that a country with 5 per cent of the world's population and around 25 per cent or less of the world's GDP could run the world, let alone 'remake it', was still being resisted.

Also, Clinton spent much of his time in his middle years in the White House resisting the insistent attempts to get the US deeply and militarily involved in the Yugoslav crisis. When it came to the question of military force he strenuously opposed the ground war option that was being propounded amongst some Europeans, and during the later air war over Serbia he determined on a plan – only high flying aircraft – that would lead to the absolute minimum of US deaths.

Yet, by the time of his second inaugural in January 1997 the new mood in Washington for 'global leadership' and 'global intervention' was running so strongly that he adapted to it. His second inaugural speech from the Capitol steps pledged the US not just to 'lead' but also to 'shape the forces of the global society' – the first time Clinton, who normally stuck strictly to domestic objectives – had gone into the 'global leadership' business.

And during the latter 1990s the idea of American global leadership began to morph into something else – the radical idea that American power was now strong enough to 'remake the world'.

This aim of 'shaping' 'global society' was hugely ambitious – even by the extravagant and visionary standards of American universalist political rhetoric. The US had a long history of political belief in 'remaking' *its own society* and the people within it (there were, after all, millions of 'born again' Americans); it also had a long history of believing itself to be the best – the 'last, best' – hope of mankind'. But this old American idea was rarely hegemonic. Americans tended to believe they should lead, but by example, not force. The rest of the world may well be mired in decadence and sin, and might, or might not, not follow the virtuous path once it was pointed out to them. But that was up to them. What was new about the gathering American mood at the turn of the century – and to many, somewhat frightening – was the view that America could *succeed* in forcing change in the world – that it had the power and tools to do so, and that all it needed to do was to try.

Clinton's tools were primarily the economic ones. Once converted to 'global leadership' he sought to exercise American power in the world through economic globalisation – and the spread of 'free-markets'. Indeed corporate support for 'free' and 'open' global markets was the major strategic aim of corporate

America. And by the time of his second term Clinton was listening to, and learning from, corporate power. His younger radicalism and populism – he was from a poor family from Arkansas – had dissipated during the skirmishes with corporate insurance companies when, with his wife Hillary, he tried and failed to seriously reform the private healthcare system.

Globalisation was to became the heart and soul of the Clinton Presidency – the underlying big idea of the second Clinton term. And Clinton found an avid supporter in Britain's new prime minister Tony Blair. At the prime minister's country home Chequers in November 1997 both leaders created the 'Third Way' programme with globalisation as its centrepiece. In his 1998 State of the Union speech, coming on the heels of a 'thinkers' dinner' at the White House, Clinton announced that 'we have found the third way' as 'we have moved into an information age, a global economy, a truly new world'. It was all very Whig in its optimism, its progressiveness, and its innate imperialism. And by December 2000, in the final weeks of his presidency, Clinton was again together with Blair in Britain when he declared, with Blair nodding in agreement, that 'globalisation was irreversible'.

According to Clinton advisor Sidney Blumenthal 'globalisation became the linking storyline for new policies in a new world.'[7] And the new world was going to be like America. Martin Albrow, a leading student of globalisation, could write that 'if globalisation was the way, America had to lead the rest of the world along the path'. In other words American norms and ways of doing things would be spread worldwide without war by the tried and true method of economic and cultural penetration – the cultural, of course, following the economic.

And the more globalisation the more democratisation, American-style, based upon 'freedom and democracy'. For many, both supporters and opponents of globalisation, the more globalisation the more the world would begin to both copy and value the American way of life and American values. Main Street would spread to every corner of the world, and in the process resistance to America would evaporate and the world would become peaceful and one. In sum, 'globalisation' would further American influence and values without the need to resort to force. America could remake the world without the Pentagon, by peaceful means.

The well-connected American journalist Thomas Friedman was to give the game away. In The New York Times he wrote that the main strategy of the Clinton era – 'globalisation' – was essentially 'Americanisation' with its 'driving idea' being 'free market capitalism' enforced through the IMF and the World Bank. And he argued that the reason for supporting multilateral institutions was that 'they make it possible for the United States to advance its interests without putting American lives or treasure on the line'. Chalmers Johnson singled out the Clinton administration and its Treasury Secretaries, Robert Rubin and Larry Summers, as subtle 'agents of [American] imperialism'. 'Clinton' he argued 'camouflaged his [American imperial] policies by carrying them out under the banner of "globalisation"'; and 'the United States ruled the world but did so in a carefully masked way that produced high degrees of acquiescence among the dominated nations'. Martin Albrow went further. For him 'globalisation' was nothing less than 'a programme for world domination'.[8] Whether 'imperialist' or not, the way in which Clinton's White House (and the economists who supported it) were viewing the 'globalisation' process was not unlike that propounded some years earlier by Francis Fukuyama, and his end of history as peaceful global liberalism.

'THE PROJECT': 'REMAKING' COURTESY OF THE PENTAGON

But on 3rd June 1997, with Bill Clinton six months into his second term in the White House, the peaceful advance of America was to be shattered – so to speak. For a new project was launched in Washington. Called the 'Project For the New American Century' it was supported by an array of foreign policy thinkers, politicians and activists, many of them luminaries of what during the Reagan years had become the influential neo-conservative movement. Included in the list of supporters were: Elliot Abrams (who went on to become George W. Bush's Middle East advisor), Jeb Bush (the brother of the next president), Midge Decter (the neo-conservative writer and wife of Commentary editor and neo-con Norman Podhoretz), Steve Forbes (the multi-millionaire Republican), Francis Fukuyama (the author of *The End of History*), Frank Gaffney (cold warrior and leading neo-conservative) Donald Kagan (neo-con Yale historian), Zalmay Khalizad (who would go on to become Ambassador to occupied Iraq, and the single most important advocate of the Iraq invasion and occupation), I. Lewis Libby (who would go on to become Vice President Cheney's chief of staff), Norman Podhoretz (leading New York neo-con polemicist), the late Peter Rodman (would later become Asst. Secretary of Defence under Donald Rumsfeld), Donald Rumsfeld (who would go on to become Defence Secretary and the architect of the invasion of Iraq) and Paul Wolfowitz (later Rumsfeld's deputy in the Pentagon and the leading proponent of the Iraq invasion).

This 'Statement of Principles' remains the boldest and clearest statement of neo-conservative geopolitical strategy that was later to inform the George W. Bush White House and dominate the US government in the aftermath of the attack of 9/11. To this day it forms the basis for the doctrine of remaking the world in America's image. In essence it is a robust call for American global leadership but it sets its strategic vision in purely geopolitical, and military, context. It does not mention American global economic power although it assumes it. It is well worth quoting in full.

American foreign and defense policy is adrift. Conservatives have criticized the incoherent policies of the Clinton Administration. They have also resisted isolationist impulses from within their own ranks. But conservatives have not confidently advanced a strategic vision of America's role in the world. They have not set forth guiding principles for American foreign policy. They have allowed differences over tactics to obscure potential agreement on strategic objectives. And they have not fought for a defense budget that would maintain American security and advance American interests in the new century.

We aim to change this. We aim to make the case and rally support for American global leadership.

As the 20th century draws to a close, the United States stands as the world's pre-eminent power. Having led the West to victory in the Cold War, America faces an opportunity and a challenge: Does the United States have the vision to build upon the achievements of past decades? Does the United States have the resolve to shape a new century favorable to American principles and interests?

We are in danger of squandering the opportunity and failing the challenge. We are living off the capital – both the military investments and the foreign policy achievements – built up by past administrations. Cuts in foreign affairs and defense spending, inattention to the tools of statecraft, and inconstant leadership are making it increasingly difficult to sustain American

137

influence around the world. And the promise of short-term commercial benefits threatens to override strategic considerations. As a consequence, we are jeopardizing the nation's ability to meet present threats and to deal with potentially greater challenges that lie ahead.

We seem to have forgotten the essential elements of the Reagan Administration's success: a military that is strong and ready to meet both present and future challenges; a foreign policy that boldly and purposefully promotes American principles abroad; and national leadership that accepts the United States' global responsibilities.

Of course, the United States must be prudent in how it exercises its power. But we cannot safely avoid the responsibilities of global leadership or the costs that are associated with its exercise. America has a vital role in maintaining peace and security in Europe, Asia, and the Middle East. If we shirk our responsibilities, we invite challenges to our fundamental interests. The history of the 20th century should have taught us that it is important to shape circumstances before crises emerge, and to meet threats before they become dire. The history of this century should have taught us to embrace the cause of American leadership.

Our aim is to remind Americans of these lessons and to draw their consequences for today. Here are four consequences:

- we need to increase defense spending significantly if we are to carry out our global responsibilities today and modernize our armed forces for the future;

- we need to strengthen our ties to democratic allies and to challenge regimes hostile to our interests and values;

- we need to promote the cause of political and economic freedom abroad;

- we need to accept responsibility for America's unique role in preserving and extending an international order friendly to our security, our prosperity, and our principles.

Such a Reaganite policy of military strength and moral clarity may not be fashionable today. But it is necessary if the United States is to build on the successes of this past century and to ensure our security and our greatness in the next.

This 'Project For The New American Century' brought together the two strands that made up the political support in Washington for the new interpretation of 'global leadership': the doctrine of 'remaking the world'. One was the neo-conservative strand. Neo-conservatives had been around in Washington and New York for some time, and had become a political genre during the Carter Presidency when, during the détente period, they broke ranks with orthodox American liberals. Former liberals and socialists, many of these neo-cons simply 'crossed the floor' to become supporters of Ronald Reagan's cold war policies towards the Soviet Union. Most of them had in their past voted Democratic, some had been socialists; they were largely, though not exclusively, Jewish; and they were intellectually inclined and fiercely articulate. Some (like Irving Kristol and Midge Decter) had gone the full ten yards and bought into the cultural conservatism of Ronald Reagan; others (like Paul Wolfowitz and Richard Perle) were largely uninterested in 'culture wars', concerned primarily with a strong national defence.

The second strand behind 'The Project' was more traditionally Republican conservatives – made up mainly of corporate and Wall Street elites and their supporters. Donald Rumsfeld, George W. Bush's first Secretary of Defence, was one such; and George Bush himself would also fit into this category. For these 'corporate conservatives' 'the business of America' was indeed business; and what was good for business was good for America. Most American corporate leaders would tell their Republican friends that with American business now global in reach America therefore needed to remain a world power. Business and empire went together.

The neo-cons were more intellectual and abstract in their approach, and introduced into the geopolitical equation an ideological battle – emphasising the superiority of American democracy over all other systems and particularly over Islamic and Arab systems. They also claimed to be universalists, seeing 'democratisation' as a global goal – an aim of all humanity – which American power was *uniquely* able to deliver.

Yet, whether business or intellectually-based or whether corporate conservative or neo-conservative, the reality was that by the late 1990s both groups supported *extending* the boundaries of the America's influence in the world, and believed in the use of American power to achieve this end.

And the key to American power was seen to be the Pentagon and its budget. US defence spending had declined significantly in the early post-cold war years under George H. W. Bush and Bill Clinton. But, following the Republican victory in the 1994 mid-terms, Clinton's January 1995 military budget proposal was $257 billion, a figure similar to that being spent during the arms race at the end of the Nixon/Ford years; and then the Gingrich Congress added on another $7 billion. Serious supporters of the use of American power were, however, reviewing the nature of this huge spending item, and were beginning to argue for real reform.

A leading advocate of reform was a former Secretary of Defense, Donald Rumsfeld. Some time before he became George W. Bush's first Defence Secretary he had advocated a reformed US military that could intervene all over the world. His thinking was later reflected in the US National Security Strategy of 2002 which declared that the US 'will require bases and stations within and beyond Western Europe and Northeast Asia, as well as temporary access arrangements to the long-distance deployment of US forces'. This was virtually the same approach as outlined in 'The Project' in 1997, which, as one left-leaning American writer argued 'desires and demands one thing: the establishment of a global American empire to bend the will of all nations...a new socio-economic Pax Americana'[9]

To secure this global reach Rumsfeld sought, and later was to secure, a US military that was both highly mobile and packed with high technology – and no longer held back by large, slow-moving standing armies. He also sought to change the old cold war US strategy based on fighting two big wars at the same time and to replace it by one favouring multiple surgical interventions.

A 'LIBERAL WAR' IN THE BALKANS
In the late 1990s 'The Project For a New American Century' secured many adherents beyond its neo-conservative and corporate conservative backers. Mainstream Democrats were beginning to talk the same language. Surprisingly some of the Project's themes were taken up by Clinton's Secretary of State, Madeleine Albright, when she argued in a somewhat discordant (to liberal ears) speech in February 1998. 'We are the greatest country in the world' she declared 'and what we are doing is serving the role of the indispensable nation...to make the world safer for those people around the world who follow

the rules.' (Whose 'rules' was not outlined; but it can be more than assumed that they would be those approved by the US State Department.)[10] Albright may well have been referring to the US being 'indispensable' to UN operations – but she made her speech at a time when the Americans were beginning to flex their muscles over the continuing crisis in Yugoslavia and were contemplating intervention outside of UN sanction (although arguments for an interventionist 'forward strategy' based upon projecting power was still somewhat overripe for the Democratic establishment).

During 1999, in Clinton's last year in the White House, there was a subtle but real change in the political atmosphere in Washington. Clinton had finally decided, after much prompting by British prime minister Tony Blair, that the US would use military power – through NATO – to force a conclusion to the long-running Yugoslav crisis. This led to the US-led air war over Serbia – an action pursued without a UN mandate! By the end of the operation it was clear that this 'military option' had been a success – and a victory for what had became known as 'liberal interventionism'. Carried through by a centrist Democratic president, this interventionist operation amounted to a huge shot in the arm for 'the Project' and the neo-conservatives who had been arguing that the use of military force abroad could be beneficial.

US action in the Balkans war helped build a consensus across the aisle in Washington. It was an unstated consensus, but a real one, and it was forged some time before George W. Bush took office in January 2001. The years of American reticence and dithering about the use of 'hard power' outside of UN authorisation was over. The lesson was clear: America was a global power – the 'indispensable' global power – and should be free to use all the weapons in its arsenal: both the 'soft power' inherent in economic globalisation (on American terms and by American rules), and, when and where necessary (as in the Balkans), military interventionism in American interests."

For the American political elite the issue was no longer whether interventionism was right or wrong. It was now a question of how to sell it. Democrats and liberals (and some neo-cons) who favoured intervening began to argue their case by using the term *'liberal* interventionism' – justifying the use of power in foreign lands on moral and humanitarian grounds. Their great hero was Woodrow Wilson, who, as the twenty-eighth president of the USA, had introduced America onto the world scene by taking the country into the First World War almost as a moral crusade – as a 'war to end wars' and to 'save civilisation'. Then, in the aftermath of war, he had set about reorganising the world, not just as a victor but as moral leader and teacher. His famous Fourteen Points were pure 'liberal interventionism'. In Wilsonian rhetoric the use of force was not a cynical exercise in national interest but rather used to secure 'democracy, open agreements and free trade', and other good outcomes, like 'self-determination'.

To his supporters and heirs Woodrow Wilson embodied American goodness delivered through the barrel of a gun to a wicked, corrupt, and violent, world. His foreign policy was an early outing for the idea that the American moral compass should guide the world and could 'remake the world'. And in the aftermath of the great war, at Versailles, and in the name of these American ideals, the world, or at least Europe, was indeed reorganised on American idealistic terms – with detailed prescriptions for the future. A host of small issues including the future of Alsace Lorraine, the Italian borders, Romania, Serbia and Montenegro were settled as well as larger ones such as dissolutions of the Austro-Hungarian and

Ottoman empires and the creation of an independent Poland with access to the sea. And all this based upon the absolute conviction in Wilson's breast of American moral leadership.

A more contemporary version of 'liberal interventionism' was unfurled by Tony Blair in a pioneering speech in April 1999 in Chicago – delivered during the non-UN sanctioned air war over Serbia. Fresh from securing Clinton's indispensable military support, Blair, seeing a vista before him of future 'liberal interventions', set out the case in some detail, using Serbia/Kosovo as a case study. He started by quoting Bismark disapprovingly for his famous anti-interventionist statement that 'the Balkans are not worth the bones of one Pomeranian Grenadier'. And he then went on argue that bombing Serbia was a 'just war' based upon 'values' and not on interests. To make his point about values he described the Serbian leader, Slobodan Milosevic, as 'an evil dictator'. And he linked him to Saddam Hussein. 'Many of our problems' he argued had been caused by 'two dangerous and ruthless men – Saddam Hussein and Slobodan Milosevic' who were oppressing their countries.

Blair conceded that 'non-interference has long been considered an important principle of international order' – indeed the bedrock principle of the United Nations. But, he argued, it should no longer be considered inviolate. He was loath to 'jettison this principle' lightly, though he argued it should be so jettisoned in some cases such as 'genocide' or 'minority rule'. Blair did not define 'genocide' or 'minority rule', nor did he argue who should so define it – the UN? Or the West's leaders? Nor did he issue a list of regimes that would fall foul of these criteria. But, imprecise though it may have been, Blair's speech was catalytic, for it opened the door to a new doctrine for the times. The old-style UN notion that force should only be used when one country had attacked another or crossed borders (as in the first Gulf War) was out: a new, seemingly more morality based, doctrine was in.

IDEAS OF GOING IT ALONE

The idea of 'democracy at the barrel of a gun' was later to be taken up by the Washington neo-cons in the run-up to the 2003 invasion of Iraq. In the Chicago speech Blair had, quite fortuitously, made the link between Slobodan Milosevic and Saddam Hussein – the 'two evil dictators'. It was comic book stuff, but in the mass media public-relations world of images and manipulated emotions it served well to make the clear moral case thought necessary by the Bush administration in order to justify the invasion of Iraq. Force in order to 'remove a tyrant' was an easy sell – certainly easier than in order to secure a geostrategic aim – such as the protection of oil interests or Israel.

Coterminous with this debate about interventionism was a debate, initiated by George W. Bush during his 2000 presidential election campaign, about unilateralism, or the unilateral use of American power. Bush made the argument that the United States was often constrained, certainly by the UN and oft times by allies, in acting in its own interests. He was drawing on a neo-conservative theme that neo-con intellectual godfather Irving Kristol had developed in the 1980s as he became disillusioned with Ronald Reagan's foreign policy. Kristol had complained about the Reagan administration. 'They're always thinking of world opinion' he argued and about 'how our allies will react, how the UN will react, what our obligations are under various treaties. They don't act in a vigorous way, which one anticipated Ronald Reagan would do.'[12]

This urge for unilateral action burst upon the top level political scene during the George W. Bush presidency in the form of the powerful axis of Secretary of Defence Donald Rumsfeld and Vice President Dick Cheney. This duo were American nationalists, quite at home with the idea of an American empire, who saw life in pragmatic, non-ideological, terms through the lens of American interests. And they believed in the efficacy of hard power when necessary to secure those interests. They were naturally attracted to the new doctrine of unilateralism. They believed that the US was militarily powerful enough to act in, and on, its own when its interests were involved. And they saw the UN as unable and unwilling to take action in American interests, and allies, even close ones, as often well-meaning but given to complicating the operations. Following the NATO air war over Serbia some Pentagon officials had complained about how the numerous American allies (particularly the French) had insisted on getting involved in detailed planning causing a cumbersome military operation.

Yet even though the Pentagon would have preferred to act alone in military operations, such a go-it-alone posture was ruled out politically. Allies were welcome. But a new Washington catchphrase emerged – the US would intervene 'with others if possible, but alone if necessary'. This was the 'coalitions of the willing' strategy that was used for the first Gulf War and would be used again, with a much slimmer coalition, for the 2003 Iraq invasion.

This new American unilateralism was much criticised in Europe. But the door to unilateralism had been opened earlier, not least by Europeans themselves. Not only had most every EU government gone along with ignoring the UN as NATO launched its air war over Serbia, but in 1956 the Franco-British invasion of Egypt was a high-profile example of an intervention (or invasion) not sanctioned by the international body or by 'international law'. European criticism of American 'unilateralism' was always somewhat contrived. For in reality, and in private, for many European leaders the issue with Bush was not his acting without UN sanction (they had done that themselves only four years earlier!); rather, it was the act itself – what they considered the foolhardy and utterly counter-productive policy of introducing thousands of western troops into the middle of Arabia without any Arab or Muslim support.

KRAUTHAMMER'S EMPIRE

American opinion following the Kosovo war was warming to the idea of – and the use of – American global power. Even before 9/11, the idea was settling that America was not just the world's dominant power, but was dominant enough to remake, even rule, the world. And should do so. Listen to Charles Krauthammer, a leading neo-conservative strategist, *six months before 9/11*. 'America is no mere international citizen,' he asserted, 'it is the dominant power in the world, more dominant than any since Rome. Accordingly, America is in a position to reshape norms, alter expectations and create new realities. How? By unapologetic and implacable demonstrations of will.'[13]

And Krauthammer was not alone. There was more, much more, where that came from – both in the Washington think tanks and in the political class generally. And when Henry Kissinger, the doyen of American geostrategy who rarely stepped beyond a consensus and always measured carefully every word he wrote, joined the argument essentially on Krauthammer's side it was clear that the 'hegemonistas' had won. Kissinger was extravagant: he said of the USA that 'at the dawn of the new millennium' the country was 'enjoying a preeminence unrivalled by even the greatest empires of the past'.[14] 'Unrivalled by even the greatest empires of the past' was pow-

erful stuff: for it placed twenty-first century America in a higher league than first century Rome – which had virtually controlled the world! In the first few years of the new century this,
though, was the ascendant view.

Such extravagant analyses were not written for effect. They
were issued by hard-nosed realists based upon a clear calculus
of hard power. And early twenty-first century America was
indeed powerful – for she stood on the shoulders of one unvarnished truth: that the Pentagon's military power and prowess
was unrivalled. The US Department of Defence (the Pentagon)
budget had fallen from its high point during the Cold War in
1985-6 (around $450 billion to a low in 1997-8 (around $300
billion), but would then increase significantly up to under
$400 billion just before the Iraq war. Just as important in the
military pre-eminence assessment was the worldwide lead the
Pentagon had established in military Research and
Development. Mobility and flexibility of armed forces was the
new name of the game in the twenty-first century – as was
advanced technology – and US spending on 'R&D' was impressive, in 2003 it would be more than three times the next competitor (all the European militaries put together).

It was a military that allowed an imperial reach. The
Pentagon's missiles, bristling with ordnance (nuclear and otherwise) could reach anywhere in the world, and with great precision; and its intelligence-gathering through its extensive satellite
system was the global best. At the turn of century, in 2001, its
empire was best exemplified by its 725 bases girdling the earth
in thirty-eight countries; and its 254,000 military personnel, over
500,000 counting civilians and dependents, located abroad.[15] All
in all, a mobile, high-technology military constructed for global
policing (with basing arrangements, for instance in Eastern
Europe, in the Balkans to allow for such mobility).

The message from the think tanks and the thinkers was cohering: America was at the height of its powers. It should go for it. All it needed, as Krauthammer argued, was an 'unapologetic and implacable demonstration of will'.

9/11

These impulsions to remake the world based on American power were the ascendant view in Washington when, in September 2001, the planes hit the Twin Towers of the World Trade Center in New York City and the Pentagon in Washington D.C. And in a fateful combination national hubris met national tragedy. It was an event that created a gripping fear throughout the continental US – fanned by around the clock mass media coverage (in which commercial pressures for sensationalism served only to increase the sense of fear).

The US population had, of course, felt fearful before – during the Cold War, when Soviet missiles were capable of reaching American cities and towns in a matter of minutes. But the Soviets were seen as a traditional power whose leadership was essentially rational and could therefore be deterred and negotiated with; and this took some of the sting out of the fear. Americans had also been warned about terrorism coming to the homeland. Six months ahead of the attack, the report of a commission chaired by former Senators Gary Hart and Warren Rudman had predicted such an event. They had argued prophetically that 'a direct attack against American citizens on American soil is likely over the next quarter century' and asserted that 'the combination of unconventional weapons proliferation with the persistence of international terrorism will end the relative invulnerability of the United States homeland to catastrophic attack.' But, according to Co-Chairman Gary Hart, in a sign of the sense of invulnerability of pre-9/11

America, a *New York Times* journalist walked out of the commission's press conference, saying – the exact words – 'None of this is ever going to happen'.[16]

In fact, differing reactions to 9/11 were a factor that was to separate Americans from Europeans in the months that followed. Europeans had never had the sense of invulnerability that for Americans was so rudely shattered on 9/11. Many Europeans had, in fact, grown somewhat used to living with terrorism. The Basque separatists in Spain, the Islamic extremist bombers in Paris, the IRA in mainland Britain and political extremists in Germany and Italy had all brought terror to European cities. These terror campaigns in Europe, together with the memories of total war, particularly the aerial bombardment during the Second World War, meant that many Europeans could not share with the Americans their sudden sense of vulnerability – nor their consequent acceptance of the radical foreign policy solutions put forward by their leaders.

AFGHANISTAN

For the hard-nosed American conservatives the horror of 9/11 was both a national humiliation and a huge political opportunity. For in the aftermath of the atrocity it was clear that their hour had come. 'The Project For The New American Century' had set out the case for a major assertion of US power well before the attacks – but until 9/11 these thinktank warriors remained marginal figures, unable to fully convince the wider American political class and public. 9/11 changed all that.

The invasion of Afghanistan in October 2001 and the removal of the Taliban regime – after it refused to yield up the Al-Qaeda leadership – was supported around the world as a proportionate response to the atrocity. But for the Washington conservatives, both the corporate conservatives and the neo-conservatives, Afghanistan was only an audition for what was to be the real 'unapologetic and implacable demonstration of will' by America.

Following 9/11 and the toppling of the Taliban, Charles Krauthammer finally got the traction he couldn't get in 1990 when he originally coined the term the 'unipolar moment'. In 2002 he could argue, to some applause, that:

> When I first proposed the unipolar model in 1990, I suggested that, if America did not wreck its economy, unipolarity could last thirty or forty years. That seemed bold at the time. Today, it seems rather modest. The unipolar moment has become the unipolar era.

In proclaiming a 'unipolar era', and a new American century, Krauthammer drew on comparisons between American power and reach in 2000 and earlier empires. He concluded that 'Charlemagne's empire was merely Western European in its reach. The Roman empire stretched further afield, but there was another great empire in Persia, and a larger one in China. There is, therefore, no comparison'.[7]

It was grandiose stuff verging on the megalomaniacal. But it was also resonating where it counted – in the White House. In the great battle for the novice president's ear between hawks and doves, the hawks could finally make their move; and in the debate about America's role those who believed in power (and power projection) could now win out over those who put their trust in diplomacy and economic influence.

Only a few days after the attack, the British Prime Minister, Tony Blair, as though sensing that the American leadership would indeed use the crisis to radically change their policy towards the world, made a huge claim – that when the dust from the terrorist attack on New York and Washington had settled, world politics could be 'reordered'.[18]

THE GLOBAL WAR ON TERROR

9/11 enabled the hawks to declare a worldwide 'War on Terror'. George W. Bush proclaimed in a solemn pronouncement before a joint session of Congress, with British PM Tony Blair looking on, that 'our war on terror begins with Al-Qaeda, but does not end there. It will not end until every terrorist group of global reach has been found, stopped, and defeated'.[19] European leaders agreed with Washington that Al-Qaeda and other groups posed a serious threat, and the EU nations gave total backing (including military support) to the US campaign in Afghanistan to topple the Taliban. But they had many reservations about the idea of a 'war' on terror, with its black and white solutions of 'winning' and 'losing' and its proclaimed goal of 'ridding the world' of terror.

A 'war on terror' posed many problems, not least that declaring a 'war' dignified opponents, like Al-Qaeda and local terrorists groups, as 'soldiers'. Britain's chief prosecutor, Ken McDonald argued that those responsible for the acts of terror on the London underground on 7th July 2005 were not 'soldiers' on a 'battlefield' but rather 'inadequates' who needed to be dealt with by the criminal justice system.[20] Also, 'terrorism' is a technique not a body of people or a cause and therefore difficult to fight a 'war' against. And 'wars' – certainly American wars – create expectations of victors and vanquished. Yet Europeans who had lived with terrorism over a number of decades tended to believe that, ultimately, terrorism could never be fully eradicated; it could only be limited – and that the best way to limit it was by addressing the causes as well as using force. And for some critics some of the causes were to be found in US foreign policy in the Middle East region; and, as time went by and the initial horror of 9/11 abated, many of these critics even began to share a sentiment held widely throughout the Middle East and the world. They argued that the Manhattan atrocity, and other violent episodes, were only to be expected as a reaction, a 'blowback' against the impositions of US foreign policy – an ugly, and horrific, side effect of the job of being a superpower. Some unfriendly critics even suggested that the US 'had it coming' – the basic reaction of the Palestinians caught on American TV screens dancing in the streets, an image which the Palestinian leader, Yasser Arafat, instantly attempted to correct by publicly giving blood to the victims.

In his speech to a joint session of Congress some ten days after the attacks George W. Bush declared that 'every nation in every region now has a decision to make. Either you are with us, or you are with the terrorists'.[21] The American president was dividing up the world between America on the one side and terrorism on the other. And terrorism was to be defined by America. And this war on terror was going to be 'won'. It was hard not to come to a conclusion that the world the US administration was seeking was a world where every government was pro-American on terms defined by the White House.

FULL SPECTRUM MILITARY DOMINANCE: DONALD RUMSFELD

It was all very imperial in its assumptions. And very ambitious too. But the foundation for this new imperial thinking that was gripping Washington was the Pentagon's global pre-eminence – and its extraordinary, and unique, ability to project power around the world. And no one understood this better than the leader of the Pentagon, and of the hawks around Bush, Donald Rumsfeld. Rumsfeld was a traditional corporate conservative

Republican, and had had been Secretary of Defense once before, in Gerald Ford's short-lived administration. With rimless spectacles and a seemingly bland demeanour, he had the deceptive look of a careful corporate bureaucrat. But in the months and years ahead Rumsfeld was to turn into a true political heavyweight, a radical who succeeded in changing American grand strategy and sold the change to the American media and public with waspish humour.

Rumsfeld saw himself as a super-realist and believed in the political power of the US military. He had once remarked, at a cocktail party in the mid-1970s, that America could' get further with a kind word and a gun, than a kind word alone'. In the months before 9/11, Rumsfeld had been attempting to reform the US military – the so-called 'Rumsfeld Lite' reforms – to enable it to more effectively project power around the world. To this end, he wanted a military that could intervene quickly and was more mobile, technologically advanced and smaller than that advocated by traditionalists in the Pentagon, who favoured 'overwhelming force'. The public mood after 9/11 gave him the chance to put this vision into practice – first in the conflict in Afghanistan, later in the war in Iraq. He was also media savvy (if not media friendly) and was able, if not to secure the full backing of the mainstream US media, at least to ensure their benign neutrality.

Rumsfeld sat atop a cadre of civilian advisors in the Pentagon – many of them neo-conservatives like Richard Perle, some traditional conservatives like Bill Schneider – who were convinced not just that America was militarily pre-eminent, but that she was able to dominate any opposition. The Pentagon's official goal on the 'battlefield ('the battlefield' was not defined) was to secure what it called 'full spectrum dominance'. The US Department of Defence asserted that:

The ultimate goal of our military force is to accomplish the objectives directed by the National Command Authorities. For the joint force of the future, this goal will be achieved through full spectrum dominance – the ability of US forces, operating unilaterally or in combination with multinational and interagency partners, to defeat any adversary and control any situation across the full range of military operations.[22]

US military supremacy – or dominance – was an integral part of the more rounded assessment of geopolitical power in the world that was shaping in Washington. The US National Security Strategy (NSS) issued in 2002 by the White House, written in the aftermath of 9/11 and the declaration of the 'global war on terrorism', remains to this day the best source for describing the imperial thinking that dominated Washington – amongst Democrats as well as Republicans – in the first years of the new century.

At the heart of this strategy was the formal and declared objective of retaining American global supremacy, although the more palatable term – 'primacy' – was used. It talked of ensuring that 'no challenger or combination of challengers...' could rival the US. And after the Europeans attempted to set up a separate defence agreement at the Franco-German – Luxembourg – Belgium defence summit in May 2003 both Condoleezza Rice and George Bush warned Europeans not to try to 'balance' the US or 'create a rival' to it.

This 2002 NSS certainly reflected the times it was written in. With America wounded and the 'amour propre' of its Republican leaders offended, it was a defensive and braggadocio document. Yet, its central postulate – that the US was the only serious global leader and should keep it that way – only made explicit what had been the implicit strategic position of the post-Kosovo Washington consensus before 9/11. A strategy of blocking rival powers even from equalling the USA was an idea given an outing a whole decade before it became official policy. In 1991 Zalmay Khalizad, a member of Dick Cheney's team at the Pentagon during Cheney's time there as Defence Secretary, outlined this kind of thinking in a book called From Containment To Global Leadership. His idea: that US strategic doctrine should 'preclude the rise of another global rival for the indefinite future'.[23] Khalizad was later to join the tight inner circle of White House power in the run-up to the Iraq war and was made special envoy to Afghanistan in 2002.

REGIME CHANGE AND PRE-EMPTION

The *2002 National Security Strategy of the United States* also outlined the rationale for the US to pre-emptively attack, and change, a regime. A state opened itself to pre-emptive attack from the USA if it possessed two characteristics: if it had the capability to hurt the USA and its allies through possessing weapons of mass destruction; and if it was deemed malign or a 'rogue'.

The term 'rogue', though, was never seriously defined. Richard Haas, a moderate conservative and Director of Policy Planning at the State Department in the George W. Bush administration, had attempted earlier in 2002 to define a working doctrine for pursuing such 'regime change' – he suggested that a regime can rightfully be overthrown by the USA if it 'massacres its own people' or 'supports terrorism in any way'.[24] For Paul Wolfowitz, a 'rogue state' worthy of regime change would be one that was a threat to peace and/or undemocratic – and its removal would allow the USA to establish a global goal of a widening 'zone of peace and democracy' in the world. These definitions were, though, so vague that opponents of the new strategy could argue that a 'rogue state' simply amounted to any regime that 'disliked' or ideologically opposed America. Initially, three states – comprising the famous' axis of evil' outlined by President Bush in his 2001 State of the Union address – came into view as members of the club of rogue states and as candidates for pre-emption: Iraq, North Korea and Iran. By mid-April 2003, two were left, and Syria, Libya, even Saudi Arabia, were being talked of as candidate members.

As Washington's new doctrine evolved in the fraught first six months of 2002, it became clear that, to the Bush administration, the threat from 'rogue states' was not so much a direct, or imminent, threat – of a Saddam Hussein lobbing a missile at the American homeland – as it was a longer-term threat. The fear was that 'rogues' could at some future date develop weapons of mass destruction and surreptitiously pass them on to terrorist groups like Al-Qaeda for delivery into American cities. No amount of containment and deterrence could stop such an event, so the USA would need to act first, pre-emptively, to remove the hostile regime and the 'gathering threat'. Critics immediately suggested that this gave the USA huge leeway to take out any regime it simply suspected of potential terrorism at some date in the distant future – a definition which could include large numbers of nation-states. Rather than adopt the new US policy these critics, principally in Paris and Berlin, tended to fall back on the traditional doctrine about containing and deterring hostile regimes.

THE BUILDUP TO INVASION

As it became progressively clear that George W. Bush was not bluffing, and the invasion of the heart of Arabia was imminent, a somewhat stunned world was trying to figure out – Why

Iraq? German Chancellor Schroeder, who supported the invasion of Afghanistan and was playing a full role in the 'war on terror' declared that that when 'out of a clear blue sky' he heard about the Iraq 'adventure' it had completely mystified him.

The real reasons for the invasion, unlike any other American military action in the postwar period, remained shrouded in mystery. There was certainly no single, clear, understandable rationale – except the imminent threat to the US of Saddam using weapons of mass destruction. And when no such weapons were found the search for clues led to a veritable industry of analyses about the underlying motivations of the leading hawks in Washington.

In the run-up to the invasion Donald Rumsfeld and Vice President Dick Cheney were the axis of power within the Bush White House. And after 9/11 they got their way in every serious debate within the administration. But they were not 'neoconservatives'. Rather, they, like Bush himself, were traditional corporate conservatives who saw big business and American interests as one, and who believed in the use of American power to further those interests. For them, universal principles – of 'democracy' or 'freedom' or anything else – were not the real issue, although they could often be an added bonus in selling policy. Nor was the security of Israel that central (although the Jewish state was seen as useful as a geostrategic asset).

For them, American interests in the region were all about economics and oil. And, crucially, and often not well understood, also about credibility. Rumsfeld and Cheney were realists, and for realists, credibility was crucial. If America was to remain a global power, let alone dominate, it could simply not tolerate small states that defied it (big states were another matter). In this category of small defiant states fell Milosovic's Serbia, the revolutionary mullah regime in Iran and North

Korea. And so too fell Syria and Saddam Hussein's Iraq. Saddam Hussein was not only small (like North Korea) but particularly weak (unlike North Korea who *possessed weapons of mass destruction*). Saddam had no aircraft to speak of, and had no control of the skies as a 'no fly zone' was in operation over Iraq. But he was still, infuriatingly, defiant. So defiant that he had attempted to assassinate former President Bush, and was simply not co-operating with Washington.

The way Rumsfeld and Cheney saw it, if Saddam Hussein could be overthrown, and a new pliant government established, then the US would not only take control of Iraq's oil supplies (with the supposed second largest reserves in the world), but the Middle East regimes would quake in their boots, and other anti-American regimes (Syria, Iran) in the region, and perhaps beyond, would either topple or fall into line. It would be a teaching strike – teaching the region (and the world) that America could change regimes at will – at 'implacable will' – and was not to be opposed. The Middle East would be 'remade' to suit American interests. Iraq was the perfect place to start.

The neo-conservatives in Washington shared the same agenda. They wanted the Middle East to be remade, and remade by the use of power if need be, but they came at it from a different angle. A radical new plan for the Middle East had been floated by leading neo-cons back in 1996 in a document called 'A Clean Break: A New Strategy For Securing The Realm'. Richard Perle (later to be Chairman of the Pentagon's Policy Board during the Iraq invasion) David Wurmser and Douglas Feith (later to become Paul Wolfowitz's deputy in Rumsfeld's Pentagon) argued that only by a daring restructuring of the whole Middle East – by transforming the existing regimes into 'democracies' – could Arab and Iranian-backed terrorism be ended.

However, the 'realm' they were 'securing' in this 1996 document was Israel; and for many neo-conservatives, many of
them Jewish-Americans, the 'transformative' power of democracy – secured through the barrel of a gun if need be – would
serve both America's and Israel's interests.

Indeed, the neo-con contribution to the party was the idea
of the promotion of 'democracy' as the key rationale for the
Iraq invasion. The vision was of American troops, as in Europe
in World War Two, being welcomed as liberators, and Iraq's
new 'democracy' becoming infectious throughout the region.

The most prominent neo-conservative was Paul Wolfowitz,
the No. 2 in the Pentagon. Bright, sophisticated and studious,
Wolfowitz was what Washingtonians call a 'defence intellectual' and he had risen to influence in Republican circles during
the Reagan years. Ever since the 1991 Gulf War, he had been a
keen advocate of a tough policy towards Iraq and the main pro-
moter in the Bush administration of regime change in
Baghdad. When, some time in the early summer of 2002, Bush
finally signed on to his plan, Wolfowitz, a keen supporter of
Israel, was dubbed by his circle, affectionately but somewhat
insensitively, as 'Wolfowitz of Arabia'.

Rumsfeld and Cheney were also strong supporters of Israel,
but not at the cost of other American interests in the region –
and during the Reagan administration they had clashed with
the neo-cons over Reagan's decision to sell AWACS aircraft to
Saudi Arabia, a policy bitterly opposed by Israel. However,
these two factions, the realists and the neo-cons, would come
together in the months following 9/11 and in the lead up to the
Iraq invasion. Cheney and Rumsfeld would get their power
projection, the neo-cons would get their democratisation. It
was an acceptable combination to both factions, and it could
be sold as: 'American power in the name of democracy'.

BUSH ON THE EVE OF INVASION

In a speech to the American Enterprise Institute on 27th February 2003, just weeks before the invasion, President Bush – and the Cheney-Rumsfeld faction – finally publicly adopted the democratisation argument. The president outlined a bold post-Iraq scenario, in which a 'democratic Iraq' would become the focal point for reordering the whole Middle East. The speculation has been that by this time the White House was fully aware that no weapons of mass destruction existed and was therefore laying out an alternative case for war. In any event, the speech was music to the ears of the neo-conservatives around Bush.

WIDER STILL AND WIDER

The neo-conservative plan for remaking the Middle East was grandiose enough; but, to European consternation, some strategists in Washington were going even further. Former Director of the CIA, the lean and incisive James Woolsey, was advocating a 'permanent war', or 'World War Four' (World War Three being the Cold War). This extraordinary advocacy of permanent war for the USA, rolled out in April as the invasion of Iraq was underway, was the brainchild of Professor Eliot Cohen, and Woolsey gave extra life to the idea by naming America's enemies in this coming conflict. They included, as of 2003: Sunni Islamists, Shiite Islamists, the Tehran mullahs, Hezbollah, Syria, Libya and Sudan – indeed anyone who opposes western-style democracy, a list which, over time, could include Saudi Arabia, Egypt, Pakistan and, maybe, even China. Woolsey, like Wolfowitz, saw the USA as creating, by force if necessary, 'a widening zone of peace and democracy' first in the Middle East and then throughout the world. And he is very hard on opponents who believe that

161

the Arab world and other non-western societies and peoples cannot be easily democratised on the American model. He called them 'racists'.[25]

This idea of 'permanent war' had considerable appeal in the White House, specifically to Bush's tough political guru, Karl Rove. Although no Republican would ever publicly advocate 'permanent war' (the American public would oppose the principle of a never-ending conflict), Rove saw the huge potential of a permanent state of wartime psychology for the re-election of the president. The permanent 'War on Terror' helped Bush, but was not dramatic enough. It was foreign threats, and invasions to remove them – particularly against easy targets like Saddam – that stirred patriotic sentiment and silenced or sidelined opposition. And if, in this permanent state of war, periods of high tension could be turned on and off at will, and at suitable times, so much the better.[26]

THE LAST TRIUMPHAL DAYS: IMPOSING AMERICA ON THE WORLD

As the American-led armies crossed from Kuwait into Saddam's Iraq in late March 2003, hopes for a reordered Middle East fuelled a renewed, and intensified, bout of American conservative triumphalism. Indeed, following the quick and incisive 'victory', and viewed from the late spring of 2003, American conservatives had much to be triumphant about. George W. Bush, 'the victor of Iraq' and slayer of the regime of Saddam Hussein, had won the 2002 mid-terms; Tony Blair, the co-victor of Iraq, was comfortably ensconced in his second term; Wall Street was bullish again; and Alan Greenspan – having gotten a new boom and bubble going by lowering interest rates to one percent in the wake of the dot.com bubble bursting – was proving nothing less than a financial wizard, his wisdom unchallenged.

These were heady days and conservative pundits were on a roll: American success in Iraq would lead to a new era of success for the global economy; a new Iraqi government would soon emerge leading to a reformed Middle East, security for Israel and, above all, another bonanza for profits as the global economy was refloated on abundant, American-controlled, cheap oil.

But for many of its supporters this was no imperial push. It was seen as an act of liberation, because American values were global values – and American business capitalist values were global values. They were held by everyone, even in those lands where they were not openly expressed (because they were suppressed by local elites).

A new western universalism was in the air. And it had clear echoes from an earlier triumphalist time when in the late eighteenth century the universalist ideas of the French enlightenment followed behind the French revolutionary army as it swept across Europe up to the gates of Moscow.

CHAPTER FIVE

THE TURNING POINT

SHOCK AND AWE

Right up until the very last minute, there were many people who simply did not believe that the Bush administration would actually launch an unprovoked attack on a Middle Eastern state without UN approval and against the fervent opposition of key US allies and an overwhelming majority of the world's peoples. They believed Bush was bluffing. But when, at 5 a.m. Baghdad time on the morning of Friday 21st March 2003, 40 cruise missiles were fired from the Abraham Lincoln battle group in the Gulf into southern Baghdad in an attempt to 'decapitate' the Iraqi leadership and the attack began, all was clear.

Bush had meant what he said; and had taken the United States of America down a new road – the raw use of power, unconstrained even by allies. Friends and opponents alike feared that this road would lead to a colonial occupation in the heart of the Arab world from which the USA could not easily extricate itself. Former US National Security Advisor, Zbigniew Brzezinski, on the eve of the Iraq war, warned his fellow Americans that the USA was more alone in the world than at any time since 1945. But the president, and the new unilateralists in the US administration, hardly seemed to care.

By Monday 24th April 2003, the US Central Command in Qatar was telling the president that the USA had defeated Saddam's army in its last holdout in Tikrit. And on that day Doug Feith, a leading neo-conservative and No. 3 at the Pentagon, was convinced that he was about to see his dream of a new Middle East come true. Feith was a jovial man, whose conviviality hid a detached, razor sharp mind, honed by his legal training. But even he was hugely excited. Some weeks before, he had been asked by his bosses, Defense Secretary Donald Rumsfeld and Deputy Secretary Paul Wolfowitz, to secretly prepare the case for an immediate war with Iraq's western neighbour, Syria. And now it seemed that, buoyed by the victory over Iraq, the president might actually order an attack on a second Arab nation and begin implementing the 'domino effect' and the neo-conservative agenda for the restructuring of the whole Middle East.

Although Feith and the neo-conservatives did not get their way that Monday – for the president decided against the attack on Syria and left Washington to campaign for his proposed tax cut – they remained convinced that the successful military overthrow of Saddam Hussein's regime had given the 'New America' – its new Middle East policy and global policy of pre-emption – a huge boost. They also felt that the Iraq war had vindicated Rumsfeld's 'light' military strategy, allowing the USA to wage war in a number of places simultaneously. To these triumphant neo-conservatives, their gamble in Iraq had paid off. America was now in the position they had worked hard for. They saw its unrivalled military power as enabling them first to remake the Middle East and then to shape a new world order.

FAILURE

But it was not to be. And within a few months of the military victory in Iraq, symbolised by the toppling of the statue of Saddam Hussein in the main square in Baghdad, the sceptics were seemingly being proved right.

By mid-2004, even though the occupation had formally ended and power had been transferred to an interim Iraq government, Washington was no longer looking to a reconstruction of the Middle East. Instead the geostrategic situation was increasingly hostile to the United States – Iraq remained a continuing sore (with Washington possessing no attractive options). Iran, now that Saddam was gone, was emerging as a regional power with its influence through Hezbullah in Lebanon and Hamas in Gaza and with Syria strengthened. US supporters in the region, in Egypt, the Gulf and Saudi Arabia, were all increasingly defensive.

By 2006 and the American mid-term elections, Iraq had become the dominant issue and the continued violence – and the lack of a political settlement – had turned the American public decisively against the war. By 2008 the Iraqi failure had became a major issue in the American presidential campaign. And even the most hawkish of the hawks were no longer talking about remaking the Middle East; instead they were reduced to the policy of 'no surrender' – a wholly different proposition.

By 2008 the full cost of the Iraq invasion and occupation to the American economy was also becoming clear. Estimates were varying, but the economist Joseph Stiglitz in a well-researched book, put the figure at over $3 trillion dollars.[1] He argued that the cost of direct US military spending, not including the long-term costs such as the continuing care of American wounded – would exceed the costs of the 12 year long Vietnam war, the Korean war, and was ten times the cost of the first Gulf War.

In March 2008 the price of oil was over $100 a barrel compared to the $25 a barrel before the Iraq invasion – a price that, before the invasion and because of the abundance of oil, was not expected to rise very much for ten years or so. Stiglitz argued that the invasion, and the instability in the region, was the 'single most important aspect' of the oil price rise. It was also a war 'totally based on borrowing' and foreign borrowing at that. The Iraq spending plus the tax cuts (largely for the upper income groups) worsened the budget deficit and was paid for by borrowing, largely from abroad. What's more, the Iraq military campaign and occupation contracts did not create the jobs at home that are often associated with wartime spending – the payoffs for allies and the global character of contractor ownership, meant that American taxpayer money was going abroad.[2]

By the final months of the Bush presidency the issues for the US were no longer about Iraqi democracy; they were about when to leave, how to leave and how to leave without creating a major power vacuum in the region.

Whatever the final outcome in Iraq, the idea that the making of a western-style democracy, radically different in style and content from most Arab states, was fanciful. Indeed the very integrity of Iraq was placed in doubt by the invasion (with the omnipresent potential to split up and draw in the neighbouring states). It was also generally considered by public and elite opinion alike that America's position in the region had been seriously set back by the invasion; that Iran had been the main beneficiary, and that she was rapidly becoming the region's superpower; that Israel's position had been weakened by this emergence of Iran; and that there was no obvious way forward for Iraq or for the United States in the Middle East; and that, at least by the objectives set out for it, the whole enterprise had been a colossal failure.

2007: THE TURNING POINT

Up until 2007 the American public had not turned decisively against the Iraq war. In a poll conducted in September 2006 the public was evenly split, 49 per cent each, on whether they approved or disapproved of the war (the approval figure had been 51 per cent in November 2004 and was 50 per cent in December 2005).[3] But during 2007 those disapproving of the war jumped significantly, and stayed high. By July 2007 62 per cent were disapproving. And by May 2007 a CBS poll showed that 76 per cent thought the war was going badly whilst only 23 per cent thought it was going well. And, more significantly, as many as 61 per cent thought that the US 'should have stayed out of the war' whereas 35 per cent thought it had been 'the right thing to do'.[4]

By 2008 opinion had become entrenched. In a poll of the American people carried out by Gallup in April 2008, 63 per cent agreed with the view that 'the United States had made a mistake in sending troops to Iraq' (with only 36 per cent disagreeing), and the numbers so believing had risen steadily every quarter since the summer of 2003. The public also supported the withdrawal of American troops, and in the 2008 campaign for the presidency the Democratic candidate for president promised a timetable for such a withdrawal.

THE BANK CRASH OF 2007

2007 was also a turning point for the American economy. And for the first time since the Great Depression there emerged in some quarters a gripping fear for the economic future. By the summer the US was witnessing the beginning of serious turbulence in the global financial system.

During the fateful month of August 2007 the strains on the American economy – principally the global imbalances and the mountainous private debt linked to the housing bubble – could no longer be contained. What bankers were calling the sub-prime mortgage crisis finally spilt out into the wider banking industry as American and then other western banks stopped lending to each other (except, that is, on terms of prohibitive rates of interest). Banks looked vulnerable for the first time since the 1930s.

The Wall Street-led capitalist debt-bubble covered the world – or, at any rate that part of the globalised world run by banks and financial institutions. Its global dimension was soon revealed when news came through of banks in trouble outside the US. A UK bank, Northern Rock, saw the first run on a British bank in living memory and had to be nationalised (by a market-friendly British government); banks from Spain to France and Germany, and Asia, including the Peoples Bank of China, were all in trouble. It had the feel of major global crisis about it.

Indeed the 2007 crisis may well have been triggered by the French bank BNP Paribas whose board took a fateful decision in early August to junk its toxic debts in the US – for reasons that are still unclear, but may have ultimately been cultural (a Gallic antipathy to Wall Street's 'Wild West' lending practices, or a reluctance to risk-take with sub-prime mortgages). In any event the board of the French bank found itself unable to properly value the assets of three sub-prime mortgage funds-and refused to play the game any longer. But, by not playing by the rules that were keeping the Wall Street bubble intact, BNP set off alarm bells all over the global banking system, directly leading to the August 2007 shutdown in global interbank lending. The European Central Bank, seeing the potential for a run throughout the system, immediately stepped in by opening $130 billion in low interest credit.

The Wall Street bubble burst over Switzerland too. At the height of the housing/debt mania UBS, the giant Swiss bank with $31 trillion in assets, had taken a large slice of American mortgage debt (reckoned to be around $80 billion dollars worth) and when the bubble burst was forced to write down $37 billion of that debt. This was a bigger write down than American banks Citigroup and Merrill Lynch. 'What happened here is a scandal' declared local lawyer and shareholder Thomas Minder at the shareholders meeting in Basel Switzerland in early April 2008. 'You're responsible for the biggest loss in the history of the Swiss economy' he thundered, and, adding a political post-script, demanded that the board 'put an end to the Americanisation of the Swiss economy.'

An important part of the new capitalist global debt bubble was the so-called 'carry trade' in which speculators and investors borrowed from low interest countries, like Japan, and placed their money in higher interest countries, like Iceland, or Turkey, or the Baltics. Massive amounts of money were involved. Iceland became what one commentator called a massive 'nordic hedge fund masquerading as a country', a fund that then invested throughout the world in such enterprises as Woolworths, Hamleys Toy Shops and West Ham Football club. The asset base of the Icelandic banking system was a world-record 8 times GDP. But it was always fragile. And Max Keiser likened the small, debt-laden country to a money geyser await-ing an eruption. In a television documentary aired just two days before the western debt bubble burst (on 7th August 2007 when bank debt literally dried up overnight) he told the story of Iceland and the carry trade – and the global financial imbalances that it represented. On the show Dr. Paul Walker of GMFS argued that 'the buying up of US debt has been a key component of the global imbalances' and that 'central banks kept putting off the day of reckoning...but the longer the put it off the more serious it will be...and it will come.' It came two days later.[5]

Previously, high inflation and a trade deficit would have brought it all to an early and abrupt end. This time, however, the low-cost Chinese would keep the system going and the American consumer buying. Americans took on huge debt and the Chinese built up massive reserves. These 'global imbal-ances' represented a dangerous and fragile balancing act, but even as American debt levels reached Himalayan proportions 'neo-liberal' policymakers in Washington, Wall Street and London remained confident and upbeat. A soothing thesis was delivered: the Chinese were recycling their reserves into west-ern system (including the US government) and would never allow their great new market to contract. In reality, though, the whole Wall Street global edifice was shaking.

It all represented a major defeat for Wall Street – and the 'neo-liberal market' capitalist economy it represented and had been vigorously promoting. And the crisis led to much public soul-searching about the causes and the responsibilities. One thing was clear. The crisis had been triggered by lending to 'sub-prime' (i.e. lower income) people who could not afford to pay back the debt – either because the teaser interest rates sud-denly rose or because of job losses or income weakness. And the banks – the lenders – were in the dock both for 'predatory' lending and for parcelling up the 'bad loans' in collective debt packages known as 'securitisation'.

Surprisingly, the bankers' bank, The Bank For International Settlements, became a harsh critic of the Wall Street-led banking establishment. Indeed, it 'startled the financial world' by pinning the blame firmly on the US central bank for what it considered to be its lax monetary policy, arguing that 'cleaning up' a property bubble once it had burst was not easy. A year later the BIS, in the form of its 78th annual report written primarily by its chief economist, Bill White, stated 'the magnitude of the problems we now face could be much greater than many now perceive. It is not impossible that the unwinding of the credit bubble could, after a temporary period of higher inflation, culminate in a deflation that might be hard to manage, all the more so given the high debt levels'.[6]

BEAR STEARNS

Bear Stearns was a Wall Street institution. Founded in 1923 it grew to become one of the largest investment banks on Wall Street – with a sizeable equities business. It employed over 15,000 people. At the beginning of 2007 its total capital was well over $65 billion and it had total assets of $350 billion. The public got to know of trouble when in 22nd June 2007 it sought to bail out one of its funds which was trading in the collateralised debt obligations. It was in real risk of bankruptcy when on 14th March 2008 JP Morgan Chase, in a highly unusual deal involving the Federal Reserve Bank (of New York), provided Bear Stearns with a mammoth emergency loan.

And on 16th March JP Morgan effectively bought Bear Stearns.

The Federal Reserve had 'tossed out the rulebook when it assumed the role of white knight', temporarily bailing out

Bear Stearns with a short-term loan 'to help avoid a collapse that might send other dominoes falling'.[7] Just days before, the Fed had announced a $200 billion lending programme for investment banks and a $100 billion credit line for banks and thrifts. And in what the NYT called a move 'unthinkable until recently' the Fed agreed to accept risky mortgage-back securities as collateral.

FANNIE, FREDDIE, AIG AND THE DISAPPEARING INVESTMENT BANKS

Three months later another shoe dropped – this time in the form of the mammoth lenders Freddie Mac and Fannie Mae. On 13th July 2008 the US government announced that they would bail-out the tottering companies. Freddie and Fannie were a hybrid organisations – they were stockholder-owned but government-sponsored companies. More importantly, they controlled just about half of the US home loan market – a total market which amounted to $12 trillion. The Bush administration agreed to an unspecified and unlimited credit line, borrowing privileges at the discount window and, incredibly, a capital-injection into the companies if needed in return for which the US government would receive shares.

So severe was the financial crisis, and the panic, that these measures were introduced swiftly in the Congress and signed with a sigh of relief by the conservative Bush administration. The US government had ditched decades of history – not to mention half its belief system – and guaranteed the debt of a private company. With the 'full faith and credit of the US' taxpayer behind them they were just one step away from socialist nationalisation – indeed, to all intents and purposes they were in fact nationalised but with shareholders continuing to take the profits – should there be any.

Later, in September, the US government went further. It effectively nationalised both Freddie and Fannie by taking it into 'conservatorship', sacking the top executives, and placing the two companies under the management of The Federal Housing Finance Agency. And then later still in September two other investment banks, Lehman Bros. and Merrill Lynch, effectively collapsed. And the 'free market' Bush administration was forced into nationalising the huge insurer AIG. This outright state takeover was a measure of how dire the US financial system had become: for, without it, the US, and the world, may well have faced an immediate financial meltdown as the now all-important foreign holders of US rushed to unload. The Chinese government was particularly interested in how the US was going to deal with the Fannie and Freddie bankruptcy – as, according to an National Public Radio report on 7th September by Adam Davidson, almost one tenth of China's GDP was invested in the outcome.

AMERICA LIVING BEYOND HER MEANS

The banking and credit crisis, serious though it was (is), was a symptom of a deeper structural economic problem facing the United States. For the explosion of domestic credit had been but a part of a policy that allowed Americans to live well beyond their means. Ever since the early 1980s – when mobile capital and 'free trade' began the process of hollowing out western jobs, and wages became static or fell – American living standards were kept high by the singular, dramatic, and ultimately deadly, growth in debt. This massive indebtedness took many forms. Two of the most dangerous were the private debt of households (causing the housing bubble) and the huge US current-account deficit which for many years remained a wonder of the world.

The country's growing current account deficit, particularly its trade deficit and the interest payments on debt to foreign investors, measures the extent to which America has been living beyond its means. And the trend has been all one way, and disastrous: for the USA was in surplus for 18 of the 22 years between 1960 and 1982 but has been in deficit every year since (except for 1991). These 'imbalances' have been a subject for urgent discussion for some years, but usually, though, only in academic circles. The Washington and Wall Street establishments have, in public at least, dismissed the idea that they represented an inherent instability that could unravel with disastrous consequences. One top official in the Clinton administration was moved to observe that 'there is something odd about the world's greatest power also being its greatest debtor.'[8] They were indeed treated as an oddity rather than a danger.

Economists tended to deal in technical talk about 'imbalances', and the new century saw the beginning of a public debate about these imbalances, but, as with all economic problems after 9/11, they were relegated as fears about security dominated the agenda. By 2004, though, the question of debt was beginning to surface. *The Atlantic Monthly* magazine, under the title 'America's "Suez Moment"', a reference to Britain's invasion of Egypt in 1956 and its humiliating rendezvous with its loss of global power, published an article which argued that 'America is like no other dominant power in modern history – because it depends on other countries for capital to sustain its military and economic dominance.'[9] In the same year the prescient analyst NYU Professor Nouriel Roubini – who became a lone voice predicting dire consequences because of the imbalances – set out the magnitude of the problem: that the current account deficit was set to rise to 7 per cent of GDP in 2006 and that the US's net investment debt was set to equal about 50 per cent of GDP and to equate to about 500 per cent of US export revenues.[10]

Bill Clinton's former Treasury Secretary, Larry Summers, was issuing warnings in 2004. In his Per Jacobsson Lecture he reiterated his serious concern about whether the foreign financing of the huge US debt could continue indefinitely. And he coined the dramatic term 'balance of financial terror' to describe the co-dependency between the foreign lenders and the US – as the US relies 'on the costs [to China and others] of not financing the US debt as assurance that financing will continue.'[11]

By 2006 the US current account deficit was topping $800 billion, this figure representing 6 per cent of US GDP. China's current account surplus was $250 billion, which amounted to almost 10 per cent of China's GDP. East Asia's surplus continued to rise during 2007 – making any global adjustment more difficult by the month. In expert testimony on 26th June 2007 to the House Budget Committee Brad Setser, a Senior Economist at Roubini Global Economics, again raised the question of American vulnerability to foreign holdings of US debt. He reported that 'since 2000, total foreign holdings of US debt have increased from $4.3 trillion to close to $10 trillion while US lending to the rest of the world has increased from $2.9 trillion to an estimated $4.6 trillion'.[12]

CO-DEPENDENCY: LIVING COURTESY OF CHINA

And then, in late 2007, as the banking and housing boom began to bust and unravel, the full importance of China to the West, and particularly to the USA, was revealed. The difficult truth was that it was China's integration into the global market during the 1990s that had allowed Americans to live beyond their means. It did so by fuelling the American (and western) private debt bubble, which in turn was only made possible because of the worldwide low inflationary environment – itself made possible by the low cost (cheap labour) economies of Asia.

It worked like this: Asian and Chinese low costs fuelled a broader global low-inflation regime which, crucially, provided the low-interest environment for the great US-UK mortgage-based housing boom. Americans (and Brits) saw their house prices rise whilst their wages were stagnant. In the US wages as a percentage of personal income fell from around 76 per cent in 1979 to 62 per cent in 2005; yet during the same period consumer spending as a percentage of wages had risen from around 120 per cent to 160 per cent.

This decline in wage income for Americans, however, was more than offset by the growth in credit – fuelled by the 'wealth effect' of higher house values. It was this credit rush which allowed a boom in consumer spending – a boom which became the life-blood of the American economy in the 1990s and into the twenty-first century.

It was this credit rush that allowed Americans (and Brits) to live beyond their means.

Starting around 1995, and lasting through to 2007, the mechanism for such living beyond means was an expansion, and explosion, of low-interest credit fuelled by a bonfire of regulations across the credit industry. As the then Chairman of the US Senate Banking Committee Phil Gramm asserted 'freedom is the answer'. And as a top lawyer for Citibank who pushed the deregulation of the credit-card industry later argued, 'I didn't realise that someday we might have ended up creating a Frankenstein'.[13]

The sheer size of this American private debt bubble slowly revealed itself. A year or so before the bubble burst leading

American political scientist Kevin Phillips was virtually alone amongst his peers in predicting real trouble ahead. He conjured up the arresting image of the 'indentured American household' with Americans becoming 'indentured servants' or 'sharecroppers' who were, in effect, spending their working lives labouring on behalf of whip-holding creditors – be they 'credit-card companies in the US or dollar-holding central bankers in Asia'. It was, as he admitted, an analogy that did not strike a popular chord. Not then.

But by 2008 it was becoming accepted wisdom that debt was at the heart of the unfolding American economic tragedy. So dire was the debt situation that it moved Ambrose Evans-Pritchard a commentator on the conservative 'neo-liberal' Daily Telegraph to write that 'the capitalist system is deformed by debt' and 'how did we ever let matters reach this pass.'[14]

'CHINUSA'

The 'lone superpower' had become the 'lone super-debtor'. And the super-creditors were in Asia. In the first few years of the new century the Asian dimension of this foreign deficit and debt was becoming alarming. East Asian countries reserve holdings rose at an alarming rate. Japan's rose from $220 billion to $834 billion, China's from $143 billion to $610 billion between 1997 and 2004. East Asian countries accounted for 80 per cent of central bank purchases of dollars and Treasury securities in the last two quarters of 2004. The US was indeed becoming locked into what amounted to a co-dependency system with Asia, and particularly with the emerging Asian giant – China.

Not surprisingly during the boom-times these global imbalances were not addressed by the politicians in Washington. They, and most commentators, still saw this system as 'mutually profitable and stable'. Yet it was becoming accepted wisdom that a correction – some kind of a resolution – was ultimately needed. Few wanted a sudden resolution – with all the attendant dangers of a collapse in confidence. The danger was that any domestic crisis could trigger a bigger Asian-US crisis.

In any such crisis few doubted that the global geopolitical tectonic plates would begin to move. And by 2007 this US-China co-dependency has become so pronounced that there seemed to be only two ways out – both fraught with danger. The first would be a rupture of the relationship. This would likely follow a precipitate act by one of the parties – say the US Senate passing a bill signed by the president that significantly upped tariffs on Chinese imports. This protectionist measure might well lead to counter-protectionism with a spiral that ultimately ended in political tension, even conflict.

Alternatively, though, a crisis could lead in exactly the opposite direction. The US and China, faced with such a break, would find it all too daunting – and pull back from the brink and deepen rather than weaken their ties. The crisis would thus be resolved by a further and deeper integration of the two dependencies. The American consumers and the Chinese producers, the US debtors and the Chinese lenders, would solidify rather than shatter their ties – and become so bound together that in effect the two economies would become one. And like the European Union, but perhaps without the formality of rules, a single market would be born and currency pegs would, over time, morph into a single currency 'CHINUSA' would be born. 'CHINUSA' would, of course, never, but never, be acknowledged. But the reality would be that the two governing leaderships in the USA and China, would, forever be constrained by Larry Summers's 'balance of financial terror', and would always act to avoid conflict. Even if it should mean a deeper and deeper co-dependency relationship.

SOVEREIGN WEALTH

And China was not the only foreign power able to provide a shock to the US financial system. For should the Gulf states, or even Saudi Arabia, adjust the dollar share of their foreign portfolios they could also shake the foundations of the US financial system, leading to a dramatic lowering of the dollar. Throughout early 2007 the financial world was replete with rumours of imminent changes of holdings out of dollars and into euros.

Chinese and Arab leverage on the mighty US – through its economy – was also highlighted by the growing controversy (and panic) over 'sovereign wealth funds' a term given by the finance industry to mobile capital owned by governments and invested abroad – much of it in the West. And there was a sudden dawning that these kind of funds were, in essence, 'political' funds, accumulations of capital controlled not by private equity owners but by such regimes as the Chinese Communist party or Middle Eastern sheiks and dictators. These 'sovereign wealth funds' were another name for funds ultimately controlled politically – by authorities ranging from basic dictatorships and to communist parties (one such being the Peoples Liberation Army Pension Fund). With continental European governments still wary of these 'sovereign wealth funds' the British government put out an official statement welcoming them; and, as of writing, in the US, Citigroup and Merrill Lynch were attempting to raise $21 billion from foreign banks in Asia and the Middle East, and the Government of Singapore Investment Corporation announced a stake in Citibank.

In a US banking committee hearing, Democratic Senator Sherrod Brown from Ohio had some fun when he asked Treasury Secretary Paulson why the Republican administration got so worried about nationalisation of banks but seemed quite willing to accept national 'sovereign' capital – as long, that is, that it was provided by foreigners. And Larry Summers, former US Treasury Secretary and president of Harvard University also sounded an alarm. He argued that the motives behind these 'sovereign wealth funds' might be questionable. Whereas capitalists invest and own companies in order to maximise their profits, any other motive distorts the proper functioning of capitalism – and he suggested that the motives behind these funds could be political, or even geopolitical. He pointed to George Soros's 'short position in the British pound in 1992' and his speculative attack on the British currency as a warning of what a sovereign wealth fund – should it have been in the same position – could have gotten up to. 'This is not conducive to the successful relations between nations' he argued.[15]

An early sign that these 'sovereign wealth' funds possessed a political content emerged when in early 2008 it was revealed that governments in Asia and the Middle East were resisting western-led IMF attempts to establish a 'code of conduct' setting out 'best practice' for their operations. It remains not without irony that some neo-liberal western governments remain hostile to nationalisation at home but welcome – as saviours – nationalised money from dictatorship and authoritarian regimes.

THE STALLING OF 'GLOBALISATION'.
Post World War Two American economic expansion was inextricably bound up with the more general process of 'globalisation'. Yet by the turn of the new century this wider project of 'globalisation' – of peaceful, largely economic, transformation – was in trouble, beginning to look somewhat frayed at the edges. An important change in the mood music surrounding 'globalisation' had taken place – for it was no longer seen as the wave of an 'inevitable' future.

For a start, by the early years of the new century there were signs of growing opposition to 'globalisation' at home – amongst the publics of the West, particularly in America, but also in some of the large southern EU nations like Italy and France. The western nations faced a catalogue of problems – manufacturing job losses, stagnant wages, unsatisfactory healthcare benefits, illegal immigration, and dangerous levels of Chinese imports – all of which, fairly and unfairly, were becoming associated in the public mind with 'globalisation'. Harvard academic Jeffry Frieden, in a comprehensive account of the history of globalisations argued that today's globalisation – the present one he suggests stretched from 1939 to its zenith around 2000 – is losing its allure and that dissatisfaction with the latest bout is now widespread. He cites the 2006 polling results about globalisation and reported that when EU citizens were asked whether globalisation is a 'threat' or an 'opportunity', 47 per cent chose a 'threat and only 37 per cent saw it as an 'opportunity'.[16]

Following the attacks on the twin towers in 2001 US opinion detoured into an overriding concern with security, but the evidence shows that even before the atrocities Americans were turning decisively against globalisation and in favour of some kind of protectionism. By early 2008 a decided shift in American opinion away from a belief in the virtues of globalisation had been detected, as had a growing support for protectionism. One of America's leading surveyors of public opinion, Norman Ornstein, the elections expert and political analyst at the American Enterprise Institute, has monitored this shift. He has suggested that 'globalisation has had a significant impact upon public optimism about the economy and public confidence in the future. 'It's given people the sense that their safety net's been shredded' he argued. And Joseph Stiglitz, the

183

Nobel Prize-winning economist, could suggest that 'we're paying the price today for the over-selling of globalisation, the fact that those who pushed globalisation in both parties were unwilling to face up to the downside risks and take actions to mitigate them.'[17]

Indeed, in recent years dangerous divisions about the merits of economic globalisation have opened up between western publics and western elites (including the super-rich elites) who, shielded from its ravages, remain insistent about its merits. Not surprisingly the lower down the income hierarchy the more hostile to globalisation people become. Asked whether they support 'a policy of restricting foreign imports in order to protect jobs and domestic industries' 53 per cent of those with advanced degrees, 61 per cent of those with College degrees, 61 per cent of those with 'some college', 71 per cent of those with high school degrees and 73 per cent of those with 'less than high school' agreed with the proposition.[18]

During the early years of the twenty-first century the evidence of serious disenchantment with global free trade was all around us. In the western world it could be seen in the high-profile middle class youth protests during the gatherings of world leaders. It could be seen also in the growing opposition from within the American political establishment to the trade regime established by successive free trade administrations. Indeed protectionist proposals from US Senators Schumer and Graham – in 2005 they introduced a bill to raise tariffs on Chinese goods in retaliation for Chinese currency policy – continues to lurk menacingly in the Senate wings.

Opposition to globalisation has many faces, and there is one such in the resistance present in the economic policies of European countries as they continue to refuse to obey globalisation's imperatives to lower their welfare provisions and tax regimes (even though, by so refusing, they risk becoming 'uncompetitive' in the global environment). Also, in the US presidential campaign of 2008 the three leading US Democratic candidates all felt the need to compete with each other in developing anti-globalisation themes – for instance, in attacking the excesses of NAFTA and promising to review US trade agreements and even US membership of the WTO. And in Europe, country after country – France and Holland in 2005 and Ireland in 2008 – found that anti-free trade opinion was a powerful factor in the serial rejections of EU treaty reform.

'BLOWBACK' AND THE END OF FREE TRADE

Resistance and opposition to globalisation outside the West became so pronounced, and sharp, that a term was coined for it: 'blowback'. 'Blowback' was originally introduced as an idea by the CIA to describe the 'unanticipated consequences of unacknowledged actions in other people's countries' and it was popularised by Professor Chalmers Johnson, in a book published in 2000. It soon spread to describe a whole host of global reactions – cultural and social as well as political – to the standardised global world that was being created.

In a sense the biggest 'blowback' of all was the increasing rejection by governments of its central doctrine of 'free trade'. Although 'free trade' remained the mantra, it was more and more often honoured in the breach. A big turning point was the death – announced in 1998 during the Asian financial crisis – of the five year long OECD-led Multilateral Agreement on Investment (the MAI). This agreement was pure 'globalisation' created to perfectly suit global capital's needs. It was bold and to the point, guaranteeing in treaty form that foreign investors 'would receive treatment no less favourable than the treatment [which a country] accords its own investors and their investments with respect to the establishment, acquisition, use, enjoyment and sale or other disposition of investments'.[19] It sought nothing less than what Thomas Friedman had described as a 'flat world'.

Yet nation-states – on behalf of their peoples and job programmes – were not seeing it the same way. One such was Malaysia in 1988 when it simply gave up on the globalisation process and rules – and to most everyone's surprise, prospered. More importantly, China itself, often considered an integral part of the globalised world, was only superficially integrated into its processes – allowed essentially to act strategically (that is picking and choosing amongst globalist and protectionist policies), an intelligent approach which allowed the Asian giant to remain intensely resistant to opening up many of her markets to western suppliers.

DID 'GLOBALISATION' EVER EXIST?

By the end of the first decade of the new century there was some clear evidence that 'globalisation' is no longer the dominant dynamic in the world economy. And, looking back, perhaps 'globalisation' was always the wrong word for the new international economic relationships that developed after the fall of communism. For there never was a truly global 'globalisation'. The figures make the point – for most of the rise in trade in the world seems to have been between the trilateral areas of America, Europe and Asia, with the rest of the world – what used to be called the developing world – not really getting a look in. And, as I argue throughout this book, the whole story is not really about a 'globalised' world, but, rather, about a much more precise development – the adhesion of Asia (and primarily China) to the western trading and financial system, a story with an obvious corollary. That, no matter its other beneficial effects, it is China's rise – and the western elites support of this rise – that has been the principal cause of the economic and social dislocations of the western world.

THE END OF AMERICAN ASCENDANCY

The world at the end of the George W. Bush presidency was very different from the world envisaged at its beginning. At its start, on inauguration day, 20th January 2000, Americans – and much of the world – still saw an ascendant America at the heart of a global economic system. The driver of this economy was something called 'globalisation' – an essentially Americanising dynamic that was fashioning the world's economy on American economic lines with American capitalist values and rules. It was also seemingly a global economy in which the US consumer was the engine driving global growth.

America was also ascendant politically. In January 2001 American influence was still spreading east through the NATO expansion into Eurasia that was inaugurated by Bush's father and continued by Bill Clinton. Poland, Hungary and Czechoslovakia had joined in 1999 and even the Baltic countries, former states of the Soviet Union, were slated to join. They were all very pro-American, seeing Washington as their liberator. And with successes in the first Gulf War and in the Kosovo campaign against Milosevic, the US stood tall. So tall that George Bush during his election campaign could promised a 'humbler foreign policy' and in his inaugural could suggest a global engagement 'without arrogance'.

But eight years later, as the Bush presidency drew to its momentous close, the promise of American ascendancy had shrivelled. The reckless 2003 attempt to remake the Middle East had failed, and the American political class was divided about how to extricate its troops from Iraq. And both big and small nations were no longer listening to the US as carefully as they used to. Iran (as of writing) was successfully rebuffing the US over its potential for gaining a nuclear arsenal; The EU leaders had turned down an American request to bring Georgia and the Ukraine into NATO; Russia was reasserting its Soviet-era influence in the Caucasus as it pressured the American satellite nation, Georgia, to disgorge two of its regions with majority Russian-speaking populations – all whilst the US was unable to offer any serious counter-pressure; and China was determining its own economic path – and had refused to revalue the remnimbi after very insistent American pressure.

And on top of all this the American economy was in deep structural recession. For the first time since 1945 American power in the world was becoming a live issue – and a question could well be asked: what kind of superpower was it that was no longer economically independent, relying for its very financial stability and living standards on another power? Of course, few were openly asking this question. London University Professor Iwan Morgan was an exception. He was suggesting that America was an 'indebted empire' and prophesied that 'when Asia stops buying dollars, the American economy will experience problems that will have implications for America's global power'.[20]

After any turning point the times that went before it can, with hindsight, look very different. And, looking back – from a vantage-point in 2008 at the end of the Greenspan/Bush regime – the great era of 'globalisation' did indeed look rather different. It looked far less comprehensive than it appeared during the heady days of expansion. In fact, it began to look as though it may never really have existed at all – at least not in the sense that the world was becoming a single global system.

What had, though, decidedly existed was a 'partial globalisation', if such a phenomenon was possible. This 'partial globalisation' amounted to an increasing trilateral integration and economic lift-off across North America, Asia, and Europe (and parts of Latin America, Brazil certainly), but it left huge swathes of the world outside the system, still without an industrial or commercial base or internal market.

What was also increasingly clear was that, whatever the precise dimensions of the power and influence of the various players in the coming multipolar world, the 21st century was not going to be the second American century.

CHAPTER SIX

AN EMPIRE IN DECLINE

WHAT AMERICA WAS

When 'Jerry' Bremer, in his desert boots, landed in Baghdad in May of 2003 to become the US 'Viceroy' in a defeated and occupied country it stirred memories of colonial times. It was strangely un-American. For, ever since 1941, in the hot war and the Cold War, the United States, with some justification and pride, could sell itself – to itself as well as to others – as the great anti-imperial power. As its troops swept through Nazi-occupied Western Europe and then manned the barricades of the West during the Cold War, the US was the 'liberator' and 'protector', spreading and defending democracy. It was a leader, the head of a grand alliance of free and democratic peoples. A leader, not a ruler.

American involvement in the world in the twentieth century always possessed a large ideological element – it was

'America against fascism' and then 'America against communism'. For many Americans, and for others too, the fifty-year
fight against fascism and communism made the US special.
She was not just another 'great power' in the mould of the
European imperial nations. She was about power certainly, but
also about 'freedom'. She had colonial possessions (The
Phillipines gained its independence in 1946) but not a worldwide colonial empire.

Indeed, in the early postwar years, during its emergence on
the world stage, Washington never tired of pointing out its history of anti-colonial struggle against the British and opposition
to the European empires. During the early phase of the Cold
War, it proclaimed itself to the leaders of the emerging 'Third
World' (to Nasser and Tito and Nehru) as an anti-colonial
power. It denounced both communism and colonialism; and
set about actively undermining the old European empires.

And in bringing Britain and France to heel after their invasion of Egypt in 1956 it earned its anti-imperial credentials.

Indeed, as it emerged as a global power in the 1950s
Washington had a very different flavour about it than did old
imperial Europe. The USA had no proconsuls and eschewed
direct rule. Instead it relied on the indirect approach, securing
power through its economic size, its societal attractiveness,
and its worldwide system of alliances. And even as it began to
dominate half the world, the term 'American empire', starkly
obvious to many in South America, continued to grate on
American ears.

EMPIRE

But in the 1990s, with the Soviet threat over, this pleasant narrative was no longer available. The USA was now the lone
superpower, and it had no communist or fascist dragons to

slay. Its overwhelming global presence could no longer be about 'liberating' and 'protecting'. And as the fog of the Cold War cleared, the US was increasingly revealed to be a power like any other – that is, acting primarily in her own interests as she saw them. Certainly, the US was still on the side of freedom – and against tyrants. In 1991 the first Gulf War liberated Kuwait from Saddam Hussein, and in 1998 the bombing of Serbia liberated the Kosovans from Slobodan Milosevic; but these were small tyrants compared to Stalin and Hitler, and their regimes were hardly about to take over the world. In this new world, more complex and shaded than the great conflicts against fascism and communism, America was becoming a nation like others.

And in this new environment, with the USA no longer 'special', those critics, domestic and foreign, who had always used the term 'empire' to describe American world involvement, were now listened to more attentively. Chief amongst them was the novelist, biographer and essayist Gore Vidal whose acerbic pen had chronicled and critiqued what he believed had been his country's degeneration from republic to empire – and to what he called 'the security state'.[1] Another is the academic and writer Noam Chomsky, who sees the history of the USA – the conquests of Hawaii, the Philippines and half of Mexico – as a colonial story.[2] As does the academic Chalmers Johnson who in *The Sorrows Of Empire* argues that 'most Americans do not recognise – do not want to recognise – that the United States dominates the world through its military power' and then goes on to set out the extent of the empire: 'our country deploys well over half a million soldiers, spies, technicians, teachers, dependants, and civilian contractors in other nations and just under a dozen carrier task forces in all the oceans and seas of the world. We operate numerous secret bases outside our territory...'[3] And from the

American right, the former Nixon aide and presidential candidate, Pat Buchanan, agreed. He saw the US as an 'empire, with America having 'inherited' the role in the world – the imperial role – from the British empire. He saw this American empire as being seriously overextended.[4]

COLD WAR EMPIRE: PUNCHING EQUAL TO ITS WEIGHT.

Of course, an American 'empire' was there from the very beginning of the United States. The expansion of the European settlements and the conquering of the American continent by force – and the subjugation of the indigenous population – was very colonial in its character. As was the expansion of the United States following the Mexican-American war. The big difference between the making of America and the European colonial expansion was that in North America the European conquerors and settlers settled, and then became the majority population.

In its first century of existence the US adopted an insular – hemispheric – attitude. And, although by 1900 her economy was by any measure the largest and most productive in the world, American strategic thinking remained essentially 'isolationist' – determined to stay out of European-dominated global politics. It was this period that allowed the idea to spread that the US – certainly by comparison with Europe – was 'exceptional', exceptionally moral that is, representing in its foreign policy – in the phrase made famous by the historian Correlli Barnett – 'all that was noble and good'.[5] The truth, however, was less uplifting, for Washington was as aggressive and acquisitive as any European colonial state. It was simply that she adopted a different – and arguably more sensible – imperial policy. She ingested what she could digest, and little more. Buchanan has argued that this traditionally careful approach by Washington has paid great dividends. He suggests that today 'America is the last superpower because she stayed out of the world wars until their final acts' and he asserts that the British, French, German, Austro-Hungarian, Russian, Ottoman, and Japanese empires are all gone today because they got involved in total wars. 'We alone remain, because we had men who recalled the wisdom of Washington, Jefferson, and John Quincy Adams about avoiding entangling alliances. Staying out of European wars, and not going "abroad in search of monsters to destroy".'[6]

America's replacement of Europe in world politics was an exercise in successful imperial statecraft if ever there was one. In the run up to the Second World War Washington manoeuvred intelligently, and then pushed decisively, to become a global power, and actively sought to undermine the British imperial economic system in order to dominate it. By entering the Second War when it did Washington was able to take full advantage of Europe's weakness and, with the Soviet Union, carve out spheres of influence throughout the world. By 1950, and the setting up of NATO, Washington's cold war boundaries were set. 'The West' was born. It was a willing alliance – a more than willing alliance – but it was also an American-led system in which American interests were well and truly served – with growing mass markets for the US corporations, and a reserve currency which allowed the US to control the financial system.

In constructing this postwar system America had half-listened to its founders. They had ignored the founders' injunction not to get involved in entangling alliances, but, on the other hand, these alliances did serve their interests, and, crucially, did not overextend the empire. For most of the cold war period America was punching equal to its weight – and Americans did not 'go abroad in search of monsters to destroy'.

The cold war policy was to 'contain' communism, not to roll it back; there were no invasions of communist-held territory; and, with the exception of the Vietnam issue, no loss of support at home for foreign policy.

THE EMPIRE'S BASES

America's cold war empire did, however, produce a monumental military-industrial complex; and Washington came out of the Cold War with unchallenged military supremacy. The Pentagon budget was so impressive that by century's turn it was more than the next 20 countries put together and three eighths of total global defence spending. The American lead on military research and development is even more impressive – four times as much as the rest of NATO Europe put together.[7] And the US military's potential reach is unprecedented in history, with a string of as many as 158 bases (or 'military installations') around the world in as many as 40 countries.

American deployments stretch across Eurasia from Western and Eastern Europe through to the Balkans (in the huge US army base at Camp Bondsteel in Kosovo picked up following the conflict with Serbia), the Middle East (including Kuwait, Oman, Saudi Arabia and now Iraq), the Indian Ocean (by courtesy of the UK in Diego Garcia) to Central Asia (with US air force bases in Tajikistan, Kyrgyzstan and Afghanistan), taking the US military right up to the Chinese border and beyond in South Korea and Japan. The only area where the Pentagon is in something of a retreat is Europe where, following the downturn in relations, US plans are to move assets out of Germany, into Poland, Bulgaria and Romania (as of 2003 the Krzesiny air base in Poznan was being prepared for the US air force).[8]

These bases were (and are) all about access, the ability at short notice for the USA's flexible forces to go anywhere in the world at any time. The architect of this new Pax Americana, Paul Wolfowitz, set out the case for them in blunt terms. 'The function of these bases he said, 'may be more political than actually military, they send a message to everyone.' And the message was clear: this new string of US bases girding the globe is very different from the system established during the Cold War (when the bases were part of a containment policy). Now, they are no longer there for containment, but rather for pre-emption – and the implied threat has been of a US administration willing to overthrow governments believed by Washington to be dangerous. As the historian of empires Paul Kennedy ruminated in front of a transatlantic television audience in April 2003, this American system of bases was beginning to look very much like an empire in the classic old European sense.[9]

The question being increasingly posed in the USA, and around the world, before and after the 2003 Iraq war, was whether this powerful US military global reach would enable the USA, even potentially, to dominate or control, even police, the world? Could the USA in fact become the famed 'hegemon' and assume the mantle of lone superpower desired by the Bush White House and Condoleezza Rice? US forces were easily able to defeat Iraq, the world's 56th military power with no deliverable weapons of mass destruction, no airforce, and a country weakened by a decade of sanctions. But could they do much more than this? And were they able, as Samuel Huntingdon asked in the mid-1990s, to fight two serious wars at the same time?[10]

OVERSTRETCH: AMERICA AS ROME?

And there was a further question. Was this global US military power sustainable? Would, in fact, US opinion allow future administrations to pay for its global network of bases, its hi-tech, flexible military, and the reconstruction costs of country after country whose regimes have been removed? Looked at another way, was the US an empire both overstretched and in decline, unable to sustain its power, like Rome or Britain before it? Was it destined to see other superpowers – maybe Europe and maybe China – rise to compete with it? And, if it continued to want to act as the world's policeman, would it need to seek to share power with Europe?

The USA at the turn of the millennium was certainly not like Rome in its latter years (Rome here meaning the empire in the West). It was not militarily weak; it had not surrendered its weapons to unassimilated bands of foreigners. It was not dependent for its supply of food on imports controlled by groups of opponents. It did not have a stagnant technology. It did not have a farm sector worked on by 90 per cent of the population held in conditions of servitude. It did not have a hugely oppressive tax system. As yet it had not directly conquered large landmasses containing restless and resentful populations. It did not have difficult supply lines. It had lost no wars (save Vietnam, and possibly Iraq). It had not yet been visited by plagues and epidemics. It did not depend on foreign mercenaries for its defence. And it did not, as yet, have a privileged, hereditary aristocracy (at least not of the type which ran Rome), nor an official and inordinately wealthy priesthood."

Nor does today's USA resemble the Soviet empire before its fall. The Soviet problem was a classic case of serious overextension. Its domestic economy was simply unable to sustain the military expenditure needed to control its empire outside of its borders. Military spending was also taking far too much out of the domestic economy – to the point in the late 1980s when the Politburo came to the fateful conclusion that the USSR could no longer compete in a new arms race in space.

OVERSTRETCH: OR THE BRITISH EMPIRE?

The US today may not resemble Rome or the Soviet Union before their falls. But it may well resemble the British empire of a century ago. Indeed the USA today bears a somewhat striking resemblance to Britain in those fateful decades around 1900, before the onset of its rapid decline. Then, whilst London ruled over a global political empire on which 'the sun never set', it possessed a home base that could no longer sustain it. The British had, by global standards, a small population. So, too, do today's Americans. Britain had serious structural economic problems – not least an increasingly uncompetitive manufacturing and industrial sector that was being supplanted by other powers. Today's US structural problems – the country's massive debt owed to foreigners and its projected deficits – are no less acute. And in one respect the US is in a worse position – for in 1900 Britain was not owned by foreigners, indeed British investment overseas was immense.

Just as crucial as the economic position was the damage inflicted by delusions of power. Imperial Britain at the zenith of empire produced an elite intoxicated with success, which slowly lost touch with reality, overestimating Britain's power and arguably leading to the blunders of the Boer War, the Great War of 1914-1918 and, at the very fag-end of empire, the 1956 Suez imbroglio. In 1921, South Africa's Anglophile Prime Minister, General Smuts, saw Britain as 'quite the greatest power in the world' and suggested that 'only unwisdom or unsound policy could rob her of her great position.' And, in the view of Britain's chronicler of imperial decline, this was exactly what happened as Britain's increasingly deluded leadership allowed 'British responsibilities to vastly exceed British strength'. They lost sight of the reality set out by Britain's nineteenth century Liberal Prime Minister, William Ewart Gladstone, delivered at the height of empire: 'Rely upon it, the strength of Great Britain and Ireland is within the United Kingdom.'[12]

HUBRIS

The American leadership in the 1990s and early 2000s was showing some of the same signs. Washington's celebration of the US 'victory' in the Cold War, and Wall Street's lauding of the revolutionary 'new economy' (which some analysts predicted was even going to bring to an end the business cycle) led to a bout of excitable hubris about the USA as the world's 'only superpower', even the world's 'hegemon'. Even the measured Henry Kissinger echoed these sentiments when he said of the USA, in an article headlined 'America At The Apex' that 'at the dawn of the new millennium' it was 'enjoying a pre-eminence unrivalled by even the greatest empires of the past'.[13] It was an environment in which grandiose ideas about the superiority of American values and the need for universal conversion took root. Just as late imperial Britain talked of 'the white man's burden' and sought to bring their form of Christianity to the world by force, so the USA sought to bring its own version of 'democracy' to the world (initially the Middle East) even at the barrel of a gun.

PROPHETS

Yet, to counterbalance these extravagances there were other, more realistic, voices. As early as 1987, at the height of the bipolar Cold War and the Reagan arms buildup, Paul Kennedy published his *The Rise And Fall Of The Great Powers*. It was a book which had real impact – not only on the academic debate, but far wider in the public policy community and beyond. For simply by setting the power of the USA in an historical context, Kennedy, implicitly at any rate, began adjusting perspectives on American power – both its real extent and its durability. He saw the US as a 'great power' rather than a global hegemon. He described what he called a 'pentarchy' of powers – the US, USSR, China, Japan and the EEC; and although there was a 'military 'bipolarity' (between the US and the USSR) what he called the 'the global productive balances' were tilting 'away from Russia and the United States, away also from the EEC, to Japan and China'.[14] The MIT economist Lester Thurow in his 1993 best-seller *Head To Head* also predicted a more modest future for America. Writing at the time of Japan's economic advance, he saw a 'trilateral' future for the world – the USA, Japan and Europe (with the vast raw materials of Russia able to enhance Europe's position).[15]

The fall of communism was to blur the impact on the public policy world of these realistic and modest assessments. For, in the aftermath of this fall, Francis Fukuyama's more expansive and imperial analysis in *The End of History* took centre stage. And in the 1990s American military 'wins' in the first Gulf War and the Kosovo crisis seemingly reinforced Fukuyama.

Yet even at the height of bullish Fukuyamaism some American policymakers were arguing against the grain. They were beginning to see long-term US weaknesses as contributing to a geopolitical decline, especially *vis-à-vis* Europe and, ultimately, China. In the short run, Europe posed the most serious challenge. Former Under-Secretary of Commerce, Jeffrey E. Garten argued as early as 1998 – prophetically – that the euro would pose a 'major challenge' to the USA, because 'when America's boom ends, it will still be the world's largest debtor, whereas the EMU region will be a net creditor.' And, echoing the view of a growing minority of worried Americans, he saw a future in which:

> the US will continue to run chronic trade deficits, while the European Union amasses large surpluses. America will not have reversed its super-low savings rates, while EMU members will

have no such problems. American companies will also want to keep an eye on European corporate goliaths…A lot of experts are pointing to the need for Europe to brace for changes ahead. So should America.[16]

Yet, even though Kosovo left an afterglow in Washington, the turn of the century saw anxiety growing about America's global economic position. And, unusually, particularly from the heart of the American bullish Wall Street business community, came a remarkable analysis for its time. The high priest of American capitalism, Morgan Stanley, issued a market commentary which suggested that 'the paradigm of US leadership in the global economy and world financial markets is coming to an end'. It made the case that the US economy was showing so many structural weaknesses that it was heading for a serious decline, and concluded that 'we are moving from a unipolar to a tripolar world, where Europe and Asia become the equals of the US in economic if not military power.'[17]

FIGURES

But it was not until the banking and credit crisis of 2007-8 that the growing decline of America as it faced the new century was fully exposed. It was a decline that was comparative, not absolute, difficult to properly measure, and the pace of which was contested. Yet, it was real: real enough to argue with certainty that the 'unipolar moment', if ever there was one, was over; that the reality was now a 'multipolar' world; and that in this multipolar world US 'primacy' was also out, and that even the US as 'primus inter pares' (first amongst equals) was in doubt.

The figures were telling. IMF figures for 2007 show world GDP standing at $64,903,263 millions. EU GDP stood at

$14,712,000, USA at $13,843,000, The People's Republic of China at $6,991,000, Japan at $4,289,000 and India at $2,998,000. On these figures the USA had only about 21 per cent of global GDP.[18]

On population the figures are just as striking: The world's population on 1st January 2008 was estimated to be 6,671,226,000. Of this total China's population was 1,324,723,000, India's was 1,134,893,000, the EU's was 497,198,000 and the USA's was 304,499,000. The USA had only 4.46 per cent of the world's population.

The figures make the point more effectively than any words. The US – with only 21 per cent of global GDP and only 4.5 per cent of the world's population increasingly inhabits a geopolitical world which is now multipolar in character. And it is clear that the EU (with a higher GDP than the US), fast-growing China and India, and energy-rich Russia, are all, in the short-term, potential competitors as global superpowers. The US lead in military strength remained impressive – twice that of the nearest spend, the 27 EU nations put together. But there remained a very big question about the exact relationship between 'hard power', even highly mobile and technologically advanced 'hard power', and real power in the world. There is obviously some relationship (this writer believes a strong one), but exactly how military spending fits into the mix of GDP, population, attractiveness, domestic tranquillity, creativity and the rest remains difficult to judge.

A POWER SHIFT

Whatever the precise figures, it amounted to a power shift, a global power shift. The 1990s western political class had been slow to recognise this shift – one effected during their watch. It was later acknowledged by one of their own, Tony Blair, when he argued, peculiarly, that he understood these global changes better after he left power. In June 2008 he suggested that 'the other change I have got to know better since leaving No. 10 is that the whole centre of gravity in the world is shifting east, that for countries like us, and Europe and America, this is a change so profound that I don't think we yet quite understand its consequences or its implications for us...We are about to enter a new epoch in terms of power relations.'[19]

Others had noticed earlier. One such was China specialist Martin Jacques who in a series of articles had made the case that 'a fundamental shift in power from the developed world to the developing world, and above all China and India' was underway and that 'we have not witnessed anything like this since the inception of the West as an industrial powerhouse in the 19th century.'[20] It was a sentiment increasingly echoed within the US itself from writers as diverse as Pat Buchanan and Chalmers Johnson. In his book, *The Sorrows of Empire*, published in 2004, Johnson, a professor at the University of California, set out the still somewhat novel case, for Americans, that America had become an empire – in the classic sense – and how this empire was now declining. He proclaimed that 'empires do not last, and their ends are usually unpleasant' and went on to argue that:

Americans like me, born before World War II, have personal knowledge – in some cases personal experience – of the collapse of at least six empires: those of Nazi Germany, imperial Japan, Great Britain, France, the Netherlands, and the Soviet Union. A combination of imperial overstretch, rigid economic institutions, and an inability to reform weakened all these empires...there is no reason to think that an American empire will not go the same way – and for the same reasons.[21]

AMERICAN WEAKNESS IN THE NEW CENTURY

And as the American economic leadership – George W. Bush, Hank Paulson and Ben Bernanke – stood astride the rubble of the American banking meltdown in 2008 and the global economic downturn, it was soon obvious that this was no short-term crisis from which America would rebound. Rather, the country's longer-term weaknesses as a power in the world – and the prosperity, and its very way of life that was linked to that power – were now becoming apparent.

At the heart of the longer-term weakness was the fact that in the new century the great engine of America, its economy, was no longer what it used to be. At any given time the raw figures of US economic strength simply did not reveal how the foundations of the American economy were being weakened and undermined.

HOLLOWING OUT THE HOMELAND

A primary cause of the weakness, and of the shift in global power, was the controversial problem of the deadly US job and wealth losses to production in the Asia. This 'hollowing out' of the US economy had been proceeding over many decades, and was for some time nigh unmentionable in polite high political circles. Imperceptible at first, it grew to the point when it became a live political issue in the early 1990s with the campaign for the USA to create NAFTA and then again in 2004 and 2008 presidential elections. The figures of job losses were alarming.[22] But the real problem was that this tide of job and wealth losses seemed inexorable, and was showing no signs of abating. Nor would it until either comparative costs equalised (China's huge reserve pool of peasant labour) or trade barriers went up and a protectionist strategy was ushered in. Ross Perot's image – used in the 1992 presidential election campaign – of a 'huge sucking sound' of jobs leaving America would grow louder and louder. And as things stood in 2008, even though opposition to this aspect of globalisation was decidedly growing, the hollowing out of the Homeland was simply set to continue and continue.

This transfer of wealth reflected itself in the twin deficits of trade and budget, the global imbalances – particularly between China and the US – and America's massive domestic debt structures. The fact was that the great job and wealth loss was being largely hidden, and even after it was well underway, Americans were still living well beyond their means. And the world outside the US had been complicit in this arrangement- for non-Americans needed high US consumption as it contin- ued to fuel world trade. It was a mutuality that many believed would ensure that American consumers could continue to live beyond their means for some time to come; but it was also a fragile mutuality that should it ever break could mean a sharp and serious readjustment.

END OF THE RESERVE CURRENCY

Because of the USA's economic size and status as a superpow- er any serious attempt to rectify these imbalances would have very harmful short-run consequences, affecting consumer con- fidence and also the broader global system where foreign busi- nesses and economies were dependent on the American mar- ket. It was a desperate situation, in which American private debt levels and the current-account deficits were getting worse and worse, and the hype and braggadocio needed for consumer confidence were getting louder and louder.

There was another, bigger, factor at work here – the fact that the yawning American current account deficit, caused by the massive gap between imports and exports, was being plugged by massive borrowing from creditor countries – mainly in Asia and the oil rich Middle East. By investing in American equities, American Treasury and municipal bonds, American mortgage-backed securities or US corporate debt, the rest of the world (or, more accurately, the rest of the world's exporters) was a complicit partner in this huge consumer binge. In this sense the world's traders fuelled the American debt binge.

The world continued to want dollars and this need meant that the US could continue for a time as a reserve currency, and could therefore finance its international deficits – and continue living beyond its means – quite easily. Yet, it was all very fragile. Jeffrey Frankel of Harvard University predicted that 'the US could lose its "exorbitant privilege" of being able to finance its international debts easily' should the dollar continue to weaken. And he predicted that the euro could surpass the dollar as a reserve currency in 2018.[23] Between 1985 and 2008 the dollar had already fallen by 52 per cent against a basket of trade-weighted currencies. And there was a growing jitteriness about big money from abroad switching to the euro – the other safe haven, and the alternative reserve currency in waiting. Indeed, by 2008, dollar holdings of the world central banks had declined significantly – down from 73 per cent to 64 per cent – whilst the euro's share had risen and was standing at 26 per cent, and was still rising.

However, switching out of dollars into euros was likely to be a slow process, as sharp changes were in no one's interest, not least those foreign holders who were (are) thinking of switching. One way in which foreigners started to switch out of the dollar in a more subtle way was simply by building up their 'sovereign wealth' funds in euros, and as the financial crisis deepened many analysts believed that many of these funds were already 'euro-heavy'.

The decline in the British pound as a reserve currency in the first half of the last century is a kind of parallel with the decline in the dollar. The sterling currency crisis of the early 1950s was fundamentally all about Britain's losing world position, and it came to a head during the 1956 British invasion of Suez and Egypt. When President Eisenhower refused an IMF loan to Britain, the country's weakened imperial position – and imperial overstretch – properly revealed itself. Britain was acting like a political hegemon but power was passing, had passed, some time before out of British hands; and the run on the pound, and Britain's capitulation to international and US pressure, simply proved the point.

ENERGY

More importantly ultimately even than currency status is energy. And even during the roaring 90s the relationship between American power in the world and its energy supplies was coming into question. And the question was: Can a global superpower retain its power and prosperity whilst it remains so highly dependent on foreign and unstable sources of energy? President George W. Bush did not think so. He argued in 2001 that 'over dependence on any one source of energy, especially a foreign source, leaves us vulnerable to price shocks, supply interruptions, and in the worst case, blackmail'.[24]

Yet during the last three decades of the twentieth century the US had increasingly become overdependent – if not on one single supplier, then certainly on foreign supplies. As of 2004 the US produced roughly only 40 per cent of the oil it consumes. Also, the US was (is) highly dependent on the health of the global economy and the 'global' economy – particularly Japan – is also highly dependent on foreign oil. And US dependence on 'unstable' countries is also pretty high. Saudi

Arabia (15 per cent of domestic consumption), Venezuela (13 per cent of domestic consumption) and Nigeria (10 per cent of domestic consumption) are not exactly stable allies. And in 2001 the Cheney report outlined how the most unstable of all oil producing regions, the Middle East, would remain the major source of foreign oil for the foreseeable future.

Looking to the medium-term future, North America, on present trends, will, by 2025, import 5.8 million barrels a day from the Persian Gulf, 0.5 from N. Africa, 1.6 from West Africa, 3.9 from South America, 0.5 from former Soviet Union (producing a total of 21.1 million a day). By comparison in 2025 Western Europe is scheduled to import 4.5 million barrels of petroleum a day from the Persian Gulf, 3.1 million barrels a day from North Africa, 1.1 from West Africa, 0.1 from South America, 3.4 from the North Sea (Norway), 3.3 from the former Soviet Union. (a total of 18.9 million barrels a day); and the Pacific Rim (including Japan) will import 8.7 million a day from Persian Gulf and 1.8 from West Africa (a total of 16.7); and China will import 6.4 million a day from Persian Gulf, 3.1 from former Soviet Union (total of 10.7).[25]

The inescapable, and daunting, conclusion is that the US is already in a serious worldwide competition with Europe and Asia for scarce energy resources. And should the coming multipolar powers continue with their existing standards of living then this competition could be sharp and turn into geopolitical conflict. As of writing, in none of the multipolar powers are politicians preparing their publics for sizeable cuts in living standards.

SUSTAINING THE EMPIRE IN A REPUBLIC?

These long-term economic weaknesses of the USA meant that sustaining the empire was becoming more difficult by the year.

But economic overstretch and energy-dependence was only part of the problem. The other was that America was a democracy. Again, modern America resembles early twentieth century Britain – this time in the challenge that its domestic democracy presents to its global power. As much as its faltering economy, it was Britain's developing democracy, with its visceral liberal opposition to 'colonialism' and the subjugation and domination of other peoples, which helped sink the empire.

Open societies – particularly republics – are bad imperialists. For in open societies news of the harshness and moral difficulties of control and occupation abroad inevitably filter back to the homeland, creating opposition to the whole enterprise. And democracies also ultimately demand public support for foreign policy, and find it difficult to sustain a consensus behind protracted wars abroad – as the Americans found out in Vietnam in the 1970s. Also, empires need elites to run them and to justify, or force through, sacrifices at home. Nineteenth century Britain possessed such an imperial elite – it was formed in a pre-democratic era when a corpus of elite schools, like Harrow, Eton and Rugby, inculcated in the young the culture of rulership and the idea of *noblesse oblige* specially so they could run an empire. But today's American elite, imbued primarily with the culture of business and commerce, rather than with imperial governance, is not comfortable with such an overt political role.

President George W. Bush did not turn up for the funerals of the American fallen in Iraq, nor did he allow opportunities for pictures of flag-draped coffins. The idea was that public opposition to the war and occupation could be contained for a time as long as its more grievous side was downplayed by the media. Over the longer term the supporters of an American presence in Iraq and Afghanistan took the view that as long as the killing of US soldiers and personnel was not at a high and continuous rate, and the US bases were operating in relatively peaceful conditions, as in South Korea or Eastern Europe or in the tiny Sheikdoms of the gulf, then domestic public support would not become a problem.

RESISTANCE ABROAD

Yet, the idea that in the Middle East or Africa or increasingly in Muslim Asia, American troops who had invaded and occupied could become a settled presence in a peaceful environment is utterly fanciful. Indeed, the opposite is the case – for indigenous resistance to empire will only likely grow. Today's Third World millions, which American neo-cons seek to remake in the interests of democracy and free markets, are simply no longer like the millions conquered by the earlier European invaders from Portugal, France, Holland and Britain over two centuries ago. Then the locals had no television, no radio, no access to what was going on about them and little ability to put it all in context. Then, too, the European imperialists did not face, as Americans do now, a highly politicised and organised religion with a gospel of resistance, and there was no international 'mullah class' of revolutionaries aiming their weapons at the heart of the homeland. Today, foreign influence and control is both immediately known and resented, and produces its inevitable reaction. The problem for the neo-conservatives in Washington who seek to 'remake' the Middle East is that they will run everywhere right up against this basic force of human dignity. Few people will agree to being 'remade', even remade into democrats – from outside. And sometimes, difficult though it may be for some western minds to grasp, even tyrants and puritan mullahs are preferable to foreigners and 'infidels'.

There is one sense in which Washington's twenty-first century form of power projection may be more sustainable than Britain's nineteenth century type. It is more subtle and indirect. Whereas imperial London (and imperial Rome) directly ruled over the lives of millions of people around the globe, Washington does not (apart, that is, from its armies in Iraq and in Afghanistan). Instead, it tends to exercise its power on local governments through trade, aid and investment and through international institutions like the IMF and the World Bank and, increasingly, by the *threat* of direct military power.

Modern Americans, brought up on anti-colonialist rhetoric, do not warm to the idea of empire. And, incredible though it seems to millions around the world, most Americans truly do not believe they possess one.

The exercise of American military power in the 1990s and early 2000s – in the first Gulf War, in Serbia and Kosovo, in Afghanistan and Iraq – has given life to the critics' assertions that the mailed fist (of empire) lies behind the velvet glove (of economic influence). Even so, US power projection at the turn of the millennium was less overt and less intrusive than that used by Europe's empires. The old-style colonial power invaded, stayed and ruled – often for centuries. Today's American power projection, apart again from Iraq and Afghanistan, is normally intimidatory, in order to get local rulers to support US policy. Or it is of the 'hit and run' variety, which entails American military intervention (based upon air supremacy) and then leaves behind American-influenced governments to look after American interests, often with little purchase outside of the capital city, as in post-conflict Afghanistan.

But the future trends are ominous. With the US military operating two 'wars' – or what are technically occupations following invasions – in Iraq and Afghanistan, the US military is now being used more and more to bolster American influence abroad. This not only causes resentment in the occupied territories but also around the non-American world. And in 2008, in its campaign against nuclear proliferation, the US was contemplating using air power to destroy the nuclear facilities of Iran, and presumably afterwards would leave a regime in power in a strategically important area of the world which would be decidedly unfriendly to the bombers.

THE AMERICAN MESSAGE?

As well as economic strength and domestic support, superpowers have normally possessed a message for the world – something they are, or an idea or ideology they stand for, that is good and positive and attracts the world peoples (or makes them temper their hatred). In the nineteenth century Britain's ideology was of good governance and Christianity; in the same era the French had 'Frenchness', its language and culture, and human rights. In the twentieth century the Soviet Union had the idea of communism – a new world of equality where no one would be oppressed; and America promoted the ideology of democracy and freedom (and mass consumer prosperity).

Positive perceptions of America were commonplace around the world during the late twentieth century. In large parts of the world, not just in advanced Europe, the country was seen as a breath of fresh air – it was a 'liberator' following its entry in two wars against dictators, its open society, with its popular films and music, was infectious, and its economic system, American capitalism, was admired and copied. And, above all, during the Cold War it was the home base for that part of the world that was non-communist.

Yet, towards the latter years of the Cold War this generally friendly disposition had begun to change. around the turn of the millennium, in the last years of the Clinton presidency and the first years of the presidency of George W. Bush. America's closest allies and civilisational partners were to be found in Europe, and in the view of many Europeans and, slowly, of many Americans too, the USA was becoming a country in trouble. In popular perceptions there was unease that the superpower that had won the Cold War was frittering away the peace in an economic bubble (fuelled by a 'hi-tech' bubble) that would soon burst. This unease was made worse by the tawdry Monica Lewinsky scandal, followed by an impeachment, and then, in 2000, by the first ever American president to be put in office by the Supreme Court (and not the people). It was all grist for the mill of a lurking, alternative, view of America – as distorted as was the earlier, rosier, view – of an increasingly uncivil society, a nation ridden with violent crime and racial tension, with cut-throat competition, huge inequalities and without a welfare state.

These changes in European attitudes towards the USA started to reveal themselves in the opinion polls in late 2002 – after 9/11 and before the invasion of Iraq! The fact that 71 per cent of French people thought the 'spread of American ideas and customs is a bad thing' was high, but not surprising; what, though, was shocking was that 67 per cent of Germans, 58 per cent of Italians and 50 per cent of British people thought the same thing.[26] All this prompted the leading neo-conservative Robert Kagan to argue, in his 2003 bestselling book *Paradise and Power*, that 'Americans are from Mars and Europeans are from Venus' and 'it is time to stop pretending that Americans and Europeans share a common view of the world.'[27] And, as Europeans began to change their views about the USA, their views about their own continent also changed. For the first time since 1945, many Europeans began to believe they lived in better societies than their American counterparts, that they had a higher standard of life – certainly in the cities – with less violent crime and racial tension and better welfare states. And, following the attack on the Twin Towers, the USA was just as vulnerable to terrorism as they had been. They also began to sense a power shift across the Atlantic and a geopolitical vacuum into which Europe could begin to assert itself, even become an alternative superpower.

More important than European opinion was the steady erosion of support for America in the Middle East. In the Arab world the US in the Eisenhower and Kennedy years was seen as a friend, even to some of the modernising Arab nationalists – certainly so when compared to the hostile European colonial powers that had ruled the region since the collapse of the Ottomans, and had invaded Egypt in 1956. But since then it was all downhill – and the descent in relations was a product of traditional 'Third World' anti-imperial sentiment. American support for Israel was seen as another example, by proxy, of western colonial rule, a sentiment made worse by the clear imperial-like Israeli occupation of Palestinian lands. And American support for the despotic Arabic sheikdoms reinforced the imperial rather than 'liberator' image, as did the invasion and occupation of the heart of Arabia in 2003.

By the turn of the century 'the Arab Street' had joined the 'Latin American Street' and the 'Pakistani Street', and increasingly 'the Iranian Street', in seeing the United States as an adversary. American talk of 'democracy' was but a mask. It was all about force. America was an empire like all the others before her. And it could be said, and was, that in 2003 the USA lost the last believers in her as a force for progress, as an 'exceptional' democratic power, in the sands of Arabia.

CHAPTER SEVEN

DISASTER FOR THE MIDDLE CLASS

The CNN commentator and presenter Lou Dobbs is an unusual journalist. Originally a fiscal conservative he describes himself as an 'independent populist'. For many years before the 2007 banking crisis forced the issue he was breaking ranks and telling Americans what he saw as some unvarnished home truths about the excesses and the weaknesses of Wall Street capitalism. For a time Dobbs was something of an eccentric lone voice in the often conformist financial media community as he pointed to the underlying structural weaknesses, the loss of jobs to low cost areas, the stagnation of wages, the growing debt, and the global imbalances – all of which, for many years, simply went unreported.

The reasons were simple. Since 9/11 the gripping fear of terrorism deflected Americans from their gathering economic troubles. But, both before 9/11, and in the years when its memory faded, these weaknesses also went largely unreported. For many commentators they were hardly discernible – after all the leaders of media corporations and many of their journalists were high net worth individuals and continued to do well and were shielded from facing the growing strains on normal family budgets. Growing poverty became something of an issue, but, as long as it was still a minority phenomenon restricted to the traditional underclass of urban African-Americans, it was not to become an urgent media concern. Another reason was more elevated. The American (or 'Anglo-Saxon') model of capitalism survives, and often thrives, on confidence, and there is an in-built mechanism in the system's news and propaganda outlets that blocks out bad news – until, that is, it becomes impossible to ignore.

Wall Street capitalism had certainly been dynamic and 'innovative'. And for its supporters, although it had produced inequalities (what didn't?) and egregious wealth for some, its growth record outweighed these problems. Tony Blair's aide Peter Mandelson, the guru behind New Labour, was famously 'relaxed' about the arrival of the mega-rich – as long, that is, that 'the rising tide lifted all ships'. Yet, as the 1990s progressed there was a growing awareness that the much-touted new capitalism had a dark social underside. It was becoming clearer by the month that some ships were beginning to sink.

And by century's turn the new, rawer, global capitalism was no longer lifting even 'most' ships. A more suitable metaphor for the new capitalism was that of a super yacht – where those who can scramble aboard are safe, secure and become increasingly wealthy – surrounded by many smaller ships in trouble, with many sinking. This 'sinking' was even confirmed by US Federal Reserve chairman Alan Greenspan, who, in 1997, conceded that during his own time at the helm America had witnessed an absolute decline – sometimes quite steeply – in the living standards of millions of US individuals and families; a similar worrying decline to that which had occurred in that other highly global-friendly nation, Britain.[1]

Lou Dobbs was starting to say, loudly, that the problem was not restricted to growing poverty. The broad American middle class itself was in danger. And when CNN allowed him to host a regular economics show called 'The War On The Middle Class' it was a sign that times were changing and myths were being bust. For a mainstream broadcaster such a title, let alone the show's often radical content, would have been unthinkable some years previously.

Dobbs's campaign started to take off when the middle class issue dominated the presidential primary election campaign of 2007/8. And these growing middle class insecurities and anxieties were directly and viscerally blamed on the actions of big corporations. One of the candidates, former Senator John Edwards, developed an anti-corporate rhetoric with a populist edge that had not been heard in America since the days of Huey P. Long in the 1930s. And some of his themes – including the need for more trade protection to save jobs – were taken up by the other candidates, Senators Barack Obama and Hillary Clinton. And in the presidential campaign itself the Democratic Vice-Presidential Candidate, Senator Joe Biden of Delaware, went even further. Brushing aside criticisms of stirring up 'class war' he raised in high-profile fashion the normally marginalised issue of the growing inequalities of America. The fact was that by the election year of 2008, the two-decade-long consensus built up behind global market capitalism was beginning to falling apart.

Dobbs saw the middle class as the great backbone of America – indeed the great achievement of postwar American capitalism. And indeed it was. But it was an earlier 'social' capitalism – that mix of private and public and social and market that operated from the 1950s to the late 1970s – that had created that most historically elusive of outcomes: rising profits and a rise in the income and living standards of almost everyone. This 'social' capitalism had certainly not banished inequality, but it was a political economy in which 'a rising tide lifted most ships'. And in the 1950s this middle class was forming the very character of American social life – a life depicted by the term 'the American dream'.

This middle class society was 'diamond-shaped' – with a large middle, and at the bottom a relatively small underclass in the inner cities, and at the top a tiny, almost invisible, group of the very rich. It was also highly stable: the stability guaranteed by wave after wave of immigrant blue-collar workers and their families as they secured rising living standards and 'improved themselves' through mass consumerism and mass education and then identified with, and supported, the system.

THE WAR ON THE MIDDLE CLASS

It is the potential end of this 'dream' that was (is) devastating news for advocates of Wall Street's global capitalism. For there is now no longer a widespread expectation that the coming generations in the West will live better than the present ones. Indeed the opposite is true. Many will have a lower living standard and increasing insecurity at work.

In the two western societies most integrated into the global economy – the US and Britain – there was clear evidence that declining or stagnant living standards for large numbers of their peoples was well underway as early as the mid-1990s. That these warnings were ignored by the policymakers of the time was, though, not surprising. To fix the problem would be difficult, indeed politically impossible – for it would mean confronting both established interests and governing ideology. And, thankfully, the politicians of the 1990s were able to avoid addressing the subject because, by the late 1990s the growth, and potential future growth, in private debt – the developing debt bubble – would bring much needed help to strained family budgets.

This fall (or stagnation) in living standards was best revealed by the official figures which showed falls in average hourly income. (Hourly income remains a good guide to living standards because although some household income might show a rise this was only because one or more family members were working harder with two or even three jobs. A 'working until they drop' culture is not a sign of rising living standards).

One startling statistic tells the story of a long-term, 20 year, downward trend: in 1997 the average hourly earnings in the US were below those in 1977! According to some calculations the average hourly earnings of production workers in private industry in the US fell in real terms between 1987 and 1996 by as much as 7 per cent (wages rose by 31 per cent but inflation, as measured by the Consumer Prices Index, rose during the same period by 38 per cent). And between 1987 and 1996 the average hourly earnings of production workers in the private sector rose from \$8.98 to \$11.81, but in the same period prices (the CPI) rose from 113.6 to 156.9.[2] The lower two-fifths of the population seem to have been hit particularly hard, with millions of US workers and their families seeing their standard of living fall as a result of the minimum wage being 25 per cent lower in 1997 than it was in 1970.

These falls often mean that, as the *Der Speigel* journalist Gabor Steingart has remarked 'the affluence on display in their [US middle class] living rooms is nothing but a modern form of fraud. And no one should be fooled by seemingly well-to-do suburbs, where banks own many of the cars parked in garages and driveways.'[3]

Ships were sinking throughout the fleet. Professor Alan Krueger, chief economist of the US Labor Department in the mid-1990s reported income falls across the spectrum:

> From 1979 to 1989, the inflation-adjusted wage rate of the worker in the bottom 10th percentile – someone earning just above the minimum wage – fell by an astounding 16%. The real wage of the median worker fell by 2%. Only higher income workers did well: at the 90th percentile pay increased by 5%. From 1989 to 1997, real wages for workers at the bottom essentially stopped falling and the growth of wages for workers at the top continued at a more moderate pace. *But the wages for workers in the middle – the vast American middle class – continued to erode, with the median workers wage falling 5% since 1989.*[4]

Harvard academic Robert Lawrence has set this dramatic fall in American wages in its proper historical context. He argues that for a hundred years, between the 1870s and the 1970s, average real wages in the US doubled every thirty-five years, and consequently 'each successive generation lived twice as well as its predecessor'. Now, however, this American dream no longer holds, for Lawrence reports that since 1973 the 'real wage growth in the US has departed sharply from its long-term trend. Between 1973 and 1994 real compensation increased by just 8.6% – less than half a percent a year...it [compensation] lagged considerably behind the 24% rise in output per hour recorded over the same period.'[5]

In new capitalist Britain there were similar disconcerting trends in wage rates. During the 1980s income inequality certainly increased – as Stephen Jenkins reported, 'income levels rose for most, but were stagnant for the poorest income groups'.[6] However, during the 1990s, as the full force of globalisation hit the British economy, some incomes began to fall, and average real earnings also fell. Weekly pay for the lowest 10 per cent of males and the lowest 25 per cent of females fell between 1989 and 1995. Also the average weekly hours worked by the lowest decile rose, whereas for the highest decile they fell.[7] Real median earnings were £228 per week in the spring of 1993 but had fallen to £225 by the spring of 1996. A spokesman for the British Labour Party, which was in opposition at the time and not yet fully Blairised, placed the blame on the 'flexible labour market'. These bleak figures, he argued, were the result of 'well paid full-time jobs…over a period being replaced by badly paid part-time jobs'.[8]

THE JOBS CRISIS

The falls in earned income during the 1990s took place in a changed environment for labour, and for work more generally. As it took hold, the new capitalism was ensuring that labour was both less secure and less valued. Increasing job insecurity followed naturally from the progressive introduction of the 'flexible labour market' – one of the central pillars of the new globalism, an approach lauded across the Anglo-Saxon political spectrum from Ronald Reagan's conservatives in the 1980s through to Tony Blair's New Labourites in the late 1990s. At the heart of the argument for a flexible labour market was the not unreasonable notion that no one should expect a job for life.

The postwar American dream was never based upon a job for life. However, for most middle-class Americans in the pre-globalisation era relatively secure work was certainly an expectation; as was the ability, if the family was prepared to move to a new location, to find equally well paid or better paid work elsewhere. And umbilically linked to this secure work – an integral part of the job, indeed often a recruiting tool – was a package of benefits, including healthcare and pension coverage. In Britain, too, relatively secure, adequately paid work, with the back-up of state health and pension benefits, was also an expectation.

The labour market created by the new era of global capital brought to an end these expectations. It did so by systematically replacing full-time work by part-time, thus creating a huge 'contingent' workforce. It has been estimated that in the US during the 1990s temporary worker agencies – such as Kelly Services and Manpower – grew twice as fast as the nation's GNP.[9] It has been estimated that all kinds of 'contingent labour' – contract and temporary workers, involuntary part-timers, employees of subcontractors, and homeworkers – grew by a staggering 120 per cent in the first half of the 1980s.[10] The US Bureau of Labor Statistics has noted that the number of part-time workers rose to 19.5 per cent of the workforce in 1994, up from 14 per cent in 1968, but according to Susan Houseman of the Upjohn Institute, such data fails to account for the 'growing number of Americans who hold *two* part-time jobs, or a full-time and a part-time job. They appear instead in the official count as full-timers, working a total of more than 35 hours per week.'[11]

In Britain in all types of household part-time work is increasing: 5.9 million worked part-time in December 1992, rising to 6.3 million in September 1996 (five million of these being women). In Britain between 1979 and 1993 full-time work fell dramatically – by a huge 10 per cent. Will Hutton has calculated that between 1975 and 1993 the proportion of the adult population in full-time tenured jobs fell dramatically from 55 per cent to 35 per cent. And many of these, he argues, were not wholly defined by their income, which ranged widely from high to low, but rather by their insecurity.[12]

And in both Britain and the US, as the economic boom of the late 1990s gathered pace – ahead of the inevitable recession – many new jobs were created, but most of these much-touted additions to the job pool were of the part-time, contingent variety. 'Contingent labour' is difficult to define properly – for instance some analysts believe it should include self-employed independent contractors (the kind of worker who is a victim of corporate downsizing). Even so, a 1995 US Bureau of Labor Statistics study, which defines contingent labour as individuals who do not possess an implicit or explicit ongoing contract of work, suggests that 15 per cent of wage and salary workers are contingent.[13]

In any event, the rise of contingent labour has produced a new pattern of corporate employment based upon an inner core and outer periphery of employees. In the summer of 1997 the *New York Times* ran a controversial series of reports from across the country on the effects of downsizing. It reported that:

> at many companies, an upper tier of full time core workers enjoys the best combination of pay, benefits, hours and job security that a company can offer. Below them is a second tier of less valued part-time, temporary and contract workers who, in addition to being less expensive, can be discharged more easily, giving corporate managers the flexibility that they say is essential to compete in an increasingly global economy.[14]

Of course this new system of contingent labour (and, more generally, the flexible labour market), which is demanded by the global economy, does in some senses serve the needs of people, of labour as well as of capital. Flexibility and part-time working appeals to many women and some men because it fits in with their family responsibilities. And in principle labour flexibility is a highly appropriate mechanism for an advanced, complex society.

However the 'hire and fire' economy of the Anglo-American globalised system is not essentially a response to changing social needs. Rather it has taken advantage of them in order to save costs. Contingent labour relieves the employer from burdensome social costs such as having to pay expensive health-care benefits or pensions. In the US this amounts to a major breach by capital and corporations of an unspoken social contract whereby the middle class, who could expect little or no state support for health, could rely upon their employer to provide healthcare benefits as part of a relatively secure job contract. In Britain the plug has also been pulled on another social contract – the increasing army of contingent workers used to be able to rely upon a relatively adequate benefit system, but now see it progressively eroded.

Flexible labour markets make it easy for capital to respond quickly to changing market conditions by being able to hire and fire easily. However this too often means that employees, rather than the so-called capitalist 'risk-takers', bear the risks of the free-market system. What is more there is no evidence whatsoever that the hire and fire economies have done any better than those with more regulated labour markets.

HIDDEN UNEMPLOYMENT

Karl Marx famously coined the idea of a 'reserve army of the unemployed' acting as a weapon that could be used by employers to discipline workers. As the number of core workers has shrunk and that of contingent workers has risen, modern global capitalism now has its own 'reserve army' available – and, in a sense unknown to Marx, on a global scale! Of course many part-time workers, unlike the unemployed of old, are not seeking full-time work and therefore cannot be counted as 'reserve' in the Marxist sense; however, many, many are, and with welfare being pared down, with more income needed in traditional households and with the growth of single parent families and people living alone (who need a proper wage, not a supplementary one), the demand for full-time, benefit-linked work will always be high.

Contingent, part-time work serves another function too. Western governments, in this media age when public relations seems all-important, are fighting a constant battle of presentation. The growth in part-time work serves to hide the extent of unemployment. During the 1970s the unemployment rate began to rise across the OECD world – up from 3 per cent at the beginning of the decade to an average of about 6 per cent at the end. The 1980s saw unemployment rise further, denting the view that unemployment was a passing phase, linked to economic cycles.

In the early 1990s, with the corporate mania for downsizing in full swing, it became obvious that structural factors such as changing technology and footloose global capital in search of low costs were causing high unemployment. Harry Shutt has pointed to technology as being partly responsible for this higher unemployment, and as a reason for the new phenomenon known as 'jobless growth', particularly in Europe. He argues that 'taking the 1974 to 1994 period as a whole, there has been negligible growth in the numbers of employed people in the countries of the European Union at a time when the level of economic activity (GDP) has expanded significantly', and he pointed to the example of Spain, where employment fell by over 8 per cent during the period whilst the economy virtually doubled in size!¹⁵

In the late 1990s the peak of the Anglo-American boom did create a tightish labour market and an American 'jobs miracle' was proclaimed. But the high employment figures hid the fundamental – and grave – changes that were overwhelming the world of work. For included in the employment numbers were millions and millions of employees who were not in full-time, secure work, were not in adequately paid work and – more harrowing even than that – were not in work that provided adequate social benefits. In fact, included in US 'employed' figures are 'day labourers and people who survive on odd jobs', for 'all it takes to be listed as "employed" is to have one hour of work a week'. This American 'jobs miracle' was a statistical con-game. And at the heart of the myth of late 1990s 'full employment' was the assumption – accepted by most of the Anglo-American media – that high employment meant high living standards. The *New York Times* issued a contrarian position when it argued that 'a lower jobless rate means little if a $15 an hour factory worker is fired and earns only half of that in his next job'.¹⁶

Rarely was the question asked of the new millions of low paid workers in Anglo-America: would you prefer to be 'in work' in the US or Britain, or unemployed and on welfare in France or Germany? Millions of those employed in Britain or the US would have answered in favour of the continental European option.

NAGGING INSECURITY

But perhaps the most important consequence of the new 'flexible labour market' at the heart of the new Wall Street capitalism was the widespread and profound insecurity it engendered. Insecurity is indefinable, and its extent is not statistically provable. Yet over the last two decades it has interwoven through the fabric of the working populations of the free-market economies. The signs of anxiety are there for everyone to see: employees work longer and longer hours, workers stay late at the office, not in order to finish necessary work but to secure their positions, and there is an increase in useless paperwork to justify jobs and salaries.

Of course job insecurity certainly keeps people on their toes, as well as on other people's toes, but there is no evidence that it produces higher growth rates than was the case in the more regulated and structured labour markets of the 1950s, 1960s and early 1970s. The jury is still out, and may always be out, on whether labour market competition and insecurity, or alternatively stability and cooperation, produce a more efficient economy.

And, anyway, aside from the economics of it all, there was the fact that in the new capitalist society insecurity was (is) unequally spread. Owning capital was supposed to be a risk-taking enterprise, but was increasingly becoming a more secure way to live than the risks inherent in the world of work. Even in a financially turbulent world, even too in a financial meltdown, the risks to capital were becoming far less than the risks associated with holding a job, particularly in the private sector. Capital ownership provided many more real choices, and opportunities for diversification and manipulation, than did (does) a job. Investments are highly unlikely to do badly in good times, and even if shares and bonds plummet there is normally some capital left. Often the worst that can happen is a reduction from a lavish to a high living standard – from a large to a small yacht, from three Mercedes to one, from three or four homes to just two. Yet the loss of a job, particularly with few state benefits available, alters a whole way of life.

For most people in the West under pensionable age, income from employment remains the very foundation of their lifestyle, if not their life. Other sources of income – dividends from shares, interest from bonds, small inheritances, rent – may help out, but tend to be marginal. Jobs remain the name of the game – and the character of employment – particularly its security – becomes important. For the employed majority, if not for those who employ them, the new capitalism's destruction of traditional job security was a real blow. And by destroying the good secure job (with pensions and benefits) it was also destroying one of the building blocks of the American and western middle class.

Flexible, 'hire and fire' labour policies may also have caused some wider problems in society. The world of disposable jobs may well have induced a short-termism into the work culture that would feed through into broader social values. Richard Sennett, in his fascinating book *The Corrosion of Character: The Personal Consequences of Work in the New Capitalism*, argues that this connection is very real. It appears that 'when people talk in earnest about family values, "no long term" is no way to raise children. We want them, for instance to learn how to be loyal; a management consultant told me he felt stupid talking to his children about commitment, since at work he does not practice it.' Sennett also argues, intriguingly, that hire and fire labour flexibility may undermine the work ethic: 'the classic work ethic was one of delayed gratification: coping with immediate frustration usually requires a sense of sustaining purpose, of long-term goals. The flexible work ethic undermines such self discipline; you must seize the moment, delay may prove fatal.'[17]

THE DEVALUATION OF WORK

The American (and western) middle class was forged on the work ethic. The capitalist system of the twentieth century, which created this middle class, differed from the old aristocratic system it replaced by exalting productivity and creativity – that is, work – over lineage. And by mid-century almost everyone – the medium and small businesses, the professional classes, even the big corporate bosses – was defining themselves by their work, and by securing their money 'the old fashioned way' – by earning it.

Yet the new globalised economy, and the new capitalism it created, was turning this value system on its head. Work itself was becoming devalued. Earning money, as opposed to making or having money, was becoming more and more difficult. It was a stark fact, but in the 1990s earned income (wages and salaries) actually fell as a percentage of total income. Global capitalism was at least becoming clear about its priorities: lower rewards from work, higher rewards from investments and inheritance. And there were big rewards too for going into debt. The average American no longer worked to pay for a house – you could buy it, and sell it, for a huge profit, all in the same week by the clever use of debt.

From 1989-95 US wages were stagnant or declining for the vast majority of the workforce – amounting to 80 per cent of working men and 70 per cent of working women. And this was during a time when profits were at a postwar high. For instance the average after-tax profit rate for non-farm businesses was 7.5 per cent in 1994 compared with an average 3.8 per cent in the 1952-79 period. 'By the close of the second quarter of 1995, the return on equity for Standard and Poor's list of five hundred major blue chip companies was running at an annual rate of 20% – the best ever for corporate America.'[18] Another estimate, reported in the *Wall Street Journal*, was that corporate profit margins in the US rose between 1989 and 1996 from 6 per cent to 9 per cent.[19] The same trend was observable in Britain. Looking at the same issue from a different vantage point, income from employment (wages) diminished as a ratio of all household disposable income from 90.4 per cent in 1977 to 73.3 per cent in 1994, while income from rents, dividends and interest grew from 10.7 per cent to 13.6 per cent and even benefits rose as a proportion of income.[20]

In the George W. Bush years the story was more of the same. US wages continued to stagnate – with real earnings over the period November 2001 to November 2006 actually falling somewhat. And between 2006 and 2007, even though growth was rising and profits were high, real wages actually declined (real hourly by 0.7 per cent and real weekly by 0.9 per cent).[21] It was a period which may indeed have seen real earnings and wages declining, but it also saw consumption rising – from about 67 per cent of GDP in 2000 to 71 per cent in 2005. It was becoming clear that the driver of this consumption was debt, including huge amounts of mortgage debt. With their real wages stagnant or falling Americans were being encouraged to live beyond their means.

WAGES VERSUS INVESTMENTS

One look at the riches and rewards created by investments – as opposed to wages and salaries – shows the advantages in the new economy of investing over working. Charles Handy calculated that 'A £10 million investment, for example, which is made on the expectation that it will recover its costs in ten years' time and provide a 20% compound return, will, in the next ten years, if the expectation is met and if things continue the same, earn an extra £26.4 million, and even more in the years following.'[22]

Of all the income coming into all the households in the US and British economies during the height of the new global capitalist boom the share of pay went down and the share from interest, dividends and straight gifts (inheritance) went up. Of course much of this was concentrated at the top. Take shares. In Britain there remained a marked difference between the wealth holdings of the top 1 per cent and the rest – the top 1 per cent holding almost half of their portfolios in shares whereas less wealthy groups held progressively less and less in shares.[23]

Inheritance payouts are also concentrated at the top but are now becoming increasingly widespread. Inherited wealth is very big business, perhaps the biggest business of all in today's global capitalist economy. The British free-market Conservative government in the 1990s talked approvingly of a future economy dominated by inherited wealth as wealth 'cascaded down the generations'. As the new capitalist era got underway in the early 1990s Robert Avery of Cornell University predicted that 'we will shortly be seeing the largest transfer of income in the history of the world'.[24] And around the same time political scientist Kevin Phillips also argued that inheritance is 'about to become a critical component of the younger generation's future, *something America has never before experienced*'.[25]

THE WORKING POOR: THE WONDERFUL WORLD OF WAL-MART

Perhaps the single most powerful illustration of global capitalism's devaluation of work, and of earned income, is the growth on both sides of the Atlantic of the working poor. These are the millions of people who put in 'a fair day's work' but end up without 'a fair day's pay'.

In the early years of the new century the American 'new economy' retailer Wal-Mart became the symbol of such low pay and conditions. There were even reports that in parts of the Wal-Mart empire their workers were depending on federal food stamps and the use of hospital emergency rooms for basic medical care. From being the darling brand of the new 'flexible economy' in the 1990s Wal-Mart's labour practices became highly controversial – so much so that by 2007 Democratic politicians in the presidential campaign found the company an easy target.[26]

In the US, the Bureau of Labor Statistics defines the working poor as 'persons who worked (or were looking for work) during twenty-seven weeks of the year, and who lived in families below the official poverty line'.[27] Where this 'poverty line' falls is obviously contentious, but what is not in dispute is the fact that large numbers of people in work are paid very low amounts of money – in 2005 42 per cent of American individuals had an income of less than $25,000 per year and about 20 per cent of American individuals (40 million people) had an income of $12,500 or less.[28]

In Britain, where there is no official 'poverty line' or count of the number living in poverty, low pay, in reality 'poverty pay', is also a feature of the employment landscape. In 1991 a staggering 28 per cent of those with *less than half average income* were in households with some kind of income from work, including a third who were self-employed.[29] Over a decade and a half later – with 'low pay' now increasingly defined as 60-70 per cent of median pay – then around 20-30 per cent of *all incomes* were in this category.[30] The low value set for the minimum wage in both the US and Britain tells the whole story of poverty pay.

Of course for some, poverty pay is simply an addition to family income. As Paul Gregg and Jonathan Wadsworth have reported about Britain, 'new jobs – often McJobs – are taken disproportionately by those with another household member already at work'.[31] For others low pay is acceptable if it places you on the ladder to higher pay. And for some, work, any work at virtually any pay, will suffice because of the need to be in a working environment. However none of these arguments outweighs the attack that low pay makes upon the work ethic. For if work is underpaid it will be undervalued. Nor do they outweigh arguments about equity. For it remains difficult to argue that the gap between the ability, creativity and dedication of the working poor and that of the modern inheriting class is large enough to begin to justify the gap between them in income and wealth.

NO WAY BACK

The new capitalism's devaluation of work – of jobs and wages – and its elevation of globally operated capital and investment, has not only eroded the traditional middle class; it is also in the process of entrenching deep social divisions. The old 'diamond-shaped' social structure, with a large and stable middle class, continues to give way to a new structure in which extremes of wealth and poverty co-exist with a disappearing middle – the bulk of which are disappearing as they become downwardly mobile. In 1991 Robert Reich designed an important graphical representation of this changing income distribution in the US which holds good for the new century as well: a sagging, elongated wave, where a 'symmetrical wave' described how the rich were getting richer as the poor got poorer, with the middle beginning to sag. He suggested that throughout the 1950s and 1960s 'most Americans were bunching up in the middle, enjoying medium incomes...But beginning in the mid-1970s, and accelerating sharply in the 1980s, the crest of the wave began to move toward the poorer end. More Americans were poor. The middle began to sag, as the portion of middle-income Americans dropped. And the end representing the richest Americans began to elongate, as the rich became much, much, richer.'[32]

As I outlined in Chapter One a mega- and super-rich class (with income deriving from inheritance and investment rather than work) is now an embedded feature of western society. The economist Paul Krugman has argued that the much vaunted 'Anglo-Saxon' new capitalism model is not only not producing the broad and vibrant middle class of so-called 'knowledge workers'; but rather the model is generating 'the rise of a narrow oligarchy' with 'income and wealth becoming increasingly concentrated in the hands of a small privileged elite.'[33]

The problem is not just growing inequality – it is much deeper, and worrying. For what the two decades of new capitalism has wrought in the West is the *entrenching of classes* and the virtual end of mobility. An American child born in the bottom fifth income group has just a 1 per cent chance of joining the top 5 per cent of American earners.[34] Today, in a startling reversal, it is Europe's so-called 'sclerotic' societies that are arguably more mobile that those of the famed 'dynamic' 'Anglo-Saxons.' The Centre For American Progress in Washington, published in late April 2006, a report on mobility which concluded that the chances of Americans remaining in the same bracket as their parents is higher than in every other developed country except the UK.[35]

GLOBAL CAPITAL AND SOCIAL DIVISIONS

There is clear evidence that the US, Britain and New Zealand are amongst the lead players in this story of rising inequality and social division. And one major reason why these 'Anglo-Saxon' new capitalist economies generate greater inequalities and social divisions than do their continental European counterparts is that they are more exposed to the dictates of global-isation with its 'free-market' imperatives.

It was during the 1980s that first signs of a difference between 'Anglo-Saxon' inequality levels and continental European ones became apparent. There were, in fact, increases in the measure of inequality for all leading western nations, with the intriguing exception of France. In the US the Gini index rose from 31 to 34 (compared with 27 to 31 for Britain, 25 to 27 for the Netherlands and 23 to 23.5 for Belgium). OECD figures also show that the US had the highest percentage of low-income persons of any of the OECD countries. And in the 1990s – as 'globalisation' grew apace – an in-depth OECD study of inequality in the leading western nations, published in 1995, showed that the US was leading the world in terms of inequality, with Canada second, Australia third, Britain fourth and New Zealand and France joint fifth. Interestingly, most of the continental European nations – those shielded from the full impact of 'globalisation' by a social mar-ket or social democratic tradition – came well down the field, and Norway, the Netherlands, Belgium, Finland and Sweden would have had to more than double their inequality ratios to match the US.[36] Latest figures, for 2007, show the United States with a co-efficient number at 45, the UK at 34, and France and Germany both at 28.[37]

During the 'Thatcher revolution' the UK adjusted to the emerging global economy more fully than any other western nation. Indeed Britain became the most 'globalised' of all major economies – and virtually a laboratory for testing the future of 'market globalisation'. Thatcher argued that 'there is no alterna-tive' to 'globalisation'. But her victory was bought at a price: a new era of growing inequality. Before 1976, and Britain's revo-lutionary 'adjustment' to global economics, life in the country had been becoming more and more equal in terms of both income and wealth. After thirty years of social democracy Britain was probably a more equal society than it had ever been before, and may ever be again. According to John Hills, the index for income after direct taxes in Britain stood at 47-59 in 1913 (the precise figure elusive for that time), 43 in 1938, 35 in 1949, 36.6 in 1964 and 32 in 1974-5. From the mid-1970s, as the social effects of 'globalisation' began to take hold, the inequality index rose dramatically and by 1984-5 it had reached 36.2. According to Hills, 'the rise in inequality after 1978 is more than large enough to offset all of the decline in inequality between 1949 and 1976-7, and almost large enough to take it back to 1938'. Similar trends towards inequality have been reported for New Zealand, another globalised 'free market' country made defenceless against 'globalisation' in the 1980s. Between 1981 and 1989 the New Zealand equality index (Gini coefficient) rose by almost three points – from 26.7 to 29.5, a larger percentage rise than that of the US in the 1980s.[38]

In the US itself, the primary driver and host to global capitalism, inequality also rose sharply in the 1980s and 1990s, a trend made more remarkable by the fact that it had also risen during the 1970s. In 1994 the Council of Economic Advisors reported that 'starting some time in the late 1970s income inequalities widened alarmingly in America'. In the 1980s the average income of the poorest fifth of American families actually declined by about 7 per cent whilst the richest fifth became about 15 per cent wealthier (a stark statistic which left, in 1990, the poorest fifth with only 3.7 per cent of the nation's income and the richest fifth with a little over half!). Among all advanced countries where data for the 1980s are available, the US showed the most dramatic expansion of inequality, a social division that one American scholar argued was 'lethal to our middle class way of life'.[39]

By 1994 the share of the US income cake held by the poorest fifth of Americans had declined to 3.4 per cent. Between 1992 and 1996 American families in all the lowest income groups – those earning less than $10,000 a year through to those in the $50-75 000 category – received a smaller share of the nation's total pretax income whereas those in the higher categories – $75,000 to $200,000 or more, received an increase. One sure sign of increasing inequality within the US was the diverging income shares of the middle quintile and the top one per cent of the US population. Between 1987 and 1998 the income share of the middle quintile fell from 16.3 per cent to 14.3 whereas that of the top 1 per cent rose dramatically, from 8.3 to 13.5 per cent.[40] By 1998 even official predictions foresaw increasing inequality.[41]

This growth of inequality in the US is closely related to education and skill levels. And there is a link between education level and 'competitiveness' in the global economy. Unskilled workers are increasingly 'uncompetitive' globally while higher skilled workers are still, for the moment, 'competitive'. The figures are dramatic. Between 1979 and 1995 real wages for workers with less than 12 years of education fell by 20.2 per cent, whilst those with 12 years fell by 13.4 per cent and those with sixteen plus rose by 1 per cent.[42]

WEALTH INEQUALITY

Of course income inequality is only one measure of the social division in western nations. Wealth also counts. And the story of wealth distribution in the 'new capitalist' states of the US and Britain since the late 1970s is a striking one. We have already (in Chapter One) recorded the egregious wealth of the mega-rich; but the extent of wealth *inequality* in the US in the last two decades is, perhaps, an even bigger story.

The situation in the 1990s is illustrated by the fact that in 1995 the mega-wealthy (the top ½ per cent, or 500,000 families) controlled 24.2 per cent of assets and 27.5 per cent of net worth, the top 1 per cent of American households (about one million) possessed 31 per cent of assets and 35.1 per cent of net worth, the next 9 per cent (the affluent) possessed 31 per cent of assets and 33.2 per cent of net worth, and all the rest (over 89 million households) only possessed 37.9 per cent of assets and 31.5 per cent of net worth.'[43]

By 2004 wealth inequality had grown even further, and there was evidence that the mega- and super-rich were pulling away from everyone else, including the merely affluent. Figures show that the top quartile (25 per cent of people) owned 87 per cent of the country's wealth, the upper middle quartile owned 10 per cent, the lower middle quartile 3 per cent and the bottom quartile 0 per cent. They also show that between 1995 and 2004 the gap between the top quarter and the 'lower middle' quarter had risen by almost a third. A 2007 report from Harvard University argued that 'by the early 1990s, the United States had surpassed all industrial societies in the extent of inequality of household wealth'; and it also argued that the economic growth of the most recent decade or so, from 1995 onwards, had seen 'growing inequality [of wealth] accompanying [this] wealth growth.'[44]

Not surprisingly Britain resembles the US in this 'wealth gap'. In Britain an unhealthy concentration of wealth is not new. Back in the 1930s the top 1 per cent owned as much 58 per cent of all the country's wealth. And the mass of Britons were capital-less and propertyless. As R. H. Tawney poignantly argued, Britons who fought during the First World War on the Somme and at Passchendale 'probably do not own wealth to the value of the kit they took into battle'. In the first seven decades of the twentieth century things changed significantly

– indeed dramatically – with the top 1 per cent's stake declining from 68 per cent in 1911 (for England and Wales) to 20 per cent in 1976 (for the UK as a whole). This half-century-long spreading of wealth, primarily the product of progressive tax policies, amounted to what Charles Feinstein has called 'a major economic and social revolution'.

However, in a clear measure of the reactionary effects of the new global market capitalism, this wealth 'revolution' stalled as the British economy became more globalised during the 1980s and 1990s when wealth distribution remained static. By the end of the 1980s – after a decade of Thatcherite market radicalism – the top 10 per cent of adults owned 45 per cent of the wealth, and 30 per cent of adults still had less than £5000 in assets. In the early 1990s the British super-rich – the top 1 per cent of the population, with an average wealth of $1.3 million each – owned a huge 18 per cent of the country's marketable wealth and the top 5 per cent owned a staggering 37 per cent of all wealth.[45] Even after Thatcher's 'popular capitalist' revolution (with its rhetoric of 'spreading the wealth' beyond the traditional landowning class) wealth and land still tended to go hand in hand. John Scott, in the most sophisticated analysis available, described the 'top twenty' of the British league of wealth as 'a mixture of urban and rural rentier landowners and entrepreneurial capitalists'. Scott argues that because research into this very murky area can only concentrate on relatively visible sources of wealth, and is often unable to penetrate into the anonymity of most shareholdings and bank accounts, rentiers, whose assets are concentrated in such anonymous investment portfolios, are normally underrepresented in any hierarchy of wealth holders. Even so, he argues that land and entrepreneurial capital remained the major sources of really large fortunes in the

1980s, and that 'the wealthiest landowners are the long established landowning families of Cadogan, Grosvenor, and
Portman, most of whom own substantial urban estates as well
as their country acres'.[46]

TOLERATING INEQUALITY, OPPOSING REDISTRIBUTION

The growing social divisions in western countries – particularly the startling, egregious concentrations of wealth amongst the
super-rich – are beginning to disturb a wide variety of people.
Many establishment figures worry about inequality in purely
prudential terms – about the point at which inequality will lead
to social upheaval, for example race riots in the US or class-
based upheaval in Europe. However there is a growing moral,
even aesthetic, dimension to this unease. Even some supporters
of the current free market system find such huge disparities
seriously troubling. Arthur Seldon has called them 'disturbing
and offensive', and Jeff Gates echoes a widespread view that the
time has come for a reassessment – 'now that these accumulations have reached what anyone would agree has no conceivable purpose other than to preclude others from the modest
accumulations essential to economic self-sufficiency'.[47]

The question for the new super-rich – 'how much is
enough?' – is now becoming insistent. Questioning egregious,
outlandish inequalities is a normal human response to excesses. It is certainly a question of taste, but also of basic social justice and an innate sense of fairness and proportion. Even
Americans, who tend to ask fewer questions than people from
other cultures about disproportionate financial rewards, 'have
a normative value set with which they judge a person's earnings as either fair, too high, or too low'.[48] This question of fairness – of proportion – particularly as sharp divisions are now
emerging in the domestic societies of the global economy, divi-

sions that may deepen with the coming downturn, is leading to a revival of the equality debate.

THE EQUALITY DEBATE

Contemporary capitalists may not much like equality, but capitalism has a surprisingly good record on the subject. In a sense, the history of western capitalism is also the history of growing equality – of the political kind. With the abandonment of slavery and serfdom the notion of equality of worth took hold. Political equality – 'one man one vote' and later 'one person one vote' – and legal equality – all are equal before the law – became fundamental precepts of western society during the capitalist twentieth century.

But political equality is one thing, economic equality another. Economic inequality, it is often said, is the price to be paid for economic efficiency; and a dynamic economy needs incentives and punishments which always produce inequality. This belief that economic equality is inefficient (it remains a belief, because equality has never been achieved) has dominated the Anglo-American postwar intellectual landscape, so much so that a firm consensus has formed behind it.

But not all the arguments against economic equality are about efficiency. Some rest upon moral propositions. Robert Nozick, echoing John Locke, believed that rights to property are so important that they should not be violated in the name of equality, as long, that is, as these rights are 'justly' acquired in the first place (but, as is usual with economic liberals, the question of whether, say, inheritance, is a 'just' method of acquiring property or capital rights, is left unanswered).[49] Another 'moral' argument against economic equality rests upon the proposition that inequality is fairer – this is the meritocratic view that it is unjust for talent and hard work to go unrewarded, the inevitable outcome in a strictly egalitarian system.

Interestingly, a presumption in favour of economic equality has not yet caught on amongst the broad mass of the western middle class. There exists a vague desire for social justice – a rejection of the unfairness and the wrongfulness of huge gulfs in living standards and life chances – but there is, as yet, no real popular support for measures of redistribution. It seems reasonable to believe that a passion for equality and the policies of redistribution will only appear when median income is falling and a large number of 'ships' are not rising but sinking. Should this be allied to an appreciation that disproportionate wealth and income is increasingly *unearned*, that upward mobility is not possible because of deep structural obstacles, then a real backlash against the inequities of global capitalism may begin.

Although the search for economic equality may not be a western ideal, a strong belief in 'equality of opportunity' certainly is – accepted by right, left and centre, Americans and Europeans alike. Yet, new global capitalism presents a real obstacle here. The new division between the global aristocracy (based on capital and inheritance) and 'sinking' 'uncompetitive' workers has so embedded privilege that it is now almost impossible to rise from bottom to top, from bottom to middle and from middle to top. Also, when the state was a serious player alongside the private sector then inequalities of wealth and income, though real, were less important, because many people of talent, ability and creativity could gain some purchase upon power and influence through public and political work (in parties, local and central government, and national and regional bodies). However in the era of global capitalism, when the state has been weakened and politics reduced, then those with wealth are the only ones with power. The old 'rags to riches' myth was never much of a reality, but today it is an utterly impossible dream.

There are now only two ways for western countries to go. They can either tolerate increasing inequality – a strategy which in the coming downturn will lead to social resentments, the growth of stealing and violence, and innumerable social problems. This route will need vast increases in public expenditure on prisons and police, if not on social welfare. Or, alternatively, we can change tack and try, by new policies, particularly tax and trade, to lessen these sharp inequalities with a degree of economic redistribution throughout the social structure. redistribution from the top to the middle will be the easy part; from the middle to the bottom will be much more politically fraught.

DEBT AND DISASTER

By the late 1990s, the gathering problem of stagnant – or falling – middle class incomes was becoming a talking point, if not in media commentary, then certainly in the world of think tanks and public policy forums. The politicians certainly knew of it. Yet, strangely, with so many family incomes in trouble, consumption levels remained high, and were fuelling what seemed to be endless economic growth.

There was a nagging question in the air: how, in these circumstances, could this extraordinary consumer boom be maintained? It remained a mystery. And no one, least of all western policymakers, was in a mood to answer it. For this was the time of the 'dot.com revolution' – in which America was leading the West into a new hi-tech world, a 'new economy', indeed a 'new paradigm' with new rules. The 'revolution' was in reality a 'bubble', and it was to burst. But soon thereafter there was another massive distraction when, after 9/11, security from terror dominated the scene.

Yet the answer to the question was not difficult. The consumer boom was floated by the stagnant incomes of the middle class being massively supplemented by bags and bags of debt. Nationally it amounted to a mountain of debt – a mountain of Himalayan proportions. Wall Street organised a private debt bonanza not seen before in American history. And it was to be engineered through the American and British love affair with home ownership. Millions of cheap mortgages (kept cheap by the low inflation environment) allowed millions of families to access cash and to borrow money as never before because of their rising house prices – the so-called 'wealth effect'. The much-vaunted American and British economic growth rates were to be underpinned by a consumption binge as western consumers used loans and credit cards mainly for holidays and shopping.

And alongside Wall Street, Washington was hugely complicit. The Wall Street-friendly governments of the time – the Clinton and Bush administrations and the Blair government in Britain – encouraged this financial services explosion through their continuing support of deregulation. As, crucially, did Fed Chairman Alan Greenspan who was reported to have 'brushed aside warnings about deceptive lending practices, including those of Edward M. Gramlich, a member of the Federal Reserve Board.'[50] The American economist Noel Roubini – the leading seer of the debt crash of 2007 – has described the major debt instrument used in the debt-boom – the SIVs – of being 'off-sheet scams' and argues they should have been regulated.[51]

The dimensions of the early twenty-first century debt boom are staggering. The pressure for the debt inflation was released through of a range of very lightly regulated new debt vehicles – with the acronyms like CDOs, MBSs, SIVs, and in the corporate sector CDSs. The US Bureau of Economic Analysis tells the incredible story. The ratio of debt to GDP stayed at a steady 1.2 during the 1950s, 60s and 70s; in the early 1980s it started to rise significantly and did not stop rising, until at its height, it reached well over 3.1; that is, 200 per cent higher than in 1979. It was 2.7 times GDP in the early 1930s. One analyst suggested that 'something big happened in the early 1980s' to cause the ratio to rise.[52]

Truly staggering amounts of money were involved. The amounts were rarely able to be calculated. Yet the London *Daily Telegraph*'s Ambrose Evans-Pritchard, whose reporting on the unfolding debt crisis was amongst the most prescient and alarming, set out some of the dimensions in a series of powerfully argued articles in 2007 and 2008.[53] When the investment bank, Bear Stearns, collapsed in March 2008 and was bought in a firesale by JP Morgan, it was revealed that its 'total position' amounted to $13.4 trillion – greater than the US national income and equivalent to a quarter of the world's GDP. And all of it built on an asset-base of only $80 billion. Warren Buffet famously described these derivatives as 'weapons of financial mass destruction'. The credit default swap market (CDSs) amounted to $45 trillion!

One of the world's leading authorities on this debt bubble, the late Professor Susan Strange, has argued that this bubble was the product of the structure of modern capitalism – what she termed 'casino capitalism'.[54] It had two main features. The first was the extreme 'financialisation' of the system – a term meaning more credit, more banks, more lending to new types of institutions like hedge funds, private equity funds and the like, and lending through an array of new and exotic types of financial instruments. And, in turn, this 'financialisation' was made possible by a systematic political programme of deregulation of financial markets – a deregulation which itself was made effective by the global nature of these markets.

It was this deregulation of capitalism (and particularly finance) that was obviously 'the something big' that had occurred in the early 1980s as part of the Reagan and Thatcher revolutions. And it was hardly surprising that the 1980s also saw the first serious rise in the ratio of debt to GDP, a ratio that has risen consistently ever since.

This 'pro-market' inspired deregulation of western capitalism was not without its early 1980s critics in the West's politico-economic establishment. Reagan's approach was famously called 'voodoo economics' by then Vice-President, George Bush, who was highly critical of 'supply side' economic deregulation and the tax policies that led to huge government debts; 'Reaganite' White House insider David Stockman was another who opposed the 'new economics' that was producing high forward trajectories for government deficits and debt; in the academic world Professor Strange who, in decrying what she came to call 'mad money' argued that 'it was, as is, wildly foolish to let the financial markets run so far ahead, so far beyond the control of state and international authorities.'[55] There were other voices too, but they remained in a decided minority – and, as the debt party got into full swing, they were drowned out, treated as curmudgeons and 'party poopers'.

Following Thatcher and Reagan, the presidencies of Clinton and George W. Bush and the premiership of Tony Blair all successfully resisted tougher regulation – surrounded as they were in Wall Street and the City of London by 'casino capitalists' and market fundamentalists. Their era of deregulation allowed what amounted to a shadow banking industry to build up – and become a primary purveyor of the 'funny money' of the 'casino'. These investment banks, hedge funds and private equity funds were, alongside the more regulated big banks, the engine drivers of this massive debt bubble. And these investment banks were allowed to take all the risk they wanted with their balance sheets without the government stepping in. Even as the banking crisis developed some supporters of the deregulation of the 1990s, like investment banker-turned Treasury Secretary Hank Paulson, were fighting a rearguard action as he tried to mitigate and water down the inevitable Congressional regulatory backlash.

THE COMING MISERY OF THE MAJORITY

The future can rarely be depicted with any precision. But should today's trends continue, then one thing is certain: the disappearing middle class will be replaced by a new social structure in which the life now lived by the West's poor will be the future lot of the majority of its citizens.

This coming misery of the majority will, though, likely exist side by side with a wealthy and self-perpetuating globally-oriented 'aristocracy' who will define themselves by their ownership of capital.

It is a combustible prospect for it will exist in an era, unlike any before, in which this poor majority will also be an assertive majority. The social and political deference to 'authority' that existed at the beginning of the twentieth century is, at the beginning of this century, as dead as a dodo. So it would seem likely that such a future majority will demand major, even revolutionary, changes in the economic and political system.

It amounts to a classic pre-revolutionary situation – as critical and as dangerous as the last time – in the 1930s – when the West faced economic collapse and total political change.

CHAPTER EIGHT

DEGENERATE CAPITALISM: THE RETURN OF 'ARISTOCRACY'

By the spring of 2008 the great debt bubble had been deflating for almost a year – and, in April, just as the unfolding banking and debt crisis was beginning to bite hard, Alan Greenspan, now a former Fed Chairman, finally surfaced to address his still loyal followers. He told a conference in Tokyo that 'the current credit crisis is the most wrenching in the last half century and possibly more'. These remarks, coming as it did from the author and architect of the long debt boom himself, were revealing; and they echoed the views of a gathering consensus that was predicting a downturn more serious than any since the Great Depression.

The economy was obviously in big trouble – but so too was the whole 'new capitalist' system ushered in during the Greenspan era. This 'new capitalism', so proudly and insistently proclaimed for over two decades by Wall Street and its supporters around the world, was now in question.

Moral condemnations of the new capitalism were becoming commonplace. The 1990s was being called 'the greediest decade in history', an era of excess neatly captured by a series of high-profile business scandals. The most sensational of these had erupted in early December 2001 when the mega-global company, Enron, filed for bankruptcy. The scam had involved the creation of off-shore units which were used both to avoid taxes and keep losses off the balance sheets. So shocking was the revelation that it also destroyed the Enron account-ants, Arthur Anderson, and even led a traumatised Congress to more properly regulate financial business through new legisla-tion known as 'Sarbanes-Oxley'.

Yet the bedrock legitimacy of western capitalism – and the worldwide appeal of the West – had not rested on capitalism's ethical standards, Rather, it had been based on the delivery of prosperity – more precisely on mass middle class prosperity. But now, the first time since the 1950s this mass prosperity was no longer a firm expectation. The middle class was fragmenting (both up and down), 'all ships' were no longer rising with the tide, and many were sinking. The living standards of millions of middle class people were falling. And, as discussed in the last chapter, a new ugly, 'un-American', feature was emerging: a rigid class system with little upward mobility. As the crisis unfolded during 2008, Main Street's troubles (mainly the collapsing hous-ing and mortgage market) were beginning to rock Wall Street too. So much so that the banks and financial institutions were run-ning to the erstwhile derided state for life-support.

Clearly, something had gone wrong with the economy. And the question that no one had thought possible was now arising: was there something wrong with the system itself? Can American capitalism any longer deliver? Alongside this nag-ging question, and just as important for capitalism's future, and for its long-term popular legitimacy as an economic model, was its moral and ideological standing. Post-1945 capitalism – the Roosevelt-LBJ 'social democratic' model – had for a time secured a popular consensus behind it. It was seen as stable, as delivering rising living standards to a mass middle class, and, crucially, as furthering American values – it was both *democratic* (certainly more so than the command economies in the East) and *meritocratic* (instilling the positive values of work and merit).

And when in the 1980s Ronald Reagan and Margaret Thatcher took western capitalism into its new rawer, and more globalised, phase, they also sought to justify it beyond its appeal as a material success story. They promoted their new brand of 'popular capitalism' as being virtuous as well as efficient. It would deliver 'freedom' as well as prosperity. Indeed, capitalism and freedom went hand in hand, and capitalism was uniquely able to preserve western liberties. This idea drew upon a deeper body of thought that saw capitalism as an historically progressive force – having broken the bonds of feudalism in the middle ages. It was not only the ally, but also the begetter, of political liberalism and democracy, indeed of the modern liberal world itself. The heroes of the 'new capitalism', economists like Frederich von Hayek and Milton Friedman, were touted as the incarnation of John Locke and John Stuart Mill.

One major achievement of the Thatcher-Reagan revolution was to associate modern capitalism – the western economic system – with 'freedom' and with 'markets'. And according to its 'free-market' supporters, the key virtue of the capitalist system, the thing that allied it to 'freedom', was that it was not based upon 'commands' – unlike in the 'command' economies. The theory was that every action in 'the market' – buying and selling – was purely voluntary.

Advocates also argued that access to capitalism and the market was both free of prejudices and unlimited. Traditional barriers based upon class and background, race and religion were all irrelevant criteria for membership of capitalist society. It was 'the colour of your money' not 'the colour of your skin' that counted. And although access through money limited the numbers who could properly participate, the great capitalist growth engine would, by 'trickle-down', allow more and more people to participate. Thatcher made 'popular capitalism' a political slogan and promised wider and wider access to capitalism and the market, based upon the idea of wider and wider shareholding.

As it turned out, though, modern global capitalism, like its nationally-based predecessor, is hardly overwhelmed with participants. Shareholding has certainly burgeoned; yet most of this growth is through pension funds – at one remove from and with no participation by those whose money is used. Just as tax dollars and pounds support programmes of which the taxpayer may not approve, so in today's global capitalist system the people's pension money might easily be supporting companies and industries of which many do not approve. (A recent advertisement by the Calvert Group in an American newspaper highlighted this problem: it asked 'Does your retirement money go places you never dreamed of?' as part of a campaign against tobacco.) Real shareholding – in which the participant knows what he or she owns and can direct his or her money to the desired location – remains a decidedly minority affair both domestically and globally, and shares remain a small proportion of the portfolios of the vast majority of those who own them.

Also, it is difficult to describe global capitalism and its markets as 'democratic' when the vast majority of western people still come to the market with next to nothing, putting them at a great disadvantage compared with those who bring substantial financial resources to the party. As I will argue later, the claim that modern capitalism – particularly when it is shorn of the balance provided by the state – is dynamic and progressive now rings hollow. Indeed modern capitalism (and the 'markets' associated with it) has become a force for stasis and tradition in that it gives a huge advantage to those with established wealth rather than those whose talent and merit will make wealth.

Some imaginative 'market theorists' have acknowledged this problem of limited access to the markets. Jeff Gates has argued that modern capitalism needs to be more inclusive but seems unable to make enough capitalists. In order to create such a capitalism he suggests a whole series of reforms, including bank credit without collateral, conditional tax relief on capital gains and a re-engineering of estate taxes to advance broad-based ownership.[1]

Others seek to rectify this deficiency in modern capitalism by using state money for vouchers or indeed cash rather than services. 'Give em the money' as a one-off in order to increase access to the markets. As Arthur Seldon suggested in the context of how to fund education, health and pensions, 'the obvious alternative [to state funding} was to provide purchasing power in cash, general or earmarked, rather than services in kind'.[2] This provision would presumably come from taxes, and be subject to downward pressure every year as the low-tax regime developed. But not even the most radical policy of income redistribution would provide those outside the capitalist world with the asset base necessary to seriously join it – to become 'a player'.

'Popular capitalism' will thus remain a pipedream as long as the global system has no way of opening itself up to mass involvement. The fact remains that mass asset ownership without a revolutionary programme of *asset redistribution* – from the asset rich to the asset poor – is well nigh impossible. Only a political programme to break up the accumulated asset base of families and companies could achieve this objective. However, no 'pro-market' theorist, not even the radical and adventurous Seldon, has proposed such a shocking departure. The idea of an existing political party taxing wealth in order, say, to fund mortgages for the young is utterly fanciful. Hardly anyone today – left or right – sees a role for government as an agent of widening the distribution of *capital*. Few supporters of the new capitalism see anything wrong with one man owning wealth equal to whole nations, or any problem with one man personally owning huge tracts of Britain's capital city – as does the Duke of Westminster. The 'new capitalism' has no use for Huey Long's cry of 'every man a King!' or Lloyd-George's aim of everyone owning an 'acre and a cow'.

THE WORK ETHIC

In her campaign for 'popular capitalism' Margaret Thatcher also portrayed capitalism as a system which protected and enhanced the Protestant virtues, including the work ethic. Certainly this idea of the 'work ethic' – that hard work, application, delayed gratification, and making sacrifices – is good for economic growth has consistently been espoused as public doctrine by supporters of Protestant, liberal capitalism. In their famous works both R. H. Tawney and Max Weber argued that Protestantism, and specifically Calvinism – with its belief in the value of work – was a crucial ideological ingredient in the rise of capitalism; and many contemporary American economic historians, like Talcott Parson and Herbert Gutman, have also tended to associate the work ethic with the US's economic success.[3]

This Protestant, capitalist 'work ethic' was, though, seen as more than simply an engine for economic and material advance: it was also a moral good, good for the person, good for personal growth, Peter Saunders has argued that Max Weber's idea that some kind of spirituality fuelled the original dynamic of capitalism – particularly in Britain – had some truth in it, but that the puritanism and dynamism may have since drained away. He presents a sad case that 'today, this religious motivation has all but vanished and we have inherited the behavioural husk having lost the spiritual kernel. We therefore continue to work methodically each day in pursuit of the next dollar, even though we may be hard-pressed to provide an adequate explanation for why we do so…This for Weber is the poignant tragedy of the modern age, that we are locked into a system which has lost its substantive meaning for us.'[4]

Whilst she was prime minister Margaret Thatcher made this Weberian moral case for the capitalist work ethic by evoking 'Victorian values'. She argued that hard work, thrift, delayed gratification and the like built self-reliance and independence; and she counterpoised all this to what she described as the 'dependency culture' – the socialist welfare state – in which hard work was replaced by inducements to idleness and sloth. (Intriguingly there was no similar rhetoric from 'market' supporters about the problematic values of the 'idle rich'. Yet, interestingly, such criticism had been a prominent feature of pro-capitalist Victorian radicalism.)

Yet, in today's economy justifying capitalism by reference to its encouraging the work ethic is becoming difficult. The popular idea that there was a link between hard work and income – that those with high incomes earn their economic rewards because they work harder than others – was always fragile; but may well have been broken altogether by the publicity surrounding some of the very large rewards 'earned' by private sector executives. Some of these egregious salaries and 'packages' enjoyed by top executives in the corporate world have raised the issue of the proportionality of work to reward, and the powerful question of 'how much is enough?' And on top of proportionality, it has been difficult for supporters of global capitalism to defend huge salary 'packages' for executives who were failing (like chief executive Roger Smith of General Motors who received a rise of half a million dollars a year following the collapse of the company's market share and the huge reduction of its workforce) or were corrupt (like the top Enron executives, paid lavishly whilst the company was cheating).

Also, the work ethic, particularly the idea of delayed gratification, has been systematically eroded by the commercialism of modern capitalism, by the instant greed perpetrated by the advertising industry, and by the search for short-term financial gain, which is now almost endemic. Indeed Michael Rose has argued that in contemporary capitalism hard work is no longer valued highly, certainly not as much as 'performance' – a very different idea no longer linked to hard work. He suggests that what matters now is 'effective work', not 'hard work'.[5]

MERIT

Linked to the work ethic is the idea of merit. British Prime Minister Tony Blair, declared on entering Downing Street in 1997 that he sought to create a 'society based on meritocracy' and that 'the Britain of the elite is over...the new Britain is a meritocracy.' This term 'meritocracy' was taken from the title of Michael Young's famous 1958 work *The Rise of The Meritocracy*; and although Young was to say 'I wish Tony Blair would stop using the term', Blair, like Thatcher before him, and like many others, saw 'opening up...old structures to uniquely reward merit and meritorious individuals as one of the key attributes of the new 'market capitalism'.

Of course what is deemed to be the core institution of capitalism, the market, is not meritocratic at all, for the market, so its supporters argue, exists specifically to cater to the public's tastes and needs, those of the majority not the meritocracy. However, from the supply side, to take *advantage* of the market some degree of merit or business acumen is needed, a characteristic that requires ability not position; and intelligence, not social standing.

The problem for contemporary capitalism is that the rewards for merit (and work), though still there, are no longer as substantial as they used to be. Rewards from other things than work and merit – most particularly from the inheritance of capital – are today often much greater, enough to secure a very, very good standard of living indeed. Without providing a real system of rewards for merit and work, the very legitimacy of modern capitalism may well begin to falter.

INDIVIDUALISM

Alongside hard work and enterprise, individualism has been at the heart of the value system of old-style capitalism. Calvinism, with its commercial values, believed in the individual having a direct line to God. 'Grace alone can save, and this grace is the direct gift of God, unmediated by any earthly institution.' And other supporters of capitalism and private property – the great English liberal thinkers like Hobbes and Locke and Herbert Spencer, the American founding fathers in the new world, the New Liberals at the turn of the century and the 'neo-liberal' (conservative) globalisers of today – all, irrespective of their differing views about the exact role of the state, have placed 'the sovereign individual' at the very centre of their worldview.

In the contemporary era, supporters of capitalism have compared, favourably, this individualist ethic with the values of socialism, and even social democracy, which were seen as weakening the sense of individuality through the conformity that, they argued, collectivism inevitably induced.

Yet in today's capitalism this polemic is increasingly difficult to sustain. The free enterprise system no longer has a lockhold on individualist values. Indeed, how can it when it was the capitalist ancestors, and not the present economic players, who were the individualists, who, by hard work or enterprise or even sharp practice, amassed the wealth. And how can individualism be such a highly prized virtue when, in our economy of inherited wealth, it is increasingly the family unit, and not the romantic, lone, individual, from which all good things, primarily capital, flow?

What's more, modern capitalism can hardly become an engine for individuality while its primary institution, the large corporation, promotes conformist corporate cultures and hierarchies that, instead of promoting individual flair and creativity, induce all the opposite attributes such as safe, bureaucratised, routine thinking, and lack of imagination and risk. These are the characteristics highlighted in William H. Whyte's classic work *The Organisation Man* – and he had corporations, not just public sector organisations in mind![6] And with corporations now triumphant and more powerful than ever, we can expect a further quantum leap in the deadening conformist hand of corporate bureaucracy. It is not a system in which the individual – at least as classically understood – will flourish.

RISK (OR LACK OF IT)
In today's capitalism the decline of creativity and the individual has gone hand in hand with the decline of risk. Risk was

always the great capitalist value; and risk-taking was always the prized hallmark of the entrepreneur, the lifeblood of the daring, the unusual, and those who stood out from the crowd and deserved – through talent and work, or even luck – their riches.

Yet more and more critics are now asking a question well worth asking – perhaps the most subversive question of all. Who, in fact, in the modern global capitalist economy is actually taking the greatest risks? Capital or labour? Corporations or employees? It is a good question. For today when companies get into trouble they can switch their investments – often abroad – with minimal losses. Or, as in the contemporary credit crunch, they can be bailed-out for fear of a more general collapse of the system. On the other hand, in the age of 'flexible labour markets' and 'downsizing', employees lose their jobs, and the loss of a job is everything, a total loss, not a partial loss suffered when capital is depleted.

In the modern capitalist economy it is now the employee who increasingly bears the risks. For when the gamble of investment fails, those without capital are laid off (or casualised) whereas those who make the investment decisions are all too often protected against loss. It is a topsy-turvy, perverse, world and another reason why modern global capitalism has lost its moral edge.

Global investors are also able to shed risk. When markets collapse it is the state, the taxpayers, that stands ready to help out the investors, and the bigger the investors the greater the state bailout. When investors stand to lose millions in low cost foreign markets, such as in Latin America in the 1980s or Asia in the 1990s, the taxpayer-backed IMF stands by to help. As Martin Wolf has argued, 'unregulated flows of short-term international capital are a license to rack up losses at the expense of taxpayers'.[7]

The 2007-8 banking and debt crisis, still unfolding as this book was written, showed up how the 'entrepreneurs' of the financial business class suddenly ceased to be society's risk-takers. As the crisis unfolded many super-rich bankers and hedge fund operators certainly lost money, but many other 'risk-takers' have turned to the much maligned state, in the form of the Federal Reserve (ultimately backed by the tax-payers) to bail them out. Worries about 'moral hazard' – the term used to describe the bail-out of risk-takers, have been set aside.

Take the case of the collapse of the venerable investment house of Bear Stearns in March 2008. Bear Stearns got into trouble with reckless and irresponsible debts which came home to roost. But instead of letting the risk-taker go bankrupt, in one fell swoop the debts of Bear Stearns were effectively nationalised. The 'risk-taking' bankers at JP Morgan, whom the government chose to take over the failing bank, were given a huge government-backed prize; they paid next to nothing. And the moral of the story: when Wall Street bankers were in trou-ble, these financiers hardly batted an eye before running to the state for life-support, the same state – the US government – that Wall Street had for years been disparaging as too big, too prone to regulation and too interfering.

Vincent Reinhardt, a former Fed director of monetary affairs, spoke for many, not just market purists, when he criticised the Bear Stearns deal on the grounds that it would set a terrible precedent for future state bail-outs. He reminded people that in 1998 the Federal Reserve had saved the hedge-fund Long-Term Capital Management but had done so without using tax-payers' money (by coaxing its creditors to save it). This time, though, the Fed had gone too far. It had, he said, 'eliminated forever the possibility that the Fed could act as an honest broker' and that the next time a big Wall Street firm was in trouble they would expect government money to come to the rescue.

Earlier, the 1998 Asian financial crisis had provided another illuminating example of how, in the new global economy, risk is no longer borne by those who are supposed to bear it: the great western capitalist risk-takers, the lenders of capital – banks and financial entrepreneurs. Instead the losses were borne by local Asian borrowers and peoples. As Edward Luce has argued, 'Apart from those who lost money on regional stockmarkets or bet the wrong way on currencies, most banks which lent money to the three economies (Korea, Thailand and Indonesia) will be repaid in full.'[8] And incredibly, following the IMF-imposed recovery programme, some creditors received a higher rate of interest than that which they had negotiated before the crisis occurred.

That tenacious critic of modern capitalism, *The Guardian*'s economics commentator Larry Elliott, focusing on this shedding of risk, reports with some glee Professor K. Raffer's 'wicked' idea that debtor governments should be able to seek protection from creditors in the same manner as US entrepreneurs are able to use the bankruptcy procedures of 'Chapter Eleven' in the US to avoid serious penalties for failure.[9]

Banks, particularly the big ones, are also in the risk-shedding business. During the bank and credit crisis of 2007-8 the full 'have it both ways' approach of the banks – particularly the big investment banks – was on display. Whilst profits were secure, 'risk-taking' was encouraged and the banks shunned the 'fearsome' state, arguing for light touch regulation if any. But when in trouble they were no longer 'risk-takers'; they demanded successfully that the public sector bail them out.

ANGLO-SAXON CAPITALISM: A RETURN TO FEUDALISM

Anyone taking an audit of corporate capitalism in the early years of the new century would not be bringing good news. The headlines told it all: global imbalances, mountainous debt, runaway profits and growing social divisions. The old style capitalism that postwar Americans so prized, the capitalism that forged modernity out of backwardness and sustained the values of the American way of life – individualism, hard work, the ethic of responsibility, merit, and rewards for talent and risk – was hardly discernable.

The truth was that today's capitalism had degenerated. It has, quite contrary to its supporters' strongly held beliefs, become seriously unprogressive. And in its new deregulated, global, phase, it had unleashed a dynamic that is, incredibly, taking us right back in time. Back, that is, to the values and society of the feudal world from which the earlier form of capitalism helped set us free. This new degeneration has a hundred causes, but at its heart is a change in how capital and money is made. About what values and skills, or lack of them, are needed in the money-making process.

As the old self-improving adage had it about success: 'he made his money the old-fashioned way – he earned it'. No longer so. Now money is made in large part through the practice and culture of inheritance. Inheriting capital and money (which amounts to a gift) may indeed be a sign of generosity, and helpful to the recipient, but it erodes the value of work – of earning money as opposed to making it. It has no connection with work – neither hard work nor Michael Rose's 'effective work' – or creativity. It is a reward for bloodline rather than merit. And in today's explosion of inheritance it is creating a class – or rather a caste – at the top of our western societies who have inherited, or stand to inherit, enough wealth and income to enable many of them to avoid work for ever.

Historically work has been the key to productivity, both material and cultural. It may be argued that in advanced societies economic productivity (though not cultural productivity) can increasingly be fostered by improved technology rather than work. However, even should this be true, a society and culture that marginalises the importance of work, relying instead for rewards based upon inheritance, will come up against the issue of the incalculable and intangible loss of human dignity.

Inheritance is very big business, perhaps the biggest business of all in today's global economy. In the US, Robert Avery of Cornell University has predicted that 'we will shortly be seeing the largest transfer of income in the history of the world'.[10] In 1973, 56 per cent of the total wealth held by persons aged 35-39 had been given to them by their parents. By 1986 the figure for 35-39 year-old baby boomers had risen to 86 per cent, leading political scientist Kevin Phillips to argue that inheritance is 'about to become a critical component of the younger generation's future, *something America has never before experienced*'.[11]

In one of the few studies of the inheritance transfers of the super-rich – in this case American millionaires – it has been estimated that, on present trends (in 1996) 'the number of estates in the $1 million or more range will increase by 246 percent during the next decade; these estates will be valued (in 1990 constant dollars) at a total of more than $2 trillion (that is $2,000,000,000,000). But nearly the same amount will be distributed by so-called pre-decedent affluent parents and grandparents to their children/grandchildren.'[12]

The amounts of individual wealth transfers by inheritance are staggering. Looking to the future, economist Edward Woolf has projected that if inheritance follows the pattern of US wealth concentration in the 1990s then in the early years of the new century the wealth going to each of the top 1 per cent of Americans will average $3 million, and the next richest 5 per cent (the 95-99 percentiles) will average $900,000 each. Also looking to the future, Kevin Phillips suggests that inheritance taxes might slightly alter the future social outcome, but that 'baby boomers would be the most polarized and stratified generation in US history', and that 'the overall pattern would be unmistakable: inherited wealth would create a hereditary caste; class lines would harden'.[13]

Yet these concerns were to fall on deaf ears. The 'new market economy' politicians in both Britain and the US, particularly those who would proclaim the merits of 'entrepreneurship' and 'hard work', were seeking the directly opposite outcome – to *increase* the pool of inherited wealth by lowering inheritance taxes even further, or removing them altogether. In Britain the free-market Conservative governments of the 1990s talked approvingly of a future economy dominated by inherited wealth as wealth 'cascaded down the generations'. And the New Labour government that succeeded it fell in behind the inheritance culture and in its 2008 budget raised the threshold for not paying inheritance tax to £600,000 per couple. In the US the Republican party successfully demonised proposed inheritance taxes by calling them 'death taxes' – even though such taxes did not fall on the dead but on their heirs (and did not apply to the vast majority of people, only to those with estates more than $4 million).

Also, and intriguingly, the intellectual leaders of the new capitalism – in the Anglo-American economic think tanks and the 'neo-liberal' university departments – put up no objections to this new inheritance culture. Few 'free-market' theorists saw any contradiction at all between growing levels of inheritance and the enterprise society they were attempting to create. Even the great man of economic liberty, Frederich von Hayek, saw no reason to oppose, or even limit, private inheritance. He supported what he called 'the transmission of material property' because 'there is a natural partiality of parents for their children', and because if inheritance was seriously threatened, people would 'look for other ways of providing for their children'. In a very, for Hayek, defensive, indeed sheepish, mode of thinking he also argued that 'men being what they are, it [inherited capital] is the least of evils', and inherited capital is a 'lesser evil' to be tolerated.

In a further line of argument Hayek revealed his near-irrational opposition to the state when he asserted that 'those who dislike the inequalities caused by inheritance should recognise that the state will not be capable of splitting up inherited capital leading to its dispersal'. (Why not? Isn't every redistribution, from inheritance taxes to lower income taxes, to welfare benefits, to road building programmes, to education, helping to split up inherited capital, and disperse it?)[14]

However, the Murdoch journalist Irwin Stelzer has recently broken ranks with many of his fellow 'free-marketeers' by suggesting that their opposition to taxes on inheritance is wrong, that 'revenues from [inheritance taxes] could be used to lower income tax rates, especially on low earners...This would reduce the tax on work by increasing the tax on the less productive activity of being around when someone dies.' He also argues that inheritance taxes do not deny children their 'endowments of family reputation and connection; [and] knowledge, skills and goals provided by their family environment'.[15]

Inheritance remains a decidedly under-researched and under-discussed subject in the debate about 'free markets' and

modern global capitalism. Grossly unjust, unfair and unproductive – as it rewards lineage not merit or work, and undermines the enterprise culture – the conservative support for
inheritance appears contradictory, if not hypocritical. So much
so, that capital inheritance has become one of the intellectual
Achilles' heels of 'free-market' theory, the 'guilty little secret' of
'progressive' modern global capitalism.

THE NEW INHERITANCE CULTURE

Of course inheritance has always been part of the way of life in
both capitalist and pre-capitalist societies. Passing on wealth
from one generation to the next (via the eldest son) kept relatively large accumulations intact, and was defended on moral
grounds by virtue of the right of the giver to dispose of 'his'
property as he saw fit. During the age of the mixed economy –
in the mid to late twentieth century – inheritance taxes started
biting into the inheritance culture, but at the same time inheritance became a feature of middle-class life, primarily through
the inheritance of housing.

Now, though, with inheritance taxes falling throughout the
globalised capitalist world – as part of the necessary 'competitive tax environment' – the actual amounts of money and assets
being handed down from generation to generation are becoming larger. Also, it is far easier to make these inherited accumulations grow than it used to be. To create a large amount from a
smallish one used to involve considerable work and talent;
now, however, huge fortunes accumulate as you sleep.

Worse still, many of today's inheritances are becoming the
sole means of income for the inheritors. A huge private dependency culture – dependence upon the family rather than the
state – is being erected. American analysts have described this
derisively as 'economic outpatient care'. And such outpatient

welfare care is now massive. It has been estimated that in the mid-1990s a huge 46 per cent of the affluent in the US give at least $15,000 worth of economic outpatient care a year to their adult children or grandchildren. If this estimate is accurate and an 'affluent' person is defined as a net dollar millionaire, then there is an annual transfer of $15 billion from the super-rich to their descendants in the US alone.[16]

This super-rich welfare state involves the transfer from one generation to another of 'entire coin collections, stamp collections, payments of medical and dental expenses, plastic surgery' as well as straight cash gifts. It has been estimated that 43 per cent of millionaire parents fund all or a large part of their grandchildren's tuition at private primary and/or secondary school, 32 per cent fund their adult children's further education 59 per cent provide financial assistance in purchasing a home, 61 per cent provide 'forgiveness loans' (those not to be repaid) to their adult children, and 17 per cent give gifts of listed stock to their adult children.[17]

All of this is producing a new generation – children of the super-rich who, because they are partly or wholly financially dependent upon their parents – even when they are well into their forties and sometimes their fifties – exhibit, and are likely to transmit to their own children, non-productive, idle and dependent values. And they are also likely to experience poor social relationships. As in any dependency culture, relationships can be distorted by inheritance. Reliance upon inheritance can induce animosity and squabbling amongst family members. As an analyst of the inheritance scene put it:

The fact is that many 'thirty something Americans' cannot maintain anywhere near the lifestyle they had while living with Mom and Dad…In fact, many are unable to purchase even a modest house without financial subsidies from their parents. It is not unusual for these 'rich kids' to receive substantial cash and other financial gifts until they are in their late forties or even early fifties. Often these UAW's [under accumulators of wealth] compete with each other for their parents' wealth. What would you do if your economic subsidy was being threatened by the presence of your equally dependent brothers and sisters.[18]

And these cash gifts often go to the less financially successful and less independent children of the super-rich – daughters who have married and become homemakers, thus losing their earning power, or less successful sons. 'Consequently, an increasing number of families headed by the sons and daughters of the affluent are playing the role of successful members of the high-income-producing upper-middle class. Yet their lifestyle is a facade.'[19] This gift culture – which is seen as an acceptable part of the contemporary capitalist system – represents not only a huge misappropriation of resources but also a distortion of values, elevating failure and idleness over personal success, merit, work and enterprise.

Such a massive inheritance economy is already polarising western societies. It has been estimated that in the US, *in early 1990s money*, the wealth given to the top 1 per cent averages $3 million and that given to the richest 5 per cent (the 95th to 99th percentiles) averages $900,000, whereas the middle fifth (the 40th to 59th percentiles) on average receive $49 000. For those further down the inheritance is negligible.[20]

The western world, already divided between the skilled and non-skilled, is now also becoming divided between inheritors and non-inheritors. Yet, in this age of inheritance even those fortunate or talented enough to acquire skills may be in for a rough time. For skills will continue to be much less well rewarded than capital or its associated professional services, and the gap between skilled employees and the rich and super-rich will probably continue to grow. The fact is that an economy that supports and nurtures inherited capital simply cannot create the right environment for skills to flourish. Global foot-loose capital, as it exerts downward pressure on the national tax regimes and hence the public education system, will inevitably limit investment in skills. (And there is also some evidence to suggest that inheritance encourages greater consumption, less savings and investment and more dependence upon credit amongst those who receive it.)[21]

The 'free-market' system, which rejects government interference in individual decision-making, *even at the point of inheritance*, is simply unable to act as the radical, democratic and 'classless' force some of its supporters claim it, and want it, to be. Instead, under the pressure of globalisation it is now becoming a conservative force, an economic system for stasis, geared primarily for the protection and inheritance of existing capital and only secondarily for the creation of rewards for work, risk and skills. The ancestry of today's American millionaires points up the inevitably conservative, aristocratic, and unproductive character of the reward system of today's capitalism. The fact is that the American super-rich scene is still dominated by descendants of the early migrants to North America – the English (21 per cent), followed by the Germans (17 per cent), followed by the Irish (12 per cent) and Scottish (9 per cent).[22]

Indeed, in one sense, 'markets' are not just 'not progressive'. They are inherently conservative in their social and cultural consequences. For to 'leave it to market forces' in the hallowed injunction of classical economics is not to submit to an impersonal and rational mechanism of allocation, but rather to ensure that *existing*, indeed traditional, patterns become entrenched. And Britain under the supposed radicalising impact of the Thatcherite capitalist revolution was a case in point. For all that privatisation and deregulation, regardless of the independent case for each of these measures, may simply have served to give an unexpected lease of life to the 'old money' conservative (and inheriting) class and culture.

THE REACTIONARY GLOBAL MARKET

The image of the 'free market' implanted in western minds by globalist intellectuals and propagandists was that of a progressive force: open, liberal and democratic, reforming old institutions, making vested interests (primarily an over-weaning public sector) conform to consumer needs through the market. 'Neo-liberal' economics – as its very name suggests – was also associated with the 'liberal' side of politics. Adam Smith, and the Manchester School of 'free traders' and 'free-marketeers', in the nineteenth century were all liberals. This derived from the historical association between capitalism and Whig, then Liberal, politics, primarily in England, where the opponents of the market and the rising merchant class were often conservative and Tory.

The political ideas and values of today's leading contemporary 'free-market' 'neo-liberals' are more difficult to identify. The Frankfurt School of economists, clustered around the legendary Freiderich von Hayek, and the later Chicago School of monetarists, with Milton Friedman at the helm, were not only disdainful of the state but also of politics and most politicians. Seeking a minimal state and a small, sometimes tiny, role for politics, their social values were normally 'liberal' in that they tended to place the 'sovereign' individual at the centre, although they believed that this individual was best protected and enhanced by the market rather than the state and a programme of rights. Hayek himself made clear in a famous postscript, 'Why I am Not a Conservative', to his major work, *The Constitution of Liberty*, that he did not stand in the European conservative tradition. The latter, he argued, lacked principles and represented little more than a 'widespread attitude of opposition to drastic change'.[23] Hayek did not seek change for change's sake, but at the time of writing – at the height of postwar social democracy – he did seek change, even drastic change.

Hayek saw himself as a liberal but not as a democrat, or at least not a modern democrat. Like his supporter, the monetarist Milton Friedman, he saw democratic politicians as demagogic, and elections as problematic because they tended to entrench parties committed to welfare and enlarging the state. In the 1970s and 1980s the politics of Chile became a testing ground for their proposition that limited democracy, or even its temporary abandonment, was sometimes necessary in the construction of a 'free-market' system.

Some of the disciples of Hayek were ultraliberal – indeed libertarian. They possessed a 'moral commitment to the idea of a polity that maximises the scope for individual human beings to give material expression to personal values and perceptions of self-interest' – a view that often led on to socially liberal policies on issues such as homosexual law reform and the decriminalisation of some drugs.[24]

During the 1970s and the 1980s this liberal and progressive image of capitalism made a lot of headway with intellectuals, journalists and the media. Leading Thatcherite Arthur Seldon was not a supporter of the Conservative Party and called himself 'Whiggish'. Thatcher herself presented some of her political battles as 'progressive' compared with the views of public school traditionalists in her cabinet, the hierarchy of the

Church of England, even the royal family. Her rhetoric praised the liberal, 'open' character of the free market, and depicted the left as socially reactionary, as favouring the trade union power of the 1950s, the old British class divisions and a bureaucratic centralisation of the state that kept 'kept people in their place'. Her Conservative government – particularly Cabinet Minister Norman Tebbit – talked of 'upward mobility' as a positive social aim and saw traditionalist upper-class England as attempting to frustrate a new social openness. (Indeed most leading market economists would tend to place themselves in support of the general liberal postulations assembled in Karl Popper's *Open Society and Its Enemies*.[25]

And the 'freer' market system she introduced certainly liberalised and modernised some aspects of traditional British society, for example its consumer laws and pub and shop opening hours; and her privatisation programme led to a managerial flexibility and consumer consciousness that had not been present under the previous regime. (Of course these liberalising changes in the 1980s were part of the deeper process of modernisation – of the sloughing off of the social stultifications of empire and class hierarchy – which would probably have taken place anyway.)

In the US, Ronald Reagan succeeded in backing his democratic opponents into a conservative corner: isolating them as supporting 'old-fashioned' spending plans and 'unreformed' welfare programmes. Part of Reagan's 'progressive' appeal was simply to do with vision. He and his 'free-market' supporters seemingly had a vision, while his political opponents, lacking anything new to add to New Deal economics, appeared to be stuck in the past, traditionalist and conservative. Reagan, like Thatcher, was also continually hitting home by counterpoising the democratic 'free market' system with the reactionary, indeed authoritarian, command economies of the Soviet Union and the Eastern Bloc (and with western leftists, liberals and social democrats who, may be more moderate, but also shared incipiently undemocratic instincts).

By the turn of the new century this perception that 'free markets' were in some senses more socially and politically progressive and liberal than the alternative models, had begun to look somewhat superficial. For after almost a decade and a half of triumphant global capitalism, as the full hand of unchecked 'free market' globalism began to reveal itself, a different picture was emerging: on the fundamental questions – the big issues of prosperity and power in society – the supposedly 'free market' was turning out to be deeply conservative, indeed reactionary, in character.

The 'free market' was sold as a challenging arena where competition erodes tradition and vested interests. But a clearer way to see it – with its deregulation and low taxation – was as a strategy for freeing up tradition, freeing up existing power centres and removing the forces that might threaten, challenge or change them. By removing the ability of politics, of the state, to encourage or institute change, it leaves existing institutions, classes and interests without challenge. Indeed, it offers existing interests greater power. The great privatisation programme of the 1980s and 90s in Britain was a good case in point – for, although it allowed space for a small number of new capitalists and entrepreneurs the bulk of the freeing-up of state assets simply allowed those with existing capital, traditional money, to make more – much, much more.

The 'free market' rarely challenges existing institutions, classes, or interests, except at the very margin; rather it operates *in their favour*. Traditional capital – in the big corporate institutions and leading families – remains largely undispersed. And in crude terms, the position of those with money, with capital, is entrenched *vis-à-vis* those without. Those with money and position are not overly challenged, and in the absence of cataclysmic financial crashes they have to work very hard to lose their capital.

THE RETURN OF ARISTOCRACY

A progressive, liberal and dynamic economic system would not freeze existing social relations. However a strong case can be made that, socially, the 'neo-liberal' global market, although encouraging upward social mobility at the margins, *has* ultimately served to bolster fundamental inequalities not only globally, but within national communities as well. Indeed, this 'new economy' may have so improved the economic power of the western super-rich that they have become entrenched in their positions at the top. Working through institutions, primarily the big corporations, but also through private capital, they have been able to effectively neuter governments by bidding down taxes, particularly business and inheritance taxes, and bidding up the rewards to private capital.

In a huge historic irony this new global capitalism is causing nothing less than a return, on a global basis, to an older form of social life – aristocracy – the very system which the rise of capitalism originally broke asunder.

If today's super-rich resemble the lords of medieval times, then the vast majority of peoples, billions worldwide, millions in the West, including many who count themselves as middle class, are increasingly like modern-day serfs, with either a minimal stake, or no stake at all, in the economic system. The political stake created for the masses by democracy – the regime of rights and votes – is still largely national and there-

fore is increasingly being either bypassed (by global corporations) or bought (by media corporations).

Just as in aristocratic times past, the few wield incredible
power. These modern-day 'lords of the universe' do not, like
medieval lords, exercise detailed, local control over most or
every aspect of the lives of others. However their individual,
personal command over the huge resources at their disposal,
gives them inordinate power over people's livelihoods, if not
their lives. It also gives them the non-economic power to construct politics, society and culture in their own image and
according to their own needs, which sits ill alongside the pretensions of democracy.

FROM NOBLESSE OBLIGE TO GREED

Of course there are some major distinctions between the old
European aristocrats and today's global rulers. The old aristocrats were, at their core, domestic, or 'national'. They identified with the nations they lived in, and rightly so, because they
owned them. Their assets were based primarily upon land.
Today's aristocrats are global, owing no loyalty or affection to
any particular landmass or group of peoples. Their assets are
financial and they make money as rentiers. French economist
Alain Parguez has called the system they operate – lending to
governments and companies – 'the international rentier economy' and the 'rentier welfare state'.[26]

The old aristocrats' social outlook was that of *noblesse
oblige* (not necessarily out of sentiment, but for sensible,
prudent reasons). Even the American robber barons, the
Rockefellers, the Carnegies, gave great sums of money to the
arts. The new aristocrats have no such condescension (or, as
some critics would put it, 'they could care less'). They have little or no social obligations – because they have no country.

Politically, the old aristocrats were conservative – believing in organic development and slow, piecemeal change, and even sometimes in moderate reform, like the English Whigs. The new aristocrats of global capitalism have no such social obligations or sense, and indeed, Gekko-style, are taught to be proud of their circumstances. For some unknown reason many modern inheritors believe, in the words of the L'Oréal ad, that 'I'm Worth It'!

The old aristocrats existed in an environment in which capital and riches needed some kind of justification – usually religious in nature. Capitalism was not only productive, but also good. Indeed, the idea that private wealth accumulation is a sign of grace goes back all the way to the puritans, arguably the founders of American commerce. Benjamin Franklin's writings, particularly *The Way To Wealth* and *Advice To a Young Tradesman*, were cited by Max Weber in *The Protestant Ethic* as portraying the essence of this ethical aspect of capitalism, a moral case – at least for self-made capitalism – that still resonates in today's America.

Peter Singer argues in his critique of contemporary self-interestedness, *How Are We To Live?*, that this puritanical religious justification for capitalism conjoined with a later, increasingly secular, ethic that also supported capitalism, the free market and the importance of wealth. Capitalism was good for character building, and good for the poor.

The idea that the market builds character was a theme pursued by Herbert Spencer, who saw a positive value in great wealth being accrued through exertion and risk – a viewpoint that, admittedly, would make him cast a suspicious glance at modern capitalism's inheritance culture. And it is also ethical because, as George Gilder argues in his influential book *Wealth and Poverty*, capitalism is good for the poor too. The wealth made by the super-rich will benefit all by 'trickle-down', and capitalism and wealth creates an incentive for the poor, who, he argues, 'need most of all the spur of their poverty.'[27]

Of course old capitalism's puritan values – independence, individuality, enterprise, risk, delayed gratification – may have told only half, or less than half, the story. Traditional capitalism was always Janus-faced, and the obverse face was of course a countenance of greed and selfishness. The late mid-twentieth century consumer culture – which spawned the label 'consumerism' – certainly emphasised material possessions and encouraged self-centredness. Critics of old capitalism made their anti-system pitches by painting capitalists – indeed even simply the ownership of small amounts of private property – as greedy. This criticism was often somewhat high-handed, for old capitalism, limited as it was by the state, had created a consumer society in which masses of people who had previously been shut off from life's material pleasures began to enjoy them. For the first time ordinary people were experiencing some limited, very limited, economic power.

NEW CAPITALISM, NEW GREED

Today's global capitalism is increasingly being shorn of its erstwhile puritanism, particularly the puritanical notion of the value of delayed gratification. The huge amounts of super-wealth now being generated need to be justified, and in the process not only do such accumulations of wealth become morally acceptable, but so too does greed itself. Greed becomes good. As Ivan Boesky, the 'king of the Wall Street arbitragers', told students at Berkeley, 'Greed is alright...greed is healthy...You can be greedy and still feel good about yourself.'[28]

Greed received a good press in the 1990s when supporters of the 'free market' suggested that greed was healthy because it recognised human nature as it was, not as we wished it to be. Greed was also sold as a spur to activity and productivity. What is more, 'free-market' apologists propounded, with some truth, that 'greed...is the motive of mankind in all economic systems, socialist as well as capitalist', but that the capitalist system succeeds in releasing it and harnessing it.'[29]

These ideas echoed an older rationale for capitalism that is no longer heard – that self-interest was positive and to be encouraged because it was efficient, and out of this efficiency would come a broader interest, some kind of 'general good'. The idea of the ultimate good being the prosperity of the people or some kind of 'general good' – achieved by an invisible hand – has disappeared under a welter of economism (of statistics, returns, performance indicators) and growing scepticism about whether such a thing exists at all. Market capitalists tend to see the general good as but a contrivance for some hidden self-interest. But if greed can no longer be justified by its contribution to the general good, then we are left with nothing beyond saying amen to individual self-gratification.

However, an insistent question about contemporary greed remains: how much money do the super-rich actually need? Is ten times the average wealth enough? Is a thousand times needed? As Bud Fox asks Gordon Gekko in Oliver Stone's movie *Wall Street*: 'Tell me Gordon...How many yachts can you water-ski behind? How much is enough?'

The view of a leading American social critic was that 'it seems safe to conclude that there is *never enough* for the very rich in our society – whether they are the chief executives of America's largest corporations, scions of the country's wealthiest families, or major recipients of the great bulk of stock dividends parceled out each year'.[30] Another late 1990s American view, surprisingly from a pro 'free-market' quarter, is that it may now be time to put 'a limit on greed' – 'now that these huge accumulations have reached what anyone would agree has no conceivable purpose other than to preclude others from the modest accumulations essential to economic self-sufficiency'.[31]

'These huge accumulations' not only raise questions about basic material greed, but also about greed for power: and about how much power is enough. The way things are developing the owners of capital are achieving inordinate amounts of power – power over individuals, power over families, power over society, even power to make history. The satirist Tom Wolfe's depiction of Wall Street financiers as 'masters of the universe' sums up this power aspect of big capital. And arguably such power is even more concentrated than that in the hands of individual politicians – those usually associated in the public mind with the ownership of power. Politicians, however, have to live within the constraints of having to share power with other politicians and other institutions. Furthermore they are accountable to their electorates. The super-rich 'masters of the universe' are, theoretically at least, accountable too – to markets. Yet this accountability is less formal than that of politicians, whose lines of authority – committees, cabinets, parliaments and ultimately voters – are clear. Financial and economic power is also far less transparent and open to the scrutiny of the media than is political power.

HOW 'GLOBAL CAPITALISM' THREATENS DEMOCRACY

Perhaps, though, the biggest problem of all posed by the new capitalist aristocracy is what it is doing to our democracy.

Democracy is ultimately all about power. Who has it? And who doesn't? And with the new capitalism placing money and power in fewer and fewer hands, in a new ruling class no less, the rest of us are beginning to resemble the mass of powerless subjects which inhabited the world before the age of democracy. There seems little doubt that the West's economic system – global capitalism – is ultimately on a collision course with the West's great political achievement – democracy.

Most capitalists – even modern Wall Street capitalists – are democrats. They see capitalism, even new Wall Street capitalism, as part of the democratic story. For them democracy and capitalism, like love and marriage, go together 'like a horse and carriage'. And they believe that the idea that politics, political ideas, government and constitutions – based upon the state, until now the nation-state – created democracy is mistaken. Instead, they argue, it was the growth of capitalism, and its idea of the market, that gave birth to the democratic society and way of life.

During the Cold War 'capitalism' and 'democracy' became synonymous, and both were claimed by people in the West to represent their system against the communist or socialist (or totalitarian) systems of the Eastern Bloc. Indeed a strong case can be made that the history of capitalism is interlinked with the history of democratic development – in the sense that, by casting aside the feudal world, capitalism helped usher in modern democratic ideas of equality and freedom. And after three centuries of capitalism it is undeniably true that democracy has become the governing ideology, indeed the very spirit of the times, almost the religion of the West.

Just as capitalism helped forward a more democratic world, so for many it remains the best bet to preserve it. Market theorists see markets as providing more democratic safeguards than government ever can. They also see 'market democracy' as more real than 'political democracy', because they see political democracy, or government or the state, unlike markets, as inherently abusive of power. When the classical liberal economist and founder of public choice theory, Professor J. M. Buchanan, presented his pioneering pro-market ideas to a British audience at the Institute for Economic Affairs in 1978 he set them in a democratic context, quoting John Stuart Mill against government. Mill had argued that 'the very principle of constitutional government requires it to be assumed that political power will be abused to promote the purposes of the holder...such is the natural tendency'.[32]

FREEDOM AND LIBERTY

At the very heart of the more serious 'free-marketeers' worldview is, intriguingly, a *political* proposition: that the most important value of all is that of individual freedom – preserving, and enhancing, the freedom of the 'sovereign individual'. Market supporters suggest that only the pluralism of the market allows this sovereign individual to develop freely. This, they argue, is because the market, unlike the state, avoids compulsion. 'Free-marketeers' proceed from the proposition that the state compels us to obey its laws by force and gathers its resources forcibly. They argue that the state, unlike the market, is backed by the law, which in turn employs the sanction of punishment, indeed jail; and that, ultimately, what lies behind the power of the state – of the world of politics – is the military.

The central 'pro-market' contention here is that the resources held by the individual (money, property, other assets) are inalienably his or hers – and that, whereas in the market the individual releases these resources voluntarily and by invitation, the state and government compels their release.

On a propagandistic and polemical level this *compulsion* argument (or, rather, anti-compulsion argument) of the global free-marketeers is very appealing – particularly when the issue is tax. People naturally tend to believe that the resources they hold are indeed 'theirs', and the idea that 'my' money is being taken forcibly by the state's tax collector taps a populist vein. Also, public bodies, unlike private bodies (even those in a monopolistic or oligopolistic position), tend to become very defensive about their use of taxpayers' money. For instance public bodies (such as the taxpayer-funded British Broadcasting Corporation) worry about accountability, where-as privately funded organisations (such as the commercially funded television companies) are much more free-wheeling, believing they are automatically accountable – to 'market forces'! (When, in fact, they are accountable to the whims and opinions of 'market-makers' like advertisers.)

Yet the intriguing questions remains: does not the private sector also engage in compulsion? To continue the television analogy: the idea that there is no 'compulsion' involved in the financing of commercial television, simply because it takes no money from the state, may be fanciful. The fact is that if the market determines television output, then in the real world it means that the advertisers – interpreting public taste – deter-mine this output. Rarely are consumers or shareholders con-sulted by the advertisers on their month-by-month decisions, and these short-term decisions can be very important indeed. The advertiser then places the costs of the advertisement onto the price, which is passed on to the unwitting consumer in the supermarket. Thus in the real world of the real market, as opposed to the imagined 'free market', a host of little 'compul-sions' are forced on the individual – acts that are not, in truth, voluntary because of shortages of time, imperfect knowledge, rigging of market entry and all the other real world constraints. Compulsion is certainly present in the market and the private sector. It is simply more subtle and circuitous than that imposed on the individual by the state.

GEORGE SOROS AND THE IDEA OF 'COMPULSION'

Intriguingly the global financier turned public intellectual George Soros (who became famous for his speculation against the British pound during the Exchange Rate Mechanism crisis of 1992) has argued that the new global market system is not only undemocratic, but also represents a threat to what he calls – taking his definition from Karl Popper – 'the Open Society'.

The kernel of Soros's argument is that the global free market is not based, as some neo-liberals would argue, upon the democratic interplay of supply and demand. 'The assumption of perfect knowledge proved unsustainable', he argues, 'so it was replaced by an ingenious device. Supply and demand were taken as independently given...[but] the condition that supply and demand are independently given cannot be reconciled with reality, at least as far as the financial markets are concerned. Buyers and sellers in financial markets seek to discount a future that *depends on their own decisions.*' (Nor can supply and demand be taken as independently given in areas other than finance; in fact there is hardly any economic activity at all in which supply and demand are 'independently given'.)

Thus according to Soros, markets, and market players, 'have the capacity to alter the subject matter to which they relate'.[33] He suggests that market players are inevitably imposing their will – in the form of their expectations, but inevitably also in the form of their values and interests – upon the rest of us. Such an imposition – arguably as much an imposition, or compulsion, as any imposed in the democratic world by politicians – affords a new view of the moral balance sheet between state and market.

It opens us to the little-heard proposition that 'the market' can limit freedom as much as can government, that the market can create a class system – now on a global canvas – as insidious as any created by old-time feudalism or the modern political class.

In other words, 'the state' – certainly the kind of welfare state created in the West during the democratic age – can be an essential bulwark in the construction of a free and democratic society. It can do so by balancing the big private sector, by acting as the last resort in a crisis (as the financial bail-outs of 2008 can testify to), and through its welfare function by *enabling* opportunity and social mobility. The problem with global capitalism is that, by eroding and demonising 'the state', it also weakens this bulwark.

THE STATE AND THE LAW

In the real world the 'sovereign individual', although sometimes, undeniably, reduced or even threatened by the state, can also be protected by it. Indeed the state may be the sovereign individual's only ultimate protector. After all the state, the polity, is the only body that can guarantee the rights of citizens and their space, not only against private interests, including big corporations, but even against itself and its own subdivisions of government. (In fact this notion of the state protecting the individual against the state is at the very heart of the American constitutional idea drawn up by the men of Philadelphia. The state would be split up – separation of powers – in order to protect the individual from any one part of it; and the state through its bill of rights, would protect minorities from majorities using the state to oppress them.)

This work of liberty is done by the law – by the state's law. That erudite political thinker, the late Maurice Cranston, has argued that the rule of law is utterly central to ensuring the liberty of the individual.[34] It is a stark fact that the more zealous marketeers sometimes overlook the fact that the state remains the only possible mechanism not only for creating law, but also for enforcing the rule of law. Thus without the state – even with a severely weakened state, as in post-cold war Russia, a society of mafias and gangs – society would be lawless. And lawlessness poses a much more serious threat to the individual – to his or her property, even life – than do the oft-cited 'excesses' of government, such as bureaucracy or tax-gathering. The rule of law is arguably the state's most profound gift to civilisation.

There is now little doubt that what William Greider called the 'manic logic' of new global capitalism seriously threatens the reign and rule of law, or at least as we have known it. Supporters of business continue to proclaim the importance of law, about the responsibility of businesses to exist 'within the law'. Yet this obeisance to the law by businesses can often be disingenuous. The fact is that many big corporations see the law as their primary threat, as they make a point of escaping, or threatening to escape, from those laws they do not like, and relocating, or threatening to relocate, to more conducive legal environments. It is a stark reality, but in this sense, for corporations, the rule of law no longer exits. In the ideal world of global capitalism the long arm of the law will not always reach. There will be no extradition treaties for mobile capital or for corporations in pursuit of lower social costs.

As well as securing the law, there is another powerful argument for the state as protector of the individual and of individual freedom. Historically, a strong case can be made that the freedom and space of the individual has best been protected, even enhanced, where there has been a balance between public and private, state and market, where the public sector can cooperate with and compete with an equally strong private sector. The pluralism inherent in such a balance can at least secure some autonomy for the domestic citizen.

Obviously for supporters of individual freedom it is the character of the state, rather than its existence, that matters. Yet in the new global order the democratic state – the state that enforces the law properly and fairly, even the state that remains in balance with the private sector – has also become the enemy, to be circumvented if possible, defeated if necessary.

PEACE, STATE AND POLITICS

The freedom of the individual can only exist if conflicts can be resolved sensibly and peaceably. The political world, rather than the economic world, was always considered the primary mechanism for such acceptable conflict resolution. After all, at the heart of the idea of the modern study of politics is both the recognition of conflict and difference and disagreement, and also the processes whereby people resolve, or do not resolve, conflicts.

Thus according to some schools of thought there is no politics in agreement, nor in forced agreement. The political philosopher Kenneth Minogue has argued that 'despots don't belong' in the definition of politics.[35] As Maurice Duverger puts it, the 'two-faced god Janus is the true image which…expresses the most profound political truth' of group conflict and its resolution based upon discussion and compromise.[36] Politics only comes into operation once a single power centre – crown, dictator, party (as in the communist system) – is removed or fades

away. In contrast, of course, a market can exist under a dictatorship, or even, as we are still seeing in communist China, a
one-party state.

The skills of the politician are democratic skills, so much so
that today the much maligned skills of 'politics' – the ability to
read public mood, the sense of what is possible and what is
not, the ability to compromise between interests, the ability to
articulate goals and values – are essential in mastering the arts
of democracy. In contrast, and it is a crucial distinction, the
skills of the business person – organisation, management, risk-
taking – are leadership skills, aimed at helping forward an
individual unit or company They are certainly creative, but
they are not particularly democratic. They are aimed at producing a product or a profit, not at securing certain values or
at resolving conflict.

However, regardless of this huge history of politics and law
as conflict resolvers, global marketeers still see the 'market' as
a much better way of resolving conflict. They correctly point to
the history of politics as being the history of the nation-state
(as much as the history of law), and to how this self-same
nation-state was the source of the great and deadly conflicts of
the past.

In contrast with this sorry history of conflict and war, they
suggest that the new world market they supported would usher
in, on a global scale, an epoch of peace (and that the global
market will ensure peace not simply because it is a market,
but because it is global). This argument, a powerful one,
rests on the proposition that it was the market, not politics,
that created one global system, and one global system is inherently more stable and peaceable than one with subdivisions –
nations – that cause emnities and conflict.

However 'one world' economically does not mean one

world politically. And intriguingly globalisers who push for and celebrate a world market do not normally also demand a 'world government'. The dynamic of global capitalism seeks no balance between public and private on a global basis, and resists – largely for tax reasons – world government. So in the real global economy that is now under construction, economic inequalities and resentments can be expected to grow; and these inequalities could spawn serious rebellions and violence.

As Soros argues: 'I can already discern the makings of the final crisis [of global capitalism]. It will be political in character. Indigenous political movements are likely to arise that will seek to expropriate multinational companies and recapture the "national" wealth. Some of them will succeed in the manner of the Boxer rebellion or the Zapata revolution.'[37] There is no reason to believe that whole nations will not opt out of the global economic system, causing conflict with their neighbours, and ultimately violence. Could Malaysia, which in 1998-9 was resisting the imperatives of global capitalism from a very, very small base, be a prototype?

And all this in an environment where there is no democratic world government to resolve these conflicts through the exercise of law. The 'one world' of global capitalism may become a very unsafe place indeed. And crucially without world government, without a global political dimension, those economic conflicts that are resolved will not be settled as they broadly are under political regimes, in favour of majorities or on the basis of rights upheld by the law. Rather they will be resolved in true market fashion, in favour of those with economic power, with that rawest of measurements: most money, most resources. Again, unavoidably, those who control the market, the super-rich with their super capital, will inevitably win.

THE STATE AND 'THE PEOPLE'

As well as securing the rights and freedom of the individual, governments – proper, democratic governments – are supposed to ensure that 'the people', rather than elites, rule. Supporters of global capitalism, however, dispute this idea that the state (and the politics it organises and protects) can ensure popular sovereignty. They suggest that only through the market mechanism can true popular sovereignty – the idea that people, rather than elites, rule – become a reality. This, as we have seen, is the notion of 'people's capitalism', made popular in the 1980s by Margaret Thatcher and Ronald Reagan. In its essentials it argued that politics and government limit, rather than enable, access to power.

This question of access is at the heart of this criticism of politics. Arthur Seldon has taken the lead in arguing, with force, that the sizeable government and state created during the post-1945 era produced a class of 'political people' who manipulated this state system in order to achieve an advantage for themselves. This idea of 'political people' could also be extended more widely to many in the middle classes, and was most evident in health and education, where the 'political people', the well-connected people, through their social status (which in the postwar period was still very, very important in European countries such as France and Britain) or contacts in the system gained what amounted to preferential treatment within the state system.

This populist appeal – that in the state and public sector, special 'elitist' people gained at the expense of 'ordinary people', or 'the common people' – subtly, or not so subtly, undercut the political left as the protector of the weak and underprivileged, portraying socialists not as caring democrats but rather as 'top people', uncaring mandarins. This was a more effective rerun of a theme from the early 1970s when the political and intellectual left were depicted as phonies: in the US as 'limousine liberals' and in Britain as 'Hampstead do-gooders'.

This right-wing populism was effective because it possessed some truth. There remains a strong case that the middle classes gained disproportionately from the welfare state, and that the welfare system was open to manipulation by the articulate and well-connected. Also, the British social democratic state, as it developed in the 1950s, 1960s and 1970s, did indeed become both bureaucratised – producing, as anyone on the receiving end could readily testify, insensitive and bossy elites – and politicised, creating political classes who saw both the state and the world of politics as exclusive preserves for their own benefit. And in the process government did indeed cease to operate as a neutral referee between private interests or as a well-organised welfare system, but instead became 'an interest', rather like a 'special interest' or a 'corporate interest'. And many of those who worked for government, who served the state, no longer saw their occupation as a special vocation – a proud vocation uniquely allowing the office holder 'to do the people's work'.

The only problem was that all these charges about state bureaucracy, about special interests and about unfair advantages gained through influence and connections in the governmental system could just as easily have been made of the market-based system. Corporations produced their own bureaucracy and organisational rigidities, inefficiencies often successfully hidden from shareholders by managers. 'Who you know', rather than 'what you know' – a corporate term called 'networking' – worked just as powerfully in the private sector. Large businesses thrived on 'connections'. Unsavoury (even

outright corrupt) connections between large private corporations and the state (such as the US Congress and executive
departments such as the Pentagon) were the routine meat and
drink of the lobbying system. Job appointments were less regulated than in the public sector, with fewer rules about inter-
viewing and discrimination. And amongst small businesses,
nepotism – almost by definition – was an acceptable form of
business recruitment.

PARTICIPATION

As well as securing popular sovereignty, marketeers claimed
that market capitalism achieved another crucial democratic
outcome: a high and wide rate of participation, higher and
wider than that offered by *political* democracy. Arthur Seldon
suggests that modern capitalism, by minimising the writ of
politics and maximising the writ of the market, 'creates a more
effective form of democracy' by enabling 'all the people, the
common people as well as the political people, to decide their
lives'.[38] He then goes on to posit what he calls 'the central question': 'is it easier for the political process to include all the
heads or for the market process to endow all the people with
money?' The obvious answer to this rhetorical question was
that the political process would include fewer.

There was a misreading of 'political democracy' here.
Modern democratic politics, political democracy, was never
just about 'counting heads' or participation. It was certainly
about allowing those who wanted to participate to do so, *and
to do so as of right*. (You had the right to vote because you were
a human being, whereas you participated in market democracy because you were endowed with money) But it was more
than that. Under the democracy of the state, access and participation were to be secured through rights, not just votes. And

rights (as I argue later in this chapter) can allow 'the common people' access to the governmental system and the decision-making forums of society just as effectively, in fact more effectively than voting every few years.

Some pro-business intellectuals believe that the private capitalist sector can help participation through means other than the 'democracy of the market' – for instance by encouraging participation through companies themselves. Company workforces already take part in company decision-making in many small ways, but Charles Handy amongst others, has suggested that a restructuring of the corporation could allow for a real advance in corporate democracy. He suggests that the modern corporation is 'inadequate for modern times', that 'a public corporation has now to be regarded as a community, not a piece of property', and that we need a 'citizen corporation' in which 'the core members of that community are more properly regarded as citizens rather than employees or "human resources", citizens with responsibilities as well as rights'.[39]

The idea here is that in these new 'citizen corporations' the private ownership of property will remain, as will the market, but that within the privately-owned unit a new sharing of power and decision-making should take place. A variant of this is, of course, the existing cooperatives. In the cooperative movement:

> the key idea is that the market mechanism is retained as a means of providing most goods and services, while the ownership of capital is socialised...all productive enterprises are constituted as workers' cooperatives, leasing their operating capital from an outside investment agency. Each enterprise makes its own decisions about products, prices, etc...net profits form a pool out of which incomes are paid...Each enterprise is democratically con-

trolled by those who work for it.[40]

One problem with this private sector model of participation is that, even if it was expanded to include public sector enterprises, the new-style market democracy it advocates takes no account of the millions and millions who have no connection with companies whatsoever – students, the elderly the unemployed. *Political* democracy, on the other hand, can include everyone. Also, market democracy – particularly in the global market – limits decision-making to economic and economic-related issues, whereas political democracy encourages participation in a range of non-economic issues, from international policy to cultural and even social and sexual issues.

Another problem with market democracy is the huge inequalities in participation. Certainly everyone who has access to the market can participate in it, but unlike political democracy, where participation is at least theoretically equal (one person has one vote, everyone has the same rights), the extent of market participation depends on the amount of resources you can bring to the market. Put crudely – for it *is* somewhat crude – big bucks mean greater participation. And under global capitalism, where capital is even more important *vis-à-vis* labour (and the state), then this inequality of participation is even more marked.

The criticism by market supporters of low participation rates in political democracy are powerfully made. However politics is open to reform. In one sense the history of government is the history of adjustment and adaptation to wider and wider participation and access, in other words to democracy. The Greek idea of the polis may have existed alongside slavery, but Greek politics gave us the word and the idea – the gripping, powerful idea of 'democracy'. Democracy remains a political word with a political meaning. The political institutions of the medieval world – kingship and the like – certainly excluded the majority of people and entrenched serfdom, yet the English Parliament was formed in this period. Although the great political/constitutional document of American independence was written in Philadelphia by English landowners, who excluded women and happily ignored slavery, it was malleable enough to become the most celebrated and mature example of democratic constitutionalism (and arguably it still is the greatest single written institutional expression of the democratic idea).

Not only is it possible to reform government and the state, to continue to adapt it to the growing modern need for ever-increasing participation and access, but reforming government in order to achieve this task is now relatively easy because of modern techniques and changing technology. The widespread use of information technology – television, computers, internet and the like – makes a surfeit of political participation now practically possible. We can participate – discuss, vote – from home. The citizen is now able to vote – monthly, weekly, daily, even hourly – both on single issues and for representatives. It is now technically possible to arrange a fairly competent referendum every day of the week. (So rather than political democracy limiting access or participation, the modern-day problem may be democratic fatigue.)

Anthony Giddens, in his theoretical book on social democracy, *The Third Way*, sees the possibilities of renewing rather than shrinking the state. 'What is necessary', he suggests, 'is to reconstruct [the state] – to go beyond those on the right who say "government is the enemy" and those on the left who say "government is the answer".' And he outlines specific strategies that the modern state should employ in order to renew itself: devolution, the further democratisation of democratic institutions, renewal of the public sphere through transparency, administrative efficiency, mechanisms for direct democracy, and government as risk manager (by which he means, in part, regulating scientific and technological change).[41]

MINORITIES

Market theorists and propagandists sometimes argue that 'political democracy' is potentially authoritarian, and therefore careless of the rights of minorities. In this mindset 'the state' is – if not exactly the door to communism or fascism – incipiently authoritarian, certainly compared with 'the market', which is viewed as inherently libertarian. Even the relatively mature democratic states – say the US or Britain – although not in themselves necessarily oppressive, have a very definite potential to be so. Their problem is majorities! Their 'working method of making decisions by majorities, or counting heads, and ignoring many heads merely because they are less numerous, is a childish and uncivilised way of deciding the use of resources'. In contrast market democracy, by 'counting pennies not heads', provides some power for 'all heads, including those of minorities and...independent and idiosyncratic individuals'.[42]

This idea that minorities and 'idiosyncratic individuals' are protected by money, even lots and lots of it, is fanciful. Stable mass prosperity, whereby majorities feel secure and unthreatened, is probably the most effective protection for minorities. But in times of economic trouble the market, by its propensity for increasing inequalities, may make life *worse* for minorities because of the creation of increasing social tensions in which minority groups become vulnerable. And it is in these difficult times for minorities that politics – in the form of an entrenched democratic political culture – and the state – in the form of a written constitution and, crucially, the rule of law is the best guarantor of minority rights. Whatever the causes of the two great holocausts – the slaughter of the Armenians in Turkey and the Jews in Germany – it was the lack of a political safety net – of strong democratic institutions, of a democratic political culture – not the lack of markets, that led economic failure and social tensions to break out into slaughter.

In a global economy in which no state is strong enough to create this political safety net, minorities may find themselves with less and less protection.

RIGHTS

The battle for individual rights has been the very stuff of the history of western civilisation. It has exercised the minds of the great liberal thinkers from John Locke to John Stuart Mill, and great polemicists such as Tom Paine and Thomas Jefferson; and it has enlivened the pages of great political documents from the Magna Carta through to *The Rights of Man* and the American Declaration of Independence, right up to the present day and the UN and EU Declarations. These traditional 'rights' – such as freedom of speech, assembly and petition, and the right to worship – are now joined by social rights such as the right to privacy, abortion and non-discrimination based upon equal rights. Even economic rights, to jobs and economic security, are now, more controversially, on the agenda. Rights are so much a part of the fabric of western life, even a measure of civilised living, that some commentators believe the culture of rights has progressed so far that the concomitant responsibilities are being ignored.

Yet rights are essentially a political idea. They are articulated by politicians and political writers. They are written down in political documents. And political, constitutional and legal systems enforce and encourage them.

It is universally accepted that the state – that is, political authority – is the only mechanism that can entrench rights.

This is so because it is the only acceptable mechanism for law-making and governing the physical forces of coercion that lie behind the law – the police, the military in 'aid of the civil power'. No one, except extreme libertarians and anarchists, suggests that the much-vaunted market – or market players – should actually make laws (although in the real world large agglomerations of private capital can control legislatures or ignore laws) or take over the role of the courts and the police (although private security services sometimes blur the distinction between state law and private rules).

The fact is that the market – and certainly the global market – cannot on its own either create or protect rights. Nor can (or should) the principal inhabitants of the market place – the large corporations! Ultimately we need to face the fact that business people are not in business to protect rights (or, more generally, to make the world a better place!) Regardless of the protestations of the business ethics industry, most honest business people will admit the truth of this. And in a world in which corporations have their way, having outmanoeuvred the state, then the future for any realistic regime of rights looks increasingly bleak.

As the claims for rights come to be extended beyond political rights to economic rights, then the very idea of rights clearly comes into direct conflict with modern market democracy and global capitalism. When, for instance, the 'right to employment' is claimed, this right is obviously denied by supporters of the global markets, and even by market democrats who see it as threatening the smooth working of market capitalism, particularly the ability of employers to hire and fire at will.

PLURALISM

For many political theorists, pluralism is the lifeblood of democracy and the democratic way of life. Plural power centres are seen as offering protection against the dangers of centralisation inherent in a single authority, and as giving the individual freedom of space and maneuverability.

And pluralism is modern capitalism's strongest suit. Whatever can be said against the global market it does not tend to centralise power – at least not during the early stage it is still in. The global marketplace is simply too big and too diffuse to allow such centralisation. So far, whatever its other democratic shortcomings, modern global capitalism remains a veritable cornucopia of pluralism: almost a bustling anarchy, with many, many decision-making centres. The sheer number of companies and units of capital competing around the world ensures such pluralism. And the new mobile capital of the global economic order also ensures political pluralism because it acts to break up political units so that it can divide and rule.

Of course modern global capitalism is witnessing an increasing number of mergers between corporations. Giant and highly centralised super-corporations are beginning to dominate the various sectors of the global economy The huge mergers of the 1990s – many of which, such as those between British Petroleum and Amoco, and Deutsche Bank and Bankers Trust, were truly transnational – all point to a worrying future of great agglomerations of economic power. Even so, there is still little prospect of that creature of the imagination, 'one great corporation', dominating the world.

On the other hand the political system, the interstate or international relations system that globalism has largely replaced, tended to concentrate power in far fewer locations. And in the Cold War's nuclear age some of these political power centres – individuals such as the president of the United States and the general-secretary of the Soviet Union, and their respective inner-sanctum colleagues – accumulated so much power that, unlike even the biggest corporation, they held the awesome power of life or death over millions. That the state can possess such an illiberal, centralising potential that may not, in quite the same sense, be present in the market is now widely recognised. Even socialists are now able to accept that in state-dominated economies there is a pluralist deficit. As Christopher Pierson has written:

> What has seemed to many commentators to be fatally damaging to this socialist argument is the continuing failure to generate a satisfactory model for the democratic control of economic life. This objection seems even more compelling now in the light of the recent experience of the two most prominent and quite divergent forms which 'real socialism' took in the twentieth century – the Soviet model and western social democracy.[43]

Of course one of the reasons why democrats and liberals support the idea of pluralism is that, by preventing the growth of any power centre from reaching the point where it can threaten the individual, such pluralism enhances individual rights. Capitalist economic pluralism, however, does not serve this function. It certainly provides many economic decision centres, and this type of pluralism certainly helps consumer choice. But extending consumer choice, important though it is, is not the same thing as protecting political rights such as freedom of speech, assembly and worship – or indeed economic rights such as a job! Political rights are protected by law and the state, and no matter how diffuse economic power may be under global capitalism, if the state is weakened, so is the ability to protect rights. And also, we should not forget that no matter the number of economic decision-makers in the market, not one of them – not one – has, *in their economic role*, any fundamental interest or motivation in protecting human rights.

Through the mists and subtleties of the great debate about globalisation and democracy there remains one very worrying political truth. Whatever the politics and values of the new world we are heading into, they will not be democratic – at least as we have known and understood the word. The kind of liberal-democratic political systems that grew from and developed out of the political upheavals of the late eighteenth century in France and North America – what we now call liberal-democracy – were coexistent with nation-states, and are likely to die alongside them.

So, as the nation-state withers on the vine under the pressures of globalising capital, so does democracy. It is a huge problem.

CHAPTER NINE

THE BUSINESS CLASS VERSUS THE WEST

THE HUMBLING OF THE STATE (AND POLITICS)

One of the great ironies of the post-cold war era is that the degeneration of western capitalism (outlined in the last chapter) has gone hand in hand with its great victory over its global opponents, communism. But this 'triumph of capitalism' was in reality the triumph of business – a victory not of a system but rather of a new class, the business class – the corporate business class. And when, following the bail-out of western business creditors during the Mexican crisis of 1994, Michael Camdessus, the chief executive of the IMF no less, could declare angrily that 'the world is in the hands of these guys' – so it was.[1] And over a decade later, with business still rampant, 'these guys' had even more power – more certainly than the leaders of most all the world's nation-states.

This victory of business, and the business class, over the state is often confused with the victory of 'the market'. But it was no such thing. For 'markets', particularly 'free markets', or 'pure markets', were always a myth – primarily an invention of intellectuals. For just as it was principally intellectuals in the 30s and 40s who put great faith in 'socialism' and 'communism', so in the 1980s and 1990s the new utopia was 'the market'.

The fact is that this corporate business class is essentially neutral as between 'markets' and the state. It would use 'markets' when they were helpful (that is when they could control them); and it would use the state too when it was helpful – when for instance the state could act in its 'handmaiden' role (with subsidies and infrastructure) or in its 'bail-out' role when business got into trouble. Business only opposed the state when it ceased to help, when it interfered in the business of business – profit-making. But as the postwar years rolled by, and the state indeed became more 'interfering' and 'burdensome', particularly through its taxation and regulation policies, tensions between business and state (and the politicians who ran the state) became endemic. And when communism finally fell and business became global the result was a weakening everywhere of governments. And with this triumph of business came a major defeat not only for the state, but for politics and politicians too.

By decade's end the reputation of politics, never held in high regard, had reached an all-time low. 'Public service' had no resonance, whereas a life in business was increasingly prized. 'Government' was a dirty word, considered inherently inefficient, if not dangerous, whereas the private sector was, by comparison, regarded as competent and dynamic. Above all, there were no role models left in the world of politics – no heroes like FDR, Kennedy, De Gaulle, even Winston Churchill; they had been replaced by business celebrities like Bill Gates, Warren Buffet and Donald Trump, in Britain Alan Sugar and Richard Branson.

The standing of politics and 'public service' had not been helped by the politicians themselves, above all by the sleaze around Bill Clinton or the 'stupid white man' image of George W. Bush. But that was only a small part of the story. When, in the mid-1990s, the American social theorist Peter Drucker suggested that 'if this century proves one thing, it is the futility of politics' he was echoing a widely held view that politics had been made increasingly redundant by the business era. That in today's world change was no longer forged by politics, but rather by the growth of markets, the privatisation of assets and the globalisation of finance; and that it took place in new arenas – primarily economic and financial, but also technological and cultural.

'Futility' was of course something of an exaggeration. For even by the end of the 'greedy decade' with global capitalism rampant, politics (and government) was still important, and always potentially able to make a comeback. What it lost, though, was its *special* quality. Politics (like the state) has lost its *special* role as the arbiter between economic interests and as the court of final appeal between business and social interests. It is no longer the ultimate forum, or the overarching way of thinking about the public world.

That arch-priestess of global capitalism, former Prime Minister Margaret Thatcher, summed up this toppling of politics from its special status with her famous dictum that 'there is no such thing as society'. She argued – and it was a powerful thrust – that politicians were nothing special, that they were little more than a vested interest like any other, an elite who evoked images such as 'society' and the 'public good' only in order to dress up their personal agendas in selfless language.

Above all the world of politics has come to be seen by influential supporters of the market as a mechanism for elitism – for the 'government of the busy, by the bossy, for the bully', while the market operated in favour of 'ordinary men and women'; the political process was constructed for elites and specialists 'in the arts of persuasion, organisation, infiltration, debate, lobbying, manipulating meetings…'[2] It was a polemical bullet that hit home, particularly in the 1980s in Britain, which had just witnessed the excesses of a minority on the extreme left in local councils and trade unions.

From this market vantage point, the world of politics has become an interest group like any other – no longer concerned with the best for the country, with 'the big picture' essentially no different from farmers, teachers, small businesspeople; politicians always have an axe to grind and a nest to feather; politics is lacking in virtue; public service is a sham, merely a cover for personal aggrandisement; the great political creed of 'rights' is a cover for selfishness (and more stress should be placed upon responsibilities). Even the political art of compromise is derided, and is often compared unfavourably – by the privately owned media – with the risk-taking of business.

It was little wonder, then, that during the high point of the victory of business in the 90s the authority drained out of politics. Political leaders were no longer held in high regard, indeed the very word 'politician' had (has) become a term of derision. The careful, contrived public language of politicians increasingly bored (bores) the public. The widespread use of public relations advisors – the politicians' response to the massive growth of the political media – tends to reduce politicians to little more than a branch of the entertainment industry. And, in the British and US systems at least, successful politicians are those who, like President Bill Clinton and Prime Minister Tony Blair, are 'PR conscious' and presentationally skilful – highly polished performers in front of the cameras, concerned to court the media elites. In a sign of the times Tony Blair as

Prime Minister even agreed to a lower billing on a television talk show than that of a popular singer.[3]

By the late 1990s the role and standing of the politician had changed radically, not only from the days of Roosevelt and Churchill, but also from those of Reagan and Thatcher. With the exigencies of the Cold War fast becoming a distant memory, the 'heroic' or 'mini heroic' style of political leadership – the attributes of distance, gravitas, character, vision – had given way to softer traits: warmth, concern, understanding, sensitivity. For the successful politician at the turn of the century 'doing the right thing', or thinking long-term and strategically is less important than the day-to-day management of the polity and society. Testing policies before they are advocated became a political must and a leadership skill: much of Bill Clinton's and Tony Blair's success for the electorate was down to Phillip Gould's and James Carville's political consultancy, GGC-NOP. And an ear to public opinion – via the use of sophisticated polling techniques and focus groups – has become a more important aspect of the job description of a politician than a grasp of the details of policy, let alone a sense of history.

This collapse in the traditional standards of political leadership is in part a reflection of a lowering of what the public expects of its political leaders. So low had these expectations become that opinion polls in 1998 showed that although a majority of Americans believed that their president had lied under oath – and to them! – they still approved of the way he was doing his job and did not want him removed from office, even though he had probably committed a crime. Politics simply matters less and less; western publics are simply not listening to their politicians about politics; instead they are turning to 'experts', journalists and a range of non-traditional authority figures – businesspeople of course, but also celebrities, royalty and talk show hosts, for social and political views and guidance.

Not only were politicians held in low regard, but so too were public servants of all kinds. And in this process even the very best examples of the public sector – the meritocrats, the highly educated achievers who ran many of the civil services of the West, even those in France and in the European Commission in Brussels – were branded as 'technocrats' and seen as much less worthy than the risk-takers in the private sector. The public servants in the American military were, though, excused, primarily because of the patriotism engendered by the 'war on terror'; but, underneath, the life of soldiering was also no longer held in high regard. Somehow the craft of administration and management in the public sector came to be labeled as 'bureaucratic', whereas the same bureaucratic functions in the private corporate sector went largely unnoticed. (And in the real world, the bosses of the public sector – the politicians, the bureaucrats – often directed far fewer resources than the chief executive officers of the private sector or the major financial families.)

THE GROWING FUTILITY OF ELECTIONS

Political institutions are also in trouble. In the global market democracies of the US and Britain, governmental institutions – from the US Congress and presidency to the British Parliament and monarchy – are losing their appeal with the public. No longer viewed as authoritative and, above all, neutral, political institutions are no longer seen as separate from the political class who inhabit them. And in the process even the institutions themselves have come to be viewed as players in a kind of market system. The US public's low regard for the

US Congress has become a settled feature of political life, and intriguingly the elected members of the Congress regularly fall well below the respect and trust ranking of the unelected members of the Supreme Court; while British opinion polls regularly report that large numbers of Britons, particularly amongst the younger age groups, no longer believe that the monarchy and royal family have much relevance to their lives.

Elections are also in trouble. No longer seen as 'democracy's great day', elections are, often accurately, now viewed as exercises in manipulation, their outcomes governed by public relations advisors and, in the US, by hugely expensive television advertising campaigns. On the right, mass democracy, and the politicians who operate within it, is seen as pandering to left-wing sectional interests and a direct cause of the so-called overblown, unfundable welfare state.[4] For many on the left, elections are dismissed as a middle-class preserve that have no meaning for large numbers of the excluded, particularly the growing underclass. Before the presidential candidacy of Barack Obama, very low turnouts in inner-city areas were part of election lore. Turnout rates in elections are generally falling. In the US, presidential election turnout percentages are normally in the low 50s. And they are in secular decline – in the three elections of the 1960s the figure was over 60 per cent in each, but every election since 1980 has seen a turnout in the low 50s (except for 1996 when it fell as low as 49.1 per cent and in 2004 when it rose to 55.3 per cent. A typical election was the 1988 contest when 91 million people voted, but *the same number* – largely composed of inner-city blacks, Hispanics and the rural and urban poor – stayed away from the polls. In elections for Congress the figures are even lower. Even after several well-publicised registration drives the turnout amongst American blacks is still alarmingly low. In Britain the numbers voting in general elections fell from a high of over 80 per cent in the early 1950s to the low 70s in the 1980s and was lower still in the two general elections of the twenty-first century (59.1 per cent in 2001 and 61.4 per cent in 2005). The European Union elections usually attract significantly fewer British voters, and voting for local elections is often in the region of 20-40 per cent.

SOCIETY AGAINST POLITICS

Some argue that this crisis of confidence in government and politics is simply a result of specific, avoidable events. Events like the deception surrounding the Vietnam War and Watergate, the 'lying' of Bill Clinton during the Monica affair or the 'lying' of George W. Bush during the Iraq invasion. Others place the crisis at the feet of what, in the fashionable arguments of the 1970s, came to be known as the 'overloading' of government, or the inability of political institutions to deal with the extent and complexity of the changing demands upon them. Others suggest it is all down to the robust health of democracy – the inherent healthy questioning of authority, the probing of leaders and public figures.

But lying politicians, or complex government, or a culture of robust anti-authority, are only part of the story. The 'free market revolution' of the 1980s and 90s produced deep social changes. These years witnessed a huge increase in small businesses, many of them sole proprietorships, started up by workers laid off by big corporations. In the process many of these new small business people allied themselves with the interests and anti-politics culture of bigger businesses. Also, the consumer and debt culture of the times naturally led to the replacing of community and citizenship values by consumer values – by a money-oriented culture over old-fashioned social responsibility. It all added up to one thing: a shift of power away from the public, or political, realm run by government to the private, consumer, realm run by business.

One of the most under-publicised social changes of the whole postwar period has been the rapid growth in the number of people who pay tax. In the 1950s tax paying used to be a concern of a 'rich' minority only. But as broader swathes of the population became subject to 'Withholding' (in the US) and 'Pay As You Earn' (in Britain) and many middle class folks started paying inheritance taxes, a rich vein of populist resentment against 'government' and its taxing powers became available for tapping. President Ronald Reagan's famous electioneering sound-bite – 'Get the government off the backs of the people' – successfully exploited this sentiment. As did presidential candidate, multimillionaire, and doyen of the low-tax regime, Steve Forbes, whose standard pitch would include the line: 'politicians say "we" can't afford a tax cut. Maybe we can't afford the politicians.'

THE CORPORATE MEDIA

This growing distaste for politics may have been down to big societal changes, but it had considerable help along the way – to the point of fanning the flames – by the ascendant business community, not least its burgeoning corporate media arm. In the age of the internet the corporate media may no longer possess monopoly power over news and information, but through their websites as well as their television and newspapers, they can still set something of an agenda. And it is often forgotten that for western publics the world of the public sector – the world of politics – is still filtered through privately owned media by a business class that can hardly help but bring its own values and opinions to bear.

In the US, television journalists, pundits and newspaper editors are employees of big business enterprises, many of them global companies. The environment is slightly more plural with the internet, but has not changed that much. Small non-corporate websites run by individuals are rather like old village meetings – good for local democracy, but rarely able to move national opinion; and bigger non-corporate websites often simply relay, through the click, news and data from bigger corporate media outlets.

Although the media class – well-off, highly educated, urban and relatively sophisticated – tend to be progressive on social issues, they are apt to reflect their employers' pro-business, and anti-politics, views on economic issues, particularly taxation (although, being high-earners, they probably come to their low tax views all by themselves, not due to corporate pressure).

Media owners are business people. And the media class is thus, in essence, a business class – and therefore naturally interested in profits. And profits lie with giving the new narcissistic consumer society what they demanded – less 'politics' and more 'lifestyle': more coverage of sex, money, fashion and sport. This kind of new news content only served to further marginalise politics, turning the world of public life into a 'boring' arena occupied by men in suits. And in the process traditional political concerns about economic and social justice became 'boring' too.

BUSINESS AND STATE: THE BATTLE FOR SUPREMACY

Yet a world without politics (and the state which allows it) is still, to westerners at least, ultimately unthinkable. We would have seen nothing like it before. From the dawn of time, certainly from ancient times – from the time when humankind began to organise itself (and arguably even before that, in the relations established between two people) – politics has existed in some form or other. In the days of the Greek polis Aristotle depicted politics as 'the master art', concerned with the allocation of resources and much more besides. The ancients seemed to possess a clear understanding of the limits of economics ('the dismal science').

In the middle ages, too, economics was subordinated to a host of social goals, such as the idea of a socially 'just price' or protectionist and producer interests (often called guilds). In medieval local communities the church often held sway over economics, and in Catholic Europe, in an approach reaching down to today's Christian democracy very definite ideas about the economy – almost amounting to a Christian code of economic policy – were propagated.

This subordination of economics to politics was inevitable in a world of traditional communities where non-economic loyalties took precedence, where community goals were seen as transcending individual economic advancement. People were loyal to their communities in a way that is difficult to understand today These communities were not instrumental or contractual, establishing obligations in return for services. Rather they were seen as living organisms which, existing long before the individual was born and surviving long after he or she had gone, could demand not only loyalty but also obedience.

Also, the sheer religiosity of these traditional medieval communities ensured the supremacy of politics over economics. Spirituality took precedence over the material world; and the debate over religion (what today we might call ideology), much of it with a highly political content, overshadowed people's vague understanding of economics.

BUSINESS, POLITICS AND THE ARRIVAL OF THE NATION-STATE

In Europe during the seventeenth and eighteenth centuries, as local markets expanded into national ones, the emerging nation-states slowly took over the political functions of the localities and the church, and began to impose their own regulations and taxes. This new world of nation-states led to, if anything, a strengthening of politics.

A transcendent sense of community remained, but was given form and life by the emergence of a new and larger political unit, the nation-state. These nations, and their states, became the primary focus for loyalty – often even competing with and overcoming the family unit. Some analysts have suggested that a sense of identity 'is inseparable from an awareness of ourselves as members of a particular family or class or community or people or nation, as bearers of a specific history, as citizens of a particular republic; and *we look to the political realm* as a way in which we can develop and refine our sense of ourselves'.[5]

In fact nowadays we tend to forget the strength of this identification with the political realm, the political community, represented as it has been over the last three hundred years or so by the nation-state. Alan Milward suggests that the ultimate basis for the survival of the nation-state is 'the same as it always was, allegiance'.[6] During the twentieth century millions of people have displayed their allegiance to the political idea of nation by making very serious sacrifices, including a willingness to make the ultimate one.

Of course the *genuine* level or intensity of political allegiance, or loyalty, is very difficult to measure. The nation-state also had ultimate legal authority over the lives of its people. It could (still can) fine, tax, imprison, even take life. There was no higher legal appeal, and most people were powerless to leave its boundaries. In such circumstances a degree of political loyalty or allegiance was hardly surprising, perhaps more as much a measure of *force majeur* than of genuine feeling.

Linda Colley has attempted to measure this political loyalty by the yardstick of willingness to serve in the armed forces. She reports that by early eighteenth century standards 'they (the statistics organised by the government in 1798 and 1803 to find out who would serve in the armed forces) confront those who argue on the one hand for widespread loyalty and deference throughout Great Britain...and those who claim on the other hand that the mass of Britons were alienated from their rulers'.[7]

BUSINESS AND THE VICTORIAN NATION

So powerful was the nation-state that even during the high point of the unfettered market relations of the nineteenth century, politics remained in charge, managing to constrain the raw economic power of Victorian capitalism. Trade and commerce may have blossomed, and increasingly broken free of borders, but in these Victorian times – in the leading capitalist nations, Britain, the United States and Germany – political sovereignty went unquestioned. The Victorian nation-state was not to be trifled with, or at least not in the way in which global capital treats the contemporary nation-state.

Of course this was the age of imperialism in which the nation-states (and their ruling groups) directly and politically controlled vast territories and peoples. The fundamental dynamic here was political – contests between peoples and civilisations, conquests, and pre-democratic values such as racial superiority and paternalist political views such as elite governance. These empires were geopolitical systems, in which trade might not always exactly 'follow the flag' but was always securely wrapped in it. Commerce played a crucial but ultimately secondary role to the political dynamic of empire, being run from London, Paris, Amsterdam, Madrid and Lisbon.

And it was politics – through imperial expansion of the European nation-states – that fuelled the globalisation of this Victorian era (whereas today's globalisation is the product of economics, of companies and capital, not nation-states).

At home, the Victorian era saw politics – in the form of an expanding political community based on the emerging middle-class male democracy – establishing ascendancy even over the confident, burgeoning capitalism of the era. Victorian capital may indeed have been confident, and profitable; but in an era of strong political loyalties, and being unable to move as freely as it can today, Victorian capital was ultimately subservient to politics, to the Victorian state, in a sense in which it is not in today's global economy. The political community through the state, could improve labour conditions, take the first tentative steps towards a welfare state, and increase public expenditure and taxes without provoking capital flight.

The great Victorian debate was not about whether society or politics existed, or should exist, but rather about how big the state should become – about how much regulation economics should endure. Even the great free-market thinkers of the Victorian era saw politics as sovereign. They may have seen the means towards achieving the free society as largely economic, but their ends were usually political.

In an interesting twist, many of these same 'free market' Victorians were political radicals whose overriding concern was not economics, but political and social change. For them the state was wrongly ordered and should be reformed, although not abolished. And, again unlike today's supporters of the 'free market', these Victorian businessmen were keen on securing rights for the broad mass of people, and saw the state – in the form of the law – as a crucial mechanism. For them the central obstacle was social: the power of the aristocracy and landed interests (reflected in the monarchy, the House of Lords and the limited franchise for the House of Commons). And it was the political ideology of freedom – of freeborn Englishmen – which fired the minds of these radicals. Certainly Tom Paine, Herbert Spencer and Auberon Herbert were supporters of minimal government. They saw the state controlled by a corrupt aristocracy, and sought a greater space for business and the market which would promote a less paternalist, less objectionable, more middle class, society, with better, more democratic values. The aim was social and political, not economic. What these anti-aristocratic businessmen would think of today's early twenty-first century entrenched and inheriting class of business people is a fascinating speculation.

Even during the so-called 'gilded age' of American capitalism in the late nineteenth century, capital was political and social – that is, bounded by the idea of limits placed upon its reach and power by the needs of a wider community. Max Weber in *The Protestant Ethic and the Spirit of Capitalism*, and the Christian Socialist R. H. Tawney in *Religion and the Rise of Capitalism* saw a direct link between religiously inspired ethics and capital, 'a code of Protestant conviction which said that gaining wealth was connected to virtue but was also a trust'.[8] There was wide acceptance of the idea that making money (profits) was morally acceptable as long as there was an ultimate social goal. In the US this notion of capital's ultimate social responsibility was given practical form in the great philanthropic trusts and foundations of the Rockefellers, the Mellons, the Carnegies and the like. These moguls were certainly not keen on state interference in the making of capital, which was often a grubby and ruthless business, but once the pile was made the idea of wider social responsibility (often in the form of charity) took over.

As an historian of the 'robber baron' period has argued:

> In short order the railroad presidents, the copper barons, the big dry-goods merchants and the steel masters became Senators, ruling in the highest councils of the national government, and sometimes scattered twenty dollar gold pieces to newsboys of Washington. But they also became in greater number lay leaders of churches, trustees of universities, partners or owners of newspapers…and figures of fashionable, cultured society.[9]

As one commentator of the time suggested, these robber barons with a conscience, and with a 'becoming gravity', offered themselves as guides 'to literature and art, church and state, science and education, law and morals – the standard container of the civic virtue'.[10]

BUSINESS AND THE TWENTIETH CENTURY NATION

The supremacy of politics over economics in the twentieth century was exemplified by the ideology of the rapidly expanding corporate world. These new corporations, which over the century had replaced the traditional family firm, were large, multi-unit operations. They represented a new managerial capitalism where month by month, year by year, decisions were increasingly taken by a race of professionally and technically competent managers. As Pulitzer Prize winning management theorist Alfred Chandler has argued, these modern big businesses were rather like independent political units, and 'took the place of market mechanisms in coordinating the activities of the economy and allocating its resources'.[11]

By controlling the market rather than competing within it, these big new corporations increasingly acted politically. As Werner Sombart argued during the 1930s, they began to take on a life of their own, the emerging managerial class having as much political and social interest in the land as any trade unionist or civil servant. They sought, and often obtained, influence over legislation by financing congressmen and senators. And, crucially, the new breed of career managers and corporate bureaucrats 'preferred policies that favoured long-term stability and growth of their enterprises to those that maximised current profits'.[12]

Although often driven by profitability, the new culture of the big, multi-unit, largely American, corporation saw the company as part of the wider political community with political and social obligations. One such political obligation was obeying the law. Of course pre-global capitalist corporations used their muscle to attempt to bend legislatures to their will and sway laws in their interests, but once political decisions had been made, the corporations, ultimately bound by the political requirements of their nations, continued their operations within the national boundaries. Although today's global corporations all make a point of declaring that they also obey the laws of the lands in which they operate, their ability to relocate in territories where laws are more amenable means that their protestations are something of an empty boast.

Some of the these big, pre-global companies operating in the Victorian and Edwardian eras saw themselves as political and social communities rather than organisations of property seeking only to make profits. The workforce – often in order to forestall trade union activity – was given the view that the company was a community, almost a family (Henry Ford even became a kind of agony uncle); and a 'community of feeling' was promoted by providing employees with long-term jobs, pensions and health benefits. This approach amounted to a form of micro-welfare capitalism. Elton Mayo, the founding father of the human relations school of management, publicised the corporate welfare practices of AT&T's Hawthorne Works in the late 1920s and early 1930s. Management theorist John Sheldrake has argued that 'the package of benefits at the Hawthorne Works was, by contemporary international standards, impressive and included a pension scheme, sickness and disability benefits, a share purchase plan, a system of worker representation, a medical department and hospital'.[13] In Britain the same kind of community attitude could be seen in the mid-Victorian mill towns where, according to F. M. L. Thompson in *The Rise of Respectable Society*, 'life centred on the mill, not simply because it was the source of work and wages but because it formed a distinct community and attracted specific loyalties'.[14] Indeed the cotton textile industry became the focus of paternalistic activity – what would later be termed 'welfare capitalism'. From the middle of the century it became increasingly common for big employers to provide reading and newspaper rooms at the mills. By the 1890s works sports grounds were common, as were brass bands.

The growth of interest by these new corporate leaders in the idea of scientific management demanded the recognition of a mutuality between managers and workers. F. W. Taylor's work on management, which advocated such a mutuality, attracted a considerable following in the US, Japan and Germany as did the ideas of his disciple, Henry Gantt.[15]

The idea of businesses as communities – of a social or political leavening of the raw economic commercialism of the corporation – did not normally go as far as seeking to involve the 'community of workers' in commercial decisions. After all, this kind of capitalism was paternalistic, not democratic. The corporation was for the workers, but not of them. Even so, after the Second World War 'co-determination', in which employees were allowed some kind of general input into commercial strategy through reserved positions on the governing boards, became a feature of West German corporations. Intriguingly, it was an idea encouraged by the victorious allies who would not have given house room to the notion in their own countries! What stopped worker participation in its tracks in the Anglo-American world was the, often visceral, opposition of some business leaders. But the trade unions were also against it – seeing their function as adversarial negotiators, not mutual builders.

Pre-global capitalist businessmen were, though, both ruthless, and often hugely profitable. Many of them had been dubbed the 'robber barons' and – by Teddy Roosevelt – the 'malefactors of great wealth'. Yet these tough-minded capitalists tended to see business as having some social function beyond the factory gates: business was seen as part of a wider community with community responsibilities. The tone was set by one such robber baron, John D. Rockefeller, a serious critic of whom conceded that his 'prodigious investments in public charities which, begun in 1890, were conducted upon a scale befitting the man's princely power, and most certainly fitted to scale Heaven's walls'.[16] And long after the age of these robber barons, the American companies of the twentieth century continued to invest in local communities – in the townships and villages in which they operated, and expected to continue to operate. All manner of local cultural services and amenities, including symphony orchestras and opera companies, were aided by large corporations.

Of course this political and social dimension of business often made good business sense. A contented workforce could be expected to work more efficiently and thus produce more profits, and, crucially would be less likely to demand trade union representation. And the local community activity would be good for the image of businesses by improving their public relations over the long-term.

For all their self-interest, pre-global capitalist businesses saw profitability and politics as somehow linked. The interest of the shareholder was not utterly paramount. The aim of the corporate game was certainly to make profits, but power, prestige, acceptability and recognition were, along with money, powerful business motives. And the path to business success did not always involve lower and lower social costs.

INTERWAR YEARS: BUSINESS AND POLITICS GET INTO BED

Of course, business concern for the wider political community was enhanced by the deepening relationship between the state and the corporations. The rapid growth in government before, during and after the Second World War opened up for the private sector, big and small, a veritable cornucopia of government contracts – particularly in the defence industry. And later, during the growth of the state after 1945, politically-driven procurement policy often became even more important to the corporations than operating in the market. In such an environment, big business increasingly saw itself, or said it did, as contributing to national (political) goals, not just profit maximisation. Business and state – and sometimes trade unions, 'business unions' – often worked together and helped each other in an 'every one a winner' kind of symbiotic relationship. A new ideology of cooperation, or corporatism, came into fashion.

The idea of cooperation between business, unions and state, much derided by today's supporters of the 'Anglo-Saxon' capitalist model, had been floated officially in Britain during the Mond-Turner talks in 1928-9, and big business organisations (such as the Business Round Table in the US and the CBI in Britain), sensing it would make life easier and more profitable, immediately warmed to the idea. In the US the business world was divided, but some of the CEOs from the biggest corporations opted for agreements with the unions and the New Deal administration.[17] In the political world, many big-business supporters of the moderate wing of the Republican Party and 'One Nation' Tories in Britain propounded these corporatist views well into the 1970s.

But in continental Europe proponents of the social market continued to stress the advantages of cooperation between what they called 'the social partners' of capital and labour; the state and big business continued to work together on long-term, strategic plans for investments and markets.

BUSINESS, DEMOCRACY AND WAR

By the end of the Victorian era the dynamic of a restless, borderless, burgeoning capitalism was well underway. And national governments were slowly losing their autonomy and authority. Some theorists have even suggested that the late Victorian economy was more globalised than that operating today.[18] It would have been a rash man who predicted that what lay ahead was a new age of nationalism. Yet, just such a new age was indeed about to dawn, and with it the continuing ability of the nation-state (and therefore of politics) to constrain the power of economics, business and the market, and to keep capitalism civilised.

This resurgence of the state (in the form of the nation-state) was the product of two extraordinary new phenomena – mass democracy and mass war. By the second decade of the twentieth century mass democracy was well under way in the advanced industrialised countries. The franchise was becoming a majority affair and the middle classes were seeking to participate. The idea of popular sovereignty – that the people owned their government – was growing: strongly in the US, moderately in some continental European countries and somewhat less in Britain. And, crucially, the nation-state became the forum – the only possible forum – for the expression of these democratic instincts and aspirations. It gave the nation a huge shot of legitimacy.

But it was war, more than democracy, that rescued the twentieth century nation-state. The sheer nationalistic fervour of 1914-18, when millions volunteered to fight (and die), remains inexplicable for many. But it existed. It produced a huge emotional commitment to the nation-state, not only during the war, but afterwards too, resting on the legions of heroes who it was claimed gave their lives for the nation, for king and country And war benefited the craft and calling of politics too – for the Second World War leaders (Churchill, Roosevelt, De Gaulle) were politicians, and their mythic status gave authority and credibility not only to the political class but, more broadly, to the state. Business and businessmen were marginalised by war, were thought to play little part in the great military clashes and political crusades, except perhaps as shadowy and sinister armaments manufacturers. The state, not the market, won wars.

The Second World War, unlike its predecessor, was a 'good war' and produced little subsequent pacifist and internationalist sentiment. A major media industry – primarily Hollywood, but television and the literary world as well – hugely reinforced national sentiment in many of the victorious countries. Patriotic themes and negative images of defeated foreigners ('Huns', 'Japs') conspired to enhance postwar nationalism. The war against Hitler was conducted by an alliance, but each nation separately was able to claim an heroic role.

The nation – with its centralised state and its politicians – not only 'won the war', but in its aftermath was also appearing to produce the economic goods. The state, like the nation, came out of the Second World War rather well. It had mobilised resources in a righteous cause, and it had been victorious. In the postwar decades it constructed a popular welfare state which brought education and healthcare to those who had been unable to afford it. The state still had negative aspects – it was seen as inefficient and ridden with bureaucracy – but as the majority of the population still did not pay a large amount of their income in taxes, it was not yet a dark force.

As a social democrat theorist Anthony Crosland wrote at the height of the postwar boom in the 1950s: 'Whatever the modes of economic production, economic power will, in fact, belong to the owners of political power' – in effect the owners of the nation-state. He believed that this political world would last, that 'political authority has emerged as the final arbiter of economic life', and that 'the brief, and historically exceptional, era of unfettered market relations is over'.[19]

Yet in the 1950s this enhanced credibility of government and the state went hand in hand with the renewal of the private sector and its enormous productive capacity. The reviving capitalism of the 1950s and 1960s, the high point of social democracy, took place in the context of an extraordinarily productive balance between economics (and the market) and politics (the state and government) that lasted until well into the 1980s.

During these decades business still deferred to national leaderships, to government and politics. Part of the reason for this was the inherited 'authority' still inherent in the idea of the nation, and in politics and the political world. The emerging big businesses, however, also found the nationally based, social democratic, 'mixed economy' conducive to its needs.

The nation-state was providing a healthy infrastructure for the private sector and was subsidising business in numerous ways. This was the age in which a Republican president (Richard Nixon) and a Conservative prime minister (Edward Heath) introduced wage and price controls; in which big business supported the election of a big-spending, 'Great Society' president (and turned its back on Reaganite Barry Goldwater); in which industrial policy or national planning was not anathema in Britain. It was an age in which business believed that trade unions had to be taken seriously indeed often appeased. And as I shall argue later, the welfare state – existing in an age when, in Europe certainly, socialism and communism were on the political agenda – was seen by many business leaders as a force for social stability.

THE COLD WAR, POLITICS AND BUSINESS

The Cold War began in the late 1940s, the same period in which huge amounts of American public and private capital were beginning to be invested around the world and later pump-primed the era of global capital. Paradoxically, it was the Cold War that staunched the process of early 'globalisation'. For the intensity of the East-West conflict locked the 'emerging markets' of Eastern Europe, the Soviet Union and above all China, out of the world economy for almost five decades. Also, the Cold War breathed life into the nation-state, and gave it a centrality that for fifty years would keep it from being overwhelmed by global capital, global business and the global market. J. G. Ikenberry goes further. He sees the Cold War as a 'long era of global struggle' that not only strengthened nations, nation-states and national governments but also 'centralised' them.[20]

Thus did the Cold War keep western politics ascendant over

western business. 'The business of America' could no longer be about business alone. It had better also be about freedom.

Government and business not only worked together to get the Marshall Plan off the ground, but saw the ambitious plan as 'a simple necessity, a down payment on the American century' From amongst the politicians Truman and many of his Democrats hardly fell in love with business – the feeling was mutual – but they saw the need to co-operate. And, later, as a key aspect of the Cold War, American policy in the Middle East, also had business and government co-operating. Daniel Yergin has suggested that US relations with the Saudi royal family and the Middle East was 'the point at which foreign policy, national-al security and corporate interests would all converge.'[21]

In the Cold War anticommunism – the great cause of the West – became a focus of loyalty. The business world, with its anticommunist instincts, naturally fell in behind the cause, and corporations, even the largest and most powerful of them, remained subordinate to the broader political, ideological and indeed cultural struggle.

Of course during the Cold War decades, particularly in the 1970s during the period of detente, business began doing what it inevitably does: breaking free from politics in search of prof-its. And even in these years of East-West tension, particularly in the later period, there was a decided increase in economic relations between western corporate capitalism and the communist bloc. Western companies were pioneering the eco-nomics of 'globalisation': in particular they were increasingly taking advantage of the Eastern Bloc's low-paid, strike-free labour. An intricate process of buy-back agreements – dubbed 'Vodka-Cola' in which 'you bottle our Coke and we'll buy your Vodka' – were developed in order to bypass the non-convert-ibility of communist bloc currencies.[22]

The advantage of western capitalist access to the low-cost, union-free command economies of the Eastern Bloc were recognised early on by such prominent business figures as Armand Hammer of Occidental Petroleum and Cleveland billionaire Cyrus Eaton. Many European business leaders also saw great benefits in dealing with the Eastern Bloc and supported and encouraged the West German policy of Ostpolitik between the Federal Republic of Germany and the Communist Bloc.

Even so, during the rule of the communist parties (in the period up to 1989) trade and capital flows were minimal, certainly compared with the opening of the floodgates following the collapse of the Berlin Wall and the dissolution of the Warsaw Pact. The requirements of politics – international geopolitics – took precedence over business. In the US, Congress politicians – as part of a major act of political interference with free trade – were able to pass into legislation 'national security' measures whereby whole sectors of western industry and commerce, particularly those connected to the defence industry, were denied trading rights with communist countries by law. These national security laws of the West, primarily aimed at denying technology transfers from West to East, were of course never fully complied with, but during the Cold War most businesses continued to place loyalty to the western political community ahead of profits.[23]

Of course this restraint of the western business class was also to do with self-interest, as corporations that skirted the legal rules and traded with the Eastern Bloc might find it difficult to secure highly lucrative defence contracts from the Pentagon. Also, because of strict western legal restrictions, the Soviet Union was unable to use its large reserves of gold as a means of financing the purchase of western technology. And capital injections into the Eastern Bloc were risky because of the inconvertibility of the communist currencies and the limits to simple barter deals in return for massive transfers of capital and services.

There was immense political and social pressure on companies not to trade with the East, pressure made all the more powerful by the anti East-West trade alliance in the US of Republicans and cold war liberals. Business leaders did not want to fall foul of Reaganite Republican sentiment or be attacked by neo-conservatives. *Vodka-Cola*, the title of an influential book published during the period of detente, became a term of abuse amongst those in the resurgent conservative and neo-conservative movement in the late 1970s and early 1980s. Armand Hammer became an American hate figure amongst Republican and Democrat cold warriors for a time. In the great cause of 'making the world safe for democracy' business was expected, even by the most pro-business elements in the political class, to toe the line.

Many western business elites, and their political allies, not only saw themselves as part of a broader political cause opposed to the Soviet Union and communism, but they also believed, certainly in the early years of the Cold War, that the West needed to be defended at home, within the domestic societies, against the spread of communist ideas. The Soviet Union, its Communist Party and its ideological and propaganda apparatus around the world, was taken extremely seriously as a threat. Its ability to attract western converts by proffering an 'alternative model' of society was not underrated.

A wide range of business people – including the 'super-rich' of the time – saw social democracy as the best antidote to world communism. A sizeable state sector, a welfare system and above all full employment (guaranteed if need be by deficit financing, some subsidies, higher taxes and even a little inflation) would ensure sufficient social stability for alternative models of society (particularly socialism and communism) to have little allure for western peoples. For the same reasons, some of the richest people in the western world promoted the politics and culture of social democracy amongst western intellectual elites in the universities, the media and politics. And of course a sizeable state – the public sector no less – was needed to organise the military opposition to the Soviet Union and communism.

THE GLOBAL WINDOW

The end of the Cold War gave western business its great chance. As capital and the corporations went global it gained power over the old nation-states, particularly the medium-sized Europeans. Business could finally start showing the nation-states who was boss. They could do so by simply threatening to leave their countries – and take some of their jobs with them – unless they got what they wanted. And what they wanted from the governments was lower taxes and lower wage costs. It was a 'race to the bottom' that governments could do nothing to stop.

The US federal government in Washington – the most powerful single political unit in the world – had the size and power to stand up to this blackmail by global capital. Yet it did not possess the political will. Ever since Reagan, American political culture and ideology was all against governments intervening in the global market and confronting, or even seriously negotiating with, big corporate capital.

So, with the European nations too small, and the US government too entranced by free trade and free-markets, global capital had the world at its feet. And for the western business class the 1990s opened up vast horizons – almost like a replay of the opportunities of the Wild West, but this time with 'the frontier' being the whole world. China, Russia, India and Eastern Europe all beckoned as markets and profit centres. But it was China that was the prize.

There were, of course, still constraints on business. In Europe, 'old' attachments to the state as a protector against the market, this time the global market, ran deep. And with the state still organised around the 'nation' so too did attachments to 'national sovereignty' and nationalism. The strongest backing for the use of the state as protector against global capital existed in France where 'economic nationalism' continued to resist what the French came to believe was a 'neo-liberal' bias in the European Commission (a reason for the defeat in 2005 of the European constitutional treaty). In Italy and Spain, the EU state was seen as protector, and populist movements began to put pressure on the EU Trade Commissioner to bring in trade protectionist measures against cheap Asian imports.

Germany remained ambivalent. Her big corporations traded around the world and supported free trade, and her governments supported, or said they supported, 'globalisation'; Germans traded with the world and did not seek state intervention in the global market to secure trade protection. But Germany also had increasing pressures for intervention, not least from a political left that saw the comprehensive German welfare state threatened by global pressures for lower taxes. Yet Germans still tended to see the EU, not the German state, as their ultimate protection in the world. Most of the expansion of German exports had been into the expanded EU rather than into the global economy, and the hard currency euro-zone was seen as sizeable and powerful enough to stand up to mobile global capital should it wish to do so. Of Europe's 'big three' Britain remained the odd man out. Its continuing Thatcherite political consensus, bound into the financial industries of the

City of London, continued to offer little resistance to the demands of global capital.

THE HUMBLING OF THE WESTERN STATE

Yet the story of the 1980s and 1990s, and of the Bush years which followed, is the story of the humbling of the state in the West – of the reordering of the erstwhile balance between state and business decisively in favour of business. The state was in some cases down-sized (losing assets to privatisation) but, more importantly, it was completely refashioned to meet the requirements of business – a relatively low business and inheritance tax regime, all the 'handmaiden state' functions (such as infrastructure, subsidies, contracts, outsourcing), and little interference in open borders for trade (and, increasingly, for labour migrants).

But the greatest achievement of all of western big business in this 'gilded era' was to add China with its millions and millions of low cost workers to its labour and cost pool. This addition of China was the heart and soul of the famed 'global economy'. It not only lowered costs (and bumped up profits) but, crucially, it created a low inflation environment throughout the western world which from the late 1990s onwards would allow another huge burst in debt and credit – a debt bubble that would fuel the consumer-driven economy, the pride of the Greenspan/Clinton/Bush/Blair era.

And when, in November 2001, China formally joined the World Trade Organisation (WTO) this new relationship was sealed.

CHAPTER TEN

RISING POWERS: CHINA IN A MULTIPOLAR WORLD

On 17th September 2001, just six days after the 9/11 atrocities in New York and Washington, the 15 year-long negotiations on China's terms of membership of the World Trade Organisation were formally concluded, paving the way for formal agreement in Doha, Qatar, later in November. Mike Moore, the WTO Director-General hailed the agreement as a 'defining moment in the history of the multilateral trading system'. And so it was.

In the agreement China committed itself to open and 'liberalise' its regime including telecoms, banking and insurance. The Clinton administration had been the engine that pushed this agreement through Congress, and Bill Clinton himself was thrilled that all his efforts had borne fruit. He had tied his legacy to the deal; and, following the US-China agreement that opened the way for the China's WTO membership, Clinton declared that 'I'll fight to make China's trade status permanent';

he argued that exports to 'China now support hundreds of thousands of American jobs' and that 'these figures can grow substantially with the new Chinese market the WTO agreement creates.'[1] In 1999 his spokesman on Asia had predicted that the WTO deal would 'clearly shrink' the US trade deficit with China – this, even though many economists believed that it would achieve exactly the opposite result.[2]

Bill Clinton could feel proud. The financial crisis of 1998 had shaken everybody – but the western-led financial system had survived. American business had broadened and deepened the 'globalisation project' and brought Asia into it. And by so doing the American financial system had been shored up; and China's addition had secured low inflation into the future and allowed the US financial system to create another credit boom and a further run up of debt.

MULTIPOLAR WORLD: CLASH OF CIVILISATIONS?
CLASH OF CONTINENT-STATES?

But things were not to work out quite the way that the pro-globalising, pro-free trade, pro-debt lobby had foreseen.

The trade deficit with China was not to come down. Indeed it was to go up – dramatically so. It rose from $68 billion in 1999 to $201 billion in 2005 and thence to a staggering $256 billion in 2007.[3] China was not to open its markets in the manner foreseen by the WTO deal. Instead, she had placed severe restrictions on western penetration of many of her service sector markets, and had helped create an Asian market for her products thus heralding the arrival of a powerful Asian internal market bloc with China at its hub.

Indeed, it was slowly becoming a distinct possibility that the western leadership class may have misunderstood the whole China process. Westerners glibly, and patronisingly, talked about 'managing' China's rise, as though they were still in charge. The truth was looking rather different, indeed the other way round. The writer Mark Leonard has reported that China's new intellectual class are beginning to exhibit the confidence of a superpower – so much so that some are now adopting the condescension of super-power thinking and seeing it as *their* duty, not just Washington's, to 'manage' change – in particular the decline of the West.[4] Whatever the real situation with China, by 2008 no one was any longer talking about an American-led world system.

The successful 2003 American military action in Iraq kept the neo-con vision of American world rule alive for a bit; but only a year later it was clear that the invasion was not going to remake the Middle East, and the dreams of 'American global leadership' – that had so infused the columns, websites and blogs of the western commentariat – were beginning to fade. And for some a new reality was dawning: that rather than the USA, it was the rise of Asia and China that was remaking the world order.

Attempts to measure this new distribution of power in the world, and particularly changes in that distribution, are diffi-cult (although the University of Michigan's long-standing 'cor-relates of war' programme has attempted an index of world power since 1812).[5] Yet, a general characterisation was becom-ing possible: one that posited that the bipolar system of the Cold War was not being replaced by a unipolar (American) structure, but rather by a multipolar structure.

The major poles of this new 'multipolarity' were generally accepted to be the United States, Europe, China, Japan and India (and, for some, a Brazil-led Mercosur and ASEAN too). Some analysts were still arguing that American power – the combination of dominant military power and leading economic power – would keep the USA pre-eminent – 'primus inter pares' or 'first amongst equals' – in power terms, although this pre-eminence could no longer be translated into 'hegemony'. As leading economics professors Ronald Findlay and Kevin O'Rourke put it in 2007, in their exhaustive look at global changes over a thousand years, such pre-eminence 'does not in any way imply that [the US] can impose its will unilaterally on the rest of the world.'[6]

There was a lively debate about the 'polar' potential of Russia. Professor Robert Skidelsky, in a paper for the Global Policy Institute in London, in late 2007, argued that 'the Russian thesis of an evolution towards multipolarity is...perfectly plausible. A separate question is whether Russia will be one of the poles.'[7] And, dependent on future trends of regional integration, Mercosur and ASEAN were also candidate members for 'polar' status.

Multipolarity had been the essential theme of Sam Huntingdon's now famous article – 'The Clash of Civilisations' – published in *Foreign Affairs* in 1993 and expanded in book form in 1996.[8] Huntingdon, though, saw the future multipolar world as being divided between cultural and religion-based 'civilisations' rather than by political units like nation-states or super-nations; and he identified eight potential 'civilisations' – western, Latin American, Islamic, Sinic, Hindu, Orthodox, Japanese and African. Huntingdon's thesis got caught up with the politically heated atmosphere following 9/11 and the US invasion of Iraq, and he became a controversial figure, more so when, in a *Foreign Policy* article in 2004 entitled 'The Hispanic Challenge' he applied his 'civilisational' thesis to the Americas by arguing that through immigration Hispanic culture threatened the 'white, British and Protestant' dominant culture of the USA.[9]

Yet, for all the controversy, Huntingdon had served to put multipolarity back at the centre of western thinking. His work contrasted nicely with that of Francis Fukuyama who, some years earlier, had unveiled his universalist analysis of *one* liberal-democratic world order which, by implication, was in effect a unipolar system led by the winner in the Cold War, the USA. This unipolar approach was scornfully dismissed by Huntingdon as possessing 'universalist pretensions' which were riddled with 'hypocrisy and double standards'. In 'The Clash of Civilisations' he had argued that examples of such 'double standards' were to be found in the western democracy debate when 'democracy is promoted but not if it brings Islamic fundamentalists to power' and in the non-proliferation argument when 'non-proliferation is preached for Iran and Iraq but not for Israel'.[10]

Yet, Huntingdon may have underestimated the resilience of the state. Some of Huntingdon's 'civilisations' may be co-terminus with states – and some, China comes to mind, might well be described as 'civilisational states' (and, should the EU or Mercosur or ASEAN become states they might also be deemed 'civilisational states'). But it is the state (and the decision-makers of the state) that remains the only player which is actually able to *do* anything, or take any action, in the international environment. And it is still the case that the state, and only the state, possesses armies and the means of compulsion; as was seen all too clearly in 2008, it is only the state that can act as the ultimate economic and financial bedrock, the bank of last resort, in any financial meltdown.

The historian Paul Kennedy in his much acclaimed book *The Rise and Fall of the Great Powers* based his approach on the 'nation-state as the central actor in world affairs'.[11] He later considered this traditional interstate approach too narrow, and, after reading widely on subjects 'that were then totally foreign to me' such as 'global warming, demography, robotics, biotech', he produced a new, more rounded, book which he finished in May 1992. Intriguingly, though, this new book, *Preparing For The Twenty-First Century*, still saw the great social, economic, environmental (and other) coming changes as best explained within the prism of the political world and political units – and assessed how these changes would affect the relative positions of 'America' (a nation-state) and 'Europe' (which he treated as a nation-state).[12]

By 2008 he had returned to a straight geopolitical analysis with nation-states as the primary actors. And, in his assessment of the future global power balance, he relegated economic growth projections in favour of a demography, arable land/water and food supplies calculation – arguing that small but well-organised political units (states) might easily wield more influence than bigger ones (in size of population and land). In this scenario the prospects of the Asian giants – China, with a projected population in 2050 of 1.4 billion, and India, with a projected population in 2050 of 1.6 billion – were not good. 'The blunt fact is that each of them would be stronger with only half their current populations.'[13]

Intriguingly, Kennedy was bullish about the prospects for Europe and the United States. The European Union (with a projected population in 2050 of 664 million) was deemed rich enough (only 'an unseen disaster' would 'set it back greatly'); and in food supply the bloc was self-sufficient and, in some places, in surplus. And the USA (with a projected 2050 population of 402 million) was also in good shape. It may well be in relative decline but Kennedy doubted that it will experience absolute decline, the 'sad decay that overcame Rome or Spain'. 'Its basic geopolitical configuration – protected by two oceans, flanked by only two, non-threatening states, and possessing the world's best balance between land size, population and agricultural output – gives it many strengths to help offset present and future stupidities'.[14]

THE RISE OF THE CONTINENT-STATE

In the latter years of the first decade of the new century – with the private financial sector in meltdown and the economy entering recession or depression – the state was relevant again. Virtually overnight the state (or 'government') became a problem-solver rather than the problem. For it was needed both to bail-out individual companies in trouble and to stabilise the total financial system. Indeed, it was becoming essential – and not just as a 'handmaiden' to an ailing private sector. It was becoming western civilisation's bedrock institution. For the first time since Ronald Reagan in the late 1970s caught the public mood with his attacks on the overblown state, the state was ceasing to be a 'dirty word'.

Yet, it was also becoming increasingly clear that, amidst all the social tribulations, only a large 'state' – with massive resources – could act to properly stabilise, reorder and relaunch the economies of the West. The old-fashioned Westphalian state – the small to medium-sized European nation-state – was simply too small. Rescue and stabilisation would need a continent-state.

Europe was at the centre of this particular story. For as the recession gathered strength it was clear that even countries the size of Britain, France and Germany were not really big enough to withstand global pressures. The EU and the euro-zone, however, were a different matter. They were both, as an internal market and as a potential global reserve currency, able to – more or less – hold their own against volatile global capital. So, too, should it wish, was the USA. These two continent-states were big enough to negotiate with global capital, big enough to regulate markets, and, crucially, big enough to survive a global trade downturn if necessary. (They both had a good balance between population, arable land and water; they both had a relatively good balance between manufacturing and services, and low and hi-tech. They would remain dependent upon foreign sources of energy – the EU on Russia, the USA on the Middle East – but in a new regime of sustainable growth they could, over time, lower their dependence on these unstable foreign sources.)

Of course, if the EU and the USA, under the pressures of a global recession, actually adopted a strategic and neo-protectionist approach to trade, then, by necessity, so too would China and India. And other trading blocs – like Mercosur and ASEAN – would, in order to join them, begin to fully integrate economically and cohere politically. Thus would emerge the real contours of the much discussed multipolar world: with blocs negotiating their futures amongst each other. The unfettered world of mobile global capital would be over.

In the early years of the new century a great geopolitical or geoeconomic drama was being played out before our eyes. By 2008, with pressure building on both sides of the Atlantic from both American and European publics, the question was: who would go first? Who would be the first to bring the global capital game to a close? Specifically, which 'continent-state' would bring to an effective end the global 'free trade regime' and replace it with a strategic view of trade and economy. As the new protectionists would put it: who would finally begin to protect its own people and no longer allow its economic and trade policy to be dictated by the ideas of extreme ideologues and the interests of super-rich globalisers.

THE DANGERS AND OPPORTUNITIES OF MULTIPOLARITY

The dangers inherent in the new multipolar reality were also becoming apparent. The era of 'globalisation' had changed the world forever, and many globalising features would remain. Cultural and technological globalisation – the huge increase in communications between people – was here to stay; as were aspects of economic globalisation (such as the increased trade and capital movements of the post-communist era). But it was also becoming clear that this new world would not be managed from one centre – either politically or economically. Neither Washington (or New York) or Brussels or Beijing would rule, let alone 'lead' or 'guide', the new world order. In this respect the new order remained a Westphalian order. It had many of the characteristics of the old 'great power' system that emerged out of the Westphalian peace in the seventeenth century and set in train an anarchic international system based upon separate nation-state 'sovereignties'.

An optimistic reading of the new multipolar world, however, was that the new multiple poles would have no alternative but to resolve differences and conflicts through negotiation and compromise, and, importantly, would be able to keep the peace – as during the Cold War – through deterrence. In a multipolar world global institutions – the UN, the IMF, the World Bank, the WTO – would no longer be dominated by one power, or one alliance of powers, but could remain fora for dialogue, discussion, compromise and peacekeeping. And, over time, a multipolar world could conceivably become a platform for convergence into some form of global governance.

In May 2004, as EU membership grew by 10 to reach 25 members, a few somewhat grandiose European thinkers were beginning to see the way in which the EU had enlarged its borders as a way forward globally. And by 2008, through the expansion of the EU (by a series of international treaties) a law-based multilateral system had spread to cover 27 nations with 500 million people – and in future it could, theoretically at least, add even more nations. This EU system could certainly see a future in which it could expand into parts of Eurasia and, maybe, even into Russia and parts of the Islamic world; but, even should it so expand, it would certainly not be able to encompass the whole world. For at some stage it would need to deal with China or the USA where, in both cases, largely unspoken Westphalian sovereignties die very, very hard.

And, as for the genuine desire held by many for a world government (or at least global governance), the new multipolar system will certainly not secure this long-held objective. Yet, it may move us a bit closer – for it is predicated on the notion that global government cannot come out of the barrel of a gun, it can only come out of genuine need and agreement. And the new multipolar system, comprising only a few major 'poles', could, just conceivably, become a realistic launching pad for some kind of global governance, if not government.

The new multipolar world now emerging may well have its dangers; but it has one great advantage over the botched attempt in the 1990s to 'remake the world' through 'globalisation'. For by recognising reality, and by recognising differences and sensibilities, it is more stable, and sustainable, as a system.

THE NEO-CONSERVATIVES AND CHINA

Even so, a realistic assessment of the coming multipolar world is one in which the emerging continent-states may well, as the competition for resources heats up, become adversarial, if not confrontational. And as the major rising power China will be at the centre of events. From a western perspective the rise of China poses a real problem. Only two decades ago the West bestrode the economic global stage with America as the lone superpower. Yet two decades later China's economy is on a growth trajectory that will take her past the US in 2050; Chinese trade and loans have tied the mighty US into a dependent financial relationship; Asian funds keep the US Treasury afloat and help stabilise US banks; and Chinese imports have so penetrated the US market (largely via the shopping giant Wal-Mart) that one wag argued that the 2008 Bush fiscal stimulus, aimed to engineer a US consumer recovery, was in fact 'a Chinese recovery programme'.

After two decades without a communist giant in the world system we now have another one, and one with more purchase on the western world. For as China moves from the margins to the very heart of the global order, it now, through trade and loans, has an economic hold on the future development of the USA.

It all amounts to a monumental geopolitical change – one that, in essence, has been allowed, even engineered, by the political leadership of the western world. In these post-cold war years the ascendant corporate business interests, in search of markets and low costs, have simply overridden those liberals and democrats in the West who have fears about the authoritarian Asian giant. And geopolitically, Washington's concentration on the Middle East has deflected serious strategic thinking away from the Asian problem. Intriguingly, during their time at the centre of events in Washington, most neo-conservatives had very little to say about China, certainly compared to their bold plans for the Middle East.

THE STRENGTH OF CHINA

The dimensions of China speak for themselves. The Asian giant has the world's largest population, reaching over 1.3 billion people, and in 2007, by one method of calculation, its economy had risen dramatically to the point where it had a GDP approaching half that of the USA (it had much less a proportion by another, 'nominal' method of calculation). It was the third largest economy in the world, after the EU and the USA, and had risen above both Japan and Germany. Its growth rates were spectacular having, over the last twenty years, averaged almost 10 per cent a year – between 1985 and 2002 averaging 9.65 per cent a year and between 2003 and 2006, 10.3 per cent a year.[15]

As a trading power China's rise is phenomenal. Her trade balance with the world in the twenty-first century has risen consistently and most recently dramatically – from $24.1 billion in 2000 to $30.4 billion in 2002 to $32.1 billion in 2004, and then to $102 billion in 2005, $177 billion in 2006 and a mammoth $262 billion in 2007. Her trade balance with the USA shows the same steep upward curve in China's favour – from $83.7 billion in 2001 to $162 billion in 2004 to a huge $256 billion in 2007. And in 2007 American consumers bought more from China than ever before – including electrical machinery and equipment (up 18 per cent on the previous year), toys and games (up 25 per cent), apparel (up 20 per cent), plastics (up 10 per cent), vehicles (up 18 per cent) and, intriguingly, iron and steel (up over 12 per cent).

Europeans had also been on a Chinese shopping spree. China saw her merchandise trade balance with the EU rise from €54.7 billion in 2002 to €79.3 billion in 2004, to €128.4 billion in 2006, a somewhat lower balance than that with the US. In 2006 China remained the EU's second largest trading partner (after the US) but displaced the US as the largest source of EU imports. In 2006 China's trade balance with the West as a whole was well over $430 billion. The story is of large tracts of American and European manufacturing facilities being effectively transferred to factories in China. And in some cases, as with ThyssenKrupp in Germany or MG Rover in England, the factories themselves had simply been dismantled and transferred to Asia.[16]

THE CHINA PROJECT

China was part of a wider 'globalisation' project which was beginning to get seriously underway as the Cold War thawed out. Even by the mid-1980s American manufacturing industry – and also Europe's – was transferring much of its production capacity from its traditional home manufacturing areas to elsewhere around the globe as corporations discovered the advantages of cheaper, non-unionised labour. Following the recovery of the global economy from the oil crisis of the 1970s, the extra costs of transporting raw materials to, and completed products from, these distant locations, were more than compensated for by the labour cost savings achievable through the use of these new locations. US automobile manufacturers, facing increasing competition from Japanese carmakers, had already begun to transfer much of their production from North to South America.

By the late 1980s 'globalisation' – as the process was called – was becoming a recognised force that had the potential to shift the balance of production from the industrialised West to the developing nations. Japan had already transformed itself from a defeated nation devastated during the Second World War to an economic giant. By the mid-1960s its electronics and automobile manufacturing was competing on a global basis. And the large Japanese corporations, from automobile manufacturers such as Toyota to electronics giant Sony, which some years previously had drawn adverse comments about their products were now surpassing their established western critical counterparts in terms of product quality.

As Bob Dylan could sing as early as 1983:

Well, my shoes, they come from Singapore,

My flashlight's from Taiwan,

My tablecloth's from Malaysia,

My belt buckle's from the Amazon.

You know, this shirt I wear comes from the Philippines

And the car I drive is a Chevrolet,

It was put together down in Argentina

By a guy makin' thirty cents a day

(Bob Dylan, 'Union Sundown', ©1983 Special Rider Music)

Though well underway as a process by the early 1980s, the pace of change pales in comparison with the changes that have taken place since 1989.

The main change has been the arrival on the global scene of China – the country tellingly absent from Dylan's new industrial litany. In the space of a quarter century the world's most populous nation has emerged from being an outsider to an industrial powerhouse which is now beginning to determine the dynamics of the global economy. The trigger for this rise was the decision of Deng Xiaoping's government – in the years following the death of the leader of China's 'Cultural Revolution' Mao Zedong in 1976 – to pursue its 'Open Door' economic policy. And the trigger was pulled because the Chinese leadership had come to recognise its limitations: that the state totalitarian model alone would be unable to meet the demands of a country with a soaring population based on an unmodernised, largely rural, economy.

But China's rise was not wholly indigenous – far from it. Nor was it an unstoppable force swept forward by a wider tide of 'globalisation'. Rather, it is more accurate to see it as the

346

product of a decision, or a series of decisions, taken by both Chinese and American leaderships. China's new economic policy –which based itself around the development of its 'generative sectors' of steel, transport and related industries – obviously had a global market in mind. Yet America's leaders could have stopped it all in its tracks. Instead they decided to smooth the way. Indeed, bringing China into the western economic system has arguably been the major project of post-1992 American economic policy, a strategy pursued with greater and greater intensity as time passed – and finally symbolised by China's entry into the WTO in 2001.

This project was sold as a 'globalisation project'; but was, in truth, 'global' only in a very limited sense. For in the so-called 'globalisation' era, development and growth in the world has remained seriously uneven – with whole areas of the world doing extremely well and others not benefiting at all. Large parts of China and India were 'winners'. But large tracts of Africa and the Middle East were not. And this new 'globalised' world was neither 'global' nor 'free-market' – as many of the big players in the system continued to severely limit market access.

China, in particular, limited market access. The country's communist leadership remained determined, almost as its principal strategic objective, to create a strong internal market, and keeping control of access was the key tool. Indeed, Dani Rodrik of Harvard has argued that those countries that benefit from 'globalisation' are not necessarily those that operate open 'free trade' and economic borders, but rather, are often those that do not play by the rules.[17]

The Chinese one-party state is best described as a command capitalist state. It is capitalist in that it has companies, a stock market, something of a market price system. It is a command economy in that the Communist Party exercises ultimate authority over most all economic units through its control of company appointments and policies, including those in the banking sector. Will Hutton has aptly described the Chinese system as 'Leninist corporatism', a system in which the communist 'party-state is at the centre of a spider's web of control' – a web, incidentally, that is extremely economically inefficient.[18]

'CHINUSA': A DEADLY CO-DEPENDENCY

By the time of the 2008 Olympic games the exact relationship between China and the so-called 'globalisation' process was starting to be reassessed. So central was China to the whole global economic regime – and also so much the beneficiary – that some in the West were beginning to believe that China was now no longer simply the grateful recipient of its benefits, but was now driving it. As Sandra Polaski argued 'the size of China's population is increasingly turning globalisation into a Chinese process'.[19]

The real story, though, may be even more dramatic. For, no matter who is driving the process, the question of its destination arises. And what emerges from under the smoke and confusion of change in the global economy is nothing less than a major change in the geopolitics of the Pacific – the arrival of an American-Chinese axis of dependency. As I described in an earlier chapter, the American debt and consumer boom built around 'globalisation' saw such high American trade deficits with Asia that the Chinese and Asians began to fund America as it lived beyond its means. Or as one of Europe's leading experts on US economic history, London University Professor Iwan Morgan, put it in 2008: 'the US is tied into a co-dependency with Asian countries, which fund its borrowing in order that their export-driven economies can have the benefit of competitive exchange rates to sell their goods to Americans'.[20]

Just as importantly, though, has been a deeper, less-remarked-upon US-China dependency – the low inflation dependency. The fact was that during the 1990s China and India, because of their low wages and costs, fuelled a world-wide low inflationary environment. This era of low inflation was a godsend to the US (and British) authorities who were bent upon creating economic growth through debt-led consumption. In any normal cycle, the steepness of the run up of debt engineered by the Anglo-American politicians would have unleashed such sharp inflationary expectations that the central banks would have needed to step in. But, thanks to China and India, the debt bonanza could continue. Thus, China, knowingly or not, played the indispensable role in the US's unsustainable housing and debt boom that burst in early 2007.

But on top of all this there was yet another drug being administered in the dependency relationship – a drug called 'sovereign wealth'. 'Sovereign wealth' funds – a Wall Street term meaning large amounts of capital in essence controlled by foreign governments – had been investing in 'small' amounts in the West for some time. Record oil and commodity prices and surging exports had transferred trillions of dollars from consumer countries to producers, mainly in the Middle East and China. These funds got recycled back to the West often through government-controlled corporations. And following the 2007 banking and credit boom collapse a series of western financial institutions, including 'giants' such as Citigroup, Merrill Lynch, UBS and Morgan Stanley, sought help from these funds. They were, in fact, partly rescued by them. By year's end in 2007 'sovereign funds' had lent $60 billion to western banks – not a huge amount but a point had been made – and there was more available.[21] The China Investment Corporation had helped bail out Morgan Stanley, while other beneficent investors such as the The Singapore Investment Corporation, Saudi Arabia's Prince Alwaleed and the Kuwait and Abu Dhabi Investment Authorities also chipped in. As *The Economist* put it, these undemocratic regimes won some spurs by 'deftly playing the role of saviour just when western banks have been exposed as the Achilles heel of the financial system'.[22]

The new century also saw China – with its vast state cash resources – looking to secure a stake in strategically important commodity corporations. China's state metals corporation Chinalco showed off its muscle in February 2008 when, after a bitter battle, it acquired a stake in mining giant Rio Tinto in a successful attempt to head off a takeover of the company by an Australian mining company, the world's largest, BHP Billiton.[23]

All this financial activity led to fears in the West about the motivations of foreign state-owned investors – and questions arose in the media about whether undue foreign political control and influence might follow in their wake. Jokes made the rounds about the image of The Peoples Liberation Army Pension Fund bailing out capitalist bankers. And ironic questions were asked about why western governments seemed to favour nationalisation only when it was under the control of foreign sheiks and dictators.

Yet many western leaders, fearing for their banks, welcomed these 'sovereign funds', no matter the regime that controlled them. When asked about growing levels of foreign investment in the UK with increasing amounts being from state-owned 'sovereign wealth funds', the UK Prime Minister, Gordon Brown, speaking on his visit to Peking on 18th January 2008, expressed himself 'relaxed about the diversification of ownership' – as did President George W. Bush. At the 2008 annual Davos get-together Aleksey Kudrin, the Russian finance minister, whose own country was seeking a stake in western energy companies, agreed with the British Prime Minister. He argued that concerns about political motivation were 'exaggerated', and that western countries should decide which of their industries were of strategic importance, and to have clear rules on what they would allow, 'rather than demanding transparency and codes of conduct'.

YOU AIN'T SEEN NOTHIN' YET

Of course, China's rise needs always to be viewed in proportion. In 2007, on one reading (of 'nominal' GDP) her economy was somewhere around a sixth of that of the USA, and she was still behind Japan and Germany; and her whole economy was not much larger than the US manufacturing sector.[24] Yet, it is the trend that matters. And – certainly by 2008 at the time of the Olympics – all the trends were still moving in China's favour.

The western leaders who pushed hard for 'globalisation' and for the 'opening to China' certainly recognised the problem. Tony Blair, one of the most insistent advocates of the Clinton/Bush 'globalisation' strategy, noted, whilst still in Downing Street, 'how great a competitive challenge the West faces from the emerging economies such as China and India'. But he, like Clinton and Bush, continued to insist that the West could compete. In a speech to the European Parliament in October 2005 he set out the case for believing that the West could meet this Asian challenge – that is remain competitive without changing the basic rules of 'globalisation', primarily 'free trade' between Asia and the West. His case amounted to repeating the tried and tested mantra: that 'globalisation' was 'inevitable', and that Europe could compete as long as it made its 'labour markets less restrictive' and its service sector more competitive by 'research and development and innovation'.[25] And Blair was far from being a lone European voice. In July 2004 the EU selected a new Commission President Manuel Barosso, who, certainly in his early years at the helm, sought to steer the Commission in a 'neo-liberal', pro-'globalisaion' direction – using the principal argument that Europe needed to 'reform' (particularly in its labour practices) in order to compete in the 'global' economy. It was a viewpoint heard throughout Europe, ranging from German Christian Democrats to Czech neo-liberals, and even in the rhetoric of the Sarkozy campaign for the French Presidency in 2007.

Yet a growing body of opinion also believed that Blair's case was flawed – that China would continue its trade advantage in manufacturing and, crucially, would later also gain a global game-changing low-cost advantage in services and technology.

In the Chinese manufacturing sector, the 'reserve pool' of labour remains deep – and costs in the southern coastal development zones and the large cities can be kept relatively low by the millions in primitive poverty in the rural areas (where nearly two-thirds of China's population still exist on just one dollar a day). As one commentator pointed out 'if all US jobs were moved to China there would still be surplus labour in China.'[26] What's more, the oppression of migrant labour, poor working conditions, extremely low wages and the absence of any serious welfare structures will continue to enable China to compete more than effectively with the West – and continue to fuel the proverbial 'race to the bottom', with all the profound effects on workers in Europe, the USA, and elsewhere.

A good measure of how China will continue to succeed in the manufacturing sector lies in its increasingly robust machine tools industry. China's machine tool industry, the fundamental prerequisite for manufacturing, is rapidly gaining ground. Through joint ventures and other co-operative arrangements, it has progressed to the mid-sector and now beyond, where it will increasingly compete in the precision sector, where European manufacturers still retain a lead. This will reverse China's demand for reliance on imported machine tools – and ultimately leave German producers, for example, unable to compete.

Globalist opinion-formers do not reject the stark reality of Chinese manufacturing ascendancy, but argue it will remain just that – a manufacturing supremacy only. 'Free-trade' theory, they suggest, will ensure that the West will retain its comparative advantage in the services and hi-tech sector which will flourish as Asia expands. This service and hi-tech sector has indeed been a success story for America and Europe – and remains a decisive voice in support of 'globalisation'. In the USA this voice is heard from the money industries in Wall Street to hi-tech California. And in the EU the power of the service sector in Northern Europe tends to take a more relaxed attitude toward trade with China than do Mediterranean manufacturers (who, displaced by Chinese imports, regularly call upon the EU Trade Commissioner for protection).

By 2008, however, as the banking and credit crisis bit hard and added to the sense of gloom, there was a growing skepticism about the validity of 'free-trade' claims. And fewer illusions remained about how the service sector (particularly financial services) could continue to rescue the West. A new, more realistic, mantra was beginning to be heard: that, contrary to some set beliefs, 'Chinamen – and Chinese women – can do services'! And they can also do banking! And, over time, they may also be able to do hi-tech! And all at a lower cost than in the West.

This new realism about China's role in the global economy led to an understanding that as the Chinese internal market grows, a flourishing indigenous service sector will grow to cater to its needs. This would dash the hopes of the West that it would be in a position to service this new Chinese market. Furthermore, the Chinese and Asian service sector, once operating, could easily start competing in the American and European markets. As the pioneering American political and social thinker Michael Lind has put it 'within a generation, the burgeoning Third World population will contain not only billions of unskilled workers, but hundreds of millions of scientists, engineers, and other professionals willing and able to do first class work for a fraction of the payment of their American counterparts.'[27]

It was also becoming clear that China was not really a 'free trade' power. That, unlike the more ideologically committed West, it was pursuing a strategic rather than a 'free-trade' and 'free-market' vision of its trading policy. China's strategic approach seemed to be: penetrate foreign markets, build up reserves, build up the internal market, and, crucially, always limit foreign access to key internal market sectors. Signs were clear and numerous that China sought to build up her own services sector by restricting market access to outsiders. An early measure of the success of this strategy can be seen in the less than dramatic growth in Chinese imports of western services compared to the merchandise trade. For instance EU-China trade in services between 2002 and 2005 showed a slight growth from €1.8billion in 2002 to €2.2billion, but was nowhere near the figure needed to close the overall trade gap.[28]

A TECHNOLOGY POWER

As with services generally, so too with the broader 'knowledge' economy. The 'globalist' Clinton/Blair/Bush/Greenspan assumption has been that the West will remain technology giants and will grow by taking advantage of its 'comparative advantage'. The clear implication is that China and other Asian countries will never catch up. Yet, in the early years of the twenty-first century China was slowly but surely becoming a technology power. And whilst it was lagging behind in certain areas, it was making every effort to correct this shortfall. Writer James Kynge in his book *China Shakes The World* pointed out that 'Chinese companies, by and large, derive their technologies by buying them, by copying them or by encouraging a foreign partner to transfer them as part of the price for access to a large potential market'.[29]

China regularly insists upon 'technology transfers' as a precondition of greater market access for western companies – whilst simultaneously expanding its research sector. The Chinese acquisition of IBM by Lenovo in 2004 is but one example. More recent acquisitions – or attempts at acquisition – have all included attempts at technology transfer. Concerns over technology transfer were seen as the 'most critical business factor' amongst German machine tool manufacturers in their recent entry into the Chinese market.[30] Technology transfer is also inherent in the relocation of aerospace manufacturing centres to China – from Brazil's Embraer, who established a production facility at Harbin in late 2002, to Europe's Airbus consortium who in 2008 were considering relocating some production to China to reduce costs.[31]

Over time these transfers could gradually erode any knowledge-based lead the West may have, while at the same time, losing manufacturing ability across the entire industrial spectrum. And with China's huge potential internal demand for passenger aircraft, and the ability to compete with western companies through its low labour costs, China's aerospace industry is set for long-term growth. Already, as early as 2004, a study for KPMG reported that China was Boeing's leading parts supplier outside the USA.[32]

COPYING

China has earned a reputation as 'the counterfeiter's paradise' with what is often seen as tacit official acceptance of wide-spread product piracy.[33] Counterfeit goods, from aircraft spares and computer software to branded consumer items pour forth from a nation which ironically is often the source of many of the legitimate versions of these products. Many though are illegitimate. For instance, Fiat's new model Panda has an uncannily similar copy – the Peri – now available from Great Wall Motors in China at a considerably lower price.[34] Fiat was not amused as there was no license deal and no apologies. The Peri is a far from unique example.

This kind of theft of intellectual property and patent infringements presents great problems for western companies; it can damage the reputation of respected brands through quality breaches, faults and failures to comply with environmental standards. The scale and sheer 'chutzpah' of China's counterfeit industry is one source of its continuing trade advantage.[35] The undeveloped nature of China's legal system also serves to advantage the Asian giant – it allows 'patent-mining', and the celebrated 'Great Wall of Patents', whereby patents can be copied and registered in China as indigenous inventions with legal action even being taken for breach of patent rights against the original foreign inventors.[36]

Some regard the counterfeiting issue as somewhat exaggerated; but a recent, 2006, report noted that counterfeit goods, and corruption in the interior, remain 'a very big problem' and that 'European businesses in 2006 identified China as by far the most problematic market for counterfeiting and abuse of IPR for European companies' and that there remained a 'continued lack of respect by some Chinese companies and regional governments for patents and IPR.' There were also examples of 'forced disclosure of highly detailed technical information; for instance, when bidding for public tenders such bids have to be prepared with Chinese partners'.[37]

Of course, copies can improve products over time. For instance, China has upgraded its PLA-AF fighter aircraft with license-built J-11 (Sukhoi Su-27SK) strike fighters, reported, it is said, by Russian observers no less, to be built to a higher standard than the originals.[38] Military aviation expert Dr Carlo Kopp notes that 'China started out in the fighter business by cloning and evolving existing Russian designs, and the J-7G is by far the best Fishbed (NATO codename for the Soviet MiG-21 original) variant ever built.'[39] By 2008, some experts were arguing that China was very close to her goal of securing military technical independence. For example the J-11 interceptor/strike fighter – the Chinese built version of the Russian Su-27 – was in 2008 being produced with domestically developed and built engines (WS-10a), avionics/radar and, air-to-air missiles (AAM's). For China, long dependent on imported technology in this field, this is a major development, both for its own use and as an exporter of such products.[40]

'CHINUSA': NOTHING THE WEST CAN DO?
Taking a quarter century view, China's rise may only be beginning. And the West's relative decline may also only be beginning. Whilst 'globalist' policies remain in place, though, there is very little that American or European leaders can do about

it. However, a change in strategic direction – away from the co-dependency and 'CHINUSA' strategy – would be another matter altogether.

One of China's vulnerabilities is that she is still too dependent on her markets in the West – a direct consequence of the tight relationship of the 'CHINUSA process'. But, should the West's politicians take a different view of trade and jobs, and start to protect the large western markets, placing clear limits on Chinese and Asian market penetration, it would bear down heavily on the Asian giant.

Yet, for the moment, such neo-protectionism is unlikely. Elites on both sides of the Atlantic are still under the sway of 'free-market' and 'free-trade' ideology; and in Washington a real fear exists that any serious trade protectionism will lead to Chinese retaliation on the funding of America's current-account deficit – as well as to serious geopolitical tensions in the Pacific.

The only other change that could halt China's rise to global leadership, and rebalance her relationship with the West, would be a deep global recession or depression. In these – not wholly unlikely circumstances – all could still fall apart for China. A scenario could be drawn in which US consumption falls and so too do Chinese exports into their biggest market. This could bring the two-decades-long Chinese boom to an end. In such circumstances China's economic slowdown would be compounded by social cohesion problems – as, say, food prices cause riots in the countryside and inflation or job losses cause living standards to fall dramatically in the coastal cities, dashing the higher expectations of China's incipient middle class. Such a future might well serve to stall China's global rise and would keep her GDP ('nominal' GDP) at about the level of the larger European nations – although she would still improve her position as the dominant regional power.

Yet, even with her exports curtailed, the Asian giant – increasingly geared to her internal and regional Asian market – will retain many continuing advantages over the United States and the West – advantages that still make her 'the globalisation era's' long-term winner, and the US, and possibly Europe too, the long-term loser.

CHINA'S FUTURE GLOBAL STRATEGY: A GLOBAL POWER

As things stood in 2008, at the time of its Olympic games, China was bound to continue to seek growing global involvement – both civilian and military. And the reason was clear. The country needed the resources of the world, and the markets of Asia and the West, in order to keep its burgeoning domestic economy on track. Whilst becoming an Asian regional power (fuelled by Asian regional economic integration) its grand strategy would remain global.

CHINA-US RESOURCE WARS?

It has been estimated that, given current growth levels, and assuming increasing levels of affluence and hence consumption, Chinese demands for oil alone could easily exceed present total world output. These predictions may seem somewhat apocalyptic, but combined with anticipated growth in developing countries elsewhere – not to mention China's billion-person plus superpower neighbour, India – on present trends demand is set to rise rapidly. While experts may dispute the details of timing, there is little doubt that the world's oil supplies are dwindling, and the competition for what remains will become ever more intense. Only a major global recession could alter this prognosis. And authors such as Paul Roberts have posed the very real potential for conflict between ever more resource-hungry energy consumers fighting for progressively larger shares of a diminishing cake.[41]

Resource wars, fought over everything from oil, gas, iron, copper and water, are now an all too real prospect – for this and future generations. As China grows, the need to compete and secure itself, both within its immediate region and also beyond, will become paramount – and it will begin acting like a normal superpower. Indeed there are parallels here between present-day China and Great Britain just a century ago, a world power completely dependent on imports for petroleum. This dependence led Britain into imperialist ventures to secure such resources, notably in Mesopotamia (now Iraq) and Central Asia (especially the Baku area, now Azerbaijan) – two petroleum-rich regions which a century later remain at the apex of international intrigue and potential warfare.[42]

As with petroleum, so with iron ore. According to Tom Albanese, chief executive of Rio Tinto, the world's second largest mining corporation, this resource competition is rapidly becoming almost a one-horse race. Speaking in January 2008, he commented that China now accounted for 47 per cent of all iron ore consumption, adding that within just a couple of years this is likely to increase to 58 per cent. Similarly, China's demand for aluminum will rise from 32 per cent at present to 45 per cent, and 25.5 of copper to 33 per cent. Rio Tinto's chief economist also commented that, within a decade, China would be likely to be consuming over half of the world's key resources, and that as a result of this there would be increased political concerns as the country seeks to ensure the security of supply of these resources.[43]

Already its enormous and growing trade surplus has given China the means to invest in regions from Africa to South

America in order to secure energy resources and commodities essential to its growing industrial sector and domestic market. From 1998 to 2003, the Middle East provided some 60 per cent of China's oil, but increasing instability in the region has led to greater diversification. Improved relations, and with it the construction of pipelines directly into China, has accounted for greater imports of oil and natural gas from Central Asia, while Africa provided 30 per cent of China's oil total imports in 2005.[44] The supply from nations with which it shares borders, and hence great influence, also lessens dependence upon vulnerable sea routes.

INTO AFRICA

In the African continent China has cleverly exploited both the West's comparative neglect of the region and Europe's history of colonialism. The need to secure the energy and commodities that it needs has prompted a 'pragmatic' approach to the politics of the continent and to the various unsavoury governments – in contrast, to what is oft-times seen as the fastidiousness and hectoring of the western approach. The fact is that China's leaders remain relaxed about regimes with poor human rights records, and about dictatorships or even worse – such as Zimbabwe, Burma and Sudan. It is a posture made easier by the fact its own political traditions are, by western standards, less than liberal.

The tragic Darfur conflict in Sudan has helped to highlight China's approach to the African continent. Whilst war raged in the area China opposed United Nations attempts to end the crisis. Though eventually relenting, and agreeing to send peacekeeping troops, China's reluctance to interfere in the region was not unconnected with the fact that Sudan is a key oil exporter to the Asian giant.

China's real-politik approach has allowed her to outmanoeuvre the Europeans in Africa as many African countries themselves, ever resentful of European colonial legacy and contemporary moralising, often prefer to deal with Beijing. In general, African states view China as either one of their own – a 'Third World country' – or as a country with no colonial baggage.[45] During Chinese premier Wen Jiabao's tour of seven African nations in June 2006 – the Angolan president praised China's 'lack of preconditions', adding that 'we hail China's pragmatism towards Angola, which has allowed us to speed up the country's reconstruction'. (This whilst Angola was being criticised by western human rights groups for abuses and corruption). By comparison with the West, Chinese rhetoric in Africa focuses on 'respecting sovereignty'.[46]

At the time of the EU-Africa summit in Lisbon, in December 2007, China's advantage over Europe in Africa was clearly spelt out by an anonymous EU official to *The Guardian* newspaper. Under the heading 'Africa's leaders look East' he was reported as saying 'Africans are full of praise for the Chinese and less happy with how we manage our aid...we moralise, we talk about human rights, we insist upon conditionality'. China, by comparison, is 'unburdened by colonial hangovers or strictures about human rights and good governance'.[47]

Chinese 'pragmatism' in Africa has helped trade. While Europe still remains Africa's biggest market, China is making serious inroads. While still behind EU levels, China's growth rate of trade with Africa had increased a phenomenal 700 per cent in 1990s and 400 per cent in the last 7 years (to 2007). Not only that, but China is now Africa's biggest lender, leading to concerns such as those voiced in September 2006 where the US Department of the Treasury was reported as accusing China of being a 'rogue creditor' and of practicing 'opportunistic lending'. The then World Bank President, Paul Wolfowitz, was no less harsh, criticising China for 'ignoring human rights and environmental standards when lending to developing countries in Africa'. Excessive Chinese loans, he feared, could just lead to yet another future debt crisis for Africa.[48]

China is also one of the world's leading arms suppliers, and these arms helps to fuel much of the continent's conflict. Beijing's reluctance to intervene in internal politics is matched by being one of the leading suppliers of cheap military hardware for both rebel forces and official regimes throughout the continent – everything from AK-47 copies to jet fighters. The Washington-based Centre for Strategic and International Studies report recently noted that 'China shipped $1 billion worth of arms to both sides in the Ethiopia-Eritrea conflict between 1998 and 2000' and that 'it supplied heavy military equipment to Kabila in Congo in 1997 and 1998, fuelled with heavy weapons the conflict in Sierra Leone, and continues to supply the Sudanese government with all kinds of military equipment'.[49]

As well as arms, China provides infrastructure to the African continent. All over the continent examples abound of largely-European funded projects linked to water, fishing, or democracy promotion which are dwarfed by the sheer scale of infrastructure projects funded by China. And as well as infrastructure there is an aid programme which derives from China's 'Third World' alignment (and its anti-western and anti-Soviet posture) during the Cold War. Items included the assigning of Chinese doctors to Africa, hosting African students in China and big-ticket items like building the first railway linking Tanzania and land-locked Zambia during the period of opposition to apartheid South Africa's regional hegemony.

China's penetration of Africa is unlikely to stop anytime soon. And it has been nurtured by some high-profile political

363

get-togethers amongst the leaders. The Beijing Summit of the Forum on China and Africa Cooperation (FOCAC), held in November 2006, was attended by 43 heads of state and a total of 48 African delegations. And this was followed soon after by a visit in February 2007 by President Hu Jintao and then-Foreign Minister Li Zhaoxing to fifteen African nations.

SOUTH AMERICA TOO

Chinese involvement in South America has also expanded dramatically. As in Africa, China is keen to improve its access to oil and other commodities, and the region is also an increasing destination for Chinese exports. From accounting for just one-third of the total of Chinese foreign direct investment in 2003, this figure had grown to one-half by 2004.[50]

Chinese influence is growing from Chile to Venezuela. Chile is the world's largest copper producer, and also an important foodstuff exporter. Brazil, meanwhile, has large markets for Chinese goods, and is the source of products as diverse – and important – as iron ore, soya, and timber. And Venezuela's leader, Hugo Chavez, has been keen to welcome China as a major trading partner for his country. As a major oil producer, Venezuela has seen Chinese investment pour in, making it the largest recipient in the continent. As in Africa, Venezuela – and other South American nations – sees its relationship with China as a means of distancing itself from US influence.

There is, however, an ambivalence in Latin America about China – not so much about China's investments in the region, but rather about the growing Chinese influence in the global economy. Hitherto Latin America has been a backyard, cheap-labour manufacturing resource for the USA, providing significant employment opportunities for the Latin American work-force. Yet, China's workers can compete with South Americans on price, with potentially serious consequences. In a glob-alised world it is not only American and European workers who are feeling the pinch of low-cost Asian labour.[51]

Washington's attitude to China in South America is some-what different to that of her hemispheric neighbours – and is mainly geopolitical in nature. Few in Washington can oppose Chinese economic involvement – 'global free-markets' are sup-posedly open for all to compete in and take advantage of – but the geopolitical implications are worrisome. Chinese influence in a region is still primarily economic, but could easily turn into something more. With already existing high levels of anti-Americanism throughout Latin America the growing Chinese presence raises considerable security implications for Washington, as it is faced with a competing superpower mak-ing serious inroads on its doorstep.

THE RED SEA ZONE

Superpower geopolitics governs China's approach to another strategically important location – the vital 'Red Sea zone' in the Middle East. China's interest here is primarily oil – and in 2007 nearly a third of China's oil imports were trans-shipped from Port Sudan. In December 2007 a Chinese construction compa-ny was awarded the contract to build a new port facility – the Red Sea Gateway terminal at Jeddah Islamic Port.[52] Jeddah can be seen in a sense as an extension of the Chinese 'String of Pearls' strategy – that is, the string of connecting strategic mar-itime locations which links China to its near neighbours in Asia and on into the Middle East.

This Chinese interest in the Red Sea zone brings China into potential conflict with the other superpower keenly interested in the Middle East – the USA. Sudan and the Red Sea are in the middle of America's intersecting interests in oil and the pursuit of the 'global war on terror'. And although so far both super-powers have avoided conflict in the region, such relatively ten-sion-free competition cannot be guaranteed forever.

THE NEIGHOURHOOD?

The other potential China-US superpower flashpoint is Taiwan, which China has long regarded as de facto part of the mainland. Increasing cross-Strait co-operation is seen by many as lessening the risk of conflict, although elements in China remain committed to full integration.[53]

Much will depend on how American attitudes to China develop. Should CHINUSA take hold, and the US find itself unable to take any disagreement with China too far, then China will ultimately get its way and, like Hong Kong, Taiwan will eventually become integrated into the mainland. Alternatively, should there be a break between the USA and China, and should a new cold war style adversarial relation-ship develop between Washington and Beijing, then Taiwan could become the flash-point for tension, even conflict, even a Pacific war.

What is undeniable, however, is that much of China's increasing military expenditure is devoted to a build-up of missile, naval and air capability tailored specifically for, and focused on, Taiwan. China's long-declared intention to reinte-grate the island fully into the mainland, confirmed by the pass-ing of the 2005 Anti-Secession Law, must be considered, and even China's defence minister has recently talked of 'armed struggle' in relation to the island.[54] As if to confirm this, the PLA Navy's first aircraft carrier, the former Soviet 'Varyag', and currently under construction, has been renamed 'Shilang' in honour of the Chinese Admiral of that name, who headed the last Chinese invasion of Taiwan.

Relations with Japan have also become a matter of some concern. Animosities have long persisted with memories of Japanese atrocities in Manchuria in the late 1930s and 1940s still fresh in many minds. The rapid rate of Chinese military growth and modernisation is of particular concern to Japan, which is at the same time being asked to take increasing responsibility for its own defence, a task hitherto largely that of the United States.[55]

Periodic tensions, such as that in November 2004 with the incursion of a Chinese submarine into Japanese territorial waters, still erupt and are unlikely to disappear with disputes over territorial rights in the waters of the East China Sea as competition for oil, natural gas and minerals become increasingly critical in a resource-hungry climate. Yet, on the other hand, since Prime Minister Koizumi left office in 2005 relations between the two Asian giants has significantly improved – and many opinion formers in Japan are beginning to look back on Koizumi's nationalism as something of a 'maverick' interlude. Whether this lessening of tensions can lead to an entente or even a co-leadership agreement remains a very open question.

A MILITARY SUPERPOWER

The Chinese leadership, like the American, sees military power as a key attribute of the modern superpower. During its economic build-up Beijing may have been more pacific and less confrontational in rhetoric than Washington – but that may simply be due to differing stages of development.

Many western geopolitical and military planners regard Deng Xiaoping's 'Twenty-Four Character Strategy' – voiced in its original form in the early 1990s – as the best indicator of current Chinese strategic thinking. It runs as follows: 'Observe calmly; secure our position; cope with affairs calmly; hide our capacities and bide our time; be good at maintaining a low profile; never claim leadership and make some contributions'.[56] Deng's approach clearly matches the needs of a rising power seeking to adapt to its new position in the world and develop its military reach – and, crucially, to do so without confronting existing powers, primarily the United States. This strategy also demonstrates a more subtle agenda. It is a subtle agenda that during the early years of the new century started to concern some western strategists.

Chinese military thinking has clearly undergone a major change in recent years. The presumption of large, drawn-out regional conflicts, fought on or in close proximity to its own borders in Asia, has been replaced by planning for short, 'intense' conflicts in a far wider context. Accordingly, and based upon the experience of observing US tactics, most particularly in the two Gulf Wars, China's leadership has grasped the need for a highly mobile force, using high-technology equipment, able to react quickly. In 2004 the Chinese Defense White Paper talked of this new style, of 'local wars under the conditions of "informationalisation"' – an awkward term meaning the use of a range of information technology.[57]

As China's economic presence has spread through the globe so it has found it necessary to widen its military reach – particularly on the seas and oceans of the world. Its increasing trade in goods and commodities, and its need for energy, demand secure sea lanes and shipping routes. Piracy is an ongoing risk in certain regions, but more profoundly worrying is the potential for political upheavals, including terrorism, to interrupt supply. The growing size of bulk and container vessels – a crucial economy of scale element to keep shipping costs competitive – means that fewer options remain for transit routes in specific areas.

To meet these threats China has transformed its armed forces from being reliant largely on manpower fighting in or near its own territory to one capable of operating in a high-technology environment in smaller-scale conflicts further afield. As a result Beijing has embarked on a strategy capable of ultimately providing a 'blue-water' force projection far beyond its borders – and is taking steps toward acquiring an aircraft-carrier, upgrading its destroyer fleet and improving its amphibious assault capabilities.[58]

The Chinese – PLA – Navy has acquired modern vessels through the purchase of new 'Sovremenny' Class destroyers from Russia, and has also been developing its own indigenous vessels of all categories, including a growing nuclear submarine fleet. China has made up for shortfalls in its own technology by a rapid 'learning curve' enabled by the acquisition of foreign military products. It has become the world's largest arms importer.[59]

On a strategic level China is already acting as a cold war style superpower – with its growing fleet of nuclear submarines carrying intercontinental ballistic missiles (ICBM's) which, crucially, give her the ability to target on a worldwide basis. At the time of the great 'festival of peace', the Olympic games in Beijing, both the United States and Europe were within range of these missiles. China's nuclear-powered attack submarines also enable a long-range anti-shipping capability far beyond her traditional radius of operation.[60]

CHINA'S 'STRING OF PEARLS'

Starting in the 1990s China has invested heavily in a series of strategically important locations beyond its own shores in order to better secure its vital energy and commodity supply routes. Described in the West as the 'String of Pearls', this is the collective term for a number of major infrastructure projects.

These stretch from the South China Sea to the Middle East, and each represents 'a nexus of Chinese geopolitical influence or military presence.'[61] They include Gwadar in Pakistan, close to the Pakistan-Iraq border and not far from the strategically important Straits of Hormuz, one of the most important oil shipping route 'chokepoints'. Here, China has almost entirely financed and constructed a huge new deep water port, able to handle oil tankers, bulk carriers and naval vessels. With new transport links inland, it is destined to become a major trading hub with access inland to Afghanistan and other Central Asian countries, as well China itself.[62]

Other pearls include a new container shipping facility in Chittagong, Bangladesh, a similar port at Sittwe in Burma (Myanmar), Port Sudan and the Red Sea ports. Such facilities have multiple value. On one hand, they are modern commercial shipping facilities able to handle the largest vessels. However, they are also ideal as naval bases for a nation which has hitherto had few 'staging posts' beyond its own shores. They thus extend the radius of operations of a navy that has previously focused largely on its own home waters. In addition, these new harbours link to other transport routes, lessening Chinese reliance upon vulnerable and congested shipping routes in the region.

An airbase located on Woody Island in the Paracel Archipelago in the South China Sea is of crucial strategic significance. It is located close to the main shipping lanes which link China – and Japan and the Pacific beyond – to the Malacca Straits. These and other projects, from the South China Sea to the Middle East, are vital elements in the establishment of Chinese power and influence as its economic might grows.[63] In recognition of this sobering fact the United States has recently upgraded its military facilities at Guam, which, as of

2008, 'is being revived as a pivot point in a sweeping realignment of US force in the Pacific area'.[64] It is an upgrading that some in Washington see as necessary to meet the 'growing challenge to the US in the Pacific and Asian region of the ...legitimate and certain re-emergence of the People's Republic of China as a global and political power.'[65]

THE 'MALACCA DILEMNA'

The classic oil routes are now vitally important to China. And almost all of the oil that China imports passes through maritime chokepoints and hence, is susceptible to serious disruption. The Straits of Hormuz, a narrow 21-mile-wide route between Iran and the United Arab Emirates; the Malacca Straits – just 1.5 miles wide at its narrowest point, the Phillips Channel – are two notable examples. The former is the sole sea route for Saudi Arabian and Iranian oil, the source of over three-quarters of China's imported oil. All its oil imports from the Middle East and Africa must pass through the Malacca Straits. Alternatives are few or non-existent: sea lanes such as the Indonesian Sunda Straits, are too small for the biggest vessels now operating.[66]

As much as 80 per cent of China's oil imports passes through the Strait of Malacca. In a 2003 speech to the Chinese Communist Party leadership, President Hu Jintao was reported as identifying 'this dependence on sea lanes as a critical vulnerability and directed national security officials to figure out a solution for the Malacca Dilemma.'[67] China has even suggested financing a canal across the Kra Isthmus in Thailand, a colossal $25 billion infrastructure project, but one which, together with new land routes through Pakistan and Burma, would offer a chance to be independent of the critical Straits. This project might never go ahead, so for the foreseeable future

China will increase its military presence in the region, particularly in the vital sea routes.

THE CHINA SEAS

Closer to home, in the waters of the East China Sea, China is looking to consolidate its presence in an area beneath which lies a rich resource of natural gas. Securing this region reaching out to what China terms the 'First' and 'Second' island chains brings with it the risk of conflict with Japan, with which it shares these waters, and which is even more dependent upon imported energy than its giant neighbour. To complicate matters, the sea lanes which serve Japan pass through both the East and South China Seas, a region which has long been the subject of disputes over the ownership of seemingly insignificant specks on the map.

Such 'specks' are the Spratly Islands and the Paracels – an archipelago somewhat closer to China's Hainan Island. The former were the subject of bitter dispute – and actual conflict – between China and the Philippines, as well as Taiwan and Vietnam, in the second half of the 1990s. China seized control of Mischief Reef, and has since occupied it with a series of concrete structures, featuring radar and defensive weapon installations, though the buildings were initially explained as 'fishermen's shelters'.[68] Chinese naval presence at the location confirms the importance of the installations, although China is as yet unable to establish an airstrip – the Reef is too small – although the Philippines have such a facility on nearby Spratly Island. The possession of such a base provides, in a time of conflict, the opportunity to deny passage through the key shipping lanes in the region – with profound consequences for a country such as Japan.[69] China does, however, have such an airbase on Woody Island in the Paracels – probably inhabited by 'Silkworm' anti-shipping missiles. She can already probably control passage – and the vital seabed resources – through the entire China Sea.

AN INCREASING MILITARY BUDGET

China's grand strategy has demanded high levels of military spending and China's military budget has increased accordingly. How much is difficult to find out. Official Chinese figures suggest that defence spending has grown from around $9 billion in 1994 to $45 billion in 2007. Highest US estimates however put the 1994 sum at $28 billion rising to $125 billion in 2007. What is not in doubt, however, is the visible scale of China's growing armed forces.[70]

In procurement policy China, traditionally dependent upon former Soviet military hardware, continues to benefit from this long-standing relationship through its links with Russia and Ukraine, as well as Israel. Despite the EU arms embargo imposed in the wake of the Tienenmen Square massacre, China benefits from close ties in the civilian aerospace and technology sectors with Europe and the United States and from co-operation prior to this date in the military sector. In addition, Pakistan and Brazil have also co-operated in the aerospace sphere. Russian Sukhoi Su-27 fighters – now built under license as the J-11 – as well as Su-30s, plus inflight refueling and AEW&C/AWACS aircraft give China a strike capability that now extends far further than before and is now sufficient to be a cause of concern for nations in the wider eastern region.[71]

In addition, China has now produced its own 'fourth-generation' fighter, the Chengdu J-10, a direct competitor for the new European Typhoon, Dassault's Rafale and the US F-16. Currently flying with Russian-built Saturn-Lyulka engines, these will soon be available with the indigenous Chinese WS-

10a 'Tai Hang' turbofan engine. This marks a crucial step forward in Chinese aero-engine technology, enabling it to be free of any externally-imposed restrictions for political purposes and spares dependability. It also opens the way to enhancing China's export potential to nations with whom it already has close trading ties and who would welcome the ability to acquire state-of-the-art fighter capability at bargain prices.

A STAKE IN SPACE

As well as a growing military budget China has sought that other great attribute of a superpower – a stake in space. In 2006 the US, in full neo-con mode, asserted that it had a right to deny space access to any nation acting in a manner 'hostile to US interests' – and this was regarded as a hostile act by China. And not surprisingly so as China had for some time been developing its own manned space programme. On 15th October 2003, the world learnt a new word: 'taikonaut', when China launched People's Liberation Army pilot Lt. Col. Yang Liwei into space in the *Shenzhou 5* spacecraft, on a flight lasting just 21 hours 23 minutes. Less than two years later, on 12th October 2005, two taikonauts spent five days in space on board, the latest stage in China's manned space programme, known as 'Project 921' which ultimately aims to put men in orbit around the moon.

China is credited with the invention of the rocket, with 'fire-arrows' being used to repel Mongol invaders in 1232, but China's modern space rocket programme began in 1970, a progression of its military 'Long March' rocket, which has now expanded into an adaptable and cost-effective family of launch vehicles. Since 1986, China has been engaged in the provision of a commercial space launch service, placing communications, weather, remote sensing, navigation, or scientific satellites for foreign countries or companies. Today, the declared aim of the Asian giant is to be able to provide, in the near future, a satellite launch service for anyone with little more than a few days' notice. Its fleet of satellite tracking ships are on permanent station around the globe, constantly monitoring the skies in which China increasingly is becoming a major player. And there is little the US or the West, even should it want to, can do about it.

CHINA IS NOT THE WEST

In 2008, as China used the Olympic stage to present herself as a new superpower, the West's leaders were unsure how to respond. In Washington the dominant viewpoint remained non-confrontational. Corporate interests were fearful of a trade and financial rupture between the USA and China; and supporters of the 'war on terror' saw tension with China as a distraction from the Middle East. Across the aisle, protection-ist sentiment in the Democratic party continued to grow dur-ing the presidential primary campaign. Human rights groups were beginning to campaign against China's human rights record, and succeeded in enlisting some high-profile media celebrities such as actress Mia Farrow and Hollywood pro-ducer Steven Spielberg.

In Europe most governments remained wary of harming relations with the Asian giant. However there was a growing undertow of sentiment critical of Peking, much of it fuelled by trade fears in Mediterranean Europe (mainly by manufacturing industries, particularly textiles and shoes, undercut by cheap Chinese imports). Human rights concerns also surfaced when in December 2007 German Chancellor Angela Merkel refused to yield to considerable Chinese pressure and invited the Dalai Lama to Berlin, setting off a controversy in which 'anti-China' sentiment was denounced by leading SDP figures including former Chancellor Gerhard Schroeder.

For many in the West human rights was clearly not one of China's strong suits. In 2007 Amnesty International listed a catalogue of abuses and extreme treatment by the Chinese authorities at variance with China's pledges made before its election to the new United Nations Human Rights Council. It reported that: 'an increased number of lawyers and journalists were harassed, detained, and jailed. Thousands of people who pursued their faith outside officially sanctioned churches were subjected to harassment and many to detention and imprisonment. Thousands of people were sentenced to death or executed. Migrants from rural areas were deprived of basic rights. Severe repression of Uighurs in the Xinjiang Uighur Autonomous Region continued, and freedom of expression and religion continued to be severely restricted in Tibet and among Tibetans elsewhere'.[72]

On top of this litany, accusations of forced confessions and torture, arbitrary detention and unfair trials are legion. China uses the death penalty for a wide range of crimes and executes more people than any other nation. In 2006 it was reported that 1,010 persons were executed and a further 2,790 sentenced to death. In Tibet, witnesses reported Chinese border guards shooting a group of Tibetans – including one child – who were attempting to cross the border into Nepal.[73]

That China did not resemble a 'free country' – as it was understood in the West – was further underscored by her approach to the internet. At the time of the Olympics China was one of the world's largest internet users – the China Internet Network Information Centre claimed that internet usage soared by 23.4 per cent during the course of 2006 and that by 2007 there were 137 million users. Yet the attitude of the Chinese authorities towards the new medium still differs fundamental-ly from much of the rest of the world. A restrictive government culture actively censors internet content, blocking access to international websites and closing down many within the country with whose output it disagrees. Yet, in a clear example of western corporate validation of China's internet culture, lead-ing American internet search providers have agreed to China's demands to censor their own output within the country. Yahoo!, Google and Microsoft all acknowledge a problem. 'Of the three companies, Google has come closest to acknowledging publicly that its practices are at odds with its principles, and to making a commitment to increase transparency by informing users in China when a web search has been filtered'.[74]

Criticism of Yahoo! in the West has gone further following the news that the company aided the Chinese authorities in suppressing dissent by providing information to them – the company allowing 'its Chinese partner to pass evidence to the authorities that was subsequently used to convict individuals, at least two of whom received long prison sentences for peace-fully exercising their legitimate right to freedom of expression'. Whilst Yahoo!, Google and Microsoft have maintained that they must comply with local law, and that it is not 'an ideal sit-uation', they continue to argue that their presence in China is 'a force for good'.[75]

THE WESTERN DILEMMA

Western leaders and analysts remain divided about how to assess and judge China. The questions were becoming insis-tent and difficult. Should China be seen through western eyes using western standards and values? In other words, should it be seen and treated as a developing state which, helped toward full 'modernisation', will over time become an adjunct of western civilization – looking, sounding and feeling like Main Street USA? Or, alternatively, will it modernise on its own, non-western, terms and put its own stamp on the world? And if so, will it be hostile? And, should we be hostile to it? And if it continues to develop in a non-western sense, continues to oppress its people, what attitude should we take towards it? How will we in the West feel about 'liberal interventionism' in the case of superpower China?

China as an entity dates from the Qin and Han dynasties in the period 221BC-220AD. Prior to this as far back as 1040-256BC, with the start of the Zhou dynasty, philosophies such as Confucianism and Daoism emerged to give this emerging nation much of its future cultural identity. The nation which we today recognise as China – Zhongghou in Chinese – became unified during this time and established a standardised legal system, bureaucracy, written language and coinage. The modern communist state as we know it today was formally founded on 1st October 1949.

Under Mao Zedong we saw the emergence of what we in the West now recognise as modern China, though there have been immense changes during that period and in particular following his death in 1976. From that time to the present, China's leaders have sought to transform the nation from an insular and economically backward regime to one which is having a profound effect upon the world's economic and political order.

The extremist politics of the Mao era were replaced by a more pragmatic regime under Deng Xiaoping, which reformed the country's agriculture, economy and scientific and technological base. However, progress towards democracy – reflecting that taking place at the time in Eastern Europe – was far more subdued, though nevertheless evident under Premier Hu Yaobang. His death in 1989 coincided with the notorious

Tiananmen Square massacre, an event which brought to an abrupt end hopes of further political concessions to a more western democratic system; at the same time, it confirmed the strength of the military.

During this period China took the first steps away from command socialism – and towards its present system of command capitalism. First, farmers were permitted to trade their production directly, and then 'town and village enterprises' were allowed to grow in the areas without the larger state-owned factories. The first of the economic development zones was established in 1980 in the Pearl River delta area and expanded as foreign companies were allowed tax concessions and other financial benefits to locate there. Yet, all the time, the Communist Party retained its tight control of the strategic development of the economy and its tighter control over politics and society.

Unlike almost any other major nation the high degree of secrecy which exists in China's political process, and its fundamentally undemocratic nature, means that it is often impossible to find out the true intentions behind policy and rhetoric. In the West a belief persists that China will change as a 'market ideology' and market system take hold, and that this will lead to political freedoms and, ultimately, to some form of democracy. Yet, China's so-called 'market economy' is so limited that the pluralism and freedom it engenders is also limited, and likely to remain so. *The Economist* has argued that 'ideally, the high-savings countries of the Middle East and Asia [will] liberalise their economies', but that we should 'not expect miracles'.[76]

Therefore, in the absence of anything even approaching a western democratic tradition, it is hard to believe that the command politics and command capitalism of the one-party communist state will easily wither on the vine – particularly whilst millions remain in rural poverty and a global recession puts a stop to raised living standards. The best bet for the future is that the West will face a China that is set to remain an authoritarian state even as it continues to play a larger and larger global role.

THE FUTURE: A NEW COLD WAR?

How the West reacts to this new communist superpower active in the world will depend upon the health of 'CHINUSA' – that is, whether America and China have become so economically dependent upon each other that there can now be no turning back. In such circumstances the American-Chinese relationship will deepen even further and may well, over time, become, in effect, a tight economic alliance – even a kind of economic NATO in the Pacific. The alternative course is just as stark – a souring of relations between the two powers that leads to a reordering of the relationship and eventually even to what amounts to a new cold war.

Andrew Small of The Foreign Policy Centre in London has pointed to the dangers ahead. 'If this were a looming conflict between two small countries in a strategically unimportant part of the world' he argued, then 'there would be people lining up to urge early interventions and preventive measures'. However, he added, 'this is a looming conflict between the two major powers of the coming century and if leaders, officials and thinkers on both sides do not work towards finding an answer to the 'big question' that everyone can live with, it is a century that could instead see everyone having to live again with systematic global insecurity and the constant spectre of war'.[77]

If a new course in American-Chinese relations is indeed ever set, then the question will arise: can it be managed? Indeed, can it be managed as successfully as the earlier Cold War between the USA and the Soviet Union? These questions

will bring to the fore the western debate about 'liberal interventionism'. Or, alternatively, it might settle it – for no one will
seek to liberally 'intervene' in China, and future interventionism for humanitarian and peace-keeping reasons will be
restricted to areas in the world wherever agreement between
the two superpowers can be reached.

A new cold war would more likely return the realist, and
realistic, approach to centre-stage in western thinking. Western
strategy towards China might then well become based upon
strategic interests, probably primarily economic, rather than
upon the attempted imposition of universal, that is western,
values. But any 'realist' grand strategy with regard to China
will need to grapple with the thorny problem of trade, and the
protectionist issue.

The western orthodoxy prevalent from Clinton to Bush (and
Blair to Brown) still has it that countries such as China can do
the jobs westerners no longer want to do, or can afford to do,
whilst western countries can concentrate and perfect their
comparative advantage in the knowledge-based and high
added value sectors. This view is now being challenged as it
becomes clear that China will soon be able to compete as effectively in the service and knowledge-based sector as it has in
manufacturing. Proclaiming an EU target of public and private
spending on R&D of 3 per cent of GDP in 2010 (up from a current 'stagnating' level of 1.9 per cent) Jan Potocnik, the EU
Science and Research Commissioner, noted that research
investment in China would grow by 20 per cent. Also,
European MP Caroline Lucas noted that 'almost 20 per cent of
China's exports are already classified as hi-tech and, with 2
million graduates a year, there's every reason to believe that
this percentage will grow'. Even arch 'free trade' advocates in
Britain are beginning to see the problem. 'There is nothing the

UK does now that China won't be able to produce in five years' commented the then Confederation of British Industries chief, Sir Digby Jones, in 2005, adding that China produced 400,000 science and engineering graduates each year, a level which the UK was failing to match.[78]

For the West, this was a sobering prospect. But, by 2008 and the Olympic games, even as the global economic downturn was adding indigenously caused job losses to those created by trade with Asia, western leaders were still talking about 'competing' with China in the 'global economy'. And geopolitically, they were still unable to come to a common view about future relations with the Asian giant. Americans, more than Europeans, were putting their faith in a future in which the 'market economy'and further global integration would modernise and democratise China, and soften her global ambitions. It was a very high expectation.

CHAPTER ELEVEN

CAN AMERICA ADJUST?
THE USA IN THE MULTIPOLAR WORLD

By 2008, in the final year of George W. Bush's presidency, with the banking and housing crisis raging and the impasse (if not actual defeat) in the Middle East becoming more and more apparent, the idea that America in the new century was in a seriously weakened condition was gaining ground.

A pervasive, and very un-American, pessimism was abroad in the land. In a *New York Times/CBS News* poll, published in early April 2008, a remarkable 81 per cent of Americans said they believed that 'things have pretty seriously gotten off on the wrong track'. Pollsters had not seen a figure as high as this since the first time the 'track' question had been asked. The negative figure had risen dramatically in the five years since the invasion of Iraq in 2003 when it stood at 35 per cent (it was 69 per cent in 2007).[1]

CAN THE USA ADJUST?

It was a climate in which the need for 'change' became a given. All the candidates for president accepted the need for 'change'; and in the Democratic primaries they were competing with each other over whose 'change' was most believable. Senator Barack Obama's slogan 'change you can believe in' struck a real cord; and the fact that this self-proclaimed 'non-traditional' candidate could do so well in the primary campaign was a sign that for many Americans in 2008 a change of course was becoming an accepted and urgent need.

The United States has a number of advantages – over other countries – in adjusting to change. The country's political culture prides itself on the ability to welcome and manage change rather than be defeated by it. And there is a belief amongst Americans in the ability to reinvent both themselves and the country.

The American historical narrative is one of optimism about change – the whole American journey is seen as a story of 'upward and onward', of problem-solving, problem overcoming and progress against the odds. The narrative is compelling: it includes – the eighteenth century victories over the British crown, the optimism of the founders, the nineteenth century victory of the liberal, progressive (capitalist) cause in the Civil War and the conquest of a boundless continent, the long course of economic growth leading to the emergence of the world's premier capitalist economy, the supplanting of Britain as the most powerful country in the world, the victory in two world wars, and in the twentieth century the leadership of the postwar western system, the beacon of democracy for the planet, the landing of a man on the moon, and, finally, victory in the Cold War.

For Americans in the early years of the new millennium, looking back, they could be forgiven for believing that their history was pure progress: and that, apart from the Vietnam imbroglio, America had suffered no serious defeat. It was a story imbibed by every American schoolchild – even the descendants of slaves.

Yet, this national cultural bias toward optimism is not an unalloyed boon. It may help to validate change, but it can also act to misread or deny a difficult reality – in this case the reality of reduced American circumstances. In sum, the culture of progress and optimism may not be the best preparation for the more realistic and circumspect approach that the times may need.

DIFFICULT

Georgetown Professor, Charles Kupchan, an eloquent and mature, but minority, voice in Washington during the G. W. Bush Presidency, has argued that the US 'cannot and should not resist the end of the American era', for such a course 'would only risk alienating and provoking conflict with a rising Europe and an ascendant Asia'. But he also suggests that 'asking the US to prepare for and manage its exit from global primacy...is a tall order'.[2]

The 'tall order' is tallest for America's political, media and financial elites. These leaders of opinion – weaned for decades on a high standard and style of living and on a sense of American global power – have felt little pain in previous downturns. And they are likely to be the last to feel pain in any coming downturn. These elites are the 'masters of the universe' – inhabiting the Washington political thinktanks, the Pentagon, the major media, the corporate boardrooms and Wall Street firms who during the 1990s set the triumphalist tone for the nation, and in very large numbers supported the invasion of Iraq.

They will, naturally, find it very difficult to adjust their thinking and aspirations downwards. And they form a powerful set of interests that still, in the early years of the American crisis, hold assumptions and illusions (if not delusions) about American prosperity, the country's unlimited power and its continuing dominant global role.

The broader American public will find it somewhat easier to adjust to a declining world role. Less invested in American global power than the elites, they also possess a strong neo-'isolationist' streak – a belief that foreign interventions should be short and sharp with no long occupations nor, outside of NATO, long commitments. They are also less likely to see the connection between securing power abroad and securing prosperity at home – polls show consistently large numbers who believe taxpayers' money could be better spent at home than on foreign aid and interventions.

Many of these 'middle class' Americans have been on the 'losing' side of globalisation and have been accommodating to lower standards for years. Struggling with multiple jobs, with longer hours, with crises over healthcare, and dealing with very tight household budgets, adjusting downwards is already an integral part of their lives.

REDUCED LIVING STANDARDS

The dimensions of the reduction in prospect for the American economy is very difficult to assess. Much depends on the exact extent of the two decades-long debt inflation, and on the extent of consequent de-leveraging throughout the economy that started in 2007. How the de-leveraging will ultimately affect the total US GDP is also difficult to predict.

The figures on the great over-leveraging are alarming. They show that by 2004 the percentage of total market credit to GDP was well over 300 per cent (a figure very likely to having risen even more since), compared to the roughly consistent 100 per cent for the first three postwar decades. New York Senator, Charles Schumer told the House Banking Committee as early as March 2000 that 'today margin debt is a greater share of total market capitalisation than at any point since the Great Depression'.[3] What precisely this means for the depth of the consequent recession or depression is difficult to forecast. As is the long-term economic effects of the winding down of the mammoth global imbalances (principally between China and the US) which is also a feature of the more general American debt crisis.

It remains very 'un-American' to look at economic life as a zero-sum game, but, as we saw in Chapter One, the era of 'all ships rising' is now over – at least for some time. And how exactly these lower US aggregate living standards will be distributed is another imponderable. Yet who gets what, who loses what, and who gains what, will have crucial social and political consequences. How the reduced American pie is distributed amongst the mega-rich, super-rich, the various middle classes, the poor, and the interlaced ethnic groups has tended to be ignored by the American political and financial elites. But, as this book has argued, the dissolution of the traditional American middle class is already underway and could have profound implications for the type of country the United States will become in the new era. Whatever happens, the big issue of the distribution of income and wealth that America has been able to avoid since the Roosevelt era will inevitably come to the fore again.

CAN BRITAIN (AND THE CITY OF LONDON) ADJUST?

Countries outside North America but in the American sphere – 'neo-liberal' casino capitalist outposts like Britain (since

Thatcher) and Spain (under Aznar) – have also been living well beyond their means. Britain and Spain have both experienced a large debt bubble based upon global low interest rates, abundant credit and hugely inflated housing costs. As in the US these economies have witnessed significant consumer-led growth rates (in part fuelled by irresponsible lending), rates that were not sustainable and have also given millions a false hope of ever-rising living standards.

Alone in the global economy, a medium-sized economy like Britain's needs to adjust to change – and in order to so adjust, the more balanced the economy the better. Yet, Britain's economy is far from balanced. As part of the late 80s and early 90s neo-liberal restructuring – when market forces eroded the uncompetitive industrial sector – Britain witnessed many decades of decline in manufacturing, and a quite dramatic switchover to services – primarily financial services. The City of London – always a large and profitable sector – became even larger and even more profitable. Britain's financial services industry has done extremely well in the post-cold war global economy. In 2003 Britain's trade surplus in financial services was reported to be 'more than double that of any other country'.[4]

In July 2004, researchers at the University of Sheffield analysed the British economy as an atlas, demonstrating that Britain was becoming dominated by London (or, rather, the City of London), and that to the north and west there was 'an archipelago of the provinces – city islands that appear to be slowly sinking demographically, socially and economically.'[5] It was an analysis which led *Guardian* economist Larry Elliott to argue that the 'City wields more power than ever' and that 'Britain has become a huge hedge fund making big bets on the markets.' And he asserted, presciently, that 'one day the luck will run out.'[6] In his powerful 2006 study of Britain's elites, Hywel Williams reckoned that 'The City, in combination with New York now controls 90 per cent of the world's wholesale financial activity.' And he recorded that at the end of 2003 310,000 people were employed in the City (and nearly 150,000 in financial services).[7] But what goes up also comes down – and by 2008 and the beginning of the 2008 financial meltdown London's financial district was already laying off large numbers of city workers.

Yet, two questions stand out: can 'the City' and its allied commerce continue to carry on its shoulders a country of 60 million people? And, what happens when China and India start seriously competing in financial services as well as in manufacturing? The mere posing of these questions may serve to show the vulnerability of a national economy which includes such a uniquely successful sector.

Whether 'the City' can or cannot continue to carry the country, its leading players will certainly remain highly influential, if not dominant, in determining Britain's foreign economic policy and alignment – more so even than the media moguls. And within 'the City' elite there was considerable support for a 'go it alone' policy, for standing off-shore (of the continent) and seeing the global economy as our market. We might be small, but we were profitable. This was the 'tiger option' – after the smallish Asian 'tiger' economies that were doing so well in the global market before the Asian financial crash. And as financial services prospered in the Blair era, then many in the square mile turned their thinking towards 'the world' and increasingly away from Europe and the EU.

This dominant view not only saw London's financial services as a global player working in a global market – very much a 'tiger' – but went further, seeing London as the world's most successful 'tiger' in the global financial jungle. And by 2007, on the eve of the global financial meltdown, all the talk was of London overtaking New York as the world's leading financial centre. By comparison, in this hubristic atmosphere, tying 'the City' down in Europe – even should 'the City' become the EU's primary financial centre (similar to 'New York' in North America) – was dismissed as too restrictive a vision. In a December 2006 after-dinner speech to London financiers, the EU's financial services action plan ('MiFID') was introduced by Charlie McCreevy, the internal market commissioner, and was given a less than enthusiastic reception – much less so than that accorded to the American comedienne Ruby Wax, who, bizarrely, but perhaps aptly, followed him with top billing.

A *Financial Times* report by Gideon Rachman at the time suggested that 'as the biggest financial centre in Europe ['the City'] would do well in a huge liberalised [European Union] market'.[8] However, the EU remains too regulated for City tastes; as does even Wall Street following the Sarbanes-Oxley Act passed in the aftermath of the Enron scandal (a tough US regulatory regime providing a huge – though probably temporary – boost for 'the City').

The successful and profitable world of British finance created, though, another vulnerability to the British economy – that of the debt culture. For it was the dynamic and innovative credit systems and culture of 'the City' that helped, together with a willing Westminster political class, to create the country's mountainous dimension of private debt. A report commissioned by the Conservative party in 2005 reported that 'personal debt levels of more than £1 trillion mean that about 15 million people are exposed to external shocks such as a sharp rise in the price of oil' and went on to call the debt issue a 'time bomb'. These debt levels had been fuelled by the 'wealth effect' of rising house prices.[9]

These vulnerabilities in the British economy – the reverse side of its successes – make Britain's 'tiger option' a huge gamble. Britain is more exposed to the global forces than any other major western country (including the US). And should the country leave the EU, then everything will depend upon a continuingly robust global economy – and one in which competition in the service sector from China and India remains weak.

Britain's 'successful' economy – no matter its vulnerable and exposed global position – will likely continue to convince a powerful faction of opinion formers that the country can, with confidence, 'go it alone'. After all, the 'tiger option' will continue to appeal to more than just the profit makers; it will have an abiding resonance with the popular instincts of English exceptionalism – of a uniquely entrepreneurial people surviving and prospering alone on the global 'open seas'. This appeal combines short-term profits and nationalist romance – the two impulses that built the empire and will be difficult to combat.

Yet the romance of the 'island story' will come face to face with the realities of the great de-leveraging, and with the lower living standards inevitably involved. Britain comes out of its 'neo-liberal' era as a more unequal society than it was at the beginning. It has, though, succeeded in building up something of an American-style 'middle class' – increasingly travelled, self-confident and with considerable expectations – based upon a mountain of debt. As they are marched down the mountain this middle class will inevitably fracture, creating a growing pool of 'losers'. For a time, Britain's welfare mechanisms will help to cushion the blows; but sooner or later, the increased pressure on the welfare services will need to be funded by higher taxes (which will be resisted by the remaining middle class and the super-rich) or, alternatively, by government deficits and inflation. Both of these courses of action will increase the uncompetitive global position of a very globally-oriented economy.

One way of limiting the damage of a global recession or depression would be to further integrate the British economy into the European market by joining the euro-zone. With a declining global demand for financial services the euro-zone would at the very least provide a hinterland for the City of London (in much the same way as New York is able to service the internal American market).

However, this radical change in the geopolitical course will be very difficult to engineer; it will run right up against the British attachment to 'sovereignty', to its history as an imperial and independent power, and to its rigid constitution based upon ancient 'sovereignties' including the monarchy and the culture of 'Queen and country'. In this sense the traditional political culture of Britain's elites directly damages the future economic health of its people.

WORLD ROLE: OVER-EXTENSION (AND RETRENCHMENT)

Both in the USA and Britain lower living standards and a reduced economy will have serious geopolitical as well as social consequences. In the USA should aggregate lower living standards lead to real political change and usher in new social priorities, then pressure will grow to cut the mammoth Pentagon budget – with all that entails for the global reach of American power. Such pressure could even come from Republican politicians.

Economic pressures on the Pentagon budget will coincide with a growing question mark over the continuing political will to sustain America's extended 'empire'. Much will depend upon how the Iraq imbroglio ends, and what toll it takes on support for America's existing global reach. In 2008, as President George W. Bush was preparing to leave office, it was clear that America's twin defeats – in Iraq and in the banking crisis – had already produced one major result: the certain knowledge that the world was not about to be remade in America's image. Nor was the US likely to retain its 'primacy' in world affairs, nor be able, on its own, to be the world's policeman. Any exit from Iraq (together with the pressures on the US Treasury caused by the banking crisis) will inevitably lead to reassessment of the role of American hard power and, consequentially, to a review of expeditionary wars, 'liberal interventionist' power projection, and even the number of American foreign bases strung out around the world.

The early years of the twenty-first century will bring some kind of reassessment, formal or informal, in Washington about the proper extent of its worldwide interests and reach. Yet, in the early years of the new century the 'over-stretch' debate was rather slow in coming. Politicians in Congress and business leaders rarely addressed the question – although, after 2003, the debate about America's future in Iraq became a kind of substitute for a broader debate about America's role in the world. Even so, there remained a general reluctance in Washington to debate, let alone set out, a new more limited US strategic doctrine.

It was down to the academy to challenge long-held strategic assumptions. 'The over-extended empire' had in fact been the theme of scholars and writers for some years past. The main protagonist of over-extension, or 'imperial overstretch', Paul Kennedy, writing as early as the mid-1980s, pointed to 'the awkward and enduring fact' that US global interests and obligations are nowadays far larger than the country's power to defend them all simultaneously. Some time later Chalmers

Johnson, in his 2004 book *The Sorrows of Empire*, set out a systematic critique of American global over-extension, arguing that one of the 'sorrows' was 'financial ruin'. He pointed out that the 2003 invasion of Iraq, unlike the first Gulf War, had not been subsidised by US allies and had been a huge drain on the US Treasury and cause of large budget deficits – and that 'at some 5 per cent of GDP, this deficit represents an unusual statistic for a country with imperial pretensions'.[10]

Other American heavyweight academics were also, at least by implication, arguing that the US was over-extended. Though rarely willing to say out loud that the US needed to systematically retrench – let alone spell out the details of such a retrenchment – they nonetheless set the stage for a debate on over-extension by their analyses of decline and their rejection of unipolarity. Huntingdon of Harvard in his famous article 'The Clash of Civilisations' in *Foreign Affairs* in 1993 saw the West (and the US) as a declining force and made a case that the US needed Europe to help out.[11] The arch-realist John Mearsheimer of Chicago saw the US as unable to become a 'global hegemon', and strong enough only to become a 'regional hegemon'. He, again, implicitly at least, saw the US as over-extended in the Middle East. He opposed the 2003 invasion of Iraq; and famously, or infamously, later argued that one-sided support for Israel, caused in part by the Israeli lobby, was not in the American interest.[12] And Charles Kupchan saw a future 'after Pax Americana' in which he argued for some forward thinking in America about how to adjust to the new multipolar world (he suggests by accepting the new, larger role of Europe and China).[13] But Kupchan, like the other multipolar analysts, was not in the business of spelling out what precisely an American retrenchment would look like, or the precise areas of the world from which America should withdraw.

US RETRENCHMENT?

By 2008 and the financial crisis, the idea of American 'over-stretch' was increasingly acceptable – and there was a sense that, sooner or later, Washington would need to return to the less frenzied period before 9/11 and construct a grand strategy that was more realistic. Yet, in the run-up to the presidential election of 2008, in the debates in the Congress and amongst the presidential candidates, no politician (or any of their advisors) outlined anything remotely akin to a comprehensive post-Iraq American grand strategy. Indeed, with the need for domestic 'change' taking precedence, strategic thinking in Washington was placed on hold – as if the legion of strategists were waiting to see how the coming domestic 'change' would put pressure on foreign policy.

It was also clear that any redrawing of the American geopolitical footprint around the world – any retrenchment – would not, at least initially, be overly dramatic. As Kupchan argued 'few in history have wilfully made room for rising challengers and adjusted their grand strategies accordingly.'[14]

More to the point, American living standards, and US trading and corporate interests, will remain dependent upon the US ensuring that it keeps a very sizeable geopolitical footprint in every continent. By 2007 by far the largest US trading partner was Asia, which dwarfed the partnerships with other continents. APEC, a grouping which includes China and Japan, dominated US trade flows. In 2007 US imports from APEC were four times those from the EU, while exports were about 3 times those into the EU. A long way behind APEC was America's second largest trading partner, non-US North America (Canada and Mexico), and some way behind Canada was the EU, with LAFTA (eleven Latin American countries including Mexico) in fourth place. The sheer size of the trading relations between the US and Asia (APEC, principally China and Japan) is revealed by the fact that in 2007 the US trade deficit with APEC was almost twice that of the *combined* deficit with the EU, LAFTA and Canada!

US TOTAL TRADE AND TRADE DEFICITS (2007)

APEC (incl. China and Japan)	463	(-127)
North America (Mexico and Canada)	216	(-35)
EU	146	(-20)
LAFTA (11 LA countries plus Mexico)	120	(-23)

Investment patterns, however, show Europe, rather than Asia, as the primary partner for the US. In 2006 US direct foreign investment in Europe was well over twice that invested in Asia, and also twice that invested in Latin America; and foreign direct investment into the US shows Europe as by far the largest investor (with almost five times as much as Asia).[15]

These trade and investment bonds will ensure that any initial US retrenchment is relatively limited. Yet, in the coming era global flows may well weaken as globalisation – global integration – falters and regional integration (in Asia and in Europe, and in the Americas) deepens. And they could weaken even further in a global recession or depression.

The extent of the coming global economic slowdown will also determine the fierceness of the twenty-first century competition among the powers for resources, particularly energy. The US is unlikely – unless it can secure energy independence – to lose its interest in the oil rich areas of the Middle East and the southern borders of Russia. And in the Middle East both the Christian Zionists and the Jewish lobby will continue to guarantee ultimate US support for Israel. Whether US support for Israel forces a peace deal with the Palestinians or translates itself into support for Israel during a wider conflict, the Israeli connection means that Washington will never be able to completely disengage from the region.

POWER, SOFT AND HARD

What, though, the US can actually *do* to enforce these continuing global interests remains the big question. America will always possess significant economic power around the world (through trade and aid), but she will be competing here with the growing economic clout of the EU and Asia whose economic sway in some parts of the world now easily matches or surpasses hers. And her forward military presence – exercised either through local bases or the mobility of armed power (particularly the threat of aerial bombardment) – will remain greater than any other global power. Even should there be cuts in the Pentagon budget, American military ascendancy is so pronounced that the cuts would need to be savage to reach the levels of her major potential challengers.

Yet, the Iraq experience has brought into question the exact usefulness of America's military superiority in securing US objectives. The Pentagon's superiority gives the US considerable political power in negotiations. And its nuclear forces still provide deterrence, and ultimate guarantees against other nuclear powers. The questions arise over the huge Pentagon spend on mobility, reach and hi-tech fighting ability. This mobility certainly allows the US, should she wish, to intervene more effectively than any other power as a worldwide 'peacekeeper' and 'peacemaker' – both for humanitarian purposes and also for her own interests – to secure resources and assets. Yet a declining economy (with only 20 per cent of the world's GDP) will mean that it becomes a US interest to encourage a multilateral approach to humanitarian intervention.

US military superiority allows the US not just to 'intervene' ('liberal' or otherwise) but to *invade* other countries to change regimes. The fact is that the mobility and technical superiority of the US military would probably allow her forces to topple most any 'Third World' regime Washington disliked. She could, as in Baghdad in 2003, use control of the air and/or an invasion to be in the capital city within days. But what then? If the invasion was for a specific and limited purpose – to remove weapons of mass destruction or to remove a leader who imminently threatens the US – then that could be achieved, although, probably, only one capital city at a time. But by the end of the Bush era the lessons of Iraq in 2003 were beginning to sink in: that invasions do not 'remake' the invaded country into 'democratic' replicas of Main Street or even simple, stable dictatorships. Over the medium to long run this kind of intervention – regime change invasion – would only make the US position weaker.

There is the further problem presented by a failed war. In their foreign interventions Americans traditionally want a quick 'in and out' victory – and such successful actions can serve to reinforce public support for military interventionism abroad. But a failure like Iraq – with no clear rationale for war, no guaranteed stable future, and thousands of troops in the middle of Arabia hostage to a great national debate about an exit strategy – only increases domestic scepticism about the use of force abroad. It is a scepticism that will be compounded by an economic downturn when public opinion will begin to insist that public spending at home should take precedence over military spending abroad.

Yet, in looking at the future US approach to military power, it is unlikely to radically change, at least into the medium future. Both US public attitudes and US grand strategy will conspire to keep the Pentagon as the world's pre-eminent military. The Pentagon remains a major political constituency with large numbers of jobs dependent on it, and its many domestic bases remain the lifeblood of local economies throughout the country (indeed, the military, together with the churches, form part of America's great undeclared welfare state).

Military superiority – in spending, technology and mobility – remains a 'card' in the hands of US policymakers which they will be very loath to discard. The US, reduced though it may be, will remain a superpower, and Washington's elites – whether Republican or Democrat, liberal or conservative – will continue to pursue a global strategy. But as economic decline and global realities press in on Washington's decision-makers, a revamped global strategy – refined, reordered, and retrenched – can hardly be avoided.

A FORWARD STRATEGY IN EURASIA?

Perhaps the best way to look at a potentially revamped US grand strategy is through the prism set out by Zbigniew Brzezinski sometime before the feverish post-9/11 atmosphere. Brzezinski, Jimmy Carter's National Security Advisor from 1976, was no neo-con hawk (and was to have severe misgivings about the Bush Two doctrine of pre-emption and regime change). Yet, like many in the Democratic foreign policy establishment, he continued to support the idea of American 'primacy' in the world and advocates an American global policy that attempts to secure that 'primacy' for the next century. Brzezinski avoids the bombastic language of 'hegemony' and 'domination' used by neo-conservatives, but only because, like his fellow Democrat former President Bill Clinton, he believes American primacy can be secured through more subtle means. In his book *The Grand Chessboard* Brzezinski argued that American primacy in the coming era needs a forward strategy for America, and that the key to such a forward strategy is US control of Eurasia.[16]

Eurasia is the key. The father of contemporary geopolitics, Harold Mackinder, argued early in the last century that whoever 'rules the world-island [of Eurasia] commands the world'. The landmass of this 'world-island' stretches in the west from the Atlantic shores of Ireland and Portugal all the way across the Urals and Siberia through to China and the North Pacific Ocean, down around the shores of South East Asia and back to India. It is, unquestionably, the key strategic area in the twenty-first century. In size it is virtually equal to the Americas (about 50,000,000 square kilometres each); but it has three-quarters of the world's population, almost 70 per cent of the world's GNP and, crucially, about three-quarters of the world's energy sources.

Washington's great unspoken fear, and Brzezinski's spoken one, is that the USA may well be marginalised in Eurasia – or, as he puts it, even 'ejected' from the continent altogether. Should this indeed happen, then, by mid-century, the USA, restricted to hegemony over the western hemisphere and influence around the edges of Eurasia (say, in parts of Southeast Asia and Australia), will return to its pre-Second World War war status as an hemispheric, rather than a global, power.

Great challenges to American primacy in Eurasia loom. China may prove to be the most formidable. But Europe is another, particularly an increasingly united EU in a strategic relationship with Russia. Brzezinski himself worries that, as Western Europe is 'America's geostrategic bridgehead on the Eurasian continent', then 'any ejection of America by its western partners from its perch on the western periphery [of Eurasia] would automatically spell the end of America's participation in the game on the Eurasian chessboard.'[17]

EAST EURASIA: CHINA RISING

And what of America's 'perch' at the other end of Eurasia – in East Asia? There seems little doubt that the coming era will see greater integration of East Asia under Chinese leadership. This integration will inevitably mean a lesser role for the US. And in military terms as the major Asian power China will continue to challenge the US. The big question remains about Japan – about whether relations between China and Japan will continue to thaw to the point of alliance, or whether the US will retain Japan as her principal ally, and a balancing factor against China, in the region.

American influence in East Eurasia will also depend on whether the US can use India as another balancing force (alongside Japan) against China, as will the future of 'American boots on the ground' in South Korea. Should Asian integration and Chinese influence over North Korea ultimately end the tension between the two Koreas (and even bring them together) then, in what will be a big moment for Asia, US troops will leave the Korean peninsular. In any event, the tides of history now seem to be running fast towards Asian integration with a lesser role for the USA and a bigger role for China, in the region.

SOUTHERN EURASIA

The American position throughout the southern rim of Eurasia will also become increasingly shaky. In the Middle East much will depend on how the US extricates itself from its heavy occupation of Iraq, and that in turn may well turn on future US relations with Iran and with other neighbouring states. It could go either of two ways: if the US continues to confront Iran it can only successfully do so by building a 'Sunni Wall' alliance throughout the region, but that in turn will demand some kind of settlement of the Israeli-Palestine issue on terms currently (2008) unacceptable to Israel. Alternatively, if the US accedes to Iran as regional superpower (it did, after all, help her into her ascendant new role) then it will have serious trouble both with Israel and with the 'moderate' Sunni Arab states.

Oil will remain at the centre of American interests in the Middle East, and the US will remain the major global player in the region. Yet she is looking at a future in which her previously dominant influence will erode, and she will no longer be able to secure her objectives as easily as in the past. Also, depending on how the 'war on terror' develops, the real centre of US interest in southern Eurasia may move further east into Afghanistan and Pakistan. American relations with Pakistan are the key here. And it must remain an open question whether America or China will become the dominant outside external influence over the country. Much will depend on the outcome of the Afghan conflict. An American 'loss' in Afghanistan could have major repercussions throughout the southern rim of the former Soviet Union where the US, since the end of the Cold War and then again since 9/11, has made some geopolitical inroads.

US power in Eurasia relative to Russia will likely decline. Already, by 2008, Russia had succeeded in drawing a line across western Eurasia. Whereas the Balkans (including Serbia) might well end up in the western orbit, the forward march of NATO was stopped at the eastern Polish border – with the Ukraine and Belarus unlikely to join either the EU or NATO in the foreseeable future.

WESTERN EURASIA: EUROPE RISING

The American geostrategic toehold in Western Eurasia is also somewhat fragile. Culturally and historically strong (with ties of kinship and ideology), the American-European relationship is undergoing a profound change – as important as anything happening in Asia or southern Eurasia. Everything in western Eurasia depends on whether the growing economic unity and integration of the EU area can develop a more serious political dimension. The core of the EU, the euro-zone, is a great success story and can be expected to become a reserve currency to rival the declining world role of the dollar. As integration proceeds pressure for an economic government for the euro-zone can only grow – and could become acute should global financial instability cause divergences between member states.

The ratification of the Lisbon Treaty will see a small, but highly significant, leap towards more political unity. The creation of a permanent presidency for the EU and a new EU Foreign Ministry, as well as some further strengthening and streamlining of EU central institutions, will give a further boost to what is already an embryonic EU government.

But it is developments on the security front that may be decisive in weakening US influence in Europe. Already, before 9/11, US troops and bases were being wound down in 'core Europe'. Following 9/11, and during the Iraq invasion and occupation, US influence in Europe was increasingly questioned in 'Old Europe', as designated by Donald Rumsfeld, but grew in peripheral Europe. The new entrants to the EU, formerly subject to and still fearful of the Soviet Union, are keen to secure continuing American support and backed the invasion of Iraq. They joined with Britain to form what amounted to 'an American camp' within the EU – not just supportive of the Iraq invasion, but also keen advocates of the American 'neo-liberal' (neo-conservative) economic model. Poland played a key role when the fiercely nationalist but also pro-American Jaroslaw Kaczynski's Law and Justice Party, joined an informal alliance with

Eurosceptic, pro-American Britain, to act as a brake on Paris-Berlin led 'core Europe'. Whilst Poland and Britain (two size-able countries) acted together to limit further European unity and integration, particularly in the defence field, the US could continue to divide and rule. At one stage, at the height of tensions over the Iraq invasion, the Bush administration even went so far as to publicly spell out its divide and rule strategy for Europe – calling the new strategy 'dis-aggregation'.

Poland, though, changed geopolitical tack in October 2007 with the defeat of the Law and Justice Party and the victory of the more pro-European Donald Tusk, the leader of Platforma Obywatelska. With the new government seemingly increasingly reconciled to the EU (and to Germany's leading role) the rest of the new EU states can be expected, over time, to lessen their suspicion of Berlin and Paris – thus making way for a clearer path to a more united Europe, but particularly to the new European Defence System (ESDP). In an early signal of a new American approach to Europe, the Bush administration in 2007, under French President Sarkozy's prompting, agreed to lift its hostile attitude to (and effective veto over) the Paris-Berlin plan for a more unified and separate European Defence and Security Policy. It was a recognition, even in Bush's Washington, of America's new geopolitical weakness. The US was beginning to need Europe as much as Europe needs the US.

LEAVING THE 'EUROPEAN SIDEKICKS' BEHIND?

As always with retreating allies, any American leaves a problem for its most loyal allies – like Britain and some of the newer members of the EU. The UK's 'special relationship' constructed around and dependent upon, cold war style heavy US involvement in Europe, could become a casualty of a weakening American presence.

In order to keep any influence over the western end of Eurasia the ideal scenario for the US would be for Britain (as well as, maybe, say, Poland) to continue its membership of the EU but, within it, to continue to act as an awkward partner and thus dilute and divide the EU as America's potential super-power rival. But should this particular move on the chessboard not work, then a good second best move would be to have Britain outside the EU – as an American satellite nation off the coast of the continent.

Should Britain's leaders opt for this wrecking role for the UK, the consequences for Britain, let alone the European continent, could be very harmful indeed. Such a rejection of Europe by Britain would probably find allies in other quirky corners of the continent, particularly in Eastern Europe, and perhaps, in Scandinavia. This could create an inner and outer Europe, with outer Europe aligning with the US against inner Europe on key global issues. If such a split became a fact, Europe could be permanently divided.

And such a Balkanised European Union would be in no shape to meet the challenges posed by the geopolitics of the coming twenty-first century multipolar world. A weakened and divided, inner and outer core, Europe would make it easier for the US in the west and China in the east to establish separate spheres of influence within Europe – to divide and conquer the continent.

The most realistic outcome for western Eurasia, however, remains a united Europe – with Britain and Poland fully reconciled to the EU, and, ultimately, to the euro-zone. This Europe will inevitably result in a smaller American geopolitical presence than at any time since before 1942.

CHAPTER TWELVE

THE RESCUE OF THE WEST?

RESCUING THE WEST?

With America weakened, and Europe not yet fully united, the new century – from the vantage point of its very early years – does not look good for 'the West', not as good, that is, as did the previous century. Of course, pessimism about the decline of western civilisation has been a constant feature of post-Victorian times – ever since Oswald Spengler's *The Decline of the West* was published in 1918. Spengler, though, was a cultural conservative (indeed reactionary) who saw liberalism and modernisation as weakening the West from the inside (and there are traces of this approach in Samuel Huntingdon's 'Clash of Civilisations' published some three-quarters of a century later). Yet today's pessimism about 'the West' is less about cultural decay and more about economics and geopolitics – about population figures, GDP statistics, military success (or lack of it) and the rise of new powers such as China and India.

Fears about the declining West have been exacerbated by growing divisions amongst the allies – most of them flowing from Washington's 'global war on terrorism' strategy. By early 2008 NATO's occupation of Afghanistan was causing serious trouble, with most European governments remaining reluctant allies and displaying this reluctance by either underfunding their own contribution to the NATO operation or refusing to send their troops into the areas of high conflict. Many Europeans saw Afghanistan as an unwinnable war, as Al-Qaeda terrorists and other anti-western elements would regroup and relocate into the western Pakistani mountains. And they also saw the ultimate war sought by the Americans as being fought out in Pakistan (against the wishes of Karachi), and such a war as an unacceptable western encroachment on Pakistani sovereign territory.

Tensions in NATO were also growing over attitudes to Russia. At the NATO Bucharest summit in April 2008 Germany and France blocked an American attempt to give the green light to immediate Georgian and Ukrainian accession to the alliance. This Franco-German reaction was bitterly resented by some Washington conservatives who considered it a sellout to an increasingly authoritarian Kremlin. Yet in Europe it was seen more positively – as Europeans, not Americans, deciding on the (albeit temporary) boundaries of Europe, and on the border between European and Russian influence, and as an example of a more independent European position.

REFORMING THE WEST? TWO EQUAL PARTNERS (ROME AND BYZANTIUM)

Fears about the declining and divided West have led to a recent revival in rhetoric about reforging and reuniting 'the West' or 'the western world' – and some of them have found their way onto the top political tables. In early 2008 the administration of George W. Bush showed some enthusiasm for the idea for a Transatlantic Free Trade Area (TAFTA) proposed by German Chancellor Angela Merkel. This sketchy but intriguing idea had been knocking around think tanks for some time; and Merkel's proposals reiterated many of them including the highly ambitious aim of creating a single transatlantic market for investors, with common rules and standards on questions such as financial regulation and intellectual property. There was little doubt that TAFTA was aimed at strengthening the West against a rising China.

At the same time the somewhat chastened Washington was engaging in new thinking about how 'the West' could be unified strategically by reforming NATO in the new century. This had been a long-term goal of French statecraft from the days of Charles De Gaulle and his vision of creating an equal partnership across the Atlantic. This would involve turning the American-European partnership into a close, highly co-ordinated, relationship of equals, something rather akin to today's Franco-German alliance. Or to the 'empire with two halves' – Rome and Byzantium.

Intriguingly, the idea of a more independent Europe was seemingly no longer discouraged in George W. Bush's weakened Washington. In fact, in late 2007, following his election, President Nicholas Sarkozy of France had flown to Kennebunkport, Maine, and had secured a general understanding with Washington that was historic by any imagining.

Under this informal agreement France would end the era of 'Gaullisme' by rejoining the military wing of NATO – but only in return for US support for a separate European Defence System (ESDP), a system which Sarkozy in early 2008 was proposing to make one of the centrepieces of his upcoming Presidency of the European Union.

As proof of the American earnest to lift their veto on the ESDP the American Ambassador to NATO, Victoria Nuland, was dispatched to Paris in late February 2008 to make the unusual announcement, for a Bush appointee, that 'I am here in Paris to say that we agree with France – Europe needs, the United States needs, NATO needs, the democratic world needs – a stronger, more capable European defence capacity...An ESDP.'[1]

By the spring of 2008 the atmosphere in Washington had changed dramatically. From the permafrost of some five years earlier, attitudes to Europe were positively warm. Besieged by the imbroglios in Iraq and Afghanistan and by the banking and debt crisis Washington was offering an olive branch to Europe. On TAFTA and a possibly reordered NATO, a new, and surprising, American willingness, even amongst the dying embers of the Bush presidency, to at least try and unify the West was on parade. However, whether Europe would salute was another matter.

OR TWO WESTS?

One potential problem, though, with a reformed West of equal partners was that, without overarching and binding political linkage, like a transatlantic single currency, this kind of equal partnership could easily dissolve into 'two Wests' – two political centres that would inevitably start competing, even possibly conflicting.

Ultimately, a common, or even single, 'West' can only be successfully constructed (like the EU itself) should the parties share interests and values in common. Obviously the USA and the EU hold some very basic interests in common – they are both advanced industrial and commercial societies, and share a common interest in maintaining their high living standards within sustainable economic development as well as protecting their free societies based upon law.

Yet, since the end of the Cold War American and European interests in some key parts of the world have begun to diverge – particularly in Europe's neighbourhood. Europe's future energy needs are increasingly linked to Russia, and a strategic long-term 'energy for markets' deal between the EU states and Russia will stabilise relations across the old cold war divide. Washington, however, sees Russia in a very different way and remains in a semi-competitive relationship with the Kremlin for influence in Eurasia. Also, Europe and America possess underlying divergent interests in the Middle East and the Mahgreb. Europe sees the region as its neighbourhood and seeks stability, whereas Washington's interest in the region lies primarily in oil and counter-terrorism. Given their druthers most European governments (even the German) would seek major concessions from Israel in order to achieve a peace settlement (which they believe would lower tensions throughout the region as well as seriously weakening Iranian influence). They would also talk to Iran as part of a regionally-negotiated settlement of the Iraq quagmire. By contrast, no medium-term future US administration can be expected to even consider forcing a real crisis with Israel in order to achieve real concessions.

The China question might also serve to open up divergent American and European interests – and can fracture the West. For instance, should a future Washington administration put up tariffs on Chinese imports, ought the EU to show solidarity with Washington, or should it seek to replace the US in China's affections? In other words, it could become very tempting for the EU to seek to replace the USA as the recipient of Asian funds – allowing Europeans to begin living beyond their means in the same manner as Americans have been doing over the last few decades.

The great transatlantic question is: are these divergent geopolitical interests between Europe and America so serious that they override the interests that they hold in common? In other words, in the coming multipolar world do the Europeans and the Americans have a 'special relationship' which sets them apart from the other multi-poles? Or, should Europe and America act independently of each other, treating each other in exactly the same way as they would treat China, India, Japan, and the rest, in the coming system of current and shifting alliances?

Yet, if interests may be diverging between the US and Europe, are their values? Transatlantic get-togethers have for some time been riddled with formulaic, cliché-ridden rhetoric about sharing values. Of course, they represent an essential truth. Americans and Europeans are more like each other, and think more like each other, than any other two peoples on the planet. Yet, even so, there are clear differences in values that appear in rhetoric and policymaking, and they are wide enough sometimes to be described as a 'gap'. Even before 9/11 a transatlantic debate about a so-called 'values gap' between Americans and Europeans was underway, one that intensified as the Iraq policy unfolded. Condoleezza Rice, then the National Security Advisor to the President even gave over part of a major speech in Washington to this 'alleged values gap' between Americans and Europeans which she suggested was centred around some specific areas of policy difference like the death penalty, gun control, biotechnology and climate change.[2]

One source of the difference over values is the continuing religiosity of modern American society. Measured simply by churchgoing the US remains a much more religious society than most of those in Europe. But it is the role of religion in the public space – the slow erosion of the separation of church and state – and its effect on public policy that is the issue. US public life used to almost define itself by French-like strict adherence to the separation of church and state, but since the rise of the Christian Right into a serious political force within the Republican party in the 1980s this separation has become increasingly blurred – with obvious effects on policy, particularly foreign policy. One very high-profile effect has been the influence of Christian Zionism (particularly when linked to the more traditional Israeli lobby) on US policy towards the Middle East.

One reason for the continuing power of religion in American society – and one not fully understood by Europeans, is the extent to which Christian churches fulfil a welfare role for many local communities in modern America, particularly throughout the American south – one which many supporters of the 'minimal state' are more than pleased for them to shoulder.

The European approach to welfare tends to give the state a bigger role, and often a redistributive role. For Europeans the state is viewed in a different light from many, particularly upper income, Americans – it is not seen as stifling enterprise but, rather, as opening up opportunities for those not able to afford private health and education. At the root of many of these transatlantic distinctions is a fundamentally different approach to questions of economic equality. Quite simply, Europeans are much less tolerant of inequality than Americans, much more fearful of its social and political consequences. Many Americans believe that inequality (even deep inequalities represented by mega-rich excess amidst poverty) is the necessary price paid for dynamism and growth; Europeans see inequalities as limiting opportunities. Americans, because of their history, are less likely to see economics as a zero-sum game whereas Europeans see a limited pie.

In the years ahead these values differences will always act as a limiting factor in any serious transatlantic economic co-operation and certainly integration. For instance, in the early discussions and debates in 2008 about the details of the projected Transatlantic Free Trade Association (TAFTA) value-laden questions such as how to harmonise tax policy, labour market regulation, and social protection were already serious stumbling blocs to agreement. Americans and Europeans may want to work together to rescue the West, but they are still looking warily at each other.

A CHANGE OF LEADERSHIP?

If an equal partnership across the Atlantic will be difficult to work, what about a change of leadership for the West? What about a European-led West, with Europe taking over the role that the US fulfilled during the Cold War?

For many, both in Washington and Brussels, even to pose the question seems far-fetched – still so even after the failure of US leadership in Iraq and the Middle East and the collapse of the American Wall Street economic model. The fact is that such a transatlantic role reversal is, at least for the next decade or two, simply not on. And the explanation is not just habit. It boils down to the same reason that Europe can no longer accept American leadership: that, over the long-run, it is simply unacceptable and unrealistic to expect one equally-sized state with an equal GDP to lead another – particularly so when the supposed follower state is a world superpower.

What's more, following the divisions over Iraq, there remains too much suppressed – and non-suppressed – hostility and scorn amongst some American elites for 'old Europe'. At the height of the transatlantic controversy over Iraq Washington neo-cons were describing Europeans as 'wimps', unwilling to recognise the global terrorist threat and unable, because of low military spending, to properly defend themselves in a dangerous world. And, more caustic of all, they saw Europe morphing into 'Eurabia' – a continent, under pressure from domestic Islamic populations, preparing to do a deal with Islam, indeed militant Islam, as part of a process of ditching its western heritage. Grisly book titles, like Bruce Bawer's *While Europe Slept: How Radical Islam Is Destroying the West From Within* and Walter Lacquer's *The Last Days of Europe: Epitaph For An Old Continent*, give the flavour of the critique.[3]

As well as scorn, large numbers of US commentators and analysts tend to see Europe as irrelevant in the global power game. In analysis after analysis of the coming global order and rising and falling powers, Europe (and the EU) is regularly treated as though it was invisible. For instance, Josef Joffe, the publisher-editor of *Die Zeit* (and a fellow at Stanford University) is not alone in writing a whole article on the coming global era as though it boils down to a contest between the USA and China (and perhaps India) only. In this carefully written piece there was not one, not one, mention of Europe.[4]

American critics of Europe also talk of a demographic timebomb – of Europe becoming unimportant globally as it declines because of its ageing population. The superpower expert Professor Paul Kennedy, though, warns us to view population alongside arable land (measuring the ability to feed) and when arable land is added to the equation, the prospects for Europe look good whereas those of the Asian giants do not.[5] However, from Washington's perspective Europe's economies are not creative or dynamic enough to offer much long-term competition to China and because of lack of unity and political will, Europe will fall increasingly under the sway of the Kremlin.

So, with these anti-European views still prevalent in Washington and Wall Street any 'new West', certainly one under European leadership, seems premature. Americans will simply not agree to accept leadership from Europeans, and some will even continue to resent a European input into a more collective system. And from the European vantage point resentment, even outrage, at the kind of Washington elite thinking that took the country into the Iraq war and occupation will live on, even through a new presidency. For many in Europe the events in 2003 meant one sure thing: that for some time the Americans have forfeited the right to a leadership role.

BUT EUROPE COULD GO IT ALONE

But what of Europe? In the coming unsettled geopolitical climate, Europe enters the twenty-first century as by far the most stable of the three new superpower regions. Whereas the USA is like a shooting star, one that is now falling to earth, Europe is more like the moon – less exciting, but always there every night.

Europe's story is remarkable. In the heated transatlantic debate and discourse it is often forgotten that historically Europe *is* 'the West' – for good or bad, its veritable beating heart. It was Europeans, the Portugese to be exact, whose fighting ships first took what we now call 'western' peoples and ideas into the heartland of Eurasia and set in train the European colonisation of the world; and it was Europeans, the

British to be exact, who founded the USA, and it was European peoples and ideas that were the dominant influence in inform-ing the political and economic development of the new world. In the twentieth century Europe stalled, nearly destroying itself in two catastrophic wars, the result of which was the division of the continent and the dominance of old Europe by the new world. But, with American help, Europe survived and prospered in the Cold War. And now it is back.

In the first decade of the twenty-first century a strong case can be made that Europe looks in better shape than does its great North American offshoot. It came out of the Cold War in relatively good shape, and in the new vacuum proceeded to further integrate and unite (through the euro-zone) and expand (into eastern Europe). But its leaders kept a sense of limits – Europe did not over-extend itself by inordinate global ambi-tions and huge deficits and debt. It did not lose its bearings.

Crucially, in the 1990s 'Core Europe' did not throw all of its eggs into the 'neo-liberal' (neo-conservative) globalisation bas-ket. Europe's core states retained a balance in their economies as they rejected the extreme financialisation of capital, the mammoth private debt levels (housing boom and bust) and the hollowing out of the manufacturing sector encouraged by the Americans and the British. Crucially, too, 'Core Europe' broke with the habits of half a century by saying 'no' to allying itself with the US president in his grievous 2003 military expedition in Arabia. Consequently, it has not suffered a geopolitical defeat, and a collapse in its credibility and reputation.

The European continent meets the twenty-first century as the most civilised major living space on the face of the globe. It is large and powerful as well as stable and prosperous (with 500 million inhabitants earning a quarter of the world's GNP). People in the EU live longer than anywhere else except perhaps Japan, and they have far more leisure time than Americans. The EU is more than self-sufficient in food, has a good water supply, and, with its strategic partnership with Russia, has relatively stable and diversified sources of energy. It has two nuclear powers and can defend itself against all-comers by the traditional doctrine of nuclear deterrence.

Above all, it is governed by consent, and protects its individual citizens through a dense network of rights. It is largely secular, separating church and state, and, crucially, is the area of the world most resistant to the rise of fundamentalist religion. In sum a strong case can be made that Europeans enjoy the best quality of life in global history. Though wracked during the early and mid-twentieth century by wars and tyrannies, Europe is now the bastion of civilised living and democratic standards.

EUROPE AT THE CROSSROADS

But can Europe keep its gains? The EU stands at a real cross-roads. It has the economic strength, political stability, human, natural and technological resources to go it alone as one of the new rising global superpowers. Since its low point in 1945 its leaders have rightly concentrated on gradually uniting the continent through economics and currency union; and through both luck and judgement they have got the balance right between building up the union's domestic prosperity and asserting a global role. To continue to set aside unrealistic global ambitions whilst tending to Europe's resources and strength, the sinews of its economic power, and keeping on this sustainable path, will remain the beginning of wisdom. As is the need to secure a strategic partnership with Russia and stabilise the southern borders – in the Middle East and the Mahgreb – hopefully without a great clash with Islam.

The good news for Europe is that because of its recent history of bloody wars and defeats, including imperial defeats, Europe's leaders – with a question mark over some British elites – show none of the imperially derived hubris (and arrogance) which so easily lead to unrealistic and vainglorious global ambitions.

There is, though, an alternative scenario. Europe could fail to take the next step and balk at political and defence union – and then slip back into quarrelling nation-states. In this outcome – and if the rise of China is as dramatic as many think – then in the long-run, even by mid-century, this fractured EU could become Balkanised, and split between rising Asian powers and a retreating USA.

ENDING THE GRIP OF GLOBALISATION

Just as important as who leads the West is its future direction, including its governing ideology. A gathering theme was emerging amongst some opinion-formers that should the West keep on the path of 'globalisation' – that is if the governing dynamic remains global integration driven primarily by the private sector (the search for low costs and high profit) then a number of dangerous developments can be expected: the West's industrial sector will continue to be hollowed out; China and India will continue to build up their internal markets which remain relatively closed to western commerce; the two Asian superpowers will also move into a dominant position in Asia both economically and militarily; and they could continue to build up their strategic control of energy supplies around the world.

The damage to the western economies caused by the hollowing out of jobs and wealth to low cost centres and the unwinding of the mammoth credit mountain was, by 2008, causing politicians to review policies. There was, though, as yet, no review of the fundamental doctrines that had guided western policymakers ever since the late 1980s. Not surprisingly so, for the course set during the two-decade-long Greenspan era, started during the Thatcher/Reagan administrations and continued and honed during the Clinton, Blair and G.W. Bush administrations, though unsustainable, seemed so successful that it was very difficult to easily challenge and change.

SHAPING GLOBALISATION

An alternative path for the West would involve a world order in which a co-ordinated 'West' attempted to shape globalisation rather than simply accepting and obeying its rules as immutable. Shaping globalisation means ending global integration as the driving force of western economic and social development. It means taking the radical step of protecting American and European jobs and American and European wealth by establishing their priority over global market integration. It means forming domestic western (US and European) policies for jobs, for healthcare, for education and for taxes – and then prioritising those policies over the private sector-led global pressures that would inevitably seek to undermine them.

STRATEGIC TRADE

For instance, trade policy would no longer be driven by 'free trade' global market ideology irrespective of the damaging domestic social consequences; rather, trade policies would be informed by, and fit in with, the employment and social needs at home, and negotiated accordingly.

A start in this direction was made with the trade policy changes developed by Democrats during the 2008 presidential primaries. It was all very general, but candidates Edwards,

Clinton and Obama all made promises to end the liberal trade era and review and renegotiate trade deals in order to protect American workers. Clinton even promised to review America's attitude to the World Trade Organisation and stated that as president she might well withdraw America from the 'Doha Round'. Obama argued that 'trade needed to be viewed not just through the lens of Wall Street, but also of Main Street, which means we've got strong labour standards and strong environmental and safety standards', and argued that he would amend the North Atlantic Free Trade Agreement (NAFTA) and 'fight for fair trade' by pressuring the WTO to enforce trade agreements and stop countries from unfair subsidies and non-tariff barriers on U.S. exports.' 2008 clearly saw an historic change of mood about 'free trade', and in the Senate, Democratic Senator Schumer's bill (Schumer-Graham) – indeed quite specifically seeking to place serious tariffs on Chinese imports – was still lurking and gathering support.

All in all the political winds of 2008 were beginning to blow the old 'globalisation' consensus away. There was considerable populist rhetoric about trade; but behind the bravado of 'change' was an awareness within the Democratic leadership that changes in trade policy could easily ignite a protectionist firestorm and a tit for tat battle of wills across the world between the great trading nations. China's reaction would be crucial here. But, no matter these concerns, with the economic clouds gathering and darkening, it was clear that the consistent and insistent push towards integrated open borders for trade was now over, and an era of managed trade was about to begin.

The Clinton/Blair/Bush mantra that 'globalisation is here to stay: accept it and adapt according' was now being challenged by a new approach which, whilst not seeking to opt out of the global economy, argued that the West should stop 'accepting' but rather start trying to 'shape' globalisation. And 'shaping' meant a new view that domestic social needs and justice, and the tax, labour and welfare policies needed to secure them, should take priority and be pursued even if they altered and hindered the global dynamic – the corporate search for lower costs and higher profits of the 'globalisation' creed.

BREAKING THE GRIP OF 'THE MARKET'

At the very heart of the Greenspan era's dramatic 'globalisation' strategy – its engine, so to speak – was the fundamentalist doctrine of the market or the 'free market'. After all, the great 1990s burst of economic globalisation was not driven by governments or trade unions, but rather by the force of the 'free market' – in reality by the big 'market makers' of the private sector. Globalisation was in a very real sense the market unbound, the domestic 'free market' transferred onto a bigger stage.

So, as economic woes in the West brought 'globalisation' increasingly into question, so too did it weaken support for 'the market', particularly market fundamentalism. Yet loosening the grip of this fundamentalist ideology on the West's economic (and cultural and intellectual) would take time. For by the turn of the century in American (and British) popular intellectual life, support for the market, particularly the 'free market', had become an act of faith, almost a religion. And it was (is) a religion that has spawned a powerful clerisy in the form of the army of economists, economic and business commentators and analysts that now so dominate American (and British) public life and public opinion. John Kay, himself a distinguished member of this clerisy, has described how public interest in economic questions is now moulded by what he calls the 'rivetingly awful' 'world of Bloomberg television'.[6]

This clerisy is not wholly united, but true believing market fundamentalism remains its most driven, most dynamic, strand. And as the 'neo-liberal' deregulated economic system they helped construct winds down they can be expected to resist apostasy and stick by the true faith, almost to the bitter end. Those economists who take a balanced view about the complexity and limitations of markets, like Kay himself and, in the US, Paul Krugman, still represent a minority view. And little will really change until the key building bloc of modern business commentary – the dominance of economics over politics – is finally challenged: a task that economists and business commentators, no matter how well-meaning, are unlikely to be able to perform.

More daunting than the tenacity of the 'free market' clerisy, however, will likely be the opposition of the rich and powerful – those entrenched moneyed interests that have done very well out of the current world economic order. This order, geared up to secure the maximum profitability for big corporate interests, is, of course nothing like a real 'free market' system. There is, in fact, no such thing in this world as 'the free market' (which is why I have put the term in inverted commas throughout this book). All kinds of market imperfections and interventions see to that. A better term would be the economic status quo. But the supporters of this economic status quo prefer to call it 'the free-market'. It sounds something worth defending.

In any event, a global order that has delivered so much will not be easily abandoned or eroded by those who have benefited from it. And the new super-rich super-class can be expected to join the 'free market' clerisy in a strong rearguard action to keep the status quo and to halt and divert change.

THE BEGINNING OF CHANGE

Yet in the early spring of 2008 events themselves were conspiring to undermine the foundations of the 'free market' status quo. For in order to deal with the American financial crisis that had broken some months before, the politicians and the central bank (the Federal Reserve) started to entertain and even implement policies that would strike at the heart of the market fundamentalist system. Market doctrine – though not the big money boys themselves – was hostile to state intervention even in order to bail-out private sector institutions in trouble. Yet this was exactly the strategy adopted by the Federal Reserve during the crisis (the American state supervised, helped and guaranteed the JP Morgan takeover of the failing bank, Bear Stearns, and the bailing out of the two mammoth mortgage institutions, Freddie Mac and Fannie Mae; and in 'neo-liberal' Britain the troubled Northern Rock was actually nationalised!). Even more potentially heretical was the infringement of free market doctrine that was contemplated by Democratic politicians in the House and Senate as they advocated intervening in the market (for housing) to help families in trouble. Serious breaches in the market doctrine of the sanctity of contracts were contemplated by plans that, in order to avoid the loss of homes, would give judges the right to vary mortgage contractual agreements.

Also, during the financial crisis, tighter and more effective regulation of the banking and financial system – a 'no-no' for market purists – began to appeal to policymakers. This, even though deregulation (or at least 'light touch' regulation) was a core principle of market doctrine. Supporters of the market, like Hank Paulson, former banker and George W. Bush's Secretary of the Treasury during the early stages of the crisis, attempted a rearguard action to keep regulation at bay when, on 1st April 2008 (April Fool's Day), he introduced a 'new' regulatory framework for the banking and financial sector – a plan immediately attacked by Democrats, including former Labour Secretary Robert Reich, as attempting to 'deregulate' rather than 'regulate'. However, all the signs were that a new consensus was cohering around the need a tighter, more robust, regulatory system for the future.

Bail-outs and regulation were one thing, but a change of course in tax policy was decidedly another. For 'neo-liberals' a low-tax regime was an utterly central article of doctrinal faith. For them, taxes, particularly progressive taxes, were a clear form of state interference in individual freedom and an unwarranted intervention in the market. And a progressive tax regime was bad for rich folk and thus for capital, and thus, so the argument progressed, for employment. Low-tax regimes had governed the 'neo-liberal' economies of the West from the late 1980s onwards – from Reagan to George W. Bush, and from Thatcher to Blair – and George W. Bush had cut taxes, primarily for the wealthiest Americans, even when the US budget deficit was becoming embarrassing.

During the 2008 presidential campaign Democrats were working on a future tax regime that would not have appealed to Ronald Reagan. Presidential candidate Senator Obama proposed a plan – similar to that of other Democratic candidates – involving billions in tax breaks for 'the poor and the middle class' whilst increasing taxes on 'the rich'. The idea was to stop 'rewarding wealth instead of work'. It amounted to a radical change in outlook at least on tax policy. Yet these plans, though promising a somewhat different course, were not radical enough to seriously erode the growing wealth and income gaps in the United States, nor to be able to deal with the government deficits over the long run (particularly should spending on the

Pentagon remain at Bush levels and, in the coming recession, spending on welfare, health and education rise). A real change in course would need more profound measures than any being offered in the election campaign of 2008.

STRATEGY NOT IDEOLOGY

Yet to secure real change nothing less than the abandonment of the governing free-market doctrines for the western world will suffice. But what was needed in its place? Certainly not a new doctrine, for it was adherence to doctrine itself that was the problem. First, the doctrinaire pushing of good ideas – the market, and globalism – to absurd extremes in order to serve a greedy and triumphalist class in a greedy and triumphalist era. And in foreign policy the doctrinaire ideology of American universalism – the notion that every part of the world should have democracy imposed on it (through the barrel of a gun if necessary).

What was needed was a new, balanced, undoctrinaire, view of the role of the state as a limiter and balancer of rampant corporate business.

CONTINENT-STATES

And by 2008 with the private financial sector in meltdown the state had indeed returned to the centre of thinking. And suddenly, with bail-outs needed, and government guarantees sought after, the state, and politics, was relevant again. 2008 was a year in which the state was needed. And more than needed – it was becoming essential, and not just as a handmaiden used to subsidise and oil the private sector. It was western civilisation's bedrock institution.

Yet, it was also increasingly clear that, amidst all the financial and social tribulations, only a large state – with massive resources – could properly stabilise the capitalist system. The old-fashioned Westphalian nation-state – that is, anything up to and including the medium-sized European state – was simply too small. With investment houses and commercial banks failing and the whole global financial system tottering, we would need something the size of a continent-state.

Europe was the centre of this dynamic. Countries the size of Britain, France and Germany were not really big enough to withstand global pressures. But the EU and the euro-zone were a different matter. Europe, both as an internal market and as a potential global reserve currency, was able – more or less – hold its own against volatile global capital. So, too, should it wish too, was the USA. These two continent-states were big enough to negotiate with global capital, big enough to regulate markets, and, crucially, big enough to survive a global trade downturn. They both still had large, prosperous, internal markets; they both still had a relatively good balance between manufacturing and services, and low and hi-tech; they both still had a good balance between population, arable land and water; they both could still draw on traditions of law and good governance. They would remain dependent upon foreign sources of energy – the EU on Russia, the USA on the Middle East – but in a new regime of sustainable growth they could, over time, lower their dependence on these unstable foreign sources.

Of course, the EU and the USA, under the pressures of a global recession, were already adopting a more strategic, more protectionist, approach to economics and trade. And China, who had never globalised as much as the West in the first place, and India, were following suit. And other trading blocs, in order to protect themselves, would, inevitably, begin a further process of economic, and maybe even political integration.

Thus – in the early years of the twenty-first century – was already emerging the much discussed multipolar world: with the 'continent-states' of Europe, the USA, China, India, perhaps Russia, perhaps Brazil, negotiating their futures amongst each other. (And, for the rest, future 'continent-states' – Mercosur? The African Union, ASEAN? – were already discernible.) It was a world – already in formation – in which unfettered global capital would no longer be king. Capital would still flow but it would need to compromise with politics and people.

ENDING THE WALL STREET GAME: WHO WILL GO FIRST?

In the early years of the new century a great geopolitical or geo-economic drama was being played out before our eyes. By 2008, with pressure building on both sides of the Atlantic from both American and European publics, the question was: who would go first? Who would be the first to bring the global capital game to a close? In sum, who would finally put the interests of its own people – their jobs, their future living standards – ahead of the needs of the 'superclass' – the new social term given to the super-rich globalisers by the writer David Rothkopf – whose clear interest was still to push on with global economic integration until one world, with no government, was run exclusively by mobile capital.[7]

Amongst the candidates to lead the change, the clear front-runner was the USA itself. It would be fitting: America had been strong enough to lead the world into the crisis of global capital, and now was, still, just, strong enough to lead it out. And the US was better at change than its competitors. As the US financial system roiled downwards, with falling 'middle class' living standards, mortgage defaults, continuing job losses, the bottom-up pressure in Main Street for change was growing to the point where even the powerful, penetrative US media corporations could no longer contain it. Americans have powerful corporations, but they also have, unlike Europe and China, a populist democratic culture. In the US there is a greater chance that change can be forced and forged from below.

In 2008 populism was in the air. And as in previous difficult eras in American history populist pressures can create a dynamic which ultimately changes the whole political direction of the country – as did the FDR coalition in the 1930s or the Ronald Reagan coalition in the 1980s. Today's existing order is a market order, and 'changing direction' will inevitably involve adopting policies for greater welfare and even for redistribution. Depending on the severity of the coming economic downturn political life could become quite dramatic, even involving a return to the FDR-LBJ New Deal-Great Society America that was abandoned in the 1980s.

CHINA'S RESPONSE: TENSIONS (CONFLICT) IN THE PACIFIC?

Such profound politically-led change in the western world would not be without its real dangers. China's response would be crucial. China is a status quo power. Having done well out of American-led 'globalisation', it seeks more of the same. And an American or European retreat from economic globalisation (whether depression-driven or not) will certainly threaten the status quo. When the Wall Street global capital game comes to an end China's growth rates will be lower, inflation may well be higher, and the end of the decade-long great Chinese boom will stoke social, even political, trouble for the regime.

Slowing growth rates may, for a time, ease potential 'resource wars' between the US and China. But what if China can de-couple from a US slowdown – in the sense that she can continue to grow her economy, without US growth, through her now large internal and Asian markets? In such an outcome she will continue to demand the resources from Africa and the Middle East and Latin America needed to fuel this growth.

Economists, who still dominate the commentariat scene in the West, rarely understand how politics in all its random and irrational guises can oft-times intervene in 'rational' economic processes. But in the kind of unstable world we are entering, political change – forced by social unrest – in China and populism in the US can easily upset the delicate economic balance between China and the US. Trade protectionist measures in the US Congress could trigger a Chinese retaliation on the financial balances it holds in the US (by, say, switching dollar holdings into euros).

A study of politics (as opposed to economics) teaches that, in a fraught environment with nationalist emotions running high, the fact that such an act might well be 'irrational' (in the short run it would hurt both China and the Americans) may not stop it from happening.

RESOLVING THE CHINA–AMERICAN QUESTION

The coming period will see the resolution of the pivotal Chinese-American relationship – one way or the other. One way forward is to deepen the existing relationship. Stasis is a powerful force; and the ties that bind may well already be too strong. Trade and debt are powerful linkages – and the two nation's elites may opt for further integration of their two nations rather than the path of conflict (hot or cold). This is the CHINUSA option in which the two countries forge their destinies together and become one great transpacific trading bloc which will morph into a Pacific version of the EU. Such a deeper integration will be good for China's development – as it will continue to grow by adding to its manufacturing supremacy by slowly penetrating the services and hi-tech sector of the

American market. It will be very bad for the domestic US population as the hollowing out, and the transfer of jobs and wealth, will continue. But it will be good for both American and Chinese economic elites, who will continue to make money.

An alternative view of the future is that the economic imbalance between the US and China is at the heart of the global economic problem and needs to be addressed, one way or another. As the political economist Iwan Morgan argues 'things that cannot go on forever tend not to, and there is broad recognition that the US current account deficit falls into that bracket'.[8] The current-account imbalance is the obvious headline behind the deeper story of the trade imbalances (massively in China's favour) and the debt imbalance (China's funding of the US Treasury and US agencies) that have so distorted US-Chinese relations since the 1990s. A badly managed unravelling of these financial imbalances, or a conflict over resources such as oil and gas, could even lead to a military confrontation in the Pacific. The potential for conflict – perhaps over Taiwan, perhaps elsewhere in the Pacific – is always a lurking presence.

DEPRESSION THE SAVIOUR?

These US-China imbalances may, though, unravel naturally – simply as a result of a global economic recession or depression, as a slowdown compresses trade and lending. As the financial crisis deepened some commentators, mainly behind cupped hands, were beginning to argue that a full blown global depression would not only solve America's debt problem but could also do the job of dealing with climate change. They had a rueful ring of truth about them. Such a tragic outcome would likely though amount to 'redemption by making things worse' – particularly so since the necessary changes might well be secured by the normal political change in normal times.

WESTERN ELITES: RESTORING A SENSE OF LIMITS

The neo-conservative era unleashed following the West's victory in the Cold War – the era of greed, arrogance and excess – is now coming to an end. Yet the features of this era will be with us for some time yet. The new global business class may well continue to set the tone, as will the mega and super-rich who will continue to amass egregious amounts of money, and will continue to remove themselves from any obligations to their own societies. The economies that they, and the political and media class that supports them, created in the 1990s – with dangerous global imbalances and mountainous debt levels – will not wind down overnight. And there can be little doubt too that the great neo-con vision of a global conquering America – of its 'full spectrum' world dominance – will, like a fire in the minds of men, continue to flicker.

Yet, the unravelling of this world order is already, clearly, underway. It will be an unwinding that will not be without its difficulties, and its pain – for millions of people.

It should not be forgotten that the era now closing did not just happen by accident. The obsession with 'markets' – and with business culture – was not just a natural outgrowth of the collapse in 1989 of command economy communism; and the dramatic push for American global domination did not have to flow automatically from the end of the Soviet Union. The fact was that politics was at work here. For the western leaders of the Greenspan era – from Bill Clinton to George W. Bush from Tony Blair to Jose Maria Aznar to John Howard – not only encouraged the new order, they seized on its possibilities to push it to its limits. They were both true believers trying to 'remake the world' and opportunists (seeking votes). Business may well have been in the ascendant, but the politicians took the decision to give business its head. Hopefully, the responsibility for the coming dislocation will not be laid at the door of the western politicians and public servants who in the next decade now have to pick up the pieces.

Endnotes

PREFACE

1 See; Francis Fukuyama, *The End of History and the Last Man*, London edition, 1992

INTRODUCTION

1 Gorbachev's remarks reported in *The New York Times*, 2nd May 2008
2 See: Francis Fukuyama, *The End of History and The Last Man*, London edition, London, 1992
3 *International Herald Tribune* (*IHT*), 24th-25th November 2007
4 Martin Lipton, financial lawyer, in *IHT*, 30th April 2008
5 Hearing before the Joint Economic Committee of the Congress, 13th November 2002
6 See: usa today.com/money/economy/fed2004-02-23-greenspan-debt

7   Speech at Federal Reserve System's Annual Community Affairs Research Conference, Washington, D.C., 4th April 2005

8   See an early criticism: Batra, R. *Greenspan's Fraud: How Two Decades Of His Policies Have Undermined the Global Economy*, NY, 2005. For a more friendly work see: Woodward, Bob, *Maestro: Greenspan's Fed and the American Boom*, NY, 2000

9   Paul Krugman, 'Blindly into the Bubble' *New York Times (NYT)*, 22nd December 2007

10 Reported in *Business Week*, 14th July 1997

11 See: Joseph Stiglitz, *The Roaring Nineties: Why We're Paying The Price For The Greediest Decade in History*, NY, 2003

12 Quotes from Stiglitz, op. cit., p. 92

13 'The Blair Court Has Presided Over This New Rottenness', Jackie Ashley, *The Guardian*, 22nd January 2007

14 See: Susan Strange, *Mad Money*, Manchester, 1998

15 Reported in *The New York Times*, 22nd December 2007

16 Reported in *The Guardian*, 10th January 2008

CHAPTER ONE

1   Thomas J. Stanley and William D. Danko, *The Millionaire Next Door* (Atlanta, GA: 1997). Some scholars have suggested defining 'the rich' not in terms of millions but rather as those with a family income over nine times the poverty line – in US terms about $95,000 a year in 1987. See S. Danziger, P. Gottschalk and E. Smolensky, 'How The Rich Have Fared, 1973-87', *American Economic Review*, vol. 72, no. 2 (May 1989), p. 312

2   From *World Wealth Report* 2007, from Capgemini/Merrill Lynch 2007. (Report available on web)

3   From Stephen J. Rose, *Social Stratification in The United*

States, New York, 2007

4 The *World Wealth Report*, Capgemini/Merrill Lynch, New York, 2007, p. 8

5 *Newsweek*, 4th August 1997 (source IRS)

6 The UN *Human Development Report* (1996) put the figure at 358, and *Forbes* magazine's 1997 wealth list put the figure at 447, up from 274 in 1991

7 Peter Kwong, 'China's billionaire bubble', *IHT*, 17th November 2007

8 Reported by BBC News, 19th April 2007

9 BBC News Report, 19th April 2007. BBC website, Business Section, 19th April 2007

10 *Newsweek*, 4th August 1997 (source: Forbes, op. cit.)

11 See also, Phillip Hall, *Royal Fortune: Tax, Money and The Monarchy* (London, 1992) for a systematic account of the mysteries of the royal finances. One fact about the Queen's money remains: since 1993 she has remained above the law as far as taxation is concerned as she is not treated in exactly the same way – with all tax laws applying to her – as every other British person. Also see; Jon Temple, *Living Off The State*, Progress Books, 2008 for a well-researched guide to royal finances

12 See: *Newsweek*, 'The New Rich', 4th August 1997. 'The richest one percent of this country owns half our country's wealth...five trillion dollars. One third of that comes from hard work, two thirds comes from inheritance...interest accumulating to widows and idiot sons'

13 John Hills, *Income and Wealth*, London, 1995, p. 9. Hills suggests that 'If Britain's richest man, Soho millionaire Paul Raymond, receives a modest 3 per cent net real return on his reported £1.65 billion fortune' his income would be £1 million a week

14 Figures from *Newsweek*, 4th August 1997, reporting Forbes in June 1997. The figures for the Queen were for 1992 (as published in *The Sunday Times'* 'Rich List', 1997), and were subsequently revised downwards following a complaint to the Press Complaints Commission

15 *World Wealth Report*, 2007

16 GDP here measured by 'purchasing power parity' method.

17 In: John Gray, 'Bill Rules the World – And I Don't Mean Clinton', *Daily Express*, 11th September 1998

18 For individual wealth assessment see: *Forbes* Rich List and *Sunday Times* Rich List – reported by BBC News, 19th April 2007. Also, see the World Bank GDP tables in World Bank's *World Atlas 2007*

19 Wealth figures from *The Sunday Times'* 1997 'Rich List', op. cit., population figures for 1995 from *World Development Report* (Washington, DC: World Bank, 1997)

20 These figures are for 1998. By 2007 they would be even more in favour of the billionaires

21 See *Sunday Times* Rich List, 2007 and 1997

22 Andrew Lycett, 'Who Really Owns London?', *The Times*, 17th September 1997

23 *The Guardian*, 23rd September 1997

24 Alan Blinder, Former Vice-Chair of the Federal Reserve Board, quoted in *Newsweek*, 23rd June 1997

25 From Stephen J. Rose, *Social Stratification in the United States*, NY, 2007, p. 27

26 The *Forbes World Wealth Reports*, 1996, 2001 and 2006

27 *2007 World Wealth Report*, p. 2. Chinese figures from Professor Peter Kwong, *IHT*, 17th November 2007

28 See: Jon Temple, op. cit.

29 *World Wealth Report*, 2007

30 *World Wealth Report*, 2007

31 In 1980, of the 252 largest US enterprises only 32 were controlled by families (only two through a majority of shares); and amongst the major shareholders in Union Pacific in 1980 were the Harriman family, the Rothschild family, the Kirby family and the Kemper family, yet not one of these families possessed more than 2 per cent of the total shareholdings, a pattern that had hardly changed since 1938. Reported in John Scott, op. cit., p. 65

32 Edward Luttwak, *The Endangered American Dream*, New York, 1993, p. 175

33 M. Soref and M. Zeitlin, 'Finance Capital and the Internal Structure of the Capitalist Class in the United States', in Mizruchi and Schwartz (eds), *Inter-corporate Relations: The Structural Analysis of Business*, (New York: 1988)

34 M. Zeitlin, cited in John Scott, op. cit., p. 300

35 *The Economist*, 27th November 2004

36 Stewart Lansley, *Rich Britain: The Rise and Rise of the New Super-Wealthy*, London, 2006, p. 67

37 For the quotes and financial details see; 'Greed of the Highest Order and the Worst Privatization Since Rail' by George Monbiot, *Guardian*, 14th February 2006. Carlyle's mission statement, size of investments and board membership are on the group's website: www.carlyle.com

38 Forbes Special Report on CEO Compensation. www.forbes.com/2005/04/20/05ceoland.html

39 *Business Week*, 21st April 1997

40 Tom Nicholas, *The Myth of Meritocracy: An Enquiry into the Social Origins of Britain's Business Leaders Since 1850*, Mimeograph, LSE, 1999. p. 26

41 Reported in *The Philadelphia Inquirer*, 26th May 1991

42 *Fortune Magazine*, 4th May 1990

43 Kevin Phillips, *Boiling Point: Republicans, Democrats and the Decline of Middle Class Prosperity*, NY, 1993, p. 190

44 See: T. J. Stanley and W. D. Danko, op. cit.

45 For discussion of twentieth-century capitalist wealth concentration see: K. Renner, *The Institutions of Private Law and their Social Function*, translation of 1928 revised edition (London: 1949); R. Hilferding, *Finance Capital* (London: 1981); A. A. Berle and G. C. Means, *Corporations and Private Property* (New York: 1947); C. A. R. Crosland, *The Future of Socialism* (London: 1956); and J. Scott, *Corporate Business*, op. cit.

46 Scott, *Corporate Business*, op. cit., p. 303

47 Ibid.

48 A. A. Berle, *The American Economic Republic* (London: 1963). See also J. Burnham, *The Managerial Revolution* (Harmondsworth: 1945); C. A. R. Crosland, *The Future of Socialism* (London: 1956); A. A. Berle and G. C. Means, *The Modern Corporation and Private Property* (New York: 1947, 1st edn 1932); A. A. Berle, *The Twentieth Century Capitalist Revolution* (London: 1955)

49 Estimates from C. Parkes, 'The Birth of Enclave Man', *Financial Times*, 20th-21st September 1997

50 Thomas I Friedman, *IHT*, 24th June 1997

51 *NYT*, 18th April 1997

52 Paul Krugman, 'From Hype To Fear', *NYT*, 8th January 2008

53 *Guardian*, 7th June 1997

54 Martin Wolf 'Leona Helmsley Is Alive in Britain', *FT*, 7th March 2008

55 IMF and Gibraltar figures in Hans-Peter Martin and Harald Schumann, *The Global Trap: Globalization and the Assault on Prosperity and Democracy* (London and New York: 1997), p. 63. Originally published in German under the

title *Die Globalisierungsfalle: der Angriff auf Demokratie und Wohlstand* (Hamburg: 1997)

CHAPTER TWO

1 See Chapter One

2 The % of net worth of Americans held in stocks and bonds rose from 11 per cent to 18 per cent between 1989 and 1995, and amongst the super-rich top half a million it rose from 17 per cent to 24 per cent. In Britain the rise was just as pronounced. US figures from Arthur B. Kennickell and R. Louise Woodburn, 'Consistent Weight Design For the 1989, 1992 and 1995 SCF's and the Distribution of Wealth', revised July 1997, for Board of Governors the US Federal Reserve System, unpublished. British figures for this period can be found in John Hills, *Income and Wealth* (Joseph Rowntree Foundation, February 1995), p. 94

3 Exact $ figures for 2006 are: USA 44,710, UK 40,560, Germany 36,810, France 36,580 and China 2,000. GNP per capita figures for 1992 were ($): China 470, USA 23,240, UK 17,790, Japan 28,190, Germany 23,030, France 22,260. In the US the average hourly earnings of production and non-supervisory workers on private non-farm payrolls was $11.82 per hour for 34.4 hours per week in 1996. All figures from *World Bank Atlas*, The World Bank, Washington, DC

4 James Goldsmith, *The Trap*, London, 1994, p. 18

5 The % figures in the mid-1990s (for 1994) were: Germany 21.6, France 28.5 (1992 figures), Netherlands 22.01, Sweden 27.5, Portugal 20.8 and Britain 12.8. From: Eurostat 1994

6 Figures from UNCTAD *Annual Survey of Global Investment Trends*

7   *FT*, 12th January 2008

8   Hans-Peter Martin and Harald Schuman, *The Global Trap: Globalisation and the Assault Prosperity and Democracy*, London and New York, 1997, p. 68-9

9   *Newsweek*, 3rd October 1994

10 Cited in Ralph Miliband, *The State in Capitalist Society: An Analysis of the Western System Of Power*, London, 1973, p. 132

11 *FT*, 8th-9th November 1997

12 These estimates, based upon a Conference Board of New York report, are cited in Mathew Horsman, *After The Nation-State: Citizens, Tribalism and the New World Disorder* (London: 1994), p. 201

13 Analysis in report by Sarah Anderson and John Kavanagh, *IHT*, 23rd October 1996

14 Robert Reich, *The Work Of Nations*, New York, 1991, p. 110

15 Reich, op. cit., p. 110

16 See: Roger Lowenstein, *Origins of The Crash*, 2004

17 David Hale, 'How the Rise of Global Pension Funds Will Change the Global Economy in the 21st Century', prepared for the 1997 Bank Credit Analyst Bermuda Conference, May 1997, unpublished, p. 10

18 John Scott, *Corporate Business and Capitalist Classes* (Oxford: 1997), p. 86

19 Hale, op. cit.

20 Peter Gowan, 'The Dollar Wall Street Regime and the Crisis in Its Heartland', unpublished, 2008

21 Quoted in Sarah Anderson and John Cavanagh, *Field Guide To The Global Economy*, New York, 2005, p. 42

22 Ravi Batra, *The Myth of Free Trade: The Pooring Of America*, New York, 1993, p. 1

23 John Gray, 'Bill Rules The World – And I Don't Mean Clinton', *Daily Express*, 11th September 1998

24 *The Global Trap*, op. cit., p111

25 James Goldsmith, *The Response*, London, 1995, p. 177

26 Luttwak, *Turbo Capitalism*, New York, 1998, p. 182

27 It has been argued that the US employment telephone surveys were not particularly useful. See: Gabor Steingart, *The War for Wealth*, New York, 2008

28 Robert Z. Lawrence, *Single World: Divided Nations: International Trade and OECD Labour Markets*, Paris, 1996, p. 8

29 Lawrence, op. cit., p. 129

30 See; *FT*, 27th January 1998

31 Gregory Clark, 'For East Asia the Western Myth of Free Trade is a Good Joke', *IHT*, 15th August 1996

32 Michael Lind, *The Next American Nation: The New Nationalism and the Fourth American Revolution*, New York, 1995, p. 203

33 See: Gabor Steingart, op. cit.

34 William Greider, *Who will Tell the People?*, New York, 1993, p. 393

35 Bob Herbert, 'How The Labor Game Is Rigged', *IHT*, 21st November 1997

36 Roger Bootle, *The Death Of Inflation*, 1996

37 See: George Akerlof and William Dickens. 'The Macro-economics of Low Inflation', Brookings Papers on Economic activity 1. D.C. 1996

38 'Leisurely Steps Towards EMU', Letters by Joel Barnett and another in *FT*, 8th-9th November 1997

CHAPTER THREE

1   29th January 2002 speech at UC Berkeley

2   Westminster Cathedral Lecture, 3rd April 2008

3   See www.edge.org 'The Second Globalisation Debate'.
    A Talk with Anthony Giddens, 30th January 2001

4   Quoted in John Ralston Saul, *The Collapse of Globalism*,
    London, p. 20

5   Ralston Saul, op. cit., p. 20

6   Joseph Stiglitz, *The Roaring Nineties*, London, 2003, p. 231

7   W. Easterly, T*he White Man's Burden: Why The West's
    Efforts To Aid The Rest Have Done So Much Ill and So Little
    Good*, New York, 2006. p. 10

8   See D. Nielson, 2003 'Delegation To International
    Organisations: Agency Theory and World Bank Reform' in
    International Organisation, vol. 57, 2003

9   Quoted in Ralston Saul, p. 34

10 Ralston Saul, p. 164

11 Speech at World Economic Forum, Davos, Switzerland, 1999

12 George Soros, 'The Crisis of Global Capitalism', extract in
    The Times (of London), 30th November 1998

13 Robert Samuelson, 'Global Capitalism, Once Triumphant,
    is in Full Retreat', *IHT*, 10th September 1998

14 'America: An Empire in Denial', *The Chronicle of Higher
    Education*, 28th March 2003

15 William Greider, *One World, Ready Or Not*, New York,
    1997, p. 473; Edward Luttwak, *Turbo Capitalism: Winners
    and Losers in the Global Economy*, London, 1998, p. 187

16 Martin J. Anderson, 'In Defence of Chaos', in Arthur
    Seldon (ed), *The New Right Enlightenment*, London, 1985

17 Robert Nozick, *Anarchy, State and Utopia*, New York, 1974

18 Arthur Seldon, *The New Right Enlightenment*, op. cit.,
    p. 250

19 See: The Institute For Economic Affairs: www.iea.org.uk

20 Ibid.

21 Quotes and examples from Martin and Schumann., op. cit., p. 201

22 CBI speech, London, 27th November 2006

23 Will Hutton, *The State We're In*, London, 1995, p. 306

24 *IHT*, 20th-21st September 1997

25 Ibid.

26 George Stigler, *The Citizen and the State*, Chicago, 1975

27 Speech by Barack Obama, 26th March 2008; and speech by Henry Paulson, 13th March 2008

28 Full speech by Lindsay Tanner is on the Australian government website – under 'de-regulation', March 2008

29 See: J. W. Burton, *World Society*, Cambridge, 1972; Quote from John Vogler, 'The Structures of Global Politics', in C. Bretherton and G. Ponton (eds), *Global Politics*, Oxford, 1996

CHAPTER FOUR

1 Remarks delivered at the CSIS, Washington D.C., 18th July 1995

2 Pat Buchanan, *Where The Right Went Wrong*, New York, 2004, p. 13

3 Reported in 'Buchanan feeds class war in the information age', *Los Angeles Times*, 31st October 1999

4 Peter Rudolf, 'The USA and NATO enlargement' *Aussenpolitik*, vol. 47, no. 4, 1996

5 Warren Christopher, 'America's Leadership, America's Opportunity', *Foreign Policy* 98 (Spring 1995), Vol 8

6 Robert Dole 'Shaping America's Global Future', *Foreign Policy*, 98 (Spring 1995), p. 36

7 Sidney Blumenthal, *The Clinton Wars*, 2003, p. 308

8   Friedman and Chalmers quotes from Chalmers, op. cit.,
    pp. 274-276. Martin Albrow, 'A New Decade of The Global
    Age, 1996-2006' in *Globality Studies*, No. 8. July 2007

9   'The Project For a New American Century' by W. Rivers
    Pitt in www.informationclearinghouse.info/article1665

10 Speech, 18th February 1998 at Ohio State University

11 The American political scientist, Joseph Nye, who intro-
    duced the distinction between 'soft' and 'hard' power saw
    'soft' as the power of attraction and example, whereas 'hard'
    as forcing other peoples to do what they otherwise would
    not do; but journalists and commentators had taken up
    these terms as shorthand for economic and military power

12 Cited in Jacob Heilbrunn, *They Knew They Were Right: The
    Rise of the Neo-Cons*, New York, 2008, p. 190

13 'The Bush Doctrine', *Time*, 5th March 2001

14 Henry Kissinger, 'America At The Apex', *National Interest*,
    No. 64, Summer 2001

15 2001 DOD Base Structure Report

16 Reports in *IHT*, 9th November 2001

17 Charles Krauthammer, 'The Unipolar Moment Revisited'
    The National Interest, Winter 2002/03, p. 5

18 Speech by Tony Blair to the Labour Party Conference,
    October 2001

19 Address to Joint Session of Congress 21st September 2001.

20 *The Times* (of London), 24th June 2007

21 Joint Session of Congress, op. cit.

22 From Joint Vision 2020, the blueprint for US DOD, pub-
    lished by the DOD, 2002

23 Zalmay Khalizad, *From Containment To Global
    Leadership?*, New York, 1995

24 Quoted in *The New Yorker Magazine*, 1st April 2002

25 CNN report, 3rd April 2003, posted on CNN.com

26 For an analysis of Karl Rove's attutide towards the 'war on
    terror' and other issues see; James Moore and Wayne
    Slater, *Bush's Brain: How Karl Rove Made George Bush
    Presidential*, New Jersey, 2003

CHAPTER FIVE

1 J. Stiglitz and L. Bilmes, *The Three Trillion Dollar War*,
   New York, 2008
2 Arguments proffered by Joseph Stiglitz to the Commonwealth
   Club of California, April 2008. Reproduced on fora.tv
3 History of tracker poll USAToday/Gallup on usatoday
   website under 'warpoll'
4 Broadcast on CBS News, 24th May 2007. See CBS news
   website
5 Film broadcast by Al-Jazeera, 20th April 2007
6 BIS report cited in, and quotes from, 'BIS slams central
   banks, warns of worse crunch to come', Ambrose Evans
   Pritchard, *Daily Telegraph* website, 2nd July 2008
7 *NYT*, 16th March 2008
8 The official was Larry Summers, former Treasury
   Secretary. Quoted in Iwan Morgan, 'The Indebted
   Empire: America's Current-Account Deficit Problem'
   in *International Politics*, 2008, 45 (92-112), p. 90
9 S. R. Scwenninger, 'America's "Suez Moment"',
   The Atlantic Monthly, Jan/Feb 2004, p. 129
10 N. Roubini and B. Setser, 'The US as a Net Debtor:
   The Sustainability of External Imbalances', 2004, pp. 4-5.
   www.stern.nyu/globalmacro/Roubini-Setser-US-External-
   Imbalances
11 'The US Current Account Deficit and the Global
   Economy', The Per Jacobsson Lecture, The Per Jacobsson
   Foundation, October 2004

12 House Budget Committee, 26th June 2007

13 Kevin Phillips. *American Theocracy: The Peril and Politics of Radical Religion, Oil, and Borrowed Money in the 21st Century*, New York, 2006, Figure 9, p. 326. Both quotes from Phillips, p. 296

14 *Daily Telegraph*, 4th April 2008

15 Lawrence Summers, 'Sovereign Wealth Funds', A Global Viewpoint Article adapted from remarks at the Davos World Economic Forum, 2008, reproduced in the *IHT*, 31st January 2008

16 See: Jeffry Frieden, *Global Capital: Its Fall and Rise in the 20th Century*, New York, 2006

17 Both quotes from: David Morgan, 'Could voter anxiety fuel U.S. isolationism?', *IHT*, 9th January 2008

18 Reported in Kenneth F. Sheve and Matthew J. Slaughter, *Globalisation and the Perception of American Workers*, Institute for International Economics, 2000

19 Ralston Saul, p. 163

20 Iwan Morgan, op. cit.

CHAPTER SIX

1 See: Gore Vidal, *The Decline and Fall of the American Empire*, New York, 1992, *Perpetual War For Perpetual Peace*, New York, 2002, and *Dreaming*, New York, 2003

2 See particularly Noam Chomsky, *9/11*, New York, 2001

3 Chalmers Johnson, *The Sorrows of Empire*, London, 2004, p. 1

4 See: Patrick Buchanan, *Churchill, Hitler, And The Unnecessary War*, New York, 2008, Chapter 15

5 This was the title of the first chapter of Correlli Barnett's *The Collapse of British Power*, London, 1972 – referring to the English sense of its special morally good imperial 'mission'

6 Patrick J. Buchanan, op. cit., p. 417

7   Figures from 'The Military Balance', 2001-2 (OUP for the IIS, October 2001)

8   For information on US bases around the world, see The Centre For Defence Information, Defence Monitor Series. Also see Chalmers Johnson, op. cit., Chapter Five

9   Wolfowitz quote to *New York Times*, reported in *The Guardian*

10 See: Huntingdon, *The Clash of Civilisations*, op. cit., pp. 83-91

11 This list of the characteristics of the Roman empire in its last years was based on an analysis by Robert Adams, *Decadent Societies*, New York, 1975

12 Both quotes in the paragraph from Barnett, op. cit., p. 120 and p. 123

13 Henry Kissinger, op. cit.

14 Paul Kennedy, *The Rise and Fall Of The Great Powers*, New York, 1987, p. 538

15 Lester Thurow, *Head To Head: The Economic Battle Among Japan, Europe and America*, New York, 1993

16 Jeffrey Garten, 'The Euro Will Turn Europe Into A Superpower', *Business Week*, 4th May 1998

17 'The Case For De-Coupling', Market Commentary Report, Global Strategy, Morgan Stanley, 25th March 2002

18 Figures are for GDP (PPP) published by IMF in 2008 for 2007. They are in millions of international dollars

19 Interview in *The Guardian*, 14th June 2008

20 Martin Jacques, *The Guardian*, 18th February 2008

21 Chalmers Johnson, op. cit., p. 310

22 For estimates of these job losses see: Gabor Steingart, op. cit.

23 Reported in *The Observer*, 30th March 2008

24 Speech by President George W. Bush, 17th May 2001

25 Figures and estimates made by the US Energy Information

Administration, Energy Markets and Contingency Information Division, release date, July 2005

26 Pew Research Centre national attitudes survey in 44 countries, published in December 2002, reported in *The Economist*, 4th January 2003

27 See: Robert Kagan, *Of Paradise and Power: America and Europe in the New World Order*, New York, 2003

CHAPTER SEVEN

1 See: Alan Greenspan's evidence to the House Banking Sub-Committee, 23rd July 1997, particularly his exchanges with Representative Sanders of Vermont

2 US Bureau of Labour statistics, data for national employment hours and earnings. Series Catalogue EEU00500006

3 See House Banking Sub-Committee report, op. cit. Quote from Steingart, op. cit., p. 78

4 Alan B. Krueger, 'The Truth About Wages', *New York Times*, 31st July 1997. Emphasis added

5 Robert Z. Lawrence, *Single World*, op. cit., p. 16

6 Stephen P. Jenkins, 'Recent Trend in UK Income Distribution: What Happened and Why', *Oxford Review of Economic Policy*, vol. 10, no. 1 (Spring, 1996)

7 Data from New Earnings Survey 01928 79 2077, Central Statistical Office, London, 1996

8 Figures and quotations from *News From Labour*, Labour Party Media Office, 29th January 1997. Figures were derived from The Labour Force Survey, supplied by the Commons Library to the Labour party

9 Denny Braun, *The Rich Get Richer*, Chicago, 1997, p. 245

10 Bennett Harrison and Barry Bluestone, *The Great U-Turn: Corporate Re-Structuring and the Polarizing of America*, New York, 1998

11 *The New York Times*, 8th August 1997

12 Hutton, *The State We're In*, op. cit., pp107-8

13 Bureau of Labor Statistics, Survey Of Contingent Workers, 1995, cited in Braun, op. cit., p. 245

14 *New York Times*, 8th August 1997

15 Harry Shutt, *The Trouble With Capitalism: An Enquiry Into The Causes Of Global Economic Failure*, London, 1998

16 *NYT* report quoted in Martin and Schumann, *The Global Trap*, op. cit., p. 122. The 'con game' employment statistics quote from Steingart, op. cit., p. 86

17 Both quotes from Richard Sennett, 'Work Can Screw You Up', *Financial Times*, 17th October 1998

18 Braun, op. cit., p. 118

19 *Wall Street Journal*, 17th July 1997

20 Paul Ryan, 'Factor Shares and Inequality in the UK', *Oxford Review of Economic Policy*, vol. 12, no. 1, Spring 1996, table 3, p. 117

21 Figures from The Economic Policy Institute, Home Page, 16th January 2008

22 Charles Handy, 'The Citizen Corporation', presented at seminar, Birkbeck College, London, 23rd April 1997

23 Figures from James Banks, Andrew Dilnot and Hamish Low, 'Patterns of Financial Wealth Holding in the UK', in Hills, *New Inequalities*, Cambridge, 1996, p. 342

24 Cited in Kevin Phillips, *Boiling Point: Republicans, Democrats and the Decline of Middle Class Prosperity*, New York, 1993, p. 191

25 Phillips, op. cit.

26 Reported by William Pfaff, 'The Enron Model of Irresponsible Capitalism', *IHT*, 27th May 2006

27 Monica Castillo, *A Profile of the Working Poor*, Report 896, Bureau of Labour Statistics, Washington, D.C. 1995, p. 1

28 US Census Bureau, 2006, Income Statistics for 2005

29 See; John Hills, op. cit., p. 33

30 Household Below Average Income Survey, DWP, 2008

31 Paul Gregg and Jonathan Wadsworth, 'More Work in Fewer Households', in Hills, *New Inequalities*, op. cit., p. 181. Quote from p. 204

32 Reich, op. cit., p. 198

33 Paul Krugman, 'America's Oligarchs' *IHT*, 29th February 2006

34 Edward Luce, Comment and Analysis, *FT*, 3rd May 2006

35 Reported in Edward Luce, 'Out on a Limb: Why Blue-Collar Americans See Their Future as Precarious'. Comment and Analysis, *FT*, 3rd May 2006

36 For OECD figures see: A. Atkinson, L. Rainwater and T. Smeeding, *Income Distribution in OECD Countries*, Paris, OECD, 1995

37 Latest figures from UN can be found at http://en.wikipedia.org/wiki/List_of_countries_by_income_inequality

38 See; Hills, op. cit., p. 45. Figures taken from P. Saunders, *Rising on the Tasman Tide: Income Inequality in Australia and New Zealand in the 1980s*, University of NSW, 1994

39 Braun, op. cit., p. 118

40 Phillips, op. cit., Appendix A

41 Summary Federal Tax Information By Income Group and Family Type, based upon Congressional Budget Office January 1997 forecast

42 Figures from Ronald Findlay and Kevin H. O'Rourke, *Power and Plenty, Trade, War, and the World Economy in the Second Millennium*, Princeton, 2007, p. 536

43 Cited in Stephen Haseler, *The Super-Rich*, 2001, p. 46. (See footnote 16, Chapter Three)

44 Zhu Xiao Di, *Growing Wealth, Inequality, and Housing in the United States*, Joint Center For Housing Studies,

Harvard University, February 2007

45 Charles Feinstein,'The Equalising of Wealth in Britain Since The Second World War', *Oxford Review of Economic Policy*, vol. 12, no. 1 (Spring 1996)

46 John Scott, *Who Rules Britain?*, Cambridge, UK, 1991, p. 83

47 Arthur Seldon, *Capitalism*, Oxford, 1990, p. 195 and Jeff Gates, *The Ownership Solution*, London, 1998, p. 217

48 Braun, op. cit., p. 30

49 Robert Nozicke, *Anarchy, State and Utopia*, London, 1904

50 Quoted in Krugman, 'Blindly Into the Bubble', *NYT*, 22nd December 2007

51 See: Roubin's RGE monitor, 22nd December 2007

52 Dr. Rodrigue Tremblay, in www.globalresearch.ca

53 See: website for *The Telegraph* (UK), Business Section, Commentaries 2007 and 2008

54 See: Susan Strange, *Casino Capitalism*, reprinted (from 1986) Manchester, 1997

55 Quote from Susan Strange, *Mad Money*, Manchester, 1998, p. 1. But see *Casino Capitalism* for her early critique

CHAPTER EIGHT

1 Jeff Gates, *The Ownership Solution* (London: 1998), p. 217

2 Arthur Seldon, *Capitalism*, op. cit., p. 278

3 R. H. Tawney, *Religion and the Rise of Capitalism* (London: 1960), Max Weber, *The Protestant Ethic and the Spirit of Capitalism*, trans. Talcott Parsons (New York: 1958); H. Gutman, *Work, Culture and Society in Industrialising America* (Oxford: 1977)

4 Peter Saunders, *Capitalism: A Social Audit*, Buckingham, 1995, p. 17

5 See: Michael Rose, *Re-Working The Work Ethic*, London, 1985

6   William H. Whyte, *The Organisation Man*, New York, 1956

7   Martin Wolf, 'Caging The Bankers', *Financial Times*, 20th January 1998

8   Edward Luce, 'Age Of Uncertainty', *Prospect*, July 1998, p. 27

9   Reported by Larry Elliot, 'Sending Out an S.O.S.', *The Guardian*, 12th January 1998. See also Larry Elliott and Dan Atkinson, *The Age of Insecurity* (London: 1998). The 'Chapter Eleven' procedure allows a business in trouble to seek protection from its creditors without necessarily closing down

10 Cited in Phillips, *Boiling Point*, op. cit., p. 191

11 Ibid.

12 Thomas J. Stanley and William B. Danko, op. cit.

13 Edward Wolf's projection and the quote are from Phillips, *Boiling Point*, op. cit., p. 192

14 Friedrich von Hayek, *The Constitution Of Liberty*, London, 1960, pp. 90-1

15 *The Spectator*, 17th October 2007

16 Estimated in Stanley and Danko, op. cit., p. 143

17 Ibid., table 5-1, p. 145

18 Ibid., p. 91

19 Ibid., p. 143

20 Phillips, *Boiling Point*, op. cit., p. 190, citing a *Boston Globe* report of 6th October 1991

21 Stanley and Danko, op. cit., p. 153

22 Figures from Stanley and Danko, table 1-1, p. 17

23 Hayek, op. cit., p. 397

24 Marc-Henri Glendening, 'Thatcherism and Libertarianism' in: Arthur Seldon (ed), *The New Right Enlightenment*, op. cit., p. 127

25 Karl Popper, *The Open Society and its Enemies*, London, 1962. For his views on the Thatcher governments' strategy

of social mobility see: Norman Tebbit, *Upwardly Mobile*, London, 1988

26 Quoted in William Greider, *One World: Ready Or Not: The Manic Logic of Global Capitalism*, New York, 1997, p. 288

27 George Gilder, *Wealth and Poverty*, New York, 1981

28 Quoted in Adam Smith, *The Roaring Eighties*, New York, 1988, p. 209

29 Seldon, *Capitalism*, op. cit., p. 311

30 Braun, op. cit., p. 32

31 Gates, op. cit., p. 217

32 J. M. Buchanan, *The Economics of Politics*, London, IEA, 1978, p. 18

33 George Soros, 'The Capitalist Threat', *The Atlantic Monthly*, February 1997 (emphasis added). Also see: Soros, *The Crisis of Global Capitalism*, New York, 1998

34 See; Maurice Cranston, *Freedom: A New Analysis*, 2nd edition (London, 1955)

35 Kenneth Minogue, *Politics: A Very Short Introduction*, Oxford, 1995

36 Maurice Duverger, *The Study of Politics*, Walton-on-Thames, 1972

37 From Soros, 'Global Meltdown', *The Times*, 30th November 1998, extracted from Soros, op. cit.

38 Seldon, *Capitalism*, op. cit., p. 98

39 Charles Handy, 'The Citizen Corporation', lecture, op. cit.

40 D. Miller, *Market, State and Community: Theoretical Foundations of Market Socialism*, Oxford, 1989

41 Anthony Giddens, *The Third Way: The Renewal of Social Democracy*, London, 1998, pp. 70-80

42 Seldon, *Capitalism*, op. cit., p. 99

43 Christopher Pierson, 'Democracy, Markets and Capital', in David Held (ed), *Prospects For Democracy*, Oxford, 1992

CHAPTER NINE

1 Quote, and for an inside story of the Mexican bail-out, see: Hans-Peter Martin and Harald Schumann, *The Global Trap*, London, 1997, p. 163

2 Seldon, *Capitalism*, op. cit., p. 11

3 On the TV show 'The Des O'Connor Show' Blair agreed to take second place to the singer Elton John (LWT, July 1998)

4 See particularly Julian Le Grand and Robert Goodin, *Not Only The Poor*, London, 1987

5 S. Mulhall and A. Swift, *Liberals and Communitarians*, Oxford: 1992, p. 67

6 Alan S. Milward, *The European Rescue of the Nation State*, London: 1992

7 Linda Colley, *Britons: Forging The Nation 1707-1837*, London: 1992, p. 291

8 Quote from William Pfaff, *IHT*, 2nd December 1997

9 Mathew Josephson, *The Robber Barons*, London, 1962, p. 316

10 Ibid.

11 Alfred D. Chandler, Jr., *The Visible Hand: The Managerial Revolution in American Business*, Cambridge, Mass: 1977, p. 1

12 Werner Sombart, 'Capitalism', in *The Encyclopaedia of the Social Sciences*, New York, 1930

13 John Sheldrake, *Management Theory: From Taylorism to Japanization*, London: International Thomson Business Press, 1996. See also R. Gillespie, *Manufacturing Knowledge: A History of the Hawthorne Experiment*, Cambridge: 1991; David Hounshell, *From The American System To Mass Production 1800-1932: the Development of Manufacturing Technology in the USA*, Baltimore, MD, 1984

14 F. M. L. Thompson, *The Rise of Respectable Society: A Social History of Victorian Britain 1830-1900*, London: 1988

15 See Frederick W. Taylor, *Shop Management*, New York: 1911. The standard biography is Frank B. Copley, *Frederick W. Taylor, Father of Scientific Management*, 2 vols, New York, 1923

16 Josephson, *The Robber Barons*, op. cit., p. 322

17 See: Kim McQuaid, *Uneasy Partners: Big Business in American Politics, 1945-90*, Google Books

18 See particularly Paul Hirst and Grahame Thompson, *Globalisation in Question*, London: 1996

19 Eric Shaw describing the views of British social democrat Anthony Crosland in 'Capitalism's Premature Mourner', *The Times Higher Education Supplement*, 3rd October 1997

20 J. G. Ikenberry, 'Funk de Siecle: Impasses of Western Industrial Society at Century's End', *Millenium*, vol. 24, no. 1 (1995)

21 Quotes from K. McQuaid, *Uneasy Partners: Big Business in American Politics 1945-90*, op. cit., p. 49

22 See: Charles Levinson, *Vodka-Cola*, Horsham, 1980

23 For a discussion of technology transfers by transnational corporations during the Cold War see: Peter Dicken, *Global Shift*, London, 1992, ch. 12

CHAPTER TEN

1 Bill Clinton 'Expanding Trade, Protecting Values: Why I'll Fight To Make China's Trade Status Permanent'. *New Democrat*, vol. 12, no. 1, pp. 9-10

2 Kenneth Liberthal, senior director for Asia affairs in the White House, on News Hour with Jim Lehrer, 15th November 1999

3 Trade in goods with China. *Federal Trade Statistics*, US Census Bureau

4   See: Mark Leonard, *What Does China Think?*, London, 2008. Mark Leonard was also interviewed on the BBC TV programme Book-Mark in May 2008

5   See: www.correlatesofwar.org

6   Ronald Findlay and Kevin H. O'Rourke, *Power and Plenty: Trade, War, and the World Economy in the Second Millenium*, Princeton, 2007

7   Robert Skidelsky, 'Russia's Place in the World in the Twenty-First Century', Global Policy Institute, London, 2007

8   Samuel Huntingdon, *The Clash of Civilisations and the Remaking of World Order*, New York, 1996

9   Samuel Huntingdon, 'The Hispanic Challenge', *Foreign Policy*, April 2004

10 Huntingdon, *Clash of Civilisations*, op. cit., p. 184

11 Paul Kennedy, *The Rise and Fall of the Great Powers*, New York, 1988

12 Paul Kennedy, *Preparing For The Twenty-First Century*, New York, 1992

13 Paul Kennedy, 'Bigger Isn't Always Better', *IHT*, 19th April 2008

14 Ibid.

15 Figures from IMF. The two methods of calculation are PPP (Purchasing Power Parity) system, which takes into account costs of living, and nominal which does not

16 US-China figures from US International Trade Commission, US Dept. of Commerce and US Census Bureau. And from http://ec.europa.eu/trade/issues

17 See: amoungst other works, Dani Rodrik, *What's So Special About China's Exports?*, CEPR Discussion Paper, No. 5484, January 2006. Harvard University, Kennedy School of Government

18 See: Will Hutton, *The Writing on the Wall: China and the*

West in the 21st Century, Little, Brown, 2007, pp147-151

19 Michael Dauderstädt and Jürgen Stetten, *China and Globalization*, Friedrich Eberty Stiftung, Internationale Politikanalyse Globalisierung und Gerechtigkeit, September 2005

20 Iwan Morgan, 'The Indebted Empire: America's Current-Account Deficit Problem', *International Politics*, 2008, 45, p. 92-112

21 See; Ashley Seager 'State investors deny political motivations', *The Guardian*, 25th January 2008

22 *The Economist*, 19th January 2008

23 Marianne Barriaux, 'Mining Giant opens biggest takeover bid', *The Guardian*, 6th February 2008

24 Manufacturing calculation was for 2005: from Robert Wang, 'China's Economic Growth: Source of Disorder?' *Foreign Service Journal*, May 2005

25 Tony Blair speech to European Parliament 26th October 2005

26 Sandra Polaski, *Job Anxiety is Real – and It's Global*, Carnegie Endowment Policy Brief No. 30, Carnegie Foundation, Washington 2004

27 Michael Lind, *The Next American Nation: The New Nationalism and the Fourth American Revolution*, New York, 1995, p. 203

28 See: http://trade.ec.europa.eu/doclib/docs/2006/september/tradoc113366.pdf. Figures: IMF and Eurostat 142 EU-China

29 James Kynge, *China Shakes The World: The Rise of a Hungry Nation*, Orion Books, 2006

30 See; *China Machine Tools Market*, KPMG, February 2004

31 R. Evan Ellis, *US National Security Implications of Chinese Involvement in Latin America*, Strategic Studies Institute, US Army War College Carlisle PA, June 2005

32 *China Machine Tools Market*, op. cit.

33 See: Hutton, *Writing on the Wall*, op. cit.

34 www.fiatforum.com/panda-new/129371-great-wall-peri-fiat-panda-copy-2.html

35 See: Testimony of Patrick A. Mulloy, Commissioner, US-China Economic and Security Review Commission before the Subcommittee on Federal Financial Management, Government Information, and International Security (Hearing on 'Ensuring Protection of American Intellectual Property Rights for American Industries in China', 21st November 2005, Beverly Hills, California)

36 See; Working Paper *A Great Wall of Patents: China and American Inventors – Selected Consequences of Proposed U.S. Patent 'Reforms'*, prepared for US-China Economic and Security Review Commission, Manufacturing Policy Project Washington, Virginia, 7th November 2005

37 Ian Harvey and Jennifer Morgan, *Intellectual Property Rights in China – Myths versus Reality*, E3G, April 2007.

38 Richard D. Fisher, Jr., *The Impact of Foreign Weapons and Technology on the Modernization of China's People's Liberation Army*. A report for the US-China Economic and Security Review Commission, Center for Security Policy, January 2004

39 Dr. Carlo Kopp, 'Analysis: China's Airpower: The Sleeping Giant Awakes', *Australian Aviation*, August 2004

40 See: David A Fulghum and Douglas Barrie, 'Peer Pressure', in *Aviation Week and Space Technology*, July 2008

41 See: Paul Roberts, *The End of Oil: On The Edge of a Perilous New World*, New York, 2005

42 Bernard D Cole, *Oil for the Lamps of China: Beijing's 21st Century Search for Energy*, McNair Paper 67, Institute for National Strategic Studies, National Defense University, D.C. 2003

43 *The Times*, 28th January 2008

44 Cindy Hurst, *China's Oil Rush in Africa*, Institute for the Analysis of Global Security, July 2006

45 See: Testimony before the Sub-Committee on Africa, Human Rights and International Operations, US House of Representatives, Washington DC, 28th July 2005, by Dr. Ernest J Wilson III, Senior Research Fellow, Center for International Development and Conflict Management, University of Maryland, College Park

46 Rory Carroll, 'Chinese premier boosts trade with seven-nation Africa tour', *The Guardian*, 22nd June 2006

47 'EU jamboree seeks fresh start – but Africa's leaders are looking east', *The Guardian*, 7th December 2007. Article quoted research by Chris Alden of LSE and Andy Rothman, a China analyst

48 'World Bank hits out at China over lending', *Financial Times*, 23rd October 2006. Also: http://chinadigitaltimes.net/2007/12/world_bank_expresses_concern_about_sustainability

49 See: Domingos Jardo Muekalia, 'Africa and China's Strategic Partnership', *African Security Review* 13(1) 2004

50 Joshua Kurlantzick, *China's Charm: Implications of Chinese Soft Power*, Carnegie Endowment for International Peace, No. 47, June 2006

51 R. Evan Ellis, *U.S. National Security Implications of Chinese Involvement in Latin America*, June 2005, Strategic Studies Institute, Carlisle PA

52 www.worldcargonews.com/htm/n20080112.194568.htm. 'China bags Jeddah deals – Saudi Trade and Development Corporation awarded the civil works contract for construction of terminal for completion in 22 months'

53 *The rise of China and its effect on Taiwan, Japan and South Korea: US Policy Choices*, CRS Report for Congress, 12th

April 2005

54 *Military Power of the People's Republic of China*, 2007, Annual Report to Congress. See also the 2008 annual report

55 *The rise of China*, DOD Report to Congress, op. cit.

56 Quoted in *Military Power of the People's Republic of China 2007*, DOD Annual Report to Congress, 2008

57 Cited in DOD Annual Report to Congress 2006

58 See: Ellis Joffe, 'The "Right Size" for China's Military: To What Ends?', *Asia Policy*, No. 4. July 2007, pp. 53-105

59 See: *Stockholm International Peace Research Institute Yearbook: Armaments, Disarmament and International Security*, 2008, p. 14

60 Ronald O'Rourke, *China Naval Modernization: Implications for US Navy Capabilities*. Background and Issues for Congress, 18th November 2005

61 Christopher J Pehrson, *Meeting the Challenge of China's Rising Power Across the Asian Littoral*, Strategic Studies Institute, Carlisle PA, July 2006

62 Zaid Haider, 'Baluchis, Beijing, and Pakistan's Gwadar Port', *Georgetown Journal of International Affairs*, Winter/Spring 2005

63 Major Lawrence Spinetta USAF, *Malacca Dilemma: Countering China's 'String of Pearls' with Land-Based Airpower*, School of Advanced Air and Space Studies Air University, Maxwell AFB, Alabama, June 2006

64 Richard Halloram, 'Guam, all over again', *Air Force Magazine: Journal of the Air Force Association*, January, 2008

65 Ibid. Above AFM article quoting Retd. Army General Barry R McCaffery

66 Mokhzani Zubir, *The strategic value of the Strait of Malacca*, Centre for Maritime Security and Diplomacy, Maritime Institute of Malaysia, April 2005

67 Reported in Spinetta, op. cit.

68 Vipin Gupta and Adam Bernstein, *Keeping an Eye on the Islands: Remote Monitoring in the South China Sea*, Sandia National Labs, Livermore, CA. May 1999

69 Christopher C Joyner, 'The Spratly Islands Dispute in the South China Sea: Problems, Policies, and Prospects for Diplomatic Accomodation', *New England Law Review*, Vol 32, no.3, Spring 1999, pp. 819-852. Comment on Spratlys also available in annual DOD report to US Congress 2008

70 Figures from DOD 'MPOPRC' Annual Report to Congress, 2007

71 Dr. Carlo Kopp, op. cit.

72 *Amnesty International Annual Report 2007*

73 Ibid.

74 *Undermining Freedom of Expression in China: The role of Yahoo!, Microsoft and Google*, Amnesty International, July 2006

75 Ibid.

76 *The Economist*, 19th January 2008

77 Andrew Small, *Preventing The Next Cold War: A View from Beijing*, Foreign Policy Centre, October 2005

78 Reported in *The Financial Times*, 8th/9th October 2005

CHAPTER ELEVEN

1 Reported in *IHT*, 4th April 2008

2 Charles A. Kupchan, *The End of the American Era: US Foreign Policy and the Geopolitics of the Twenty-first Century*, New York, 2003, p. 247

3 Quoted in Kupchan, op. cit., p. 93

4 See: Hywel Williams, *Britain's Power elites: The Rebirth of a Ruling Class*, London, 2006, p. 163

5 Daniel Dorling and Bethan Thomas, *People and Places: A*

2001 Census atlas of the UK, Bristol, 2004

6   *The Guardian*, 5th July 2004

7   Williams, op. cit., p. 163. See his Chapter Four on 'The Financial and Business Elites; Dividing the Spoils'

8   Reported in, and quoted from, Gideon Rachman, 'How The Square Mile Fell Out Of Love with Brussels', *FT*, 12th December 2006

9   Reported BBC News website news.bbc.co.uk/1/hi/business/4366225.stm

10 See Kennedy, op. cit., p. 514, and Chalmers Johnson, op. cit., p. 307

11 Huntingdon, *Foreign Affairs*. vol. 74, no. 3, summer 1993

12 See: John Mearsheimer and Stephen Walt, *The Israel Lobby and US Foreign Policy*, New York, 2007. An article on the same topic entitled 'The Israel Lobby' appeared in September 2006 in *The London Review of Books*

13 Kupchan, op. cit., p. 160

14 Ibid. p. 247

15 Figures for trade and for investment from US Bureau of Economic Statistics, US Census Bureau. Figures for 2007 are in US$ billions

16 Zbigniew Brzezinski, *The Grand Chessboard: American Primacy and its Geo-Strategic Imperatives*, New York, 1997

17 Brzezinski, op. cit., p. 61

CHAPTER TWELVE

1   From US State Department website, 22nd February 2008

2   Speech to National Press Club, 13th July 2001

3   Bruce Bawer, *While Europe Slept: How Radical Islam Is Destroying the West From Within*, New York, 2007, and Walter Lacquer, *The Last Days of Europe: Epitaph For An Old Continent*, New York, 2007

4 Joffe, *IHT*, 10th-11th May 2008

5 Paul Kennedy, 'A Bigger Nation Isn't Always Better', *IHT*, 18th April 2008

6 John Kay, *The Truth About Markets: Their Genius, Their Limits, Their Follies*, London, 2003

7 David Rothkopf, *Superclass: The Global Power Elite and the World They Are Making*, New York, 2008

8 Iwan Morgan, op. cit., p. 106

Index

Young, Michael, 258

Zedong, Mao, 346, 378

Printed in the United Kingdom
by Lightning Source UK Ltd.
134733UK00001BA/106-171/P

9 780955 497568